Shakespeare's Contested Nations

Shakespeare's Contested Nations argues that performances of Shakespearean history at British institutional venues between 2000 and 2016 manifest a post-imperial nostalgia that fails to tell the nation's story in ways that account for the agential impact of women and people of color, thus foreclosing promising opportunities to re-examine the nation's multicultural past, present, and future in more intentional, self-critical, and truly progressive ways.

A cluster of interconnected stage and televisual performances and adaptations of the history play canon illustrate the function that Shakespeare's narratives of incipient "British" identities fulfill for the postcolonial United Kingdom. The book analyzes treatments of the plays in a range of styles—staged performances directed by Michael Boyd with the Royal Shakespeare Company (2000–2001) and Nicholas Hytner at the National Theatre (2003, 2005), the BBC's *Hollow Crown* series (2012, 2016), the RSC and BBC adaptations of *Wolf Hall* and *Bring Up the Bodies* (2013, 2015), and a contemporary reinterpretation of the canon, Mike Bartlett's *King Charles III* (2014, 2017).

This book will be of great interest to scholars and students of Shakespeare, theatre, and politics.

L. Monique Pittman is Professor of English and Director of the J. N. Andrews Honors Program at Andrews University, USA.

Routledge Advances in Theatre and Performance Studies

This series is our home for cutting-edge, upper-level scholarly studies and edited collections. Considering theatre and performance alongside topics such as religion, politics, gender, race, ecology, and the avant-garde, titles are characterized by dynamic interventions into established subjects and innovative studies on emerging topics.

Shakespeare's Contested Nations
Race, Gender, and Multicultural Britain in Performances of the History Plays
L. Monique Pittman

Performing the Wound
Practicing a Feminist Theatre of Becoming
Niki Tulk

Butoh America
Butoh Dance in the United States and Mexico from 1970 to the early 2000's
Tanya Calamoneri

Deburau
Pierrot, Mime, and Culture
Edward Nye

Performance at the Urban Periphery
Insights from South India
Cathy Turner, Sharada Srinivasan, Jerri Daboo and Anindya Sinha

Australian Metatheatre on Page and Stage
An Exploration of Metatheatrical Techniques
Rebecca Clode

For more information about this series, please visit: https://www.routledge.com/Routledge-Advances-in-Theatre–Performance-Studies/book-series/RATPS

Shakespeare's Contested Nations

Race, Gender, and Multicultural Britain in Performances of the History Plays

L. Monique Pittman

Routledge
Taylor & Francis Group
LONDON AND NEW YORK

First published 2022
by Routledge
4 Park Square, Milton Park, Abingdon, Oxon OX14 4RN

and by Routledge
605 Third Avenue, New York, NY 10158

Routledge is an imprint of the Taylor & Francis Group, an informa business

British Library Cataloguing-in-Publication Data
A catalogue record for this book is available from the British Library

Library of Congress Cataloging-in-Publication Data
A catalog record has been requested for this book

ISBN: 978-0-367-48831-4 (hbk)
ISBN: 978-1-032-25248-3 (pbk)
ISBN: 978-1-003-04306-5 (ebk)

DOI: 10.4324/9781003043065

Typeset in Bembo
by Taylor & Francis Books

For my beloved parents,
Maxine Dowden Pittman & Thomas D. Pittman

And for Paul, partner in all things ever and always

"...the will to give ourselves to others and 'welcome' them, to readjust our identities
to make space for them, is prior to any judgment about others, except that of identifying them in their humanity."
(Miroslav Volf, *Exclusion and Embrace* 19)

Contents

Acknowledgments viii

1 Introduction: Representing the Nation's History 1

2 Staging the Multiethnic Nation: Boyd and Hytner at the Millennial Threshold 49

3 Shakespeare and the Cultural Olympiad: Gender, Race, and the British Nation in the BBC's *Hollow Crown*, Series One 94

4 *Hollow* Refuge: The BBC's *The Wars of the Roses* and This Fortress Built by Nature 128

5 The Disappearing Moor: Race, Authenticity, and the Nation's History in *Wolf Hall* and *Bring Up the Bodies* 157

6 The Trouble with History: Intersections of Nation, Race, and Gender in *King Charles III* 182

7 Epilogue: The Case of Two Richards 207

Works Cited 221
Index 238

Acknowledgments

Like so many, I have found writing during a global pandemic unbelievably difficult—overwhelmed by the speed with which universities pivoted to online teaching in spring 2020, troubled by the profound peril in which we all found ourselves (fearful for the lives of those we loved and dreading the possibility that we might infect them), powerless against the confused approach to mitigating the COVID-19 pandemic, and distraught by displays of unethical human behavior all around. In the summer of 2020, when I was originally meant to be finishing this book, the school year and its disruptions had just ended when, with a terrifying rapidity, white supremacism, racism, and sexism emerged ascendant once again in the clashes over institutional racism and the systematic police murder of black Americans. This reality made writing about Shakespeare's history plays seem unimportant, a futile speaking to the smallest of gatherings.

However, as I adjusted to new norms, returned to the classroom in fall of 2020, masked and socially distant but mercifully in person, I found the will to return to this project which comes from the heart of who I am and what I believe. Put simply, this book manifests from my love of art and literature, from a belief in their transformative powers, and from a commitment to using that numinous power to acknowledge privileges, errors, and sins that thwart our shared life together as humans on an oh-so-vulnerable planet. I want to state humbly from the start that though this book centers on performances of Shakespeare's history at and on British institutional venues and outlets that too often fail to speak the heterogeneity of the nation, the dynamics of exclusion and disharmony catalogued and analyzed are, sadly, just as prevalent in different iterations in the United States. I would never argue otherwise nor deny the tragedies in my own nation. The dynamics of New Nationalism constitute an imminent threat to democracy in my homeland as well.

And now I turn to gratitude for those who've supported this project and made the home—material, intellectual, emotional, and spiritual—from which I safely write.

It is my great honor and joy to learn from former students, now esteemed early modern and Shakespeare scholars, the Andrews University Shakes Squad: Vanessa I. Corredera, Kristin N. Denslow, Shanelle Kim, Adrienne Redding, Emily Shortslef, and Samantha Snively.

My professional life has been enriched immeasurably by the friendship and collaboration of one colleague in particular, Vanessa I. Corredera, a friend, co-laborer, and treasured hermana. This book would not be the same without you, nor would I have survived a year and a half of pandemic teaching without your companionship. What can I say, my friend but, "thanks, and thanks, and ever thanks."

Kristin N. Denslow has, likewise, been a co-author on multiple projects throughout the writing of this book—some of which she had to bear the burden of as the book came to its final stages of completion. Thank you for your collaborative wisdom and genial forbearance.

Thank you to Louise Geddes who has been the most generous of friends, who connected me to Laura Hussey at Routledge, and who possesses the gift for gathering that embodies the spirit of hospitality we should all practice as individuals, professionals, communities, and nations. Thank you to Louise and Valerie Fazel and all who've broken bread at one of Louise's amazing SAA dinners.

A group of talented undergraduate research scholars and student assistants have contributed towards this project: Matthew Chacko, Alaryss Bosco, Shanelle Kim, Samantha Snively, Emma Magbanua, Ingrid Radulescu, Elianna Srikureja, David Forner, Daniel Self, Taylor Uphus, and Isabella Koh.

Every chapter in this book began life as a conference seminar or panel paper. Profound thanks to all the seminar organizers and participants who helped improve these ideas:

Shakespeare Association of America 2013: Wrong Shakespeare organized by Katherine Scheil and Margaret Jane Kidnie.

World Shakespeare Congress 2016: Reading Shakespeare Adaptations Historically organized by Deborah Cartmell and Maurizio Calbi; respondents Zoltan Markus and Ayanna Thompson.

Shakespeare Association of America 2017: Renaissance Afterlives Revisited organized by Chloe Kathleen Preedy and Joseph Sterrett.

Shakespeare Association of America 2018: Remediations of Early Modern Drama organized by Sally Barnden and Nora J. Williams, respondent Alexa Alice Joubin.

Shakespeare Association of America 2019: Refuge in Shakespeare's Europe organized by Stephen O'Neill, respondent Kristin N. Denslow.

British Shakespeare Association 2019: Shakespeare, Race, and Genre organized by Dennis Britton.

Shakespeare on Screen in the Digital Era Montpellier Congress 2019: Royal Bodies in Shakespearean Adaptations on Screen organized by Anna Blackwell and Marina Gerzic.

Thank you to the journal editors and reviewers of the pieces that originally appeared as articles: the editors of *Borrowers and Lenders*, Sujata Iyengar and the much-missed Christy Desmet, and the editor of *Adaptation*, Deborah Cartmell, and special issue guest editors, Maurizio Calbi and Douglas Lanier.

For access to archival materials, thanks go to the staff at the National Theatre, Shakespeare's Globe Theatre, and the Shakespeare Birthplace Trust. Thank you to the humane understanding of Laura Hussey and Swati Hindwan and the insight of the anonymous reader for Routledge who have all helped these words find an audience.

I first imagined life as a professor and scholar in Meredith Jones Gray's classroom; she again created space in which to flourish when, as my chair, she proposed I take a sabbatical semester. Thanks to Meredith and to Dean of Research, Gary Burdick, for locating the funds necessary to support the sabbatical and the archival trips that formed the beginnings of this project. Provost Christon Arthur's support of the J. N. Andrews Honors Program provided me with a full-time administrative assistant in Ms. Maxine Umana whose attention to detail and commitment to the mission of Honors created time in which I could write. My dear friends and research workshop buddies, Karl Bailey and Vanessa I. Corredera, read many of these words which benefitted substantially from their wisdom and expertise.

Charles Stanley Ross remains the beginning point for my development as a scholar and professor of Shakespeare studies; he first empowered me to pursue questions of gender, identity, and equity. All thanks go to him.

I will never be able adequately to express gratitude for my incredible students in the J. N. Andrews Honors Program learning family, my colleagues in the English Department, the students in my Shakespeare and Film courses, the members of the Honors Faculty, and the Honors Council who have all pushed me to be a better thinker, scholar, and human being. During the pandemic, you behaved in the best of ways. I am humbled by your goodness.

Many partners in the pandemic stayed in touch through Zoom, FaceTime, and socially distant patio visits even on exceptionally cold Michigan winter days: The members of the Humans in Blazers squad, Ante, Dubravka & Elisabeth Jerončić, Sonia Badenas & Davide Sciarabba, Rosemary, Karl, Lily, and Anna Bailey, Anneris Coria-Navia & Benjamin Navia, Vanessa Corredera, Gabriel Montes & Levi Montes, Rebecca and Donald May, Christina Marsa Carlton, Beverly Matiko, Rebecca Wright, Jillian Imes, Haley Butler, Ingrid Radulescu, and the Karpliuk family.

My parents, Maxine Dowden Pittman and Thomas D. Pittman, endured such intense constraint throughout the pandemic so that we could be assured they would remain safe. Thank you, Mom and Dad, for being our neighbors in lockdown, for all the shared meals (even when we had to mask to keep you safe), digitally streamed concerts, Euros football matches, and home improvement projects we embarked upon together. And, as ever, thank you for setting for me a remarkable life foundation valuing excellence, learning, and the grace of hospitality.

Though I hesitate to be grateful for anything in the context of the tragic loss of life throughout the COVID-19 crisis, one of the few bright spots of completing this book during the pandemic has been the joy of working and writing alongside my beloved partner-in-all-things, Paul D. Smith, Jr. Working just across the hall from me since the first lockdown commenced, Paul has been an unparalleled example of ethical responsibility, kindness, and human goodness.

Paul, I feel so privileged to have borne witness to the consummate professional you are and now to know your "office voice"! Thank you for your constant support and investment in what is right and good.

These words come from the home you all have made for me. They are an invitation to the table. Thank you for partaking.

1 Introduction
Representing the Nation's History

"Glory is like a circle in the water,
Which never ceaseth to enlarge itself
Till by broad spreading it disperse to nought."
(*I Henry VI*)

Prologue: "All the Henrys and Richards, too, for that matter"

The 2002 Season Three finale ("Posse Comitatus," first aired May 22, 2002) of Aaron Sorkin's television series, *The West Wing*, scaffolds its plotting on a presidential outing to a conflated performance of William Shakespeare's Wars of the Roses plays, a production featuring, as the fictional President Bartlet (Martin Sheen) says, "All the Henrys and Richards, too, for that matter." The presidential theater-going serves as a signifier for Bartlet's status as "an academic elitist and a snob," Shakespeare as a "stuffy, socially exclusive affair" (Purcell 148). In contrast, the president's political opponent, Governor Ritchie (James Brolin), attends a Yankees' baseball game. In the episodes preceding the season finale, various White House staffers whinge about attending the lengthy performance, much as children might protest eating green vegetables. But *The West Wing* does not interpolate Shakespeare's ghostly and corporeal presence—as author *and* literary body—exclusively as stand-in for high culture, nutritional enrichment; more provocatively, "Posse Comitatus" appropriates the poet's cultural capital to conjure nostalgia for a heroic past and myths of the nation as rubrics by which the incipient War on Terror could be measured. Shaped in the crucible of loss immediately following the September 11, 2001 attacks, Season Three of *The West Wing* illustrates how the pressures of a new kind of war—the war against terror—would undermine and even undo the progressive accomplishments of the 1990s and provoke a steady drift towards aspects of a far-right nationalism once deemed soundly dormant in a rapidly globalizing and digitally expanding era.[1] The role of Shakespearean history in the season's final episode predicts not only the retreat of multicultural progressivism but also the vexed way in which the West's great dramatist and historian, Shakespeare, would operate as vehicle for nostalgic longing and all too rarely as goad to critical self-examination.

DOI: 10.4324/9781003043065-1

Season Three of *The West Wing,* aired after the September 11 attacks in New York, Pennsylvania, and Washington, D.C., began with a specially scripted prologue episode, "Isaac and Ishmael" (originally aired October 3, 2001). Written by Sorkin, the prolegomenon, in muted tones suited to the national mood, gave voice to an American siege sensibility and parsed (perhaps a bit pedantically) the difference between Islamic extremists and moderate Muslim people of faith. Well-intentioned, the episode sought to stem the tide of anti-Islamic sentiment while giving voice to a nation's grief. The episode features a wrongful interrogation of an Arab employee at the White House, obviously aimed to instantiate the *incorrect,* witch-hunt response to terror, though subsequent episodes in the season would trouble the clarity of that message. Despite that effort at self-critical analysis and judicious differentiation of others, Season Three developed a plotline centered on an Islamic extremist, Abdul Shareef, the Defense Minister of a fictional Arab state, Qumar; that terrorist mastermind became the object of a covert operation in the season's culminating episode and illustrated how the fog of fear surrounding the 9/11 attacks smothered the more generous-minded multicultural national project. In the season finale, the president debates the ethics of a Shareef kill order, jousts with his political rival, passes a welfare funding bill, and attends *The Wars of the Roses* (a production transferred from England to New York for a Catholic Charities fundraising event).

As a demonstration of the ways in which the terror threat propelled the liberal left closer to the right's primed nationalism, the episode's contradictions and blunted ironies inadvertently predicted the political fallout fifteen years later when 2016 saw Vote Leave's success in the United Kingdom European Union membership referendum (Brexit) and the election of Donald J. Trump in the United States. Early in the episode, the president tells his therapist that he anticipates the musical additions in the evening's *Wars of the Roses* program, particularly a rousing chorus already running through his mind; President Bartlet describes the song as an Edwardian "song I love," and quotes two lines, "And victorious in war / Shall be made glorious in peace." He comments, "It always reminds me....It makes me think of college. Like, I don't know...Like, they should be singing it in the dining hall at Christ [sic] College at Cambridge." The therapist (Adam Arkin) redirects the president's air of wistful longing for more honorable times, prompting Bartlet to hint at the choice he must make to assassinate the terrorist Shareef. In the context of the scene, the remembered patriotic anthem comforts the president but also highlights the gap between the ethical clarity of the past and the moral quagmire of a war on terror where, the implication is, defeat of this enemy requires the sacrifice of older virtues.

In the hands of Sorkin, Shakespeare's history of Henry VI's reign transforms into a piece of Victorian-era medieval nostalgia, "an insipid, stodgy costume drama" (Hampton-Reeves and Rutter 13). The intercut performance of Shakespeare's drama appears in three different snippets over the course of "Posse Comitatus"—a tableau staging of Henry V's funeral (*I Henry VI*, 1.1.1–6,

9, 16), the death of Richard Plantagenet, the Duke of York (*III Henry VI*, 1.4.106–112), and an interpolated closing chorus not taken from Shakespeare. The first scene—that of Henry V's funeral—not only mourns the dead king but, in light of 2001, also eulogizes a mode of heroic masculinity out of sync with combat against the often-unseen threat of terror. Treating as a single speech the words of the Duke of Bedford and the Duke of Gloucester, the episode stages lines such as "Virtue he had, deserving to command" and "He ne'er lift up his hand but conquered" (1.1.9, 16). A far less straightforward moment constitutes the second performed scene, the death of Richard Plantagenet. In this famous confrontation between Queen Margaret and the Duke of York, Henry VI's wife (the outsider and dowerless Frenchwoman) taunts the Duke over the death of his younger son, Rutland. This moment of civil strife vilifies the queen who is simultaneously an insider (Queen of England) and outsider (adulterous Frenchwoman) and, more importantly, unspeakably cruel as she flourishes a handkerchief dipped in young Rutland's blood. The scene justifies tacitly the masculinist construction of authority pervading *The West Wing* by finding a Renaissance-filtered, medieval exemplar of the dangers of women on top. Nonetheless, in its fuller context, the moment *does* generate moral ambiguity since the Duke of York and his family suffer, in part, because he has made a bloody claim against the Lord's anointed monarch, the pious Henry VI. The second scene, thus, could hold a mirror up to the post-9/11 West, forced to consider the causal role of its own international alliances, policies, and actions in relation to the growth of Islamic extremism. The confrontation between Queen Margaret and York encapsulates two opposed (though not mutually exclusive) responses to attack—scapegoating the figure of otherness or, the more difficult option, evaluating the internal causes and complicities that result in such violence.

Unfortunately, the final staged scene and its intertextual references cut short such self-critical analysis, though in their banner-waving enthusiasm, these elements highlight the challenges of gender, class, and racial representation persistent in third-millennial stories of the nation. Rather than stage another scene from the first tetralogy, "Posse Comitatus" returns in its fictional theater performance to the patriotic song President Bartlet has previously remembered with fondness. The episode implies that, like the patriotic chorus ringing through the president's mind, this cycle of history plays confronts short-lived strife but arrives at triumphant and abiding peace.[2] In the episode's performance, a young boy of African descent begins the final musical number, and, eventually, a large gathering of Caucasian characters joins him in song to the waving of red, white, and blue banners. The boy's presence triggers a musical intertext from 1980/85, *Les Miserables*, in which the street urchin, Gavroche, and his barricade-mounting, Tricolour-waving compatriots voice the cry for working-class freedom and equality. However, applied to a series of plays dramatizing the conflict between the contending royal Plantagenet cousins, the Gavroche reference seems more a hegemonic appropriation than genuine class resistance. Furthermore, like much of the colorblind casting of *The West Wing* and, indeed, too often much of performed Shakespeare, the black boy at the close of *The Wars of the Roses* interpolation attempts to paper thinly over persistent inequities in racial representation. The anomalous appearance of a single non-white face in the staged scene replicates the tokenism often associated with colorblind casting practices. Furthermore, his casting illustrates the way in which visible differences of race prompt questions about the accuracy and authenticity of historiographic enterprises. Should the black body of the boy be "seen" by an audience in order to make viewers wonder, "Were there blacks in medieval England," or should it be "invisible"—incidental to the historical narrative in much the way the interpolated song operates? Or should the casting reside in between those poles of visibility and invisibility, asking an audience to conceive of the contemporary nation as one in which all multicultural citizens partake in history and share in its reproduction and representation? The degree to which that remediative option thrives certainly depends upon more than a tokenism of multiethnic casting.

In addition to its questionable reliance upon a single actor of color, the production's final musical number raises eyebrows with its jangling rhymes and faith in divinely ordained dominion, embodying a chest-thumping patriotism. The imported song is actually Stephen Oliver's send-up of Victorian imperial confidence from David Edgar's two-part stage adaptation of Charles Dickens's novel *The Life and Adventures of Nicholas Nickleby* for the Royal Shakespeare Company (1982–1983). Performed on *The West Wing* and jump-cut with the successful assassination of the terrorist, Shareef, the song seems, on the one hand, intended as ironic—its genial platitudes a fiction from the start and most certainly impossible to uphold in a post-9/11 world. However, given President Bartlet's moral stature in the series and his earlier affirmation of its refrain, the closing number functions as nostalgic rather than wholly ironic. In fact, the song ensures that Shakespearean history operates as more than a marker of elitism, invoking the poet's *oeuvre* instead as a vital mode of national and popular pride. The blush-inducing words as sung in "Posse Comitatus" declare:

> Every garner filled with grain,
> Every meadow blessed with rain,
> Rich and fertile is the golden corn that bears and bears again.
>
> Where so many blessings crowd,
> 'Tis our duty to be proud:
> Up and answer, English yeoman, sing it joyfully aloud!
>
> [Evermore] upon our country
> God will pour his rich increase:
> And victorious in war shall be made glorious in peace.
>
> (Edgar 209)

What should be dismissed as imperialist tripe, instead serves as a tool for measuring the moral diminishment of a war on terror, leaving valid, unquestioned, desirable, and operational a vision of the blithe "providential" prosperity of an earlier time in England and the West. If, as seems likely, the primary goal of the song in the episode was to stress a falling off from the medieval heroism of Henry V and the moral rectitude of imperial hegemony, such deployment leaves dangerously unchecked the song's oxymoronic punchline that "victorious in war / shall be made glorious in peace." Just such contradictory assumptions about the peace secured through warfare would, of course, surface in debates over when exactly to declare "mission accomplished" in the War on Terror that followed the September 11 attacks.

Vexing further a critical dismissal of that final pseudo-Shakespearean chorus is the murder earlier in the episode of a member of the president's security services detail. Simon Donovan (Mark Harmon) dies in a convenience store robbery which he has, with an almost cavalierly confident do-good impulse, attempted to thwart. Jeff Buckley's cover of Leonard Cohen's anthem, "Hallelujah," plays throughout the death and aftermath, its wrenching tones silencing questions regarding the remaining action and content of the finale. The episode's musical elegy for Secret Serviceman Donovan, like the corporate mourning for the thousands killed on September 11 (and in particular the first responders who rushed into the World Trade Center), forestalls the self-critical mechanism that would inspire a judicious consideration of terror. Like the first responders, Donovan is the Henry V who cannot be resurrected. With the haunting acoustic strains of "Hallelujah" still echoing in the episode, the production's chorus, "The Patriotic Song" (so named in Edgar's *Nicholas Nickleby),* cannot be resisted or adequately dissected.

This American borrowing of Shakespearean history and performance neatly introduces the concerns central to *Shakespeare's Contested Nations*—English history, nationhood, multiculturalism, and the ethics of literary representation on stage and television. "Posse Comitatus" reveals that 400 years after they were written, Shakespeare's dramas of late medieval English history remain a touchstone for the often contradictory impulses of imagining nationhood. Part of that persistence stems from the capacity of Shakespearean history to accomplish competing and ostensibly opposed functions: constructing, protecting, shoring up, and strengthening the nation while simultaneously examining, questioning, or exposing the oft-obscured mechanisms by which nationhood endures, operates, and conceals its createdness. Shakespearean history masterfully illustrates the ways in which mythologizing narratives construct and sustain nationhood. These plays also dramatize the communal tendency to suppress the fact that nations are not *a priori*, divinely mandated givens but carefully crafted entities wrought out of an array of exclusionary practices rooted in gender, class, and racial differences. Despite its heterogeneity and multi-directional ethos, Shakespearean history has long been re-tuned in performance to singular notes of unison, and Sorkin's *West Wing* episode illustrates the instinct to seek shelter within such uncomplicated hymns of nationhood during moments of extreme crisis—especially after the terror attacks that quickly clouded the optimism of the third millennium.

Shakespeare's Contested Nations

The third millennium has been marked by contrary movements—a softening of borders through globalization, the European Union, multiculturalism, migration patterns, and the digitization of knowledge and commercial content—and a simultaneous hardening of nationalism in the face of this diffuseness. In reaction to a perceived dissipation of white, male, hegemonic power, New Nationalism and ultra-right-wing political parties have gained traction in Europe and the United States, and the War on Terror has pushed some neoliberals to reject elements of the multicultural project—blaming such openness, rather than Western overt and covert actions in the Middle East, for the rise of Islamic terror. The racism-fueled Vote Leave campaign of the Brexit referendum, likewise, manifests a reactionary backlash against the multicultural, postcolonial state and embodies renewed contestation over definitions of Britain and its people.

In his well-known lecture, "What is a Nation?", Ernest Renan parses the formative interrelationship between memory, historiography, and national identity. Renan identifies both "a rich legacy of memories" and "the desire to live together, the will to perpetuate the value of the heritage that one has received in an undivided form," as fundamental to the nation (52). Echoing Renan, Kwame Anthony Appiah elaborates, "What makes 'us' a people, ultimately, is a commitment to governing a common life together" (*The Lies* 102). Significantly, Renan acknowledges the violence undergirding nation-formation and the selective remembrance essential to national life:

> Forgetting, I would even go so far as to say historical error, is a crucial factor in the creation of a nation.... Indeed, historical enquiry brings to light deeds of violence which took place at the origin of all political formations, even of those whose consequences have been altogether beneficial. Unity is always effected by means of brutality.
>
> (Renan 45)

As Benedict Anderson famously asserts, the nation "is an imagined political community," adding that, "regardless of the actual inequality and exploitation that may prevail...the nation is always conceived as a deep, horizontal comradeship" (6–7). The will to live together involves both remembrance of what Renan calls, "common glories in the past," as well as selective amnesia concerning the nation's violent origins and enduring inequalities.

For example, nations find it convenient to ignore the degree to which the "imagined community" depends upon the subordination and control of females to advance the patriarchal project. Anne McClintock addresses this forgetfulness, declaring, "All nationalisms are gendered, all are invented and all are dangerous" (352). Arguing that "nations have historically amounted to the sanctioned institutionalization of gender *difference*," McClintock catalogues the instrumental service women provide the nation by defining borders, differentiating power status between men, emblematizing the nation itself, and reproducing citizens all while "denied any direct relation to national agency" (354–355). Arguing for a more robust theory of gender and nation, McClintock stresses that such a "feminist theory of nationalism" must give "scrupulous attention to the structures of racial, ethnic and class power that continue to bedevil privileged forms of feminism" (357). Primarily concerned with gender in the formation of postcolonial nations, Elleke Boehmer characterizes the nationalistic and gendered structures inherited by young, newly independent countries: "The male-dominated family drama of most nationalisms embodies, justifies and *reproduces* the organisation of power within nationalist movements and in nation-states, and delimits the national participation of women" (31). An opportunistic ideology, nationalism seizes upon the family as a malleable reinforcing analogue: "It was relative to the private, hierarchical collectivity of the family, ostensibly a natural or given structure, that the horizontally organised nation found an ideal way to sanction its structures of power and to impose its boundaries" (Boehmer 31). Reliant upon this inherited and gendered structure, "men defined national agency and apportioned the rights of citizenship by and between themselves" (Boehmer 32). However, as Floya Anthias and Nira Yuval-Davis point out, women have not been uniformly objectified or entirely disempowered agents in nation-formation; "it is clear that women themselves participate in the oppression and exploitation of women from other ethnic groups as well as from other economic classes" (2). Indeed, though women function as seeming passive cyphers and conduits for the nation's identity and endurance, "the roles that women play are not merely imposed upon them" (11). Anthias and Yuval-Davis explain: "Women actively participate in the process of reproducing and modifying their roles as well as being actively involved in controlling other women" (11), especially women of color and lower socio-economic status. But these contradictory and complicating strands interleaving gender, the nation, and white female complicities are often ignored or forgotten in the process of narrating a people's history.

For Western liberal democracies such as the United Kingdom in the twenty-first century, a related form of amnesia, particularly about a colonial-imperial and slave-owning past, demands a proper reckoning, an accounting that reads the current geopolitical turmoil in light of past crimes and the tainted character of nationalism itself.[3] Identifying nationalism and racism as inseparable and interdependent ideologies, Étienne Balibar asserts, "...the discourses of race and nation are never very far apart" (37), and "...the seeds of racism could be seen as lying at the heart of politics from the birth of nationalism onwards, or even indeed from the point where nations begin to exist" (47).[4] Balibar explains that the racism evident in colonial-imperial nations, manifests as both externally targeted against exploited native populations and internally focused against those immigrants of an "equivocal interiority" assimilated within the post-colonial nation (42–43): "The heritage of colonialism is, in reality, a fluctuating combination of continued exteriorization and 'internal exclusion'" (43). Exploring this phenomenon, Achille Mbembe observes that those external and internal others offer both a handy scapegoating mechanism and a means to avoid the sins of colonial-imperialism: "Wanting not to remember anything any longer, least of all their own crimes and misdeeds, they dream up bad objects that return to haunt them and that they then seek violently to rid themselves of" (2). By linking a resistant memory to the vilification of "outsiders," Mbembe efficiently pinpoints twinned habituations of the third millennium in which atavistic nationalisms, "retreat behind metaphorical and actual walls and seek a return to a romanticised and idealised past when the nation was reputedly great and its culture homogenous" (Clements 2).

Paul Gilroy has labeled this move "postcolonial melancholia," "an unhealthy and destructive post-imperial hungering for renewed greatness" (*Postcolonial* 95). Characterized by a "morbidity of heritage" (*Postcolonial* 100), postcolonial melancholia relates in highly ambiguous ways to the narration of the past, longing on the one hand for lost glories but suffused with a guilt over the atrocities that made that once-greatness possible. Patrick Wright explains the industry largely responsible for recirculating such ideas of the nation through highly curated history, a representational economy that gathers meaning in contrast to the crises of the contemporary moment: "National Heritage is the backward glance taken from the edge of a vividly imagined abyss, and it accompanies a sense that history is foreclosed" (66). From this vexed relation to the past, emerges a mindset hostile to the very victims of colonial aggression who have migrated to the motherland and claimed rights as citizens. Gilroy contends that third-millennial British nationhood develops,

> in opposition to the intrusive presence of the incoming strangers who, trapped inside our perverse local logic of race, nation, and ethnic absolutism not only *represent* the vanished empire but also refer consciousness to the unacknowledged pain of its loss and the unsettling shame of its bloody management.
>
> (*Postcolonial* 101)

As reminders both of lost pre-eminence and of moral culpability, postcolonials provoke the harkening back to imagined homogeneity both Mbembe and Gilroy describe, insisting on a reconsideration of the narratives inscribed about the past.

The long performance record of Shakespeare's history plays—on stage, film, and television—demonstrates that totalizing, though often divisive, tellings of history provide both an essential shape to national self-definition *and* much matter for debate. Recent performances of Shakespearean history revisit the playwright's incipient Britain now inflected by the traumas of the third millennium and an attendant crisis of national self-definition. As Peter Womack argues, "...given Shakespeare's continuing presence in the construction of English identity—given, too, the undiminished strength of nationalism as a political motive across Europe and the world," the questions raised by the dramatist's chronicle plays, "refer, not only to the audiences of the 1590s, but also to ourselves, studying, performing and watching the plays now" (96). The mechanisms of nation-building so influentially detailed in Shakespeare's histories and recycled through performance and adaptation provoke scrutiny, particularly in light of the geopolitical events of the third millennium. At a crucial moment for Western liberal democracies, *Shakespeare's Contested Nations* examines how performed Shakespearean history replicates those exclusionary pasts, critiques the omissions of those narratives, and affords opportunities to tell new stories about the nation as an ever-changing, heterogenous multicultural body. A cluster of loosely interconnected stage and televisual performances and adaptations of the history play canon (the plays of the first and second tetralogies, *Henry VIII*, and *King John*) between 2000 and 2016 illustrate the function Shakespeare's narratives of incipient "English" or "British" identities fulfill for the postmodern and postcolonial United Kingdom.

With that aim, the book considers the following questions: How do performances of Shakespearean history establish and reinforce who belongs to the nation and who speaks for the nation? How do representations of Shakespearean history empower or constrain human ethical action within multicultural Britain? What aesthetic criteria dictate the representational modes of staged and televisual Shakespearean historiography? When retelling Shakespeare's history, how do identity categories such as gender, race, ethnicity, and class intersect with one another and shape concepts of the nation in the third millennium? In performance, why does the history play prove so resistant to reappraisals and redistribution of roles, focal points, and voices to represent a multicultural present? Why do the representational modes of history on stage and screen remain limited in their re-vision of the past, present, and future of Britain? Put most bluntly, what is the trouble with history? And, finally, how might staged and filmed productions of Shakespearean historiography address that trouble?

Divided into three segments, *Shakespeare's Contested Nations* focuses on performances and adaptations from 2000–2005, 2012, and 2015–2016; each major section begins with a framing contextualization related to the questions of nation, historiography, and representation: 1) the release of *The Future of Multi-Ethnic Britain* (2000); 2) the Cultural Olympiad (2012); and 3) the Brexit referendum (2016). Performances by institutions with substantial heritage caché and an ever-expanding digital impact—the National Theatre, the Royal Shakespeare Company, Shakespeare's Globe, and the BBC—constitute the prime focus. These institutions transmit Shakespeare and Shakespearean acting as vital components of Brand Britain and boast global reach and influence in a digital media market. The selected productions form a loose intertextual web through the borrowed acting bodies and creative talents who move between the tightly interconnected worlds of British stage and television. Furthermore, the artifacts chosen reflect the influence of Douglas Lanier's directive to "conceive of our shared object of study not as Shakespeare the text but as the vast web of adaptations, allusions and (re)productions that comprises the ever-changing cultural phenomenon we call 'Shakespeare'" ("Shakespearean Rhizomatics" 29). Indeed, as Margaret Jane Kidnie argues,

> a play, for all that it carries the rhetorical and ideological force of an enduring stability, is not an object at all, but rather a dynamic *process* that evolves over time in response to the needs and sensibilities of its users. (2)

Thus, this book analyzes treatments of the plays in a range of approaches that expand conceptions of the Shakespearean *oeuvre* and adapted text: from staged performances in London and Stratford-upon-Avon, to BBC television projects such as the "faithful" adaptations of the two *Hollow Crown* series, to heritage-style, "looser" adaptations of the *Wolf Hall* variety, to contemporary reinterpretations of the history play canon such as Mike Bartlett's *King Charles III*. Putting the interrelated strategies of stage and televisual performance in dialogue, *Shakespeare's Contested Nations* assesses the mimetic modes deployed for telling the nation's stories and examines the persistence of a nostalgic heritage style that blunts the interrogative potential of the history play canon—particularly after the 9/11 and 7/7 terror attacks. *Shakespeare's Contested Nations* spotlights gaps, omissions, and erasures in representation and posits a nexus of institutional racial insularity, generic limitations, received aesthetic strictures, and audience expectations as partial explanation for the era's failure to create a more thoroughgoing reconception of Shakespearean historiography and the nation on both stage and screen.

Read in light of the third millennium's troubled multiculturalism, the selected performances underscore Shakespeare's enduring role as marker of belonging, sometimes expanding that category and at other moments reinforcing the line between "us" and "them" in British cultural life. In their work redirecting the focal attunements and methods deployed by Shakespeare scholars, Valerie M. Fazel and Louise Geddes rightly assert, "In the postmodern era, finding the 'truth' of Shakespeare's text is no longer the endgame of literary criticism. Instead, Shakespeare is the conduit for the exchange of ideas, a facilitator for explorations of methodologies" (7). By focusing on English stagings and televisual adaptations of Shakespearean history between 2000 and 2016, I hope to demonstrate how the cultural capital of Shakespeare operates in the third millennium to define, reinforce, and, occasionally, facilitate critique of British nationhood. Thus, *Shakespeare's Contested Nations* joins the work of Alexa Alice Joubin, Elizabeth Rivlin, Christy Desmet and others pursuing the ethical responsibilities of art to address the unjust histories and institutional structures that bedevil flourishing human communities.[5] This book does not argue that Britain makes a steady march towards New Nationalism between 2000 and 2016 but rather that elements of 2016's fractious Brexit debate and atavistic nationalism can be found throughout the period and are reflected in the approaches to adaptation and the practices of representation seen in the treatment of Shakespearean history.

The introduction that follows endeavors to establish the intersecting and foundational assumptions that animate the ensuing close readings of individual theater and televisual performances. Beginning with a discussion of the 2000

Runnymede report, *The Future of Multi-Ethnic Britain*, the chapter turns to the debate over Britain's multicultural status at the start of the third millennium and in the wake of the 2001 terror attacks. The chapter then tracks the emergence of New Nationalism, coinciding with both the economic austerity following the 2008 global financial crisis and the rise in refugees from the extended wars in the Middle East. With that context set, the introduction considers historiography as a highly perspectival, selective, and contingent means by which the past becomes legible to, and constitutive of, the incipient British nation. In this light, Shakespearean history, understood as a dialectic of remembrance and forgetfulness, functions as a definitional locus for the nation, its communities, and its citizens. I shift from theorizing historiography, Shakespearean history, and incipient British nationalism to the assumptions about human identities, culture, and ethics that inform close readings of casting and the representation of race and gender in the cluster of productions to be analyzed. After a consideration of so-called colorblind casting and the unique problems of racial representations in performances of the history plays, I close with chapter and methodological overviews.

Multiculturalism, the Nation, and Representation

Stock-taking at the beginning of the third millennium confirmed a vision of postcolonial Britain as a resolutely multiethnic nation with room for continued improvement in the area of integration and equality. Most notably, the 2000 Runnymede Trust report, *The Future of Multi-Ethnic Britain*, offered a thorough-going audit of multicultural policies and practices and articulated a vision for an ever-improving future. From 2009 to 2011, the BBC launched its own assessment of inclusiveness practices and offered a renewed commitment to representation of all British people through its various media outlets and programming. Between 2000 and 2016, however, the attacks in New York, Washington, D.C., and Pennsylvania on September 11, 2001 and in London on July 7, 2005, the extended wars in Iraq and Afghanistan, the unforeseen consequence of the invasion—the rise of the Islamic State—and the concomitant tidal waves of civil and military conflict in the Middle East, prompted a people movement on a scale that has threatened the aims and ideals of new-millennial multiculturalism in Great Britain. Thought leaders differ vocally on the relative and ongoing success of British multiculturalism with the hardest blow to its ideology and practices occurring on June 23, 2016, the successful Brexit referendum to leave the European Union. Stoking the fires of far-right nationalism, Nigel Farage (leader of the UK Independence Party, 2010–2016) appropriated the mass migration of Middle Eastern refugees as campaign fodder to influence the vote, this despite the fact that the UK had granted asylum at a much lower rate than other countries such as Germany and Sweden.[6] The Brexit vote in the UK, much like the Donald Trump election in the same year in the United States, signaled the emergence of a New Nationalism determined to invigorate concepts of the nation-state that multicultural policies had endeavored to soften and render more inclusive.[7]

In 2000, *The Future of Multi-Ethnic Britain* summarized the findings of the commission on the Future of Multi-Ethnic Britain (FMEB) chaired by Bhikhu Parekh and originally commissioned by then-Home Secretary, Jack Straw, in 1998.[8] At the outset of the FMEB's work, Prime Minister, Tony Blair, issued a statement of support: "'we can build a nation which respects diversity and provides social cohesion. The work of the commission is at the heart of the government'" (qtd. in McLaughlin and Neal 162). In his preface to the final report, Parekh defines a successful multiethnic or multicultural society as one

> in which all citizens and communities feel valued, enjoy equal opportunities to develop their respective talents, lead fulfilling lives, accept their fair share of collective responsibility and help create a communal life in which the spirit of civic friendship, shared identity and common sense of belonging goes hand in hand with love of diversity.
>
> (*The Future* x)

Parekh summarizes the obstacles to a "vision of a relaxed and self-confident multicultural Britain": "racial discrimination, racial disadvantage, a racially oriented moral and political culture, an inadequate philosophy of government, a lack of carefully thought-out and properly integrated administrative structures at various levels of government, and a lack of political will" (*The Future* x). Parekh argues that addressing these obstacles requires "not only appropriate legislative, administrative and other measures, but also a radical shift in the manner in which British identity and the relations between different groups of citizens are generally defined" (*The Future* x). According to the commission, during the second half of the twentieth century, multicultural Britain "evolved as an unplanned, incremental process—a matter of multicultural drift, not of conscious policy"; as a result, in 2000, "Much of the country, including many significant power-centres, remains untouched by it" (*The Future* 14). The report condemns the worrying resilience of a colonial mentality, "that involved seeing the white British as a superior race"; "It remains active in projected fantasies and fears about difference, and in racialized stereotypes of otherness. The unstated assumption remains that Britishness and whiteness go together, like roast beef and Yorkshire pudding" (*The Future* 24–25). As will be discussed below, claims such as this one brought down the ire of Home Secretary Straw and others in Blair's administration who resented the report's "grudging" attitude toward "what's been achieved already" (Straw 4).

In addition, the report highlights the failures of arts and media outlets to tell a more complex and inclusive story of British nationhood and identities. A tension between the universal and the particular threads through the recommendations for arts organizations in a multicultural context. A narrative of national identity tends to smooth over the rougher edges of difference in the service of a jingoistic universality. When that universality simply normalizes the experience of the English, claiming their stories as the story of all British people, "a particularism masquerading as the universal" (C. Taylor 44) results;

this faux universalism then mutes the distinctive differences of a vast immigrant population. That failure of representation in arts and media stems, in part, from poor diversity at the highest levels of arts administration in the United Kingdom. The Runnymede Trust report notes that the Department of Culture, Media and Sport (DCMS) issued a self-study in 1999 that claimed commitment "to equal opportunities but indicated also, without a shred of embarrassment or regret, that of the top 20 posts in the department...every single one was held by a white person" (*The Future* 161). Furthermore, "At senior decision-making levels in Channel 4, ITV and the BBC there were even fewer black and Asian people in 2000 than there had been 10 years earlier" (*The Future* 161). The Parekh report concludes that

> Inadequate attention is paid to issues of race, racism and whiteness in British culture, and there are insufficient representations, through the performing and visual arts, of the increasingly hybrid society that Britain now is. *We recommend that a national cultural policy be developed through widespread participation and consultation. It should pay particular attention to issues of cultural inclusion and identity.*
>
> (*The Future* 161–162)

In addition, the commission insists that these matters cannot be viewed in isolation from the rise of digital technologies that render immediately global the conversation on cultural representation:

> The arts and media are currently affected by rapid technological and commercial change: the synthesis of information technology with satellite and cable television, and commercial mergers concentrating decision-making power in the hands of a small number of companies. Companies think and plan globally rather than nationally or locally. Britain's diverse communities and cultures mesh with global networks of great economic significance.
>
> (*The Future* 160)

Repeatedly, the authors of the report champion the economic benefit to the United Kingdom accruing from a better cultivation of multicultural richness:

> ...artistic influences are international and flow across boundaries... In an increasingly global yet diverse world, it is societies that know themselves to be internally diverse, and are at ease with their internal differences, which stand the best chance of economic success.
>
> (*The Future* 163)

To give teeth to its proposals, the commission recommends that national funding be cut or restricted to those institutions that do not address inequities of employment, power-sharing, and the artistic representation of multicultural British identities.

Though the commission offered a roster of policy reform recommendations across sectors to nurture a flourishing multicultural Britain, backlash against the report centered on its assertion that "British" and "English" carried within them troubling racialized connotations. In their analysis of the report launch, Eugene McLaughlin and Sarah Neal explain that the right-wing press outlets "savaged" that claim, "deploying their considerable discursive resources to not just discredit the report's views on the need to re-imagine British identity but to ridicule the authors of the report" (156). The press officer overseeing the commission's launch identifies the *Daily Telegraph*'s headline on the day prior to the release (10 Oct. 2000)—"Straw Wants to Rewrite Our History: British is a Racist Word, says Report"—as "the beginning of the breakdown of the planned news media strategy" designed to control the public's reaction to the document's detailed proposals (McLaughlin and Neal 164). Gilroy ruefully opens *Postcolonial Melancholia* noting resistance to the rather mildly worded FMEB findings: "There was a depressing and deeply symptomatic counter-reaction against the publication of The Future of Multi-Ethnic Britain: The Parekh Report in 2000" (xi). Though the commission's report had pre-circulated to enthusiastic government support, Home Secretary Straw jettisoned his prepared public statement to "openly reject the FMEB Commission's apparent stance on national identity" (McLaughlin and Neal 156). Straw revealed early in his speech at the launch how much the *Telegraph* headline had shaken his endorsement of the policy publication:

> Yesterday the headline in the *Daily Telegraph*, to my absolute astonishment, was that I was through the launching of this report, intending to rewrite history! In any event, it's not my report, nor do I have any interest in the rewriting of history.
>
> (2)

While substantial portions of his speech underscored overlapping sympathies and strategies between New Labour government policy and the FMEB's work, Straw drew his words to a close by returning to the infamous discussion of "English" and "British" as racialized terms:

> ...where I do strongly part company with the Commission is over the view that's expressed in Chapter 3 of this document about Britishness. I frankly don't agree with the Commission in what it says at the end of Chapter 3.
>
> (4)

Straw argued that though past definitions of "British" might have been exclusively white, such was not the case in 2000:

> ...we were overwhelmingly a white society so people were bound to think that being British or English also was synonymous with being

> white…but these days that is changing and it's changing very rapidly and it's changing for the good and I firmly believe that there is a future for Britain as an idea worth celebrating, and a future for Britishness.
>
> (4)

Roundly criticizing those on the left for abandoning nationhood and patriotism, Straw sinisterly turned the tables to suggest in closing that the racist tendencies of nationalism derived precisely from liberals "who left the field [of national pride] to those on the far right" (4). He declared:

> I don't accept the argument of those on the narrow nationalist right, nor on part of the left that Britain, as a cohesive whole, is dead. I am proud, I am English and I'm proud to be English. I'm proud to be British and I'm proud of what I believe to be the best of British values.
>
> (4)

Straw named values such as "fair play, open-mindedness and rights coupled with responsibilities" (4). Damning both with faint praise and outright rejection, Straw ensured that the Parekh report's proposals would flounder in the maelstrom of rhetorical skirmishes.

The media characterization and Straw's disavowal rapidly defanged the FMEB's more robust recommendations. McLaughlin and Neal explain:

> In relation to formal policy arenas, the Parekh report was transformed in a matter of days from being an "inside track" visionary policy template for twenty-first century thinking on "race", national identity and citizenship to a politically untouchable document that was now part of the contested terrain.
>
> (156)

They conclude: "The Parekh report seems to provide one of the clearest examples of how right-wing news media bias can not just *shape* public reactions, but *determine* the political fate of, high profile policy initiatives on 'race'" (159). In his own account of the report's reception, Parekh summarizes:

> The report was much misunderstood, grossly misrepresented, and often deliberately distorted. Even the Home Office, which had warmly welcomed the report after a careful reading of its final draft, gave in to the pressure of the rightwing media and sought to distance itself from parts of it.
>
> ("Reporting" 1)

In his post-hoc diagnosis, Parekh indicts journalistic laziness which forestalled unpacking the assertions of the *Telegraph* article, opting simply to repeat its inflammatory and willful misreadings. In addition, the clamor of the 24/7 news cycle provoked hasty publication so as not to miss what one journalist described as the "fun of the frenzy" (qtd. in Parekh, "Reporting" 6). Understandably,

Parekh laments that the din of controversy neutered the commission's contribution to racial dialogue. Describing what he sees as the unique strength of the FMEB's approach, Parekh explains: "Instead it used race to prise open the history, culture and inner structure of British society, and locate its discussion within a wider debate around British national identity and historical self-understanding" ("Reporting" 5). However, in retrospect, Parekh recognizes the disruptive nature of any attempt to interrogate nationalism and cultural cohesion:

> The very act of raising questions about British nationhood, the best way to read its history, the nature and sources of its unity, the contestability of what are assumed to be its shared values, and so on, especially from an ethnic minority perspective, was subversive.
>
> ("Reporting" 7)

In many ways, the furor over the Parekh report predicts trends in the first years of the new millennium—a growing skepticism regarding the viability of multicultural societies, thinning liberal alliances with that cause, and a subterranean right-wing recourse to atavistic nationalisms, all of which acquired a new character once the planes flew into the World Trade Center on September 11.

British Multiculturalism in the Wake of Terror

Throughout the first decade of the 2000s, debate over multicultural values and the definition of "British" persisted. Gilroy succinctly observes,

> Multicultural society seems to have been abandoned at birth. Judged inviable and left to fend for itself, its death by neglect is being loudly proclaimed on all sides. The corpse is now being laid to rest amid the multiple anxieties of the "war on terror."
>
> (*Postcolonial* 1)

Arun Kundnani notes that while in the past, conservative voices dominated critique of multiculturalism, advocates of liberalism have joined the chorus of concern:

> Multiculturalism is no longer criticized for destroying conservative ideas of English civility, but for destroying liberal ideas of the open society. Moreover, left-wing themes of social solidarity, welfare rights and anti-fascism also have been hitched to an anti-multiculturalist discourse. Thus, multiculturalism has lost many of the friends that it had among liberals and the Left, and faces rejection from across the political spectrum.
>
> (156)

Kundnani's account charts a shift in attitudes, rhetoric, and policies, particularly after the 7/7 attacks: "Trevor Phillips, then chair of the Commission for Racial

Equality, argued that multiculturalism had allowed Islamist extremism to fester in British society" (157). To combat the so-called "fragmentation" associated with multiculturalism, nationalism dressed in terms such as "Britishness" emerged "to recharge the batteries of national belonging" (157). The joining of hands between conservatism and liberalism was driven by the perception of Muslims as a highly visible minority, resistant to core, definitional values; conservative and liberals alike asserted that "…the country's generosity and tolerance were being taken advantage of by people who did not share the same liberal values" (157). In particular,

> The rebalancing of tolerance is regarded as a necessary response to a clash between a separatist Muslim communal identity (sometimes defined as "Islamism"), and the liberal values of women's rights, gay rights, freedom of expression, secularism and anti-totalitarianism. Muslims – or in some accounts, certain kinds of political Muslims – come to symbolize the danger of cultural difference and become the focus for a project of producing good, liberal individuals who have absorbed British, European or western values.
>
> (158)

Kundnani points out that, in many ways, this multicultural backlash has replaced the colonial-era prejudices with a "rearticulation of notions of racial and civilizational superiority in an ostensibly liberal idiom" (159):

> the liberal discourse of integration emphasizes the Enlightenment and its legacy of secularism, individualism and freedom of expression. This liberal discourse has displaced an older conservative nationalism and does the same work of marking out racial difference, now through a notion of British values counterposed to a Muslim communal identity.
>
> (160)

Essentially, a new form of racism masquerades as a defense of liberal values and evades the name of "racism" by suggesting that these differences with Muslim traditions are not racial but rather religious—"hostility to religious beliefs rather than to a racial group" (160). Though studies show that Muslim immigrants do readily self-identify as British, the question of what constitutes "British" and whether or not that concept should be flexible or rigid has come under further scrutiny.

In a number of essays, including, "Too diverse?", David Goodhart has argued that the liberal welfare state of Great Britain cannot survive the fragmentation of multicultural policy and practice, in fact that "common culture is being eroded." Goodhart explains:

> In the rhetoric of the modern liberal state, the glue of ethnicity ("people who look and talk like us") has been replaced with the glue of values

("people who think and behave like us"). But British values grow, in part, out of a specific history and even geography. Too rapid a change in the make-up of a community not only changes the present, it also, potentially, changes our link with the past.

Goodhart worries that the reciprocity essential to the welfare state cannot survive a large influx of immigrants who cannot be trusted to share the same liberal values upon which the welfare state was founded. Curiously, he regards the insular nature of immigrant communities as both a threat to and an object of envy for the poor white laborer:

> This can be another source of resentment for poor whites who look on enviously from their own fragmented neighbourhoods as minorities recreate some of the mutual support and sense of community that was once a feature of British working-class life.

In this sentence, Goodhart inadvertently reveals the jealousy and base insecurity operating here, not to mention a nostalgic fetishizing of the working class that similarly accompanied Trump's brand of nationalism in the United States. According to Goodhart, cohesive communal life—a distinctly British trait and value—exists in the form of lively immigrant enclaves but because these groups are of a different complexion and religious affiliation, they cannot be considered part of the national identity and economic structure. Rather, they constitute a threat.

Similarly, Martin Amis's casual conflation of all forms of Muslim practice and belief throughout his influential post-9/11 essays fuels the backlash chronicled by Kundnani. Amis describes Islam as authoritarian at its core and when doing so offers no variation in degree or practice: "Like fundamentalist Judaism and medieval Christianity, Islam is totalist. That is to say, it makes a total claim on the individual. Indeed, there is no individual; there is only the *umma*—the community of believers" (77). Citing gender equality as a wedge issue, for example, Amis insists:

> All men are my brothers. I would have liked to have said it then, and I would like to say it now: all men are my brothers. But all men are not my brothers. Why? Because all women are my sisters. And the brother who denies the rights of his sister: that brother is not my brother. At the very best, he is my half-brother—by definition.
>
> (49)

Indeed, when discussing sexual and marriage mores in Islam, Amis contends, "It is difficult to exaggerate the sexual invasiveness…of the Islamic system, even among the figures we think of as moderate" (64). Though advanced in the name of universal human rights, such liberal positions in the 2000s eroded sympathy for and support of the multicultural agenda.

Responses to these liberal critiques of multiculturalism point out both logical fallacies and insufficient facticity in assertions that Muslim immigrants undermine British national identity and values. Pathik Pathak sees Goodhart's position as far from benign: "scapegoating immigrants for everything from the sustainability of the welfare society to the survival of democratic society leads us down a dark and dangerous path to the psychology of majoritarian fear" (261). Contending that Goodhart and others ground their skepticism about multiculturalism on baseless anxieties, Pathak argues, "This reveals the hazard of being accountable to anxieties: they rarely have any basis in fact" (265). Instead, Pathak suggests that a polity of empowered participants from many backgrounds and a commitment to universal human rights can provide the "social glue" necessary to a thriving British culture and policy:

> We need to recognise this moment for what it is: not a time to reassure majorities by shrinking into familiar, comfortable positions that relieve the burden of responsibility, but empowering more people with a say in the shape of our collective future through a strong culture of human rights embedded in a diverse civil society. This is the kind of community to which we should be aspiring.
>
> (270)

Parekh's *A New Politics of Identity* similarly questions the false binary advanced by writers like Goodhart who pit economic justice and state-sponsored redistribution of wealth against multiculturalism. Indeed, Parekh contends that social and economic justice gain sharpest moral clarity and pressing relevance when placed in dialogue with and enriched by diversity: "The politics of identity does not militate against social cohesion or redistribution; rather, respecting the legitimate claims of the groups involved is an important step towards integrating them into an expanded basis of solidarity" (*A New* 47). Sociological data offers the clarity of fact as a crucial means to dismantle the false binaries presented by Goodhart and others.

Several studies confirm that multiculturalist policies do not undermine the welfare state nor demolish British national identity and cohesion. Varun Uberoi and Tariq Modood note that proponents of multiculturalist policy and ideology also value national solidarity and interdependencies: "Contrary then to what various critics claim, multiculturalists have long acknowledged the importance of a nation's identity and people's sense of it, but they also note how both can come to include cultural minorities as they do change" (132). Uberoi and Modood contend that "Policies of multiculturalism are thus a means to help make a nation's identity and people's sense of it more inclusive over time—but not wholly different" (132). Despite the backlash and a loudly touted retreat from such policies, Uberoi and Modood point out that politicians still advance multiculturalism, and important protections remain in place for religious and ethnic minorities in the United Kingdom (134). By analyzing the UK Labour Force Survey data, Alan Manning and Sanchari Roy test identification with "Britishness." They conclude that,

> New immigrants rarely think of themselves as British but the longer they remain in the UK the more likely they are to do so. Second generation immigrants are only slightly less likely to think of themselves as British than the white UK-born population and it seems that the gap narrows further with each generation.
>
> (F74)

They also note that "Muslims do not stand out as having especially low levels of British identity" (F80); rather, the main hold-outs to self-identifying as British are the inhabitants of Northern Ireland (F80). Manning and Roy suggest that immigrant identification with British values may not be a large concern; however, "A more serious culture clash may be the refusal of the majority population to see minorities as British and it would be useful to think about how people see others as much as how they see themselves" (F97). Thus, though immigrants in the survey appear eager to continue and refine a tradition of British national identity, their contributions may not be welcomed or desired by others, a possibility borne out by the discourse surrounding the Brexit vote.

Sivamohan Valluvan's recent work examining the rise of New Nationalism across Europe and manifested in the successful Brexit referendum confirms that racial prejudices more than an often-cited economic disenfranchisement triggered the march to the right: "Brexit, and the feelings of resentment and powerlessness that fueled it, was primarily framed by issues of ethnic difference and immigration" ("Defining" 232). Valluvan cites a range of themes that captured anti-EU voter fervor: "immigration, refugees, Muslims, the spectre of Turkey, the Roma, the tyranny of anti-racist political correctness" (232). In many ways, Valluvan contends that the road to the Brexit vote was paved by the liberal backlash against multiculturalism in the first decade of the third millennium: "Brexit represented the formal consolidation of a new electoral coalition in the UK: middle-income conservatives dotted across the green shires and provincial towns of England hitched to swathes of previously Labour-voting working-class Britain" (232). Though Valluvan acknowledges benign and well-documented components of nationalism—"the entire aspiration for peoplehood, community, and the attendant expression of sovereignty" ("Defining" 233)—he quickly offers a more pressing definition and warning about its current ascendency:

> Namely, western nationalism can be read as the formation by which a self-appointed normative community attributes its putative socioeconomic, cultural and security concerns to the excessive presence and allowance made to those understood as not belonging. Those who comprise the relevant field of non-belonging include the variously constituted insider minorities but also various foreign peoples and international forces, some of which intertwine with and reinforce the pathologies attributed to those internal, generally non-white groups.
>
> (233)

Valluvan stresses that blaming economic pressures and the laboring classes for New Nationalism ignores the substantial number of affluent conservatives who supported Brexit; furthermore, in a country like Norway, where standards of living are fairly high and evenly distributed, nationalism has still gained momentum ("Defining" 235). Rather, "Muslims and multiculturalism…are definitive of the nationalist formation" ("Defining" 236). Troubled by the alignment of liberal and conservative agendas in the New Nationalism, Valluvan reminds readers, "that nationalist sway at any given historical moment requires a particular kind of racial othering" (238) and "is always, in the final instance, about its own exclusionary racisms—anything else is simply a convenient bedfellow rallied to make its appeal more likely" ("Defining" 239). A faulty sense of history—one that fails to represent the enduring role played by refugees and immigrants in the country's development—empowers a racist vision of the nation as an all-white affair.

The nature of the campaigning and the result of the Brexit referendum cast new light on the challenges to the 2000 Parekh report; in many ways the distorting media response to its gentle critique of the coded racisms embedded in definitions of "British" predict the battle lines that hardened in 2016. The racism and defensive post-imperialism driving the Vote Leave campaign's furor over immigration, the refugee crisis, and Turkey's prospective membership in the EU find analogues in the hysterical reaction against the FMEB commission's request that British history and identity be reconsidered to account more deliberately for the country's multiethnic communities. The fate of the 2000 report demonstrates the subversiveness of such a suggestion and illuminates the high-risk stakes of recalibrating and retelling a nation's story. Such tellings invariably formulate a nation's identity, reifying borderlands of difference, and determining who does or does not belong. But those re-presented histories also may unearth fault lines within a people's self-conception and expose the fictionalized and arbitrary nature of cultural givens and national pride.

Shakespeare Telling the Nation's History

George Eliot begins *Daniel Deronda* (1876) with this epigraph: "Men can do nothing without the make-believe of a beginning." She elaborates by comparing the search for an origin in two seemingly opposed disciplines—science and poetry:

> Even Science, the strict measurer, is obliged to start with a make-believe unit, and must fix on a point in the stars' unceasing journey when his sidereal clock shall pretend that time is at Nought. His less accurate grandmother Poetry has always been understood to start in the middle; but on reflection it appears that her proceeding is not very different from his; since Science, too, reckons backwards as well as forwards, divides his unit into billions, and with his clock-finger at Nought really sets off *in medias res*. No retrospect will take us to the true beginning; and whether our

> prologue be in heaven or on earth, it is but a fraction of that all-presupposing fact with which our story sets out.
>
> (1)

Eliot's characterization of beginning points as "make-believe" and her insistence that "No retrospect will take us to the true beginning" anticipates, in many ways, understandings of history that emerge with twentieth-century critical theory. Perhaps most apt about her assertions is the recognition that humans crave a beginning—that even arbiters of objectivity invent an origin and define the units by which that point will be accessed and referenced. Her epigraph understands that discourse weaves the fabric of remembrance and as a means of mediation will impose arbitrary decision points upon the "real" of the past, going so far as to invent a "naught" or point zero of an unreachable infinite regression. In other words, history-telling requires a set of epistemic functions that irreparably change the "real" that is narrated.

Just over a hundred years after Eliot wrote those words, Michel de Certeau's *The Writing of History* unpacks that mechanism by which an origin point takes narratological being. He characterizes the historiographical task as a recuperation into consumable narrative of "the real" by means of the "unreal" of discourse (xxvii); in this way, he foregrounds the mediating constructive act and the series of "as if" actions embedded in the narration of the past. These "as if" actions allow the historiographer to proceed in history's telling without admitting at every turn to the fragility of that story, a vulnerability in history exacerbated by the very act used to preserve it. Further defining the historiographical labor as a series of decision points of differentiation, de Certeau elaborates:

> But whatever this new understanding of the past holds to be irrelevant—shards created by the selection of materials, remainders left aside by an explication—comes back, despite everything, on the edges of discourse or in its rifts and crannies: "resistances," "survivals," or delays discreetly perturb the pretty order of a line of "progress" or a system of interpretation.
>
> (4)

Inherent in the shaping of the past is the decision to include or exclude and to define against the Other:

> In the West, the group (or the individual) is legitimized by what it excludes (this is the creation of its own space), and it discovers its faith in the confession that it extracts from a dominated being (thus is established the *knowledge* based upon, or of, the other: human science).
>
> (5)

In his well-known work, "The West and the Rest," Stuart Hall describes this very "system of representation" (277), which "produced knowledge" and "became both the organizing factor in a system of global power relations and the organizing concept or term in a whole way of thinking and speaking" (278). For de Certeau, the historiographical endeavor is thus complicated by 1) an assertion of truth that papers over the gap between past and present and between "the real" and discourse, 2) a series of inclusions and exclusions, and 3) definitional acts predicated upon dominated groups.

As a reflection both of what a society wishes to be and fears it is, historiography can also provoke acts of painful self-reflection:

> If, in one respect, the function of history expresses the position of one generation in relation to preceding ones by stating, "I can't be that," it always affects the statement of a no less dangerous complement, forcing a society to confess, "I am other than what I would wish to be, and I am determined by what I deny."
>
> (de Certeau 46)

In other words, though history serves a self-definitional function for a dominant group, its gaps, fissures, shards, and denials inevitably surface to provoke troubling questions about that group and its efforts at self-narration. These interrogations reveal that the stories of a dominant class silence other histories and severely circumscribe the agential capacities of those others. Thus, even as historiography serves hegemonic powers, its excesses and remainders trouble monolithic assertion: shards remain after the refining and serve as a "fragile witness and necessary critique" of social praxis (de Certeau 48). Recognizing those shards and hearing voices of dissent in the historical and cultural record fulfill an ethical duty by which the dominant or privileged class can begin to atone for being "other than what I would wish to be." The ten plays we know as "history plays" by Shakespeare instantiate the range of contradictions and uncontainable excesses de Certeau identifies as endemic to the historiographic enterprise. In these works, the real of medieval historical event transforms at the hand of the playwright and through the bodies of actors, and in the case of every play, the "shards" of an unofficial history disrupt the uniformity of a narrated past.

In the 1990s, critical theory instigated a significant transformation in approaches to and understanding of emergent British nationhood in the historiography and literature of the early modern period. The work of Richard Helgerson, David Baker, and others explores how sixteenth- and seventeenth-century literature contributed to the formation of a "British" national identity, with particular focus on the losses and gains of that often violent process. Daniel Woolf argues that during the early modern period,

> the English developed a more or less coherent—which does not mean "uncontested"—historical sense of a national past. This includes not merely the particular history of England itself and its relations with its British and Continental neighbours/enemies, but also the place of England, and

> eventually Britain, within a world history that includes the classical and pre-classical eras.
>
> (12–13)

In particular, though the distinct people groups of Ireland, Wales, Scotland, and England make up the British Isles, the Renaissance crafted myths of British identity rooted almost exclusively in English stories and thus silenced the minority groups of the island's sister nations. From its beginnings, Britain was an uneasy knitting together of disparate people groups—Irish, Welsh, Scottish, English—into a singular entity, "British." But the degree to which "British" meant little more than a normative "English" has long been debated.[9] David Baker explains: "Being English in the time of Shakespeare, Spenser, and Marvell meant taking part in nation-creating traditions of exclusion and denial" (12). As Baker indicates, Shakespeare's history plays in particular contribute to that formulation of a British identity, but Shakespeare's plays also simultaneously begin the long process of interrogating the exact nature of that nationalist formulation.[10] The performance of those plays has been a reference point over the past four hundred years for British self-perception, cultural status, and colonial-imperial power. To read *Henry V*, for example, is to witness the birth of a fledgling Great Britain and to encounter the questions and fissures that persist throughout its ensuing histories.[11]

Early modern emergent national historiography charts its own limitations and the stubborn inaccessibility of its subject matter. Phyllis Rackin observes in the time period, "an increasing sense of alienation from the past, of its ineluctable otherness, even while the desire to know and recover that past remained intense, lending a deep poignancy to the entire historiographic enterprise" (*Stages* 12). Andrew Escobedo also reads this frustrated access to the past as characteristic of the period and demonstrable in its historical metanarratives:

> The sense of temporal provisionality fostered by early national consciousness forces many historical writers into a double gesture of recognition and denial, a process in which reuniting the novel present with its estranged history calls uncomfortable attention to the chasm between now and then that the writers were attempting to close.
>
> (Escobedo 6)

Escobedo reviews long-acknowledged factors contributing to a nascent national identity in early modern England: the rise of Protestantism, the political, literary, and artistic influence of the Tudor and Stuart dynasties, and the revived Arthurian legends that conjured a point of origin for Britain. However, he notes, those constitutive elements also undermine the attempt to establish a point of connection with the past: "Yet every one of these nationalizing developments brought along with it a sense of historical discontinuity" (4). For example, just as Protestantism plays such a crucial role defining England as distinct from the Catholic sovereignties of Europe, reformation practice also cuts off the nation from hundreds of years of its own religious traditions.[12] Escobedo describes an oxymoronic interdependency between history and nation: "...English nationalism did not only compensate for historical loss but also helped to create it, depending on this gap between past and present as the condition of its success" (20). The gapped nature of historical narrative inevitably attaches to the nation such stories underprop; as a result, for both history and the nation, the means of access to a collective past and identity, historiography, also operates as the mechanism that denies access, a problematic replicated in the staged history of Shakespeare and his contemporaries.

Historiographical work when translated to the stage provokes a related "consciousness of doubleness," as explained by Brian Walsh, capable of generating critical and ethical interventions. Both actors and audience members experience doubleness as they cycle between immersion in the enacted narrative and awareness of the real bodies who perform and consume the drama; "this doubleness opens interstices in which to think critically about the concept of the past" (Walsh 27). The play of history on stage thus exposes the Certeauvian gap between the past and the present:

> Shakespeare and others harnessed the potential of dramaturgy and dramatic poetry to respond to widespread feelings of historical loss with the power of aesthetic experience: an experience that revels in imaginative gestures toward a past that is always out of reach but that promises the possibility that such enjoyable experiences can be continually recreated through the collective will to have a past.
>
> (Walsh 13)

"In other words," Walsh summarizes succinctly, "the theatrical experience of the past taught early modern audiences that history needs us as much as we need it" (21). In this way, "stage performance was, for Shakespeare and his contemporary playwrights, an opportunity to think *about* the notion of historical consciousness—indeed, to use theater to interrupt, trouble, contemplate and even help to create it" (Walsh 27). Walsh's formulation thus opens up space for actor and audience to play agential roles in the construction of history and the nation. No human involved in the theatrical display of history functions passively—not the actor who delivers pre-scripted lines nor the audience who listens to and must interpret those words. Shakespeare's embodied history invites actors and audiences alike to participate in contesting the nation:

> Standing at the beginning of the era of European nationalism, his plays empower us to see the "imagined community" of the nation as in large part a forgery or imposture, founded on a forgetting that frequently masquerades as remembrance. Even as Shakespeare's histories help to fashion the early modern nation, they subject that construct to critical exposure and scrutiny.
>
> (Baldo 8)

The danger in performance is to downplay the uncertainty and provisional status of that nation and its represented history and to ignore the transformative pressure of human agents.

Furthermore, ethical performance must engage with the fact that these history plays inevitably and lamentably ground concepts of the nation within networks of opposition and difference. The foundational work of Jean E. Howard and Phyllis Rackin establishes the central role of Shakespearean history in defining gender norms within concepts of the incipient nation: "The history plays Shakespeare wrote in the 1590s helped produce what are now regarded as 'traditional' gender relations and the divisions between what we now call the public and private domains" (10). They explain that,

> this genre, in telling stories about England's past and in using those stories to create an imagined community in the present, inevitably also told stories about gender: that is, about how masculinity and femininity differ and about the ways those differences are to be linked to specific social arrangements involving work, marriage, citizenship, and cultural power.
>
> (29)

Likewise, Jennie M. Votava asserts: "In their original contexts, these plays helped formulate the distinction among English, Irish, Welsh and Scottish peoples, the invention of Great Britain as a unified state, and the gender-based division between the public and private spheres" (172). Given their status within a "great men" tradition of history, these plays in performance too often reinscribe the site of national significance as relentlessly masculine. Unsurprisingly, as Lois Potter notes, "the histories in general…have always had a reputation for being unpopular with women." Potter suggests that the "male-oriented subject matter" and "the limited opportunities" for female actors may explain that disinclination ("The Second" 297). Francesca T. Royster identifies another element plaguing Shakespearean history by pinpointing the gender *and* racial hierarchies constructed in and through the genre:

> We might think of one of the central functions of the history play as rehearsing mythic pasts to support national, racial, and gendered hierarchies. Early modern English history plays, like Shakespeare's *Henry VI* plays, present mythic (white, male, English) heroes, ordering those "others" who might support the English cause…and casting out those who threaten the stability of the nation.
>
> (221)

Indeed, Geraldine Heng identifies racism's harmful opportunism in "the ability of racial logic to stalk and merge with other hierarchical systems—such as class, gender, or sexuality" (20). Thus, just as in conceptualizations of the nation so in Shakespearean history, gender and race inflect "belonging," very much in step with an exclusionary national historiography.

Artistic representation is by no means an ethically neutral act, particularly when a nation is being created through performance and at the expense of women and non-whites. Competing denotations of the term "representation" inhere in the enactment of historical drama. As Gayatri Chakravorty Spivak has famously pointed out, such narratives operate first as artistic representations (*darstellen*). In addition, as stories that give selective voice to some figures of the past and not to others, the history plays also reflect and determine who does and does not benefit from political representation (*vertreten*) (276). In the third millennium, as the British people debate the status not only of refugees from ongoing global conflicts but also of its citizens descended from empire's end, the representation of the nation's histories of inclusion and exclusion has implications for the quality of political representation such groups do or do not enjoy. The Parekh report very directly insists, sadly to its detriment, on the causal connection between the stories of a nation and its policies of education, criminal justice, healthcare, employment, and immigration. Isabel Karremann's dialectic between remembering and forgetting in the formation of history demonstrates how dramatic representation takes on such political dimensions:

> ...memories that deviate from the official version are subjected to acts of silencing such as censorship, taboo, or iconoclasm. By the same token, forgetting an official version of historical events and providing a set of counter-memories allows for the constitution of alternative accounts and legitimations of authority, and can thus also be seen as a strategy of resistance to structures of violent suppression. We must therefore be aware of the fact that remembering and forgetting are not only complementary processes in society, but that they are also instruments of domination or of resistance to its underlying power structure.
>
> (11)

On the stage and on film and television, performance practices can alternatively spotlight or obscure the Certeauvian shards of history and Karremann's suppressed narratives. As an artform of human embodiment, performance inevitably manifests the politics of identity regardless of whether or not creatives acknowledge this responsibility and shape the fluid semiotics of human subjective representations accordingly.[13] Karremann describes the impact of these representational choices on national culture; "Returning again and again to definitive moments in history that haunt the collective imagination," Shakespeare's history plays "highlight that there is no such thing as historical truth and that the theatre is not simply a mirror held up to nature but rather an institution and practice that actively participates in the shaping of cultural memory" (30). A production's choice of time period, representational style (naturalistic or non-naturalistic), editing decisions (both of text and filmed diegesis), the ethnicity of performers, and the costuming and props choices that mark gender, sexuality, ethnicity, race, class, ability, and religion all work to define who belongs in the story of a nation, what a nation chooses to remember, as well as what it wishes to forget.

Deeply indebted to scholarship concerning the nature, performance, and representation of the nation's historiographical memory, this book operates upon a set of related analytical assumptions: 1) Any staging of the past constitutes a staging of the present; 2) Stories of the past form the record of a nation's attempt at self-knowledge and coherent self-identity; 3) Historical narratives take shape in the borderland between in and out, inclusion and exclusion, belonging and exile; 4) Those stories of the past have victors and victims; 5) To be left out of narrated history or kept on the margins is to have one's subjectivity and value as a person assaulted; 6) Historiography relies on an assemblage of facts mediated through the fiction of a form; 7) Historical authenticity depends upon the spotlighting of select facts and a seeming transparency of form; 8) Shakespearean history weds the authority of historiography with the iconic status of England's greatest canonical author; and 9) How we tell a uniquely Shakespearean history matters for the nation and its people groups.

Intersubjectivity, Ethics, and Human Culture

By insisting that contemporary performance of Shakespearean history entails certain responsibilities of representation and recognition, I ground the analytical work of *Shakespeare's Contested Nations* in several key assumptions about the nature of human subjectivity, ethical obligation, and culture. Emmanuel Levinas understands human responsibility as fundamental to subjectivity, indeed as the very beginning of human being: "I speak of responsibility as the essential, primary and fundamental structure of subjectivity. For I describe subjectivity in ethical terms" (*Ethics* 95). As Lisa Starks-Estes explains, "For Levinas, then, ethics or moral behavior is not a supplement or an add-on to an already fully-formed subject; conversely, it is the basis upon which the subject is formed, the primary philosophy itself, the foundation of all." Levinas characterizes such foundational obligation to the face of the other as being hostage: "It is through the condition of being hostage that there can be in the world pity, compassion, pardon and proximity—even the little there is, even the simple 'After you, sir'" (*Otherwise* 117). Michael L. Morgan clarifies the hostage state of Levinasian subjectivity:

> ...in everyday life every social interaction, every encounter between one person and another, is always *already* such a nexus of plea, command, and inescapable responsibility, *before* it is anything else—which it always is. Only once the self is confronted by a face can it be responsible and must it be responsible—for and to that other person.
>
> (66)

He offers concrete precision to the Levinasian pleas made by the face of the other: "do not kill me," "make room for me," "feed me," "share the world with me," "reduce my suffering" (Morgan 68). This understanding of mutual obligation as self-constitutive then must be situated within the larger context of communities and the nations they comprise.

Levinas's conception of the "essentially social nature" of human being (Morgan 128) finds further development in the discourse ethics of Seyla Benhabib and her advocacy for deliberative democracies. She defines with more precision the nature of the social self:

> I assume that the subject of reason is a human infant whose body can only be kept alive, hose needs can only be satisfied, and whose self can only develop within the human community into which it is born. The human infant becomes a "self," a being capable of speech and action, only by learning to interact in a human community. The self becomes an individual in that it becomes a "social" being capable of language, interaction and cognition.
>
> (*Situating* 5)

Benhabib reasons that since the human being as a social subject takes form within intersubjective transactions, the capacity to challenge, pressure, and correct one's personal set of known and unknown prejudices and privileges inheres in the phenomenology of human intersubjective identities. She writes:

> In fact, all selves are constituted by complex and multiple narrations and perspectives. The perspectives of constitutive others are fundamental to my own self-narration.... If the other is already within me, why should it be so difficult for me to recognize the other outside me?
>
> ("In Defense" 188)

In the discourse ethics of Benhabib, one human imagines the world from the perspective of another, checks that conjuration through dialogue with other humans, and adjusts behavior accordingly. Benhabib extends these basic premises regarding the intersubjective nature of selfhood to her sociology of culture.

For Benhabib, individual human interactions require conversation and a constant recalibration of mutual understandings; culture necessarily magnifies and repeats the process. Disputing epistemic fallacies defining culture as a uniform entity, Benhabib argues that culture can only be described as a monolithic whole, and falsely so, from the outside; rather, experienced from within, culture will always be constituted by competing and contradictory narratives. She asserts that members of a culture, "experience their traditions, stories, rituals and symbols, tools, and material living conditions through shared, albeit contested and contestable, narrative accounts" (*The Claims* 5). She describes a "double hermeneutic" foundational to the sociology of culture: "We identify *what* we do through an *account* of what we do; words and deeds are equiprimordial," and, human actions "are also constituted through the actors' evaluative stances toward their doings" (*The Claims* 6–7). Here the words that memorialize deeds occupy equal status with the deeds, actions, and events of a people. In this, Benhabib relies upon Hannah Arendt's assertion that, "With word and deed we insert ourselves into the human world" (176). According to Arendt, each human contributes to the ever-expanding cache of stories that trace human interconnectivity:

> The realm of human affairs, strictly speaking, consists of the web of human relationships which exists wherever men live together....Together they start a new process which eventually emerges as the unique life story of the newcomer, affecting uniquely the life stories of all those with whom he comes into contact.
>
> (Arendt 183–184)

By deeming both deeds and words foundational, Benhabib insists on the prime role of narrative in establishing the boundaries and terms of culture for its participants. Historiography in Benhabib's framing then becomes one of the modes equiprimordial with action and constitutive of that action.[14]

Since humans live in Arendt's "web of narratives," as Benhabib suggests, then differentiation and interpretive judgement determine the horizon of culture. These evaluative stances Benhabib describes as "second-order narratives" circulate and inform the binaries that determine "in" and "out" in any given culture:

> What we call "culture" is the horizon formed by these evaluative stances, through which the infinite chain of space-time sequences is demarcated into "good" and "bad," "holy" and "profane," "pure" and "impure." Cultures are formed through binaries because human beings live in an evaluative universe.
>
> (*The Claims* 6–7)

She acknowledges the biases coded into these first- and second-order "texts": "Whether in the psyche of the individual or in the imagined community of a nation, it is very difficult to accept the 'other' as deeply different while recognizing his/her fundamental human equality and dignity" (*The Claims* 8). Practices of cultural exclusivity flow then from the double hermeneutic in which first-order narratives exist in parallel with these second-order evaluations. However, Benhabib remains optimistic about how the social and situated human can counteract and respond to the threat of a "closed" system of culture. Much as the situated self diffuses anxiety about the concrete other by recognizing the other as self-constitutive, so cultures must continually ingest new narratives and reform, reshape, and re-evaluate previous stories of cultural distinctiveness and superiority:

> We should view human cultures as constant creations, recreations, and negotiations of imaginary boundaries between "we" and the "other(s)."

> The "other" is always also within us and is one of us. A self is a self only because it distinguishes itself from a real, or more often than not imagined, "other." Struggles for recognition among individuals and groups are really efforts to negate the status of "otherness," insofar as otherness is taken to entail disrespect, domination, and inequality.
>
> (*The Claims* 8)

This understanding leads Benhabib to reject the "mosaic" notion of multiculturalism in which definable, unified, and wholly separate cultures function side by side within the state; such is not the aim of her discourse ethics.[15] Instead, she asserts, "that the task of *democratic equality* is to create impartial institutions in the public sphere and civil society where this struggle for the recognition of cultural differences and the contestation for cultural narratives can take place without domination" (*The Claims* 8). Historiography—the representations of a people group's cultural narratives—thus takes on appreciable ethical dimensionality precisely because humans live within and through this network of story and second-order evaluative texts that influence and even determine attitudes, behavior choices, and governmental policies.

Like Benhabib, Parekh also strives to recognize the complex networks comprising individual distinctiveness while respecting universal human value, doing so without blunting the distinguishing features of particularized selfhood. Parekh's *A New Politics of Identity* explains that all humans exist as intersectional beings with competing identity vectors. Understanding that humans belong to a range of affiliations and embody distinctions of gender, ethnicity, sexuality, class, religion, and more, Parekh sees these components of identity operating within the individual and across communities, ultimately meeting in a complex, ever-changing nation that should defy hegemonic and totalizing conceptualizations: "Identities do not co-exist passively: their interaction pluralizes each of them, and discourages their essentialization and reification" (*A New Politics* 23–24).[16] He argues that the individual must negotiate between his/her various social affiliations to harmonize a personal identity, simultaneously recognizing that the personal and the social aspects of selfhood also entail a "human or universal" element (*A New Politics* 28). This crucial third component of identity for Parekh ensures moral and ethical encounters with other humans far different from the individual:

> As we define ourselves and others as human beings, we see ourselves not merely as unique persons and bearers of particular social identities, but also as particular kinds of beings who share a common humanity with others and are subject to their claims.
>
> (*A New Politics* 29)

Thus, human identity involves a constant renegotiation of self across any number of competing and contradictory component parts all while maintaining an ethical stance vis-à-vis the common demands of universal human beingness.

The danger embedded within that necessary recognition of human value and similitude across selves, communities, and nations, is that a turn to the universalizing always threatens to homogenize and reify. Benhabib's discourse ethics seeks to counter that danger through dialogue between "moral conversation partners" (*The Claims* 14). Representations of the stories a culture tells must, in turn, reflect these complex negotiations of self and national identities.

Performing the Multiethnic Nation's History

In *The Human Condition*, Arendt describes theater as "the political art par excellence," explaining that, "only there is the political sphere of human life transposed into art." She adds that, "By the same token, it is the only art whose sole subject is man in his relationship to others" (188). The "Shakespearean theatre," Peter Erickson likewise insists, "cannot be a pristine space hermetically sealed off from ordinary social discourses." He continues: "The border between theatre and society, culture and politics, is porous, and the meanings cross back and forth. Theatre can aspire to renegotiate the terms, but it must first recognize rather than evade the problems" (242). As an artform concerned with the social and political self, theater inevitably debates the ethical framework governing communal interdependencies of the kind described by Levinas, Benhabib, and Parekh. Shakespeare's performed dramatic history intensifies such debates by scrutinizing how the social coalesces for better and worse into the larger concept of the nation. In performance, generalities about the nation's makeup take on particularity as historical personages from the collective British past are performed through and by the individual body of an actor. That individual actor functions within a fictionalized yet tangible and visible landscape thanks to the *mise-en-scène* imagined by a creative team; the degree of naturalism invoked through design, lighting, and music then influences the audience members' perceptions of the real and the historically true. The presence of the particularized human enacting a role begs the question of which bodies may perform this shared national record and assume certain historically factual roles. Afro-British actor, David Oyelowo, retells a story that haunted him when first taking on the title role of Henry VI in 2000:

> I had heard of a production of *Henry V*—I think at the RSC—where a black actor was playing the French king. As he made his entrance, an audience member was heard to say, "This is a disgrace," before very publicly making their exit.
>
> (28)

Indeed, Oyelowo himself experienced a similar initial reaction from an unnamed Oxford don quoted in a newspaper article about Oyelowo's casting as Henry VI: "We should aim to be accurate in our representation of the text. Moves like these leave us open to ridicule. King Henry VI wasn't black and shouldn't be cast as such" (qtd. in Oyelowo 27–28). Ruben Espinosa frankly characterizes such responses from disgruntled audience members accustomed to, in his evocative phrase, "seeing…through the eyes of whiteness" (*Shakespeare* 24):

> In so many ways, Shakespeare embodies whiteness and exists as a cultural icon that many aspire to access. Unsurprisingly, the ambitions of people of color who seek to access Shakespeare—actors, dramaturgs, critics, scholars, and students alike—are often trivialized. Quite often, people of color are made to feel that their renditions, adaptations, readings, and understandings of Shakespeare are inauthentic, and that, in many ways Shakespeare does not belong to them.
>
> (*Shakespeare* 7)

Here the intransigence of historical fact and an imagined representational authenticity operate as easily available and yet specious bars to full participation of some British citizens, in this case those of non-white descent, in the narrated story of a nation's identity. This is why, Erickson argues, colorblind casting necessitates "analysis and evaluation" in order "to explore, acknowledge, and confront Shakespearean blind spots regarding race" (241), blind spots that occur not just in the received dramatic texts but replicate and amplify in audiences as well.

Quite often, casting freedom—or the question of which bodies may perform shared history—tracks with the degree of naturalism posited by a given production's *mise-en-scène*. The more dependent a production becomes on naturalistic style and staging or on-location filming, the less likely a production may be to cast against the historical grain of representation.[17] Though not always the case, the visual landscape does often signal a degree of historical veracity that cross-racial or cross-gendered casting might be seen to violate. Colorblind casting (casting the most eligible actor for a role regardless of his/her ethnic and racial identities) has long served as an answer to the problem of broadening the representation and reach of Shakespearean drama in general. However, for the reasons cited above, the history plays have been a subgenre within the canon more resistant to the inroads made by colorblind casting on stage. Angela C. Pao characterizes the cognitive demands colorblind casting places on an audience, especially when non-white actors play historically white kings and queens:

> …the actors' bodies become "unmarked" in terms of race or ethnicity. This dissolution of markers relies on the audience's capacity to separate the fictional world of the stage from the world of lived experience and to give it precedence over a received body of historical knowledge.
>
> (29)

However, she quickly notes that, "the racialized body or the markers of race cannot be made to disappear" (29), as Oyelowo's anecdote above highlights.

Worryingly, the fiction of such race-blindness caters to a dangerous "post-racial," liberal self-satisfaction, one that encourages viewers to act "as if" race and ethnicity do not exist and do not inflect the meaning of history.

Such practices actually work to strengthen and perpetuate the white supremacist structures a progressive theater should, in fact, endeavor to confront, and, which, in theory, their colorblind casting practices may be intended to target and invalidate. As August Wilson famously declares, colorblind casting denies the African-American actors and creatives he addresses,

> our humanity our own history, and the need to make our own investigations from the cultural ground on which we stand as black Americans. It is an assault on our presence, our difficult but honorable history in America; it is an insult to our intelligence, our playwrights, and our many and varied contributions to the society and the world at large.
>
> (31)

Crystal M. Fleming argues that this form of "color-blind racism" advances white supremacy, "through repertoires of silence, denial, misrepresentation, disinformation, deflection, [and] willful ignorance" (44, 41). Fleming identifies colorblind racism as particularly prevalent in European countries, which "can more convincingly frame 'race' as a distant issue (both geographically and politically)" (44). Because white supremacism—"a system of power designed to channel material resources to people socially defined as white" (Fleming 24)—thrives on a "widespread ignorance [that] sustains the racial power structure" (35), productions reliant upon colorblind representational strategies, sadly, undertake racist work.

Ayanna Thompson cogently articulates the failure of colorblind casting to correct problems of multicultural representation and to account adequately for the way in which an actor's skin color sets in motion unintended racialized meanings. Thompson explains:

> it has become clear that the various models of nontraditional casting can actually replicate racist stereotypes *because* we have not addressed the unstable semiotics of race (when we see race; how we see race; how we make sense of what race means within a specific production).
>
> (*Passing* 77)

In fact, Thompson contends that colorblind casting often reads in performance as highly color-conscious casting, especially when an actor is the only person of color within a given cast or when the role overlaps with cultural stereotypes associated with the ethnicity of the actor in question. Thompson proposes a model for theater companies to follow that would be similarly useful to televisual production teams. In order for theaters to adopt mindful creative habits that anticipate the complex semiotics of race, Thompson suggests that a diversity director should facilitate ongoing conversations between members of the production team and cast to articulate, anticipate, and shape the semiotics of race on stage:

> While it is imperative that the director [of diversity] advocate for the diversification of the company, it is not enough to achieve the numbers (a target percentage, diversification beyond black and white, etc.). As part of advocating for the diversification of the company, the director must facilitate the dialogues about what this diversification means.
>
> (*Passing* 93)

According to Thompson, the testimonies of numerous black actors confirm that only rarely will a production team discuss the meaning of an actor's race within the narrative arc of a given play (*Passing* 85).

A recent public row over multicultural casting illustrates the unresolved tensions and habits of willful misunderstanding that plague an effort to represent more fully Britain's history and population on stage. In a fairly uncharacteristic move, the Royal Shakespeare Company issued a statement (April 2018) responding to a racist review by Quentin Letts of *The Fantastic Follies of Mrs. Rich* (Dir. Jo Davies). In his *Daily Mail* review, Letts observes of one black cast member, "poor Leo Wringer is miscast as the older Clerimont." Letts elaborates, "There is no way he is a honking Hooray of the sort that has infested the muddier reaches of England's shires for centuries. He is too cool, too mature, not chinless or daft or funny enough." That mixed praise precedes a direct attack on the practices of multicultural casting at the RSC:

> Was Mr. Wringer cast because he is black? If so, the RSC's clunking approach to politically correct casting has again weakened its stage product. I suppose its managers are under pressure from the Arts Council to tick inclusiveness boxes, but at some point they are going to have to decide if their core business is drama or social engineering.

Letts's review exemplifies one form of audience response to such strategies of colorblind casting—the argument of historical veracity (for a cool black man to play a particular archetype of British upper-class elitism defies facticity). The second rhetorical move deployed by Letts reduces the RSC's institutional multicultural mission to insincere and feeble "social engineering" designed to ensure continued public funding. In that accusation, Letts also establishes a false binary between the theater and social structures, suggesting that the theater has nothing to do with reflecting upon or influencing the individuals and people groups who find entertainment on the stage.[18] In an open letter signed by Gregory Doran (Artistic Director), Catherine Mallyon (Executive Director), Erica Whyman (Deputy Artistic Director), and Jo Davies (Director of *The Fantastic Follies of Mrs. Rich*), the RSC expressed shock at the "blatantly racist attitude to a member of the cast," and reiterated the aims of their casting policy and practice:

> Our approach to casting is to seek the most exciting individual for each role and in doing so to create a repertoire of the highest quality. We are proud that this ensures our casts are also representative of the diversity of the United Kingdom, that the audiences which we serve are able to recognise themselves on stage and that our work is made and influenced by the most creative range of voices and approaches.

This unified endorsement of its practices does not, however, fully acknowledge the vexed history of the RSC's approach to multiculturalism on stage.[19] The full-frontal attack of Letts's bigotry rightly sparks a cogent defense of alternative representational modes that tell cultural history through diverse bodies; however, those very efforts at diversifying bodies on stage and in film may have problematic knock-on effects because of the instability of racial semiotics.

Shakespeare's history plays confound a casting director's commitment to diversity since their status as instruments of historical narration establishes a different level of expected verisimilitude than does a comedy or tragedy. Multicultural casting clashes in these plays with the authorizing gestures to authenticity so often made when national history-telling takes center stage. Here the recent non-Shakespearean example of Lin-Manuel Miranda's musical, *Hamilton* (2016), proves instructive. Loosely translating Ron Chernow's popular biography of the founding father (*Alexander Hamilton*, 2004) into a hip-hop musical, Miranda's approach to staging history not only cross-references varied and racialized music genres but also disrupts the Caucasian identities of the founding fathers. Played by African-American, Asian, and Latinx actors in the Broadway production, the founding fathers represent American identities as radically altered. The musical's popularity and persistence stem, in part, from this effort to represent the faces of all Americans in a telling of national origins. Members of the multicultural cast testify to the personal impact of seeing a story of America's past embodied through persons who look like them. For example, in a *Wall Street Journal* interview by Kathryn Lurie, Leslie Odom Jr., the actor portraying Aaron Burr, answers the question, "Were you a student of history before this show?" in the following way: "I was a student of African-American history. I cared way more about the achievements and hard-won battles of black people in this country than I did about the founding fathers. But this show has been such a gift to me in that way because I feel that it's my history, too, for the first time ever." The ownership of shared history that accrues from diversified racial representation thus enhances minority group belonging as well as influences majority groups to rethink the complexion of the nation's contemporary identity. However, several historians contend that *Hamilton* delivers a thinned-out progressivism, one dressed up in the high-profile hues of a diverse cast but essentially traditional in its valorization of the heroic fathers who crafted a strongly federalist nation (Waldstreicher and Pasley 140). Though Lyra Monteiro admits that, "Race is, in some ways front and center in this play, as the founding fathers are without exception played by black and Latino men" (60), she chastises the production for a "truly damning omission." Monteiro observes: "despite the proliferation of black and brown bodies onstage, not a single enslaved or free person of color exists as a character in this play" (62). Broader racial representation makes an important step in expanding ownership of shared history and spotlighting the epistemics of historiography. As Vanessa Corredera argues regarding "seeing" race in the works of Shakespeare: "locating race in canonical texts forces us to identify the long-standing and potentially transhistorical practices used to discriminate against those considered foreign Others" ("Not" 45). The stories thus represented must then also attempt to trouble the institutional assumptions that have for centuries silenced people of color and their unique histories.

And this is where the history plays of Shakespeare have a distinct advantage; contesting the nature of authority, the qualities of rule, and the exclusionary frameworks governing nationhood, the history plays afford opportunities to interrogate the structural components and mechanisms that stifle alternative voices. Since Shakespearean history from its inception questions how history is made and the purposes to which it is applied, contemporary performances of that history should likewise experiment with representational strategies that echo the playwright's own suspicions about a coherent national story. "Shakespeare demonstrates throughout the history plays," argues Andrew Hadfield, "that not only are nations never inviolable fortresses with impenetrable borders, but also the peoples they contain are never pure either" (73). This potentially radical content of Shakespearean history deserves an approach to casting and mimesis that mirrors the interrogative quality of the play texts.

A Word on Terminology

In his introduction to *Forms of Nationhood*, Richard Helgerson begins by noting that, "the England Shakespeare and his contemporaries represented was as various as their representations of it. Not even its name remained fixed." His list of variants includes John Speed's "Empire of Great Britain," William Camden's "Britannia," Edmund Spenser's "England" and "Britayne land," and William Warner's "Albion" (8). With such a subject matter, consistency in terminology can prove difficult to achieve, but since discourse determines ontology, I aim for deliberate and mindful usage. I will use "British" to refer to the national identity emergent in Shakespeare's era and persistent into the present history of staged productions. Since I am interested in the ethics of this concept, I will endeavor to clarify throughout the project that a monolithic "Britain" results from fictionalizing and mythologizing constructs that are not always concealed in Shakespeare's text or subsequent performances. A prime objective of this book is to examine how performance reifies or troubles the seeming unity of what it means to be "British" and of who belongs to "Britain." I will use "England" to refer to the geographical location and ground in which the concept of "Britain" took root. The customs, traditions, legal practices, forms of government, and values that come to be known as "British" will be assumed to have originated in England primarily, and my language will reflect that sad fact; in other words, this project aligns with the substantial scholarship discussed above that recounts the ways in which "English" was often elided with "British." Such usage does not validate the silencing of other voices and versions of "Britain" that might have fought for recognition but were ignored, muted, or forgotten. Rather, from the outset, I assume the contested nature of the concept and seek to explore how the problematics of its origins manifest anew in productions of Shakespeare's history plays throughout the troubled years of the third millennium's beginnings.

Methodology and Chapter Outline

This book places a selection of staged performances and televisual adaptations into dialogue with one another probing questions of British nationhood and citizenship. Andrew James Hartley has pointed out that a theater performance, unlike a printed literary work, becomes "generically different" after the fact, its experiential component forever dissipated: "After it closes, the production may live on in memory, in reviews, in archive photographs or video, but it loses its kinetic immediacy, its presentness" (11). I want to suggest that another way in which staged performances endure is through the network of theater artists—both actors and directors—who also produce televisual adaptations. As Pascale Aebischer asserts, "the crossover between stage and screen is more complex than has been hitherto acknowledged" (*Screening* 6).[20] Though this project does not intend to trace every interconnection between the stage and televisual adaptations to be discussed, the analysis that follows will capitalize on linkages between stage and filmed productions as a mechanism for examining how the history plays may, successfully and/or unsuccessfully, expand their representational capacities across gender, race, ethnic, and religious lines of difference. Furthermore, the two performative modes serve as assessment tools for one another as we consider how history-telling can reinvigorate debates about national identity, practices of exclusivity, and the responsibilities of representation.

Boundary-drawing always involves an element of the arbitrary. This project does not aim to offer anything akin to a complete catalogue of history play performances in the United Kingdom during the fifteen years between 2001 and 2016. Rather, from a selection of moments central to the nation's self-definitional project, I will consider history play performances on stage and television that meet a number of additional criteria. Performances by institutions with substantial visible presence in the capital and an ever-expanding digital impact—the National Theatre, the Royal Shakespeare Company, Shakespeare's Globe, and the BBC—constitute the primary focus. These institutions transmit Shakespeare and Shakespearean acting as crucial components of Brand Britain and boast global reach and influence in a digital media market. As larger arts corporations, these entities operate in paradoxical ways, fulfilling the remit of art to level social critique but often shying away from counter-cultural resistance to protect the income generation necessary for a complex aesthetic ecosystem. Financial imperatives tend to make institutions risk-averse and drive aesthetic choices to safe, often more traditional ground. The selected productions form a loose web and create rich intertextuality through the borrowed acting bodies and creative talents who move between these tightly interconnected worlds. Roughly speaking, the productions to be examined date from the following pressure points for third-millennium Britain: 1) 2000–2005 and the release of *The Future of Multi-Ethnic Britain* (2000); 2) The Cultural Olympiad (2012); and 3) 2015–2016 and the Brexit referendum (2016). The story that emerges of British identity through the selected performances of Shakespearean history does not recount a goose-stepping, direct march from multicultural enlightenment to Brexit xenophobia. Rather, the selected productions demonstrate that the seeds of conflict, which grew so rapidly in the referendum vote of 2016, germinated throughout the fifteen-year period's troubled attempt to articulate Britain's national identity in a postmodern and postcolonial era. Though a nostalgic conservatism dominates much of the history-telling in the artifacts selected, glimpses of more thoughtful encounters with the legacy of Britain's colonial-imperialism can be seen, particularly in the Globe Theatre's *Richard II* (Dir. Adjoa Andoh and Lynette Linton, 2019) with which the book concludes. Performances that deploy a range of alternative adaptational approaches to and representational practices of Shakespearean history point the way forward for practitioners and creative teams seeking to exert pressure upon the dominant stories of the nation, imagining the British in more flexible terms of gender, class, ethnicity, race, and religion.

Chapter Two begins with *The Future of Multi-Ethnic Britain* as an informing context. A cluster of history play stage productions at the start of the new millennium instantiate provocative experimentation with the rules of colorblind casting and visual codes of race. By casting actors of color in lead and important secondary roles, these productions manifest a turn-of-the-century optimism about the multicultural society and third-millennium British inclusivity mirroring the best hopes of the FMEB report. The Royal Shakespeare Company crossed a major color barrier when director Michael Boyd cast David Oyelowo as Henry VI in three plays spanning 2000 and 2001; however, the productions demonstrate that navigating the politics of identity can pit protected groups against one another in a battle for status. While the Boyd productions ask audiences to reconsider the color of British historiography, they demonstrate worrying myopia concerning the vexed status of women, class conflict, and regional chauvinism. The September 11, 2001 attacks in New York and Washington, D.C. and the coalition invasions of Afghanistan and Iraq complicated the multiethnic optimism at the start of the millennium and inspired Nicholas Hytner's 2003 staging of *Henry V* at the National Theatre. With Adrian Lester as King Henry, Hytner demonstrates how Shakespearean history can be reimagined to comment on national identity and contemporary geopolitical alliances through a multiethnic cast; however, with his turn in 2005 to the two parts of *Henry IV*, Hytner heeds the compelling call of nostalgia as a ready escape hatch from the fraught realities of the extended War on Terror and the growth of Islamophobia. These staged performances provide key examples of how to rethink the representational strategies deployed to tell history even as they illustrate how difficult it may be to account for intersectional identities and move outside the verisimilitudes of authentic history-telling.

In Chapter Three, the Olympic Games of 2012 and Queen Elizabeth II's Diamond Jubilee inform a reading of gender and race in Series One of the BBC's *The Hollow Crown*. As host of the summer Olympic Games in 2012, the United Kingdom unfurled a wide range of Cultural Olympiad activities designed to foreground British influence and to welcome the world to the island nation. Though the Cultural Olympiad featured contributions from many countries and varied artistic traditions in the UK, its partnership with the BBC returned to the great playwright, Shakespeare, as definitional of Britain. At the time, the BBC was also defending its special status and financial reliance upon licence fees. In that context, the BBC conducted a self-study and diversity audit to recommit itself to the principles of a multicultural Britain and to the representation of that varied population. However, the crown jewel of the BBC's Olympiad season, *The Hollow Crown* adaptations of the second tetralogy, did little to advance that institutional goal or to expand upon the representational styles instantiated by the Boyd and Hytner productions at the start of the millennium. Relying upon a heritage England visual verisimilitude and on-location filming, *The Hollow Crown* tested colorblind casting very tentatively and to some devasting results in the context of a digital viewing global market. Continuing to confine women to the domestic sphere and deploying the racist stereotype of the magical negro, Series One instantiates worrying recursions to nostalgic conceptualizations of the nation unwilling to represent more fully a multicultural population.

Chapter Four grounds analysis in the decision on 20 February 2016 by Prime Minister David Cameron to call for a national referendum determining whether the United Kingdom should leave or remain in the European Union. The Brexit campaign's tendency to tap into deep-seated racisms to vilify an imagined "brown" invasion of refugees manifested in its print and video advertising and intensified as the vote date of 23 June drew nearer, highlighting the nation's own multicultural discomfort. Despite the uncertain future of the United Kingdom's relationship with the European Union, 2016 was scheduled as a worldwide commemoration of William Shakespeare's 400th deathiversary. Programs across the country and on a variety of media outlets chose to mark the occasion, and the BBC's signature celebration was a second installment of *The Hollow Crown*, this time adapting the lesser known plays of the first tetralogy. To compensate for the less familiar and dense historical material, Neal Street Productions assembled a highly recognizable cast and selected Benedict Cumberbatch to anchor the series as Richard, Duke of Gloucester and King Richard III. Once again, Heritage England—its landscapes, great houses, castles, and cathedrals—functioned as another character of the series. With minor characters played by a handful of actors of color, the series achieved some visual diversity; however, as with Series One, a failure to think carefully through the visual coding of race results in films that stage 2016 British anxieties about the non-white immigrant and her threat to domestic well-being. With Sophie Okonedo in the role of Margaret of Anjou/Queen Margaret, the series assigns a British woman of color a leading role but because she operates as an anomaly rather than the norm, her skin color difference triggers unintended racist meanings especially in the context of the Brexit debates and campaign rhetoric. In addition, Series Two of *The Hollow Crown* avoids grappling with the persistent class struggle of the nation by entirely excising the Jack Cade rebellion from its plotting arc; though such a cut might be defended as necessary plot compression for television, its absence fits hand in glove with the class complexities that also played a role in the Brexit results. Thus, though Series Two makes the seemingly bold step to cast "blind" the role of Queen Margaret, it falls into racist and stereotypical tropes much as in the first series and sadly replicates the ascendant fortress mentality of the Vote Leave campaign.

With the next two chapters, the book considers slant televisual engagements with Shakespearean history. Chapter Five turns to multiple adaptations of Hilary Mantel's Thomas Cromwell novels, *Wolf Hall* (2009) and *Bring up the Bodies* (2012). Indebted to the history plays in their intertextual descent from *Henry VIII*, Mantel's novels acquire their own generic status as staged history in their adaptation by Mike Poulton into a two-play suite for the Royal Shakespeare Company (first produced in 2013). When picked up by the BBC (2015), Mantel's novelistic historiography fits neatly into the generic conventions of heritage film. The creative migration from novel, to stage, to televisual series reveals persistent problems with casting and racial representation in staged history and heritage filmmaking. While a troubling reference to blacking-up in *Bring up the Bodies* appears in the staged adaptation, the BBC series quietly deletes that detail. Tracing the sanitized fate of this reference to blacking-up—the disappearing moor—illustrates the BBC's recognition of racially problematic tropes but also exposes the limits of its creative imagination when conjuring an "authentic" English past. In its representational choices, the BBC adaptation denies the impact made by persons of color on the emergent early modern English nation and insists on a dubious historical authenticity.

Chapter Six concludes with a final example of the history play reimagined. By means of five-act structure, iambic pentameter verse, and title and subtitle, Mike Bartlett deliberately positions his *King Charles III: A Future History Play* (2014) in the tradition of Shakespearean history. *King Charles III* imagines a constitutional and monarchical crisis rooted in contestation over how best to protect and defend Britain as a liberal democracy. Unfortunately, the BBC's televisual adaptation (directed by Rupert Goold) in 2017 recirculates Gilroy's "postcolonial melancholia" through an act of ventriloquism and cultural appropriation. In addition, though Bartlett clearly redresses the history play habit of sidelining women, the revisions for the BBC version fail to account for intersectional identities when the Afro-British actor, Tamara Lawrance, takes the part of Prince Harry's girlfriend. The play and BBC televisual adaptation depict a nation suffering an identity crisis and seeking comfort in a recycled and unironized nostalgia for lost empire and self-righteous moral rectitude. By failing to confront the racisms long-embedded in the narration of history and sheltering once again in a wistful nostalgia, the BBC's *King Charles III* cannot body forth sufficiently the very Britain it ostensibly seeks to underprop—an inclusive, welcoming liberal democracy comprised of many cultures and ethnicities, each member enjoying full subjectivity and historicity. Chapter Six closes by returning readers to the trouble with history—to the reasons that representation of Shakespearean history has remained so disappointingly impervious to aesthetic experimentation in the service of social justice. I conclude Chapter Six with a list of strategies for rethinking how to stage, film, and enact Shakespeare's history plays and the nation they speak into being. A brief epilogue reflects on two final *Richard IIs*—one, Josh O'Connor's rendering in *The Crown* ("Tywysog Cymru," 2019), and the second, the staged performance directed by Adjoa Andoh and Lynette Linton at the Sam Wanamaker Playhouse (2019), which points a constructive way forward for inclusive historiography.

Coda

Shakespeare's history plays anticipate an ambivalence central to nation-making that Homi K. Bhabha characterizes as a form of "double-time" in which a people require the archaic for self-definition but simultaneously bury that past to affirm the vibrancy and viability of the present national iteration. He explains:

> We then have a contested conceptual territory where the nation's people must be thought in double-time; the people are the historical "objects" of a nationalist pedagogy, giving the discourse an authority that is based on the pre-given or constituted historical origin *in the past*; the people are also the "subjects" of a process of signification that must erase any prior originary presence of the nation-people to demonstrate the prodigious, living principles of the people as contemporaneity.
>
> (208)

In this ambivalence and temporal agon between past and present, Bhabha finds that "As an apparatus of symbolic power," the "narrative strategy" of nation "produces a continual slippage of categories, like sexuality, class affiliation, territorial paranoia, or 'cultural difference' in the act of writing the nation" (201). Bhabha's stress on the temporal and hence shifting, changing, altering understanding of the nation likewise finds kinship in Shakespearean history that dramatizes both the birth of modern nations and the concept's strangely potent fragility. In differentiating between the "pedagogical" and the "performative," Bhabha also highlights two aspects of nation-building under contest in Shakespeare's plays of incipient nationalism. In addition to the pedagogical which signifies "the people as an a priori historical presence," Bhabha ascribes "a temporality of the 'in-between'" to the performative and critically troubles the monolithic nation through this aspect which is "*internally* marked by the discourses of minorities, the heterogeneous histories of contending peoples, antagonistic authorities and tense locations of cultural difference" (212). In this, Bhabha astutely argues, "We are confronted with the nation split within itself, articulating the heterogeneity of its population" (212). Thus, Bhabha offers an informing framework through which to consider the emergent nation in Shakespeare's history plays as both pedagogical and performative—with an ambivalence towards the past and even more importantly a performative element manifesting the heterogeneity of the present. Shakespearean historiography intuits the dialectic of remembering and forgetting endemic to nation-building as well as this multi-directional, ambivalent, and heterogeneous stance towards a past; furthermore, in performance, the Shakespeare history canon can confront the contradictory internal fissures ever present in the nation and give the lie to the repressive ideology of nationalism's always-already coherence. Unfortunately, all too often in the first two decades of the third millennium, productions of Shakespeare's history canon failed to capitalize on that potential, instead returning to versions of history rooted in nostalgia for a fantasized white, masculine unity as one final example illustrates.

The 2019 Channel 4 and HBO film, *Brexit: The Uncivil War* (Dir. Toby Haynes), starring Benedict Cumberbatch as the Vote Leave campaign architect, Dominic Cummings, details the opportunistic partnerships and diabolical strategies employed by the Vote Leave camp—from the ambivalent alliance with Farage and UKIP to the unholy reliance upon Cambridge Analytica's data mining and social media technologies. The film depicts Remainers as smug and asleep-at-the-wheel while Vote Leave strategists and call centers discovered under-engaged voters smarting from the sting of class inequalities and primed for xenophobic blame-shifting. As the results of the June 23 vote sink in, the film toggles between the respective campaigns. Using disorienting techniques such as super slow-motion, extreme close-ups, and a distorted, electronic mix of Thomas Arne's anthem, "Rule, Britannia," the montage crafts a carnival-of-horrors effect. The Arne anthem's well-known assertions of a triumphant, free, and imperial nation, ring ironic harmonies in the scene just as the country votes decidedly, if heedlessly, for a cataclysmic disruption to free people movement, a mobile workforce, and economic partnership with its nearest neighbors. In fact, "Rule, Britannia" echoes through the moment as a reminder of Gilroy's, "postcolonial melancholia," the nation's residual mourning over its contracted influence on the global stage, "the great transformation that quickly reduced the world's preeminent power to a political and economic operation of more modest dimensions" (*Postcolonial* 12). The film couples Arne's imperial hymn with a reference to Shakespeare as a reminder of the country's enduring cultural capital just as its economic capital slides into jeopardy.

A cameo appearance of Shakespearean history as the film draws to a close establishes a nostalgic metonymic chain that stretches from medieval history to Shakespeare's early modern England to the Battle of Britain to the third-millennial Brexit decision. In Vote Leave headquarters, Conservative MEP, Daniel Hannan (Tim Steed), stands atop the call center tables, celebrating with the team and quoting Shakespeare's *Henry V* as rallying cry: "If I may borrow from England's greatest wordsmith, 'From this day to the ending of the world but we in it shall be remembered.... this band of brothers.'" The double nature of Shakespeare's history speaks even as the film's Hannan relies on the Bard of Avon for an unironic valorization of England's band of brothers bravely severing ties with the continental nations. Too often, Shakespeare's history appears ripe for just such excision, quotation, and recycling in service to a monolithically uniform and isolationist nation. However, this brief reference and its performance history simultaneously bear detectable Certeauvian gaps and fissures that can turn Shakespearean history from resounding praise to self-critical interrogation. *Henry V*'s narration of an English high point from the Hundred Years' War reinforces the long history of animosity between England and her European neighbors, one that dwarfs the much shorter term, uneasy alliances of the late-twentieth century. The film's Hannan deploys the Shakespeare icon of Agincourt in his truncated quotation and metonymically invokes Britain's most famous mobilization of King Henry, Laurence Olivier's 1944 film adaptation dedicated to the "Commandos and Airborne Troops of Great Britain." In this association with World War II, the cameo quote allusively gestures to the aims of the European Union as well, an entity conceived of and imagined as a correction to the catastrophic conflicts of the early twentieth century. Here then, Shakespearean history may not only serve to perpetuate a vision of Great Britain as superior island nation but also may prompt vital questions about the country's tendencies to xenophobia and isolationism, a self-sabotaging compulsion writ large in the vote to exit the European Union. Such radical potential implicit in Shakespearean history requires an interrogative and resistant hermeneutic alert to the variety of ways in which the poet's historiography both reifies nationhood and queries the mechanisms by which people groups imagine themselves as sovereign, united, and free.

The "racial nonracialism" of the third millennium's first two decades left democracy unready to combat the threat of New Nationalism and its misogynistic and race-baiting strategies as instantiated by the Brexit campaign. David Theo Goldberg explains,

> Racial nonracialism takes up race more or less explicitly not to identify and address racially produced historical inequalities and inequities, more or less irreparable violent harms and their cumulative effects. It takes up race much more modestly to identify those excluded so as to bring them into the fold of a society no longer seen as racially unjust.
>
> (20–21)

Goldberg parses a crucial distinction between anti-racism and racial nonracialism: in the place of directly anti-racist practice, nonracialism expands concepts of belonging but ignores provocations to expose the structural inequities baked into the long history of the nation and that have simply manifested in new and monstrous excrescences in the twenty-first century. The "belonging" achieved in this patently ahistorical manner—whether in governmental policy or practiced in Shakespearean performances—fails to transform the nation into a thriving multicultural and inclusive society, one armed with a careful knowledge of the sins and violations of the past not to be repeated in a shared future.

The history plays' performances examined in the chapters that follow consistently instantiate this form of "racial nonracialism" that steadfastly refuses an accounting of past and ongoing harms, assuming that parceling out to underrepresented persons a few more prominent roles in the nation's narrative will heal old wounds and confirm belonging in the present moment. Furthermore, these productions repeatedly demonstrate that gender and race still too often operate as competing identity categories rather than as allied forces in a battle to reclaim authority from a patriarchal hegemony. *Shakespeare's Contested Nations* argues that such performances track with the tactics of avoidance Goldberg describes and habitually foreclose promising opportunities to re-examine the nation's past, present, and future in more intentional, self-critical, and truly progressive ways. Too often strides in alternative casting function as window-dressing rather than as thoroughgoing reimaginations of history's story; a closer examination of the cultural surround of these performances illustrates their limitations. Archival and historicist methods dominate the field of Shakespeare scholarship, but I would like to suggest that when we attend to performances and their semiotic resonances we likewise build an alternative archive for these productions and adaptations that includes governmental policy documents, sociological data, and the range of paratextual materials informing performance—playbills, DVD extras, YouTube tie-in videos, cast and crew interviews, podcasts, and intertextual ghostings that filter through the performative choices. When performances and adaptations are located and analyzed within such a signifying field of reference, we are better prepared to ask, "What national story is advanced by the accumulation of these details?" And, more importantly, "Can we live with that story?"

Notes

1 Christie Carson neatly articulates the contrasting dynamics of a post-9/11 world: "The sense of the world becoming smaller and more democratic as a result of the speed and scope of digital technology in this period was overshadowed by heavy-handed governmental action in North America and Britain which limited the rights of citizens in the name of protecting them" (228).

2 Patrick Finn aligns the "Posse Comitatus" episode with a muscular liberalism typified by Michael Ignatieff. This mode of liberalism, "upholds the standard tenets of European liberalism, that is progressive reform of society with an emphasis on the rights and freedoms of the individual," with the added imperative that "general and human rights in particular should be pursued across national borders" (12). Finn thus reads the "Patriotic Song" as typical of the episode's appropriation of Shakespeare to defend "war in the name of peace," a position Finn attributes to the Shakespearean text as well. However, Finn's excellent reading of the episode's liberal politics does not pursue precisely enough the contradictions and heterogeneity of the quoted Shakespearean material (14).

3 Such may prove difficult given the fact that, "A poll conducted six months prior to the [Brexit] referendum found that 44 per cent of the British public were proud of Britain's colonial history and 43 per cent considered the British Empire to have been a good thing" (El-Enany 213).

4 Tabish Khair also links racism and nationalism through their shared ontologies as naturalizing frameworks rooted in mystifications of history: "One major similarity is the existence of certain assumptions that, both in racism and in nationalisms, tend to 'naturalize' various ideological underpinnings with reference to a hoary past" (58). Like racism, Khair reasons, nationalism "depends on similarly vague but powerful bids to naturalize itself with reference to an ancient, and often a physical, inheritance of difference" (59).

5 In the introduction to their influential essay collection, Alexa Alice Joubin and Elizabeth Rivlin make a strong case for evaluations of the ethical in performance: "In an age when Shakespeare is increasingly globalized, diversified, spread thin, and applied in service of a multitude of agendas, it is more urgent than ever to analyze the ethical ramifications, byproducts, and problems that inevitably attend such appropriations" (2). Likewise, Christy Desmet and Sujata Iyengar conclude their systematic parsing of the terms "adaptation" and "appropriation" by asserting that, "Shakespeare has become more central than ever to debates over the ethics of appropriation" (8). Desmet's formulation of the ethical dynamics mobilized by recognizing Shakespeare in a range of appropriative artifacts also informs the current study's interest in both traditionally "faithful" performances of Shakespearean history as well as "slant" manifestations (55).

6 The Pew Research Center reports that in 2015, of the 1.3 million refugees entering the European Union, Norway and Switzerland, "more than half of asylum seeker applications" were submitted to just three countries, Germany, Hungary, and Sweden. The UK experienced a 0.2% change in foreign-born population while in Sweden the jump was a dramatic 1.5 % (16.8 % to 18.3 %) (Connor and Krogstad).

7 Just after Trump's win, Nigel Farage met with the newly elected president (even before Trump met the sitting Prime Minister Theresa May), and in February 2017, Farage addressed the Conservative Political Action Conference in the United States, gloating that 2016 was "the beginning of a global political revolution and it's one that is not going to stop, it's one that is going to roll out across the rest of the free world." The chauvinist definition of that revolution emerged in his claim, "Our real friends in the world speak English, have common law and stand by us in times of crisis" (qtd. in Owen and Smith).

8 Parekh summarizes the makeup of the commission: "For those who aren't familiar with its background, the Commission on the Future of Multi-Ethnic Britain was made up of 25 individuals, including seven well-known academics, three distinguished journalists, two senior police officers, representatives of different communities, one senior and recently retired civil servant, and several distinguished public figures including the President of the Liberal Democratic Party, and two retired chairs of the Commission for Racial Equality. It had eight women members and ten members from the ethnic minorities" ("Reporting" 1).

9 J. G. A. Pocock has argued, in fact, that works claiming to recount "British" history have only recorded "English" stories due to a profound imbalance in power between England and the other nations of the island, a disequilibrium that historiography has perpetuated (311, 313). Baker adds: "Inevitably then, I realized, in writing the history of England as a nation-state today what we are writing is the textual history of the English rulers writing their own textual history, and doing so, quite often, by 'unwriting'—suppressing, assimilating, ignoring—the textual histories of the other not yet or never-to-be nations that also existed (or might have existed) among the British Isles" (4).

10 Willy Maley and Margaret Tudeau-Clayton summarize the contradictory impulses of Shakespearean nation-making: "What we offer are views of Shakespeare and his playtexts not as sops to nostalgic longings or xenophobic mythos of Englishness with which, as we have argued, they are rather critically engaged, but as discursive negotiations which 'show' not an essential character of the English and England, but how a sense of nationhood is constructed, just as 'Shakespeare' is constructed as the figure of a 'core' national identity and culture—British and/or English—as well as a figure of a shared European and world—global—culture" (19–20).

11 In his contribution to the recent essay collection examining immigration in Shakespearean drama, Ruben Espinosa stresses the in-process and networked emergence of English nationhood in the early modern period: "Englishness in *Henry V*, on the other hand, is still being wrought, and its interconnection with otherness—be it with the French, Irish, Scots, Welsh, and even Turks—reveals the influence and importance of the foreigner in understanding the self" ("Fluellen's" 74).

12 The exhaustive work of Eamon Duffy catalogues the way in which the iconoclasm of reform painfully altered the connection between the living and the dead, between the present and the past. While reformers viewed the wholesale destruction of chantries and the elimination of the prayers for the dead from the Prayer Book liturgy as purification, these changes deeply altered how the English knew and perceived the once-superable barrier between living and dead. Duffy expresses this reformation in the customs of devotional grief as "an act of oblivion, a casting out of the dead from the community of the living into a collective anonymity" (494), and Stephen Greenblatt similarly reads the Protestant rejection of Purgatory as a collective trauma (*Hamlet* 21).

13 Concerning the political impact of performed representations, Peggy Phelan writes: "Representation follows two laws: it always conveys more than it intends; and it is never totalizing. The 'excess' meaning conveyed by representation creates a supplement that makes multiple and resistant readings possible. Despite this excess, representation produces ruptures and gaps; it fails to reproduce the real exactly. Precisely because of representation's supplemental excess and its failure to be totalizing, close readings of the logic of representation can produce psychic resistance and, possibly, political change" (2).

14 In this context of the "web of human relationships, with its innumerable, conflicting wills and intentions," Arendt defines history as "the great story without beginning and end" (184).

15 Steven Vertovec offers a practical example of how multicultural policies that avoid the "mosaic" or separatist approach, lead to healthier communities, citing the shared governance and grassroots organizational structures created in Leicester, England. Rather than homogenizing into an undifferentiated whole the city's Muslim population, the "Leicester model" succeeds thanks to "a pattern of effective, multifaceted incorporation among localized institutions, an umbrella organization, and strategically placed and symbolically powerful individuals" (238).

16 As Kimberlé Crenshaw has argued persuasively, "The problem with identity politics is not that it fails to transcend difference, as some critics charge, but rather the opposite—that it frequently conflates or ignores intragroup differences" (1242); she continues, "My focus on the intersections of race and gender only highlights the need to account for multiple grounds of identity when considering how the social world is constructed" (1245).

17 Writing in 2000, Deborah Cartmell laments, "In spite of recent readings of the representation of race in Shakespeare, films of these plays, no matter how experimental in form, remain fundamentally conservative in their representation of race" (67). Though her comments focus on screen adaptations of the so-called "race plays" from prior to 2000, her observations could as easily be applied to more recent televisual adaptations of Shakespeare's history.

18 Letts's absurd binary opposition between theater and society may well be a disingenuous argumentative strategy since the long history of theater confirms its enmeshment in social and political struggle. For example, Pao argues, "As a socio-cultural institution, the theater has always been closely linked to the political aspects of civic, state, and national life" (27).

19 Jami Rogers notes: "The twenty-first century has seen the ratio of black/Asian/mixed race to white actors at the RSC tick upwards as cast sizes have continued to shrink, with the total number of actors in productions in the vicinity of 20 performers per play between 2000–2012. The percentage of white to black/Asian/mixed race actors has shifted very little, however, which is an indication of the presence of a glass ceiling when it comes to employing black and Asian actors" (420). According to Rogers, ratios typically run at "10%-20% ethnic minority actors to 80%-90% white performers" (426).

20 In her study of Jacobean drama on film, Aebischer enumerates the connections between British stage and film: "This is not only a matter of filmmakers also being theatre-goers. It is also a matter of shared personnel: many films liberally borrow performers with Shakespearean pedigrees to initiate a complex 'haunting' of the films by their Shakespearean intertexts" (*Screening* 6).

2 Staging the Multiethnic Nation
Boyd and Hytner at the Millennial Threshold

> "O peers of England, shameful is this league!
> Fatal this marriage, cancelling your fame,
> Blotting your names from books of memory."
>
> (*II Henry VI*)

A suite of productions by the Royal Shakespeare Company and the National Theatre in the first five years of the third millennium helps illustrate both the promise and disappointment of the new millennium's recursion to Shakespearean history: promise, on the one hand, as those called upon to embody that history were not exclusively white, and disappointment, on the other hand, that such striking experiments in colorblind or color-conscious casting did not initiate a large-scale change in representational practices in staging and filming Shakespeare's history. That these staged attempts to diversify the casting of lead roles in the history plays did not transfer readily to small-screen adaptations may be traced, in part, to problems with gender, class, and race lurking in those productions. Another culprit might well have been a failure to recognize how race would signify in the telling of medieval English history through the voice of Shakespeare. Director Michael Boyd's *Henry VI* plays (2000–2001) marked a watershed moment with the Afro-British David Oyelowo starring as the titular medieval monarch, and at the National Theatre, Nicholas Hytner's inaugural season as artistic director featured the Afro-British Adrian Lester in the lead role of a much-admired *Henry V* (2003). However, by 2005, Hytner's productions of *I* and *II Henry IV* (National Theatre) muted their political commentary on the contemporary moment and kept ethnic diversity outside the royal court.[1] The 9/11 attacks, the invasion of Iraq, and the unspooling War on Terror inevitably impacted what might be identified as the optimism of the millennial moment and an initial, if admittedly limited, willingness to reconsider the makeup of British national identities. Although Hytner's 2003 production enacted a frontal assault on the "dodgy dossier" that led to Britain's partnership with the United States in Iraq, his 2005 productions sought refuge in a neverland bricolage of past and present—a timeless region of disillusionment and decay. The stereotypes triggered by inattentive colorblind casting found in the 2005 *Henry IV* productions predict troubling aspects of the Shakespearean historiography to follow on the small screen.

DOI: 10.4324/9781003043065-2

A consideration of these productions in relationship to each other and in the context of British multiculturalism in the first five years of the third millennium illuminates the competing demands of gender, class, and racial equity when telling the nation's history through the authoritative constructions of Shakespeare. These productions highlight an inadequately formulated theory of colorblind performance in operation, one that does not account for how gender, class, and race intersect on stage and signify to an audience. This inadequacy might have been addressed systematically over time had not the crises of the early 2000s intervened and thoroughly unsettled the nation's perceived security, exposing the various rifts only thinly papered over by Tony Blair's New Labour government and multicultural policies, which focused on populations that had self-excluded from economic opportunities.[2] Since New Labour spotlighted so-called "self-exclusion," its policies framed deprivation as a choice and deemphasized systemic inequality (Mckenzie S270).[3] Because of this, Oyelowo and Lester stand as anomalous—exceptions to the rules of historical representation but not rule-changers in terms of how English history may be told. Examined together, the six Boyd and Hytner productions in question predict the retreat from more radical representational approaches to a post-imperial nostalgia that threads through the adaptations that follow. As Jami Rogers notes in her exhaustive study of casting practices in the United Kingdom, "...colorblind casting has only inched forward since the 1970s....the glass ceiling remains in evidence through myriad practices of non-traditional casting, which collectively indicate little progress has been made since David Oyelowo's Henry VI at the RSC" (418). Thus, though the six productions in question—three directed by Boyd and three by Hytner—constitute significant milestones in the representational strategies of Shakespearean history, they also instantiate the challenges and competing concerns that thwart a more thoroughgoing transformation of the performed authority of Shakespeare's nation-building and nation-defining history plays.

By failing to consider with greater complexity not just the representation of the black male but also depictions of the historicity of women, women of color, and persons of the lower classes, these productions undermine the promise of the millennial moment. A politics of identity, though grounded in the desire to recognize and validate unique and characterizing differences, at the same time can put various minority groups in competition with one another rather than in partnership against hegemonic domination. This is especially so given the vital role white women play in the perpetuation of white supremacy as both members of a dominant race and subordinate participants in that race's perpetuation:

> There are special anxieties surrounding the whiteness of white women *vis-à-vis* sexuality. As the literal bearers of children, and because they are held primarily responsible for their initial raising, women are the indispensable means by which the group—the race—is in every sense reproduced.
>
> (Dyer 29)

In addition to underplaying the subordinated yet often complicit function of white women, a politics of identity can also occlude the ways that multiple lines of marginalization—such as being black and female—impact human agency and access to political and juridical resources. As Kimberlé Crenshaw famously explains, "The problem with identity politics is not that it fails to transcend difference, as some critics charge, but rather the opposite—that it frequently conflates or ignores intragroup differences" (1242). She writes: "My focus on the intersections of race and gender only highlights the need to account for multiple grounds of identity when considering how the social world is constructed" (Crenshaw 1245). Seyla Benhabib similarly observes that, too often, the interests of women within minority communities are ignored in the name of a broader, patriarchally motivated multicultural respect: "Debates around feminism and multiculturalism get quickly polarized, because so little attention is paid to this aspect of cultures as riven by internal contestation" (*The Claims* 103). In a politics of identity where marginalized persons may well be pitted against one another for access to scarce resources and status, groups that should be natural allies against hegemonic power vie with one another rather than operate as an oppositional collective. The six productions directed by Boyd and Hytner illustrate that competing interests in a politics of identity and the complexities of intersectionality may undermine the best intentions of a director to cast in such a way as to provoke rethinking about who belongs to British history.

The Future of Multi-Ethnic Britain

In *The Claims of Culture*, Benhabib articulates the high-stakes nature of historiography as a tool of self-narration and cultural authority:

> Any complex human society, at any point in time, is composed of multiple material and symbolic practices with a history. This history is the sedimented repository of struggles for power, symbolization, and signification—in short, for cultural and political hegemony carried out among groups, classes, and genders.
>
> (60)

The published report of the Commission on the Future of Multi-Ethnic Britain (FMEB) chaired by Bhikhu Parekh, *The Future of Multi-Ethnic Britain* (2000), likewise positions history as central to both the nation's self-definition and the full political subjectivity of its citizenry.[4] The report gently proposes strategies to broaden the narrowly racialized definition of "English" or "British," particularly through retelling the nation's history to account for the diverse people groups making up the United Kingdom. In a chapter entitled, "Rethinking the National Story," the commission asserts that,

> Many reforms are needed to convert multicultural drift into a concerted drive towards a Britain with a broad framework of common belonging—

> one in which all citizens are treated with rigorous and uncompromising equality and social justice, but in which cultural diversity is cherished and celebrated. One critical prerequisite is to examine Britain's understanding of itself.
>
> (15)

For many generations, the very specifically "English" story of nationhood came to embody what was normalized as "British" identity. Those narratives of Britishness have historically silenced the dissenting perspectives of the Welsh, Scottish, and Northern Irish not to mention those points of views represented by black and Asian communities (16).

> The so-called "united" kingdom contains not one nation but four (five, if the two communities in Northern Ireland are counted separately), each with its own specific history and culture. The danger is further compounded in the case of an imperial or post-imperial nation like Britain, where the differences between "us" and "them" are imagined to be racial, rooted in unalterable nature.
>
> (18)

The danger the report refers to is an entrenched acceptance of a very specifically "English" identity that prevents reflecting upon and critiquing the "nation" as a malleable and constructed concept worth revisiting and renegotiating over time and as the complexion of a country alters. Compounding this problem, according to the report, is a cultural tendency of avoidance:

> Race is deeply entwined with political culture and with the idea of nation, and underpinned by a distinctively British kind of reticence—to take race and racism seriously, or even to talk about them at all, is bad form, something not done in polite company. This disavowal, combined with "an iron-jawed disinclination to recognize equal human worth and dignity of people who are not white", has proved a lethal combination.
>
> (38)

The commission identifies arts and media outlets as a crucial platform to combat both a poisonous reticence and a lingering colonial ideology through improved representation of British multicultural identities.

The FMEB recommendations opened the new millennium with clearly articulated principles to guide public policy and a mandate to arts outlets to conduct a substantial recalibration of history and its narrative representations. In Chapter Eight, "Summary of the Vision," the Parekh report recalls problematic and debunked myths of the British past that thwart the multicultural present, noting particularly those stories of a "fortress Britain" untainted by its own tendencies to violence and inequality.

> With regard to the past we have recalled a range of myths: that the history of Britain goes back many centuries; that it has always been a basically

> peaceful and lawful place, untroubled by internal dissent or strife; that there is a single true version of the national story; that until recently Britain was culturally homogeneous; that the sea round Britain aptly symbolises its independence and isolation from the rest of the world. These myths feed the imaginations of millions of people. As long as they are dominant in British recollections of the past the country cannot be a just and inclusive society in the present, for from these myths large numbers of people and many experiences are omitted.
>
> (103)

To replace those harmful narratives of the past, the FMEB advocates for sufficient funding to "attend to issues of cultural recognition, inclusion, identity and belonging" (160). The report calls upon arts outlets to follow key policy recommendations, asserting that "the whole mainstream canon needs to be reinterpreted," to account for "Britain's growing internal cultural diversity" (162). In addition, the FMEB authors insist that historical events be re-examined and retold to better address "the issue of racism," "Britain's selective amnesia about its former empire" (163), and a studied forgetfulness about the more recent struggles experienced by immigrants to "fortress Britain" (165). The FMEB urges a substantial intervention in the canon and historiography, linking a multiculturally confident nation to an artistic and historical reckoning.

As discussed in the first chapter, these recommendations were among the most incendiary of the report's findings, prompting politicians such as Home Secretary Jack Straw to distance himself from the commission and vociferously deny that white supremacism was a deeply entrenched element of British national identity. In his speech at the report's launch, Straw insisted that since Britain was no longer, "overwhelmingly a white society," the nation's self-construal had naturally expanded (4). In a display of accomplished vagueness, he glanced at the report's suggestion that British history required retelling to account for its colonial-imperial sins and frequently inhospitable immigration policies. Straw mused, "There are as many views about the interpretation of history as there are individual historians and there can never be a single view of history, nor has there been" (2)—thus clearly denying the report's argument that a hegemonic narrative of British colonial beneficence still shapes remembrance of the nation's past.[5] Though Straw underscored in his speech the variety of "facts" that historiography might amplify or choose to mute, he persisted, "there is no reason at all for us to be trapped by one view of our past as we look to the future" (2). Such defensiveness only confirms the accuracy of the FMEB's repeated concern over a national tendency to avoid the self-scrutiny necessary to a healthy post-imperial and multiethnic nation.

On Seeing and Not Seeing: Race, Gender, and Class in Michael Boyd's *Henry VI* Cycle (2000–2001)

In significant ways, Michael Boyd's cycle of *Henry VI* plays for the Royal Shakespeare Company in 2000 participated in the new millennial commitment to fresh, inclusive representations of the nation's identity and historiography—most notably by casting the Nigerian-British David Oyelowo as Henry VI. Placing center stage an actor whose heritage invoked the traumas of British imperialism, the RSC performances insisted that the storied past belongs to all British people.[6] Stuart Hampton-Reeves and Carol Chillington Rutter note that in the RSC's millennial "This England" season, a program of productions concerned with the question of British national identity, "Boyd was the only director in the cycle to suggest that 'who we are' could be responded to with a colour-blind cast production of Shakespearean history," adding that, "Even if the world onstage was a medieval one, the ethnic mix in the cast placed it visually within the politics of the present" (189). Indeed, "For the first time in the RSC's history, audiences watched a staging of the nation that not only included non-white actors, but even seemed to privilege them" (Hampton-Reeves and Rutter 190). Citing Parekh, Hampton-Reeves and Rutter also locate Boyd's productions in the furor raised by the release of the FMEB report:

> Where the Commission's recommendations had proved an easy fall guy for editorials to rant about "politically correct garbage", the casting of a black actor as an English king was a more confrontational way of exposing latent prejudices and of exploring the true meaning of Britain's multi-ethnic status.
>
> (191)

However, Hampton-Reeves and Rutter do admit that,

> The effect of the colour-blind casting policy was not in any real sense an appropriation of British history for a new, multicultural agenda; there was no effort to translate a white mythology into a new national history of which a multicultural audience could claim ownership.
>
> (191)

In truth, the production instantiated problems to be repeated throughout the era and associated with a too-simplistic colorblind casting approach. Such approaches asked audiences to note the progressive politics of casting non-white actors for parts in the history plays but then expected those viewers to be blind to the signification of race in performance. Oscillating between claims of not seeing race and evidence that race was very much seen, these important productions also missed opportunities to consider more carefully how the categories of identity politics compete for priority. Especially problematic representations of gender and class in the Boyd cycle indicate that though these productions powerfully drew attention to the mediations of historiography in forming the nation, they fell back upon familiar stereotypes that deny equal access to that history.

The RSC's choice to cast Oyelowo as Henry VI addressed what critics have observed as a failure at institutional levels to invest in and nurture black, Asian, minority ethnic actors (BAME). Rogers writes:

> While performers such as Mike Gwilym, David Suchet, Roger Rees, Barbara Leigh-Hunt and Helen Mirren were nurtured within the system, continuing to gain larger roles, the company's black and Asian actors were rarely provided the same chances. For example, although Nunn had hired a total of seven black actors for The Romans season [1972], Lockhart, Angadi, Burton, Osoba and Rose never returned to the company.
>
> (413)

In that context of institutional neglect and racism, Oyelowo describes the significance of the coronation scene in *I Henry VI* for him personally as a black actor of color in the title role:

> This point in the play was always quite emotional for me in an almost inexplicable way. I often couldn't believe how fortunate I was to be living out a daydream I had often had, but I also felt that there were those in the audience who were in just as much disbelief at the fact that the RSC would let a black man be crowned on the famous Swan stage.
>
> (27)

Oyelowo invokes interconnecting authorities—the institution of the RSC as a company, a stage, and a venue where luminaries of performance history have previously acted, stars who were overwhelmingly white. His affective response to being in that spot performing the lead role of Henry VI demonstrates on an individual and personal level why advances in diverse casting matter: such practices signal belonging, ownership, and access. As Lynette Goddard explains,

> Casting practices raise questions about access and cultural ownership, and the extent to which non-white performers are granted equal opportunities to perform some of the most coveted stage roles. Issues around race and casting seem to become most prominent in relation to Shakespeare's plays because the tendency towards casting white performers conflicts with ideas about the cultural legacy of his work and the supposed "universality" of his plays.
>
> (82)

Oyelowo's feelings mirror comments by members of Lin-Manuel Miranda's *Hamilton* cast who, for the first time, came to consider revolutionary American history their own history as persons of color.[7] Inadequate though colorblind casting may be, the experience of Oyelowo illustrates the critical importance, for both performers and spectators, of inclusive representation on stage, particularly in the history plays which can then redress the transhistorical erasure of non-white citizens and subjects from the stories of a nation.

At the same time, Oyelowo's reflections highlight that this achievement in casting Shakespeare's historic kings is tempered by anticipated audience resistance. Susan Bennett explains that theater audiences generate interpretation in a liminal space, "between the inner frame of the fictional stage world, the audience's moment by moment perception of that in the experience of a social group, and the outer frame of community (cultural construction and horizons of expectations)" (156). The individual's experience of the enacted fiction, his/her awareness of reactions from other members of the assembled audience, and his/her culturally conditioned expectations necessarily shape reactions to performance, especially those casting choices that obviously contradict the long-standing whiteness of Shakespeare's history plays on stage. Oyelowo articulates a double awareness, even in his moment of achievement, that members of the audience, thanks to established "horizons of expectations," might still be affronted by a black man playing a historically white king. This recognition qualifies such achievements and illustrates that actors of color may be cast "blind" but perform very much aware that not all audience members will choose to be "blind" to color. Indeed, Oyelowo continues the remembrance by citing "an Oxford University don" who declared in a *Daily Telegraph* comment, "We should aim to be accurate in our representation of the text. Moves like these leave us open to ridicule. King Henry VI wasn't black and shouldn't be cast as such" (27–28). This leads Oyelowo to recount what he admits might be an apocryphal story of a black actor who played the French King in an RSC production of *Henry V*: "As he made his entrance, an audience member was heard to say, 'This is a disgrace,' before very publicly making their exit" (28). At this point in his short memoir of the Boyd production, Oyelowo does not comment further except to reveal that the coronation scene always brought that story to his mind. This detail highlights the competing energies at play in colorblind treatments of history—that of belonging and professional accomplishment when a leading role in Shakespearean historiography goes to a person of color and that of simultaneous anxiety regarding the predominantly white theater-going audiences who might hide underlying racism within the defensive shelter of historical accuracy.[8] It is a peak moment of both pleasure and pain.

Likewise, the complicated response of the individual actor of color to reviews should qualify celebrations of colorblind casting as the singular achievement of a progressive multicultural society. Oyelowo describes his reaction to the positive reviews:

> I was so relieved, not just that we had been received well but that not a single one of them [reviews] mentioned the colour of my skin in relation to my performance. For me, this was the biggest compliment of all.
>
> (56)

Oyelowo's relief that his performance was judged on its own merits, not filtered through the mediation of his race nor objected to in reviews because of his skin color, underscores the ethical and aesthetic intentions behind colorblind casting—to select the best actor for the role regardless of race. However, such "colorblind" evaluations, though welcome, allow often-white theater reviewers to participate in a broader cultural avoidance of matters of race and to leave undisturbed a disinclination to wrestle with histories of racism. Ayanna Thompson has argued, in fact, that,

> Performance reviewers must be more attentive to the way in which a production makes race semiotically (ir)relevant. Thus, it should never be a mere matter of noting an actor's race in a review; rather, it should be a matter of assessing what and how a production renders the semiotic value and meaning of that actor's race.
>
> ("To Notice")

Unfortunately, a tacitly accepted deception that audiences do not "see" race remains embedded in far too many reviews—an unwillingness to confront the signification of race within the larger multicultural society of Great Britain, what the authors of the Parekh report characterize as, "a distinctively British kind of reticence" when it comes to talking about race (38). In her analysis of colorblind semiotics and reviews, Goddard writes:

> Concerns about whether British-Nigerian actor David Oyelowo should play an English king also suggest that anxieties remain about how a performer's race interacts with certain parts.... Although his performance was highly acclaimed, debates about his right to play the role demonstrated an unease that suggests that audiences and critics were not completely "blind" to colour or to associations between race and role.
>
> (85)

Thompson adds that companies must utilize their promotional materials, "to explain their own philosophies with regards to race and performance," as a means of facilitating both audience and reviewer education on the intersection between race and Shakespearean authority in performance ("To Notice"). A more deliberately theorized understanding of the semiotics of race on stage should have been part of Boyd's productions, a landmark moment in British theater history, in part to ensure they had a more lasting impact not just on stage practices but also on the representational strategies of filmed and televised Shakespearean history.

Various decisions taken by the production creatives reveal that though colorblind practice was followed by the RSC, the company was, at the same time not truly blind. Boyd repeatedly contended that race did not factor in decision-making. For example, a BBC article from September 2000 and headlined without nuance as "Black actor cast as English king," reported, "The production's director, Michael Boyd, said the casting had not been about colour but had been conducted on merit." The BBC piece quoted Boyd justifying his decision: "David really is a bit of a genius. It is colour blind casting, his son will be white and there is no hint of illegitimacy." Of course, given the sexual dalliances of Henry VI's white on-stage wife, Margaret of Anjou (Fiona Bell), with the Duke of Suffolk (played by the white actor, Richard Dillane), Boyd's insistence on the invisibility of race and the legitimacy of Henry VI's white son rings as overly optimistic and naïve, an avoidance of the multifarious meanings of performed race as well as gender. That Boyd and his team intermittently saw race emerges through other evidence; though the director may insist that audiences would not question the whiteness of Henry VI's son, the casting of other parts suggests that skin color factored into assignments. For example, to avoid the common pitfall of "diversifying" the cast only to place persons of color in smaller or even non-speaking company parts, two high-status characters, Henry VI and Warwick (Geff Francis), were played by Afro-British actors. By casting Warwick as a person of color, the production also endeavored to avoid a neat moral differentiation by color or the implication that race motivated in some way the civil strife between the York and Lancastrian affiliates. When these productions were revived for The Complete Works Festival in 2006, the racial representation was replicated as well, again implying that the RSC casting was by no means colorblind; Chuk Iwuji (Nigerian-British) replaced Oyelowo as Henry VI, and BAME actor, Patrice Naiambana, played Warwick. Amanda Penlington pointedly summarizes the implications of such quota-style re-casting:

> Oyelowo and Iwuji do not look alike but their similar backgrounds and the production's deliberate repetition of costumes, lighting, blocking, and the selection of moments chosen for production photographs typify them as interchangeable black English Kings, rather than as individual performances of the same role.
>
> (182)

In his "Director's Note" to the program book for the three *Henry VI* plays in 2006, Boyd states forthrightly and accurately, "They [the four plays of the first tetralogy] throw an unforgiving beam of light on our understanding of Englishness" (6). However, nowhere in the 2006 program does material address the long-standing elision of English with British or the deep-seated assumption that whiteness features as definitional of "British." While racial replication in casting patterns between 2000 and 2006 establishes the production team's awareness of racial representation, the silence of the printed paratextual materials does not further a carefully self-reflective engagement with who counts as "British."

Though the production design and costuming of the three plays did not draw attention to the visible fact of Oyelowo's race, in his pious submission to death in *III Henry VI* could be read a recognizable tableau—one that underscored the violence done on the black body over the course of British colonial history. With sand poured on the stage, Henry VI stood spotlighted in surrounding darkness as Richard, Duke of Gloucester (Aiden McArdle) approached from the set's Hell mouth to circle the king and then kill the anointed sovereign. Oyelowo collapsed facedown onto the stage as blood poured from him; the regicide Richard then sat down next to the corpse, relishing his handiwork. For the following and final scene, Act Five, Scene Seven of *III Henry*

VI, a substantial blood smear visible in the center-right of the stage remained throughout Edward's kingship celebrations—a reminder of the dead black body that facilitated, in this case, York ascendency. While most other actors avoided treading in the blood, Richard walked unapologetically directly on the pool, taking his nephew "Ned" from Queen Elizabeth's arms and dandling the baby over the blood before shouting "Now" just as the lights went down. Though little would have directed audience thinking towards such a possibility, in many ways, the stained stage could not have been a more apt representation of the way in which the British Empire derived its strength and economic resilience from the blood of black humans stolen, transported, and enslaved as unpaid labor. Indeed, that the remaining actors in the scene were white underscored the sense that white hegemonic power presses on, heedless of its black and brown victims, heedless of the, "sins for which no one has the power to make amends and which can never be fully expiated" (Césaire 42). Hampton-Reeves and Rutter remark on the lasting imprint of that image since the in-the-round configuration of the Swan Theatre forced audience members "to step over" that "large pool of blood left by Henry's murder" as they made their exit. Hampton-Reeves and Rutter suggest that, "the 'national' theatre itself was bleeding" (197) and point to fractures at the RSC. However, if Oyelowo's skin color and heritage were allowed to resonate more precisely, the stained stage also gestured towards the ways in which the institutional theater has been complicit with the silencing of black bodies and stories when narrating the nation.

Gender and Nation in Boyd's Cycle

In addition to missing such opportunities to spotlight Britain's painfully racist past and present, the Boyd productions in 2000 also failed to account for intersectional identities by including no women of color in the large casts. This oversight demonstrated that at the start of the new millennium, institutional Shakespeare still had not thoroughly explored the way in which multiple lines of marginalization—being both a person of color and female, for example—further vexed understandings of the nation. Goddard argues that inclusive casting not only "raises complex questions about when we are to see race or when we are to ignore it, about the extent to which directors are in fact colour-blind" but also, "about how underlying assumptions about race and gender might unwittingly inform casting decisions" (83). In 2000, the three *Henry VI* plays relied upon a total of four Caucasian women (Bell, Sarah D'Arcy, Aíslin McGuckin, and Elaine Pyke), and the 2006 revival program listed one woman of color, Ann Ogbomo, who played one of Joan de Pucelle's fiends, the Countess of Auvergne, Margaret's Attendant, and Elizabeth. This particular failure of casting further qualifies the progressive achievement of the 2000 Boyd productions and actually directs attention to a second significant problem that would be predictive of unresolved issues in televisual adaptations of the history plays throughout the era—specifically gender trouble. Boyd's casual comment that Henry VI's son was in no way illegitimate (despite his whiteness) actually ran counter to the cycle's overt staging of female sexual promiscuity and endangerment of masculine enterprises. Put simply, these productions appeared blind to the politics of identity and intersectionality. On the one hand, the productions attempted to "correct" racial inequality through the casting of a black monarch; however, in their failure to diversify female cast members, the productions ignored how women have been continually "othered" in the patriarchal nation's history. In the case of Boyd's productions, responsible representation extended only to black men but not to women of color nor women, in fact, of any hue who constitute the nation.[9]

Indeed, through their compulsive repetitions, cast doublings, and stylized design, the Boyd productions enacted the deep dependence of national identity upon the containment and conveyance of the female body, doing too little to counter the traffic in women so often constitutive of the nation.[10] Anna Kamaralli roundly critiques Boyd's treatment of female characterization, focusing on the parts doubling of Bell as Joan de Pucelle and Margaret of Anjou: "Boyd drew on selective moments of the text to confirm a negative perspective on the characters, instead of engaging" the more ambiguous depictions of these two Frenchwomen found in the first tetralogy (175). The testimony of Bell herself bears out Kamaralli's assertion that bluntly stereotypical constructs infected the production's staging of female characters and their modes of power. Kamaralli points out that Bell's reflection, "reveals much about the attitude to female power that fueled the rehearsal process" (175) and, sadly, that Bell accepted certain of those disturbing assertions. Indeed, the archived promptbooks testify quietly to the pervasiveness of casual sexism on the set; promptbook descriptors of the female players who fill roles such as serving women or the Countess of Auvergne's attendants in (*I Henry VI*, 2.3) repeatedly identify these players as "girls." Such latent and overt chauvinism, sadly, infused the cycle's diegetic techniques as well.

The casual brutality of the Boyd cycle's access to the female body replicated the strategies of history-telling that reify female subordination as nation-building precondition. More precisely, the staging choices associated with Joan de Pucelle catered to hegemonic anxieties about female authority. The production did so by grounding the young warrior's authority not in a woman's potential prowess or leadership ability but in Joan's sexuality.[11] Bell's memories of the rehearsal process confirm that Joan would be the hyper-sexualized, Amazonian threat of England's nightmares. For example, Bell recounts that in discussions regarding Joan's sexuality and her eroticized encounters with the Dauphin,

> Michael [Boyd] went one step further than Shakespeare and intimated that she was in fact sleeping with several members of the French court. This was not a moral judgement or a comment on her sexual appetites, but rather showed just how expedient she was politically.
>
> (167–69)

According to Bell, the production assumed the villainy and specious piety of Joan from the outset:

> The play isn't about whether Joan of Arc is good or not: as I have said, an Elizabethan audience would have expected her to be a villain. By objectifying her magic in the shape of the "fiends", Michael relieved me of the burden of having to give a modern audience hints as to her true nature. (167)

That these assumptions successfully transmitted to the audience can at least be partially confirmed by audible reactions. On the archived recordings, the audience consistently laughed at moments of comeuppance—when male figures of authority put Joan in her biologically-determined "right place."[12] Although the cycle staged shocking violence against women (acts that should have triggered audience outrage), the underlying sexism of the production did not provoke righteous critique from the audience but rather laughing acceptance of the status quo gender roles, especially when filtered through the long-standing and contentious history of Anglo-French territorial conflict.

When Joan de Pucelle first appeared in Act One, Scene Two of Boyd's *1 Henry VI*, her divine mandate and physical might were undermined by blocking that staged the penetrable female body and the shepherd-warrior's sexual availability. Joan asserts the transformative power of the Virgin Mary's appearance to her: "And whereas I was black and swart before, / With those clear rays which she infus'd on me / That beauty am I blest with which you may see" (1.2.84–86). Casually invoking the black/fair beauty binary (which Kim F. Hall has so convincingly identified as an ideological "conduit through which the [early modern] English began to formulate the notions of 'self' and 'other'") (2), Joan constructs her appearance as a manifestation of divine blessing—not, it must be insisted, as an object of sexual attraction but as devout sanctification.[13] On stage, this moment gained an aspect of coquettish flirtation that drew audience laughter as did any attempt on Joan's part to assert martial prowess. For example, laughter ensued when Joan ran to raise her sword for single combat, when she flourished the sword in victory over the Dauphin Charles (Aidan McArdle), and when the Dauphin in defeat acknowledged her "Amazon." On stage, Charles emphasized his declaration of service, "Impatiently I burn with thy desire; / My heart and hands thou hast at once subdu'd" (1.2.108–109), by crawling on top of the prone warrior, placing his hand on her chest and then up her skirt while the audience laughed at this easy transition from combat to coitus. The promptbook notes confirm the scripted nature of this moment: "C caress P's body hand goes toward crotch. P stops C's hand." Though Shakespeare's Joan declares, "I must not yield to any rites of love, / For my profession's sacred from above" (1.2.113–114), on stage she and the Dauphin assumed post-coital postures, sprawled on the floor, arms behind heads (all that was missing was a cigarette). Kamaralli notes that this test of Joan's strength reduced her status as it took place (in contrast to the text) without a public audience; the members of Charles's retinue exited and, "This results in an uncalled-for diminishment of Joan's power, especially given that she is supposed to be impressing the French army enough for them to follow her into battle" (175). But, unlike male contenders for power who were accompanied on stage by an actual armed force, Joan was followed by a stylized coterie—red-clad fiends who mimed and magnified her movements. As Bell explains, these "fiends" were the textual Joan's "spirits" but their attire left no doubt about the Hellish origins of their nature and thus their contradiction of the Frenchwoman's claims of divine inspiration.

Boyd's imprisonment and execution of Joan staged the female body subject to and simultaneously essential for nation-building and power consolidation. In order to accommodate for the doubling of Joan and Margaret of Anjou by Bell, the capture and death of Joan were rearranged so that Suffolk's proxy wooing of Margaret took place after Joan's execution (5.4). In this production, which imaginatively used the vertical as well as horizontal space of the theater fully, the subdued Joan was tied to one of the vertically descending ladders (metaphors of ambition and hierarchy, and literal remnants of medieval siege-warfare). Her ladder of imprisonment, which had ropes attached to it, could be pulled and released at the whims of her captors and denied Joan the sureness of firm footing. Warwick signaled this vulnerability when he motioned for the ladder to be pulled toward him, at which point he placed his dagger first at Joan's throat and then at her crotch—seemingly provoked by her decision to plead her belly ("I am with child, ye bloody homicides!") (5.4.).[14] York (Clive Wood) continued the taunting brutality begun by Warwick, when at, "And yet forsooth she is a virgin pure," he conducted what looked like a "virginity test," thrusting his hands up Joan's skirt and body ("Y hand up skirt," according to the promptbook) and then flourishing his fingers after the act. Joan's piercing screams garnered no sympathy from York who concluded, "Strumpet, thy words condemn thy brat and thee. / Use no entreaty, for it is in vain" (5.4.83–85). Bell remembers the staging:

> The burning scene was directed to be very vicious. With the words "And yet, forsooth, she is a virgin pure!" (Part One, v.iv.83) York would stab me in the genitals and show his hand with the blood on it, ironically suggesting that he has broken her hymen.
>
> (171)

Whether a virginity test or genital mutilation, the excruciating staged violation of Joan took to an extreme the verbal diminishment she had been subjected to by her English antagonists; though it may well have been a literalization of their abusive epithets, this on-stage rape sullied the stature of these two English "patriots," a fact even Bell notes: "Their [Warwick's and York's] cruelty helps set these Englishmen apart from the likes of Henry V and the two John Talbots, and shows they are no better than the young girl they are torturing" (171). Though the scenes leading to death stressed Joan's martial and erotic behaviors as a danger requiring containment, Boyd's addition of genital mutilation and assault replicated the long-standing reliance upon sexual violence as an implement of warfare and nation-building.

Despite the sexist assumptions rampant throughout the production, the mechanisms of Joan's death offered a recuperative depiction of the Frenchwoman contrary to much of the earlier stage business. In the contrast between her overall representation and the elegiac moment of her death, the production briefly presented an alternative history in keeping with the complex and contradictory historiographical work of the Shakespearean text. Whether deliberate or inadvertent, the burning of Joan illustrated the tendency of historical narrative to paper over details such as the sexual violation of Joan to inscribe justificatory, though often unstable, differentiations between an "us" and a "them." Joan's torments reached an end as she was lowered into a blazing trap, her screams amplified by the troop of "Fiends" who had been her familiar spirits throughout the play. The production's habit of "ghosting" actually exposed, in the case of the Frenchwoman Joan, the ontological flimsiness of an English versus French designation. The limits of the playing space dictated that Joan descended into the same trap where the sainted Henry V was interred in the cycle's opening scene. Musical cues heightened this visual and aural remembrance. Though previously staged as the sexually rapacious Amazonian witch threatening the English, Joan was lamented by a haunting acapella chant that hovered with sacral texture in the space after the trap closed on the site of her immolation. Though the site-specifics of her death might invite differentiation (Joan as distinct from Henry V), such contrast was muted by the musical cues and offered a possibility that the heroism and nationalist spirit of a Henry V and a Joan of Arc might have commonality, despite all the production had done to sexualize, vilify, and undermine the Frenchwoman's military leadership.[15]

On the one hand, self-aware and keenly insightful, Boyd's reliance upon reused playing spaces (such as the trap), provocative doubling of parts, and ghostly reappearances stressed an understanding of history's cyclical nature and often arbitrary classification of "good" and "evil," "in" and "out." On the other hand, maddingly myopic at times, these very techniques (so well suited to the metahistorical interrogations of the Shakespearean texts) cut short, in crucial cases, a self-critical investigation by reinforcing gendered and nationalist stereotypes. This occurred, most notably, in the case of Bell's doubling as Joan and Margaret. Bell recalls the feat of quick-change that her doubling required: "I entered as Margaret literally thirty seconds after the last of Joan's executioners had left the stage" (171). Joan thus remained on stage as a palimpsest inscribed on the body of Margaret, Bell containing the dual French female threat in one body.[16] As with the portrayal of Joan, the cycle's treatment of Margaret conformed to English chauvinism (the would-be queen as an outsider threat) and instantiated the compulsive repetitions endemic to nation-building and nation-telling. Bell's reflections confirm that she also conceived of Margaret as other:

> Was I just Margaret, or Joan in Margaret's body, or Margaret with a vague sense of Joan? And then I realized that it didn't matter: the effect that

> Michael wanted from the transformation was beyond my control; it created an "otherness" about Margaret, but that was a by-product and could only affect the audience, not the actors involved. I had to play the two women as separate entities but at the same time had to allow them to be the same person when the production dictated.
>
> (171)

Despite the elegiac sympathy conjured by the staging of Joan's final rest, her status as immoral threat to England dictated how the playing company regarded her ghostly presence in Bell's body as Margaret. Bell explains that Boyd and she imagined Joan and Margaret as manifestations of evil only surpassed by Richard, Duke of Gloucester: "I think it was Michael's intention that Margaret was, to an extent, a conduit for evil. Joan was alive and had crossed the Channel and until we encounter Richard III no-one can match her for badness" (172). Running counter to that implicit judgement, however, was the persistent question of York and Warwick's ethical rectitude once Joan's death was staged. This nuance, however, was simply not recoverable in light of the pervasive alignment of Joan's perfidy with Margaret's. Oyelowo underscores this moral evaluation: "The idea behind having the actress playing Joan reemerge as Margaret was so that the audience would make a connection between these two characters, who both in their own ways are England's nemesis" (45). Reviews likewise accepted this judgement. For example, Russell Jackson echoes this assessment in his review of the doubling as a transition "from one French sorceress to another" (385). Thus, with cast and creatives convinced of a similitude underscored through doubling, the production shortchanged the historiographic polyvocality its own techniques rendered possible.

Bell played Margaret with a confident, agentive sensuality from her first appearance with Suffolk (Richard Dillane) that rehearsed familiar tropes of dangerous female sexuality and capitalized on the previous, eroticized construction of Bell's Joan. However, as with Joan, some striking stage business occasionally punctured that construction to offer a counter-narrative literalizing the constraint of and traffic in women upon which the nation depends. One particularly lasting *coup de théâtre* was Margaret's descent from the rafters in an over-sized gilt frame—an object to be inspected and evaluated by Henry VI. Suffolk and Henry's uncle Gloucester (Richard Cordery) argued the merits of Margaret versus the prior claims of the Earl of Armagnac's daughter all while Margaret stood within the frame which settled on stage. Competing semiotics ran throughout the moment: Margaret's red velvet plunging V-necked gown and her assured stance with arms carefully stretched to the sides of the frame for stability insisted on her own agential will, while at the same time her scripted silence necessarily highlighted her role as pawn in the power-jockeying between the king's uncle and Suffolk. Much as Joan had been pinned down quite literally to the ladder on which her sexual assault took place and contained in the pit that consumed her, so her reincarnated self—Margaret-in-the-body-of-Joan—appeared as property claimed by the men debating who would be her next owner. Once the frame landed on the stage, Suffolk easily moved with the air of ownership to the back of the frame to release Margaret from the safety catches—a fascinating example of overt theatrical mechanism working to the advantage of the fictional diegesis. This "cut" into present time—the moment of 2000–2001 and its pesky health and safety regulations that required the restraint—actually crossed epochs in ways that suggested the persistence of woman's subjected state within power relations, a subjection often relied upon to disguise the fragility of and fractures internal to the patriarchal nation itself.

The nation's additional internal fractures emerged in a key detail of Bell's doubled performance of Joan de Pucelle and Margaret of Anjou. Boyd and Bell opted to signal Joan's lower-class, French otherness through Bell's native Scottish accent, a choice that exposed fissures within the United Kingdom's own constituent nations: "An early decision we made was that Joan would have a Scottish accent (my own) and that Margaret would have a 'Received Pronunciation' English accent" (Bell 164). Bell elaborates: "The Scottish accent seemed immediately to make her [Joan] working- or peasant-class next to the aristocrats of the French and English courts" (164). For Bell, her own voice and natural accent marked Joan as lower-class other, and in defense of such ingrained accent snobbery, the actor cites the dictum that "it worked" on stage (164).[17] Even though her native accent signals citizenship in the United Kingdom, Bell deemed it a more suitable stage shorthand to convey Joan's peasant-class origins and thus revealed the deeply internalized nature of such exclusionary classifications and the way theater actually depends upon them far too frequently.[18] In performance, Carol Chillington Rutter argues, the accent rang as monstrous, creating an "unsettling" acoustics: "That accent that marked her strange branded her more menacingly. Every time she opened her Scots mouth the English heard her as a witch" (194). The Parekh report authors note ruefully that, "the UK is thought of as an essentially English nation-state, which happens for odd historical reasons to have Celtic fringes" (21), an assumption highlighted by the use of Bell's Scottish accent to "other" Joan's lower-class status, tapping into an English national chauvinism that deems Scotland a lesser-than partner of the United Kingdom.

Class Resistance in History

The Boyd cycle's competing representational strategies—ones that asked audiences to "not see" Oyelowo's race as a violation of historical accuracy but also heralded the casting as epochal, to laugh at Joan's female prowess even as it staged gruesome violations that should goad sympathy, and that emphasized Margaret's constraints while simultaneously presenting her as agential threat to the pious king and English monarchy—persisted into its treatment of the second play's depiction of class struggle. The matter of Bell's accent as Joan and Margaret signaled underlying problems with how the nations of the United Kingdom rate and rank within the social hierarchies—a native Scottish accent somehow better suited than RP to enacting a peasant-class French female.

Similar unease with where the lower class fits within a nation's self-conceptualization emerged in the staging of the Jack Cade rebellion. Indeed, the Boyd production opted to link lower-class resistance to the disruptive unruliness of gender by means of color. The promptbook indicates a red cloth carried onto stage to mark the transition to the rebellion scenes; the red glow of the downstage Hell mouth, in Act Four, Scene Two of *II Henry VI* associated the lower-class rebels with the violence and demonic threat of Joan and the disruptive sexuality of both Joan and Margaret. The degree of this threat was underscored by the red-clad murderers who destroyed Gloucester in 3.2 of *II Henry VI* as well. Thus, the predominance of red aligned Cade with Joan, Margaret, and hired assassins as threats to national order.

Furthermore, by appropriating the visual vocabulary of carnival, Boyd amplified the textual Cade's absurdity and muted the legitimate call for equality also present in the rebel's confused rhetoric.[19] In the play text, Cade's carnivalesque excess and inversions constitute another form of internecine conflict that burlesques the high matter of the aristocratic contests.[20] A force set in motion by York, Cade's oppositional fury soon exceeds the would-be king's control. In the Boyd production, relying once again upon the possibilities of the vertical space, Cade's class resistance could be seen in his effort to climb the space of the stage—not on the sides where elevated balconies existed—but in the airy nothingness above the playing space and up into the flies. For substantial portions of the uprising, Cade sat, stood, and climbed on the swinging trapeze over the central staging area. The trapeze rendered literal the carnival upside-down of Cade's rebellion and continued the production's visual language of ambition and advancement but in a different key from the ladders and ropes of medieval scaling and siege warfare used elsewhere in the cycle. Like the evocative color red predominantly associated with Joan and now transferred to the class unrest of the rebellion, the trapeze signified in ways that downplayed the legitimacy of the contestation. Hampton-Reeves and Rutter confirm:

> The riot was a dark carnival, a Hallowe'en parade that owed more to popular entertainments than to political theatre. There was little in the staging that gave any insight into the reasons *why* the commoners revolted: on the contrary, the production stressed the demonic aspects of anarchy. Audiences were invited to loathe the rebels, who in turn taunted members of the audience as if they were the lords and ladies whom they hated.
>
> (195)

The textual Cade's unruly demands, catalyzed by the shadow manipulations of the Duke of York, manifest in admittedly absurdist and counterproductive ways; however, that does not necessarily mean that the contentions lack merit or that the plea for equality is utterly irrational. The play text repeatedly captures that double-speaking of the rebellion in Cade's social-leveling rhetoric and simultaneous personal aggrandizement: "I thank you, good people—there shall be no money; all shall eat and drink on my score, and I will apparel them all in one livery, that they may agree like brothers, and worship me their lord" (*II Henry VI* 4.2.72–75). Cade's oratory intermixes conflicting political frameworks and claims: equality for all who wear "one livery" and exist as "brothers" but a continuation of servitude as implied by the very wearing of that livery and the subjection to Cade as a new "lord." The rebellion can confound the best production efforts to treat with dignity the plea for human equality, particularly in the face of its flat anti-intellectualism, mob-think, and brutality. The gleeful absurdity and blunt cruelty of even the briefest sampling of Cade's dictums—"let's kill all the lawyers" (4.2.76–77); "and more than that, he can speak French, and therefore he is a traitor" (4.2.166–67); "Away with him, away with him! he speaks Latin" (4.7.57–58)—complicate representational approaches. But from that confused rhetoric and violence emerges an indictment of income inequality, a rigged judiciary, and the complicity of the church with the courts and crown. Unfortunately, what the production ensured through its deployment of Joan's scarlet and the trapeze mechanism was that the legitimate complaints regarding food dearth and income inequality received short shrift. The trapeze device insisted on a clownishness to the rebellion that delegitimized those grievances.

At the start of the millennium, the Boyd cycle, in many ways, sought to foreground more inclusive representational choices, ones that placed the country's multicultural population at the center of power with Oyelowo as King Henry VI. However, just as the production failed to invest adequate time in formulating its inclusive casting choices or educating an audience about the semiotics of race, Boyd's plays did little to problematize the audience's willing complicity with the overt and latent sexism flowing through the performances. Many details, including the recycling of actor's bodies, staging motifs, color schemes, and blocking rightly insisted on history's cyclical nature, on its fictionalized differentiations, and perspectival "truths." However, the evidence of laughter during moments of sexism and even sexual violence implied a failure to educate audiences about the relationship between racism, sexism, and the compulsive contestations for power constituting history. The productions similarly failed to recognize how multiple lines of marginalization must be simultaneously accounted for when recalibrating a foundational history upon which a healthy multicultural society can grow. As the Parekh report insisted in the same year, "Struggles for race and gender equality can illuminate and strengthen each other. However, there are significant differences between the two, for in most contexts the experiences, interests and perceptions of women are different from those of men" (67). Furthermore, a general myopia concerning class persisted in the staging of the Jack Cade rebellion, a blindness to how racial uplift such as that achieved by the casting of Oyelowo must be accompanied by a clearsighted examination of poverty's tendency to exacerbate racism. The FMEB report endeavored to make this point in its critique of the Blair administration's Social Exclusion policies: "Street racism and violent racism arise and flourish in situations of economic disadvantage and inequality"

(106). For the report authors, failing to take seriously the economic structures that maintain social class disequilibrium has knock-on effects on multicultural thriving. By associating class struggle with the female threat of Joan and Margaret or with clownish absurdity, the Boyd productions ignored the underlying economic frustrations of the working classes in Britain, resentments simmering at the seemingly optimistic start of the third millennium. Over the next sixteen years, a large group of disaffected working-class voters would be mobilized to strike a heavy blow against the integrated global economy of the European Union. Though extraordinary in its creative exploration of historical representation, the Boyd cycle's failure to consider how race, gender, and class intermix to complicate the narrative of a triumphant British multiculturalism now looks predictive of the prejudices and conflicts that would, indeed, lead to the Brexit vote of 2016. In some ways, Boyd's colorblind casting would be more progressive than the televised Shakespearean history to come, but the neglect of multiple lines of marginalization predicts patterns visible in those subsequent adaptations.

The Color of War: *Henry V* at the National Theatre (2003)

As with the Boyd *Henry VI* productions in 2000 and 2001, Nicholas Hytner's *Henry V* (2003) disrupted representational traditions by casting Afro-British Adrian Lester in the titular role and exerting pressure on received understandings of this iconic work. Abigail Rokison-Woodall asserts:

> By casting a black actor as Henry, Hytner was making both a political and a theatrical point. Clearly Lester was going to look nothing like the real Henry V. Hytner was casting "the best actor" for the role, irrespective of the colour of his skin, something that David Lister saw as part of a wider policy plan by Hytner "to show from the start that he is going to bring a more radical approach to casting and choice of productions."
>
> (111)[21]

Even in 2003 with colorblind casting already over forty years old as a practice and even with the fairly recent example of Oyelowo as Henry VI at the RSC, applying the principles of "best actor for the role" to the history plays was still regarded as a politically "radical" decision. Such noteworthiness highlights the persistent elision between "authentic" British historiography and Shakespeare's fictionalized accounts of the nation's past. In contrast to the lesser-known *Henry VI* cycle, Hytner's production confronted both deep audience familiarity with the play and long-standing assumptions about its operation as a nation-defining touchstone.

Like the Boyd cycle, this important early 2000s production instantiates both achievements and missed opportunities that would characterize the third millennium's televisual adaptation of Shakespearean history in Britain: a tentative movement into cast diversification, a tendency to underplay the significance of a non-white actor's race even while experimenting with noticeable and so-called colorblind casting, and a mixed effort to address the politics of identity and thereby represent the stories of heterogenous minorities variously disadvantaged by the white, male hegemonic center of nation and power. In one very significant way, however, mainstream televisual adaptations would not follow Hytner's example; rather than adopting a contemporary setting and modern dress costume design, third-millennial televisual adaptations of Shakespearean history would opt for the remoteness of a medieval *mise-en-scène*, one that inevitably whitewashed multicultural Britain.

The beginnings of the Iraq war in 2003 very much informed the production choices of the National Theatre's *Henry V*. Hytner originally chose *Henry V* as a play relevant to the post-9/11 coalition invasion of Afghanistan:

> we had not long ago been at war in Afghanistan. It seemed likely that in the wake of 9/11 we would be marshalled by our leaders to go to war again. It obviously felt like a play that would speak very directly now.
>
> (Hytner qtd. in Rosenthal 694)[22]

With the invasion of Iraq, the director opted to heighten the parallels through modern dress and drew deeply from media representation of desert warfare. Lester adds: "I think the situation we found ourselves in as a country, at the time we did the play, helped to scrape off a kind of romantic veneer that the play can sometimes have. Performances can get lost in poetry and the beauty of the language."[23] Thus, from the very early days of rehearsal, the Hytner *Henry V* endeavored to disrupt the play's mythologized past through the race of its lead actor and through a design aesthetic appropriating the war underway in the Middle East.

Radical in casting choice and historiographical approach, Hytner's appropriation of the contemporary context spotlighted the narrative control exerted by the powerful and bridged the gap between the assumed whiteness of medieval England and the nation's multicultural present, making Lester's blackness as Henry V more plausible. Even so, the Hytner production oscillated between seeing and not seeing Lester's race—marking it briefly and muting it in other seemingly "blind" moments. In addition, the production emphasis on reportage and the recirculation of news in sound bites and clips astutely translated the play text's preoccupation with historiography into a contemporary idiom. Much stage business thus referenced the heavily mediatized Western experience of the conflicts in the Middle East. However, in the context of the post-9/11 resurgent Orientalism of the Afghanistan and Iraq wars, Hytner's *Henry V* did *not* choose to represent persons of Arab descent, making those victims of violence a present-absence beyond the parameters of the tightly controlled narrative. While the production denied Muslim voices despite appropriating the referents of the wars in the Middle East, other casualties of warfare, especially women, were given sympathetic and intentional development. In contrast to the Boyd productions, Hytner recognized more explicitly the high cost paid by women in the nation-building and power-brokering of men at war.

Mission Accomplished?

Throughout his tenure at the National Theatre (2003–2015), Hytner sought both to improve the financial resiliency of the institution and attract a more broadly diversified audience—goals that he saw as absolutely interconnected. To transform the class, complexion, and age of a typical theater audience, Hytner approached the currency exchange corporation, Travelex, seeking sponsorship to underwrite a £10-ticket scheme. Initially, the company agreed but rapidly retracted when the Iraq war forced budgetary retrenchments. However, by April, when Allied Forces had entered Baghdad and a coalition "victory" seemed imminent, Hytner endeavored one more time to convince Travelex to sponsor. With the end of the military campaign seemingly in sight, Travelex agreed to a three-year, one million-pound sponsorship (Rosenthal 693–94). Hytner recalls his anxieties in light of the first Travelex Season venture:

> When the first preview [of *Henry V*] arrived, I was more nervous about what was going on in the auditorium than what was on the stage. I lurked behind the sound desk at the back of the stalls, watching the audience arrive, counting the house.
>
> (60)

The *Henry V* run ended with ninety-six percent of seats sold, and in addition to the high number of daily attendances, Hytner relished the fact that the subsidized tickets attracted a different audience: "They [the Travelex audience] seemed new to us, and so was the buzz. Large numbers of them weren't middle-aged. Some of them weren't even white" (60). For Hytner and others, the demographic expansion of the National Theatre audience confirmed the relevance and appeal of its casting decisions and the power of the arts to reach multicultural British citizens: "More than thirty per cent of the Travelex audience had never come to the National before," and return NT visitors observed that the lower ticket price allowed more frequent attendance (60).

The Travelex ticket scheme very much aligned with the proposals of the FMEB body to adjust funding priorities allowing for greater "access to those arts usually thought of as elitist, particularly theatre and classical music, and most museums and galleries" (166). Parekh's FMEB report catalogued the substantial barriers in the form of institutional racism that would need to be brought into the light and corrected as part of sustained efforts to render the arts more widely accessible. Specifically, the authors argued,

> institutional obstacles must be addressed in all the main arts bodies. There is an operational inertia—a preference for business as usual—which discourages key professionals from re-examining their practices from scratch and from trying to alter the habits of a professional lifetime.
>
> (166)

The entrenched forms of institutional racism cited by Parekh and his co-authors include hiring discrimination, an advancement glass ceiling for BAME British citizens, and an almost exclusively white management and leadership infrastructure across industries and services (74). Thus, the FMEB report called for diversified artistic representation, improved popular access to fine art venues, and correction of institutional structures limiting opportunities for BAME artists and creatives.

Hytner and BAME members of the *Henry V* cast publicly heralded the production, its creative team, and the broadened audience as signs of healthy British multiculturalism. Catherine Silverstone argues that the production positioned itself, "as bringing people of different backgrounds together for a common (English) cause," quoting the BAME actor Faz Singhateh (Westmorland) who described Hytner's *Henry V* as,

> an updated version of what it is on the streets of London, in their own towns, there are black people everywhere [....] I think as young kids that's quite an important thing that they see the world as it is on stage.
>
> (qtd. in Silverstone 112)

Silverstone parses this optimism:

> In Hytner's, Lester's and Singhateh's comments, the work of the National—and *Henry V* in particular—is offered as a positive model of national unity, smoothing over traumatic histories of racism in Britain... and historical inequalities in the British theatre industry in relation to ethnicity and national identity.
>
> (112)

Indeed, Charles Spencer's highly enthusiastic review for the *Telegraph* claimed, "The casting of a black actor to play Henry V may raise eyebrows among some but here it seems like a celebration of the multicultural nature of Britain today." In his praise, Spencer invokes the judgmental few while assuming multicultural Britain as an accomplished mission and successful fact. But, of course, this should be tempered by the considerable ire and policy pullback provoked by the very gentle chiding of the Parekh report regarding the lingering white supremacism encoded into definitions of Britain. The hindsight of 2016 confirms that such celebrations were decidedly premature.

In the British theater where creatives, cast, and crew have been overwhelmingly white, one side-effect of a major casting decision like hiring Lester to play Henry V is a tendency to then assume that racism has been successfully addressed, if not solved. A false sense of accomplishment may then preclude the detailed self-examination needed to transform entrenched biases within the fine arts. On occasion when discussing issues of audience and cast diversity, Hytner adopts a casual tone that similarly forecloses more systematic reflection on pervasive racism. For example, in his almost flippant comment that some of the new audience members for *Henry V* "weren't even white" (60), Hytner delivers an aside without working through the underlying white supremacism and racism he ostensibly targeted with the Travelex sponsorship and casting choices. Hytner does admit concerning the broader Travelex audience and the casting of Lester,

> A few [NT regulars] were less comfortable, maybe feeling the theatre was slipping from their exclusive grasp. Some indignantly pointed out that Adrian Lester was black, and Henry V wasn't. Lucy Prebble, the office assistant, put their letters gingerly in my in-tray...
>
> (Hytner 60)

Without further reference in his memoir to those disgruntled subscribers or to the complex question of how humans "see" race, Hytner's truncated engagement with the signification of Lester's identity downplays the layered meaning of race and the range of reactions provoked by non-traditional casting. Such habits, rightly pinpointed by Toni Morrison as the "silence and evasion [that] have historically ruled literary discourse," prevent a more incisive exploration of liberal race myopias (9). Too often, directors and theater companies can easily attribute racist responses to a clutch of older, white querulous patrons who issue complaints—those "letters gingerly" placed in Hytner's "in-tray." But this self-satisfied liberalism (firm in the belief that "the habit of ignoring race is...a graceful, even generous, liberal gesture" (Morrison 9–10)) does not allow for audience education or for a sustained meditation on the stories that shape the nation and determine in- and out-groups. Furthermore, by recognizing racism only in the cranky letters from a certain, "unenlightened" audience demographic, theater practitioners cut short more self-critical reflection on the structural and institutional inequities that limit broader access to the arts.

Lester's more extensive remarks about his casting as Henry V better acknowledge that his performance provoked audience perspective-shifting and exerted pressure on historical authenticity, a standard often raised to prohibit persons of color from taking on the history canon in performance. In an extended interview, Lester addresses colorblind casting: "It's strange, because as I carry out my job I don't see the performance. But I know that some people will make judgements in connection with my skin colour, and for them the performance will become something new." Lester points out that since the play itself is not documentary history, skin color should not be a determining factor in casting:

> You have to think "It's not real, it's not a documentary." In the theatre you sit beside strangers watching a stage, we are telling you a story. Nowadays, people say "Oh, that's fine, that's great, yeah, tell us a story." But earlier on it was "You can't really tell us that story cos you're not white."

Insisting on the agreed-upon and fictionalized nature of the entire enterprise—the conventions of theater-going itself and the narrativizing of the past—Lester suggests the standard of historical accuracy should not even apply to the representations and transactional exchanges of Shakespearean history in performance. Lester asserts that race-specific casting may well have been an expectation in the past but that contemporary audiences no longer see such "accuracy" as a bar to performance.

Puncturing the Colorblind Claim: Seeing the Performance of Race

Despite the general suggestion that it was a mark of achieved and healthy British multiculturalism not to "see" Lester's race, Hytner's production did disrupt this predominant diegetic principle on two notable occasions—at the Boar's Head Tavern and on the battlefield of Agincourt. These "breaks" into the overtly recognizable and stereotyped performance of race confirmed lingering, unfinished race work in the United Kingdom. At the same time, these "breaks" charted an approach to adapting the histories that could invite viewers to "see" more critically the associative resonances they bring to an actor's visible race, the racial stereotypes they accept, and the feigned race-neutrality of whiteness. In the first examples, *Henry V* utilized signifiers of racial difference as a shorthand for the contrast between the former prince and the reigning monarch—between the milieu of the Boar's Head Tavern and that of the English court. The production appeared to conceive of Prince Hal's past as one defined by a Windrush-generation Caribbean enclave culture typified by Pistol and Hostess Nell Quickly. The Boar's Head Tavern, the world that Prince Hal had forsaken to assume his rights as King Henry, took on a pointedly black racial identity since both the Hostess (Cecilia Noble—Afro-British) and Pistol (Jude Akuwudike—Nigerian-British) were played by persons of color, with Pistol speaking in an identifiably Jamaican accent. The rehearsal diary kept by Peter Reynolds and Lee White indicates that Akuwudike "'was encouraged to play the part with a strong Jamaican accent, and inflect his delivery with the speech rhythms and cadences of patois'" (qtd. in Penlington 178). Given Pistol's association with the gang of thieves surrounding Falstaff as well as his final words after the victory at Agincourt, "To England will I steal, and there I'll steal" (5.1.87), the specifically racialized accent tapped into myths of black male criminality, which as Paul Gilroy has demonstrated tracked with the immigration of West Indian British subjects to the United Kingdom after World War II and evolved over the late twentieth century: "Crime, in the form of both street disorder and robbery was gradually identified as an *expression of black culture*" (*There* 140).[24] The archived costume bible lists components of Pistol's tavern wardrobe that underscored a stereotype of the urban black man living on the margins of lawful society: black zip tracksuit, orange paisley shirt, black trainers, black socks, gold chains. The tracksuit and chains gave a black street hustler character to the Boar's Head Tavern of Hal's misspent youth.

Act Two, Scene Three explicitly identified this racial context as Prince Hal's rejected past. The scene opened with a "home video" of Hal and the Eastcheap crew in days gone by. Labeled in the promptbook as "home video Falstaff stuff," the film depicted the gang in a pub drinking together, performing a portion of the play-acting scene from *I Henry IV* with Desmond Barrit as Falstaff. As others have noted, in this flashback video, Prince Hal sports dreadlocks, and the Hostess also wears braids. Imagining the Boar's Head Tavern as a site of the Caribbean diaspora might offer audiences a shorthand to the Prince's wayward youth (especially since Hytner's production was not performed as part of the *Henry IV* cycle). However, because Lester as the reigning monarch, Henry V, bore no sign (other than skin color) of those ethnic identifiers, the result of this far-from-blind detail was to align non-white culture with a misspent youth, one antithetical to the nation's rule. Juxtaposed video images made this contrast all the more noticeable at the end of the scene. Nell resumed playing a few more lines from the *I Henry IV* home video, beginning with, "A goodly portly man, i'faith," and culminating in a jubilant chorus, "his name is FALSTAFF" (2.4.422, 426). As the on-screen laughter died out, the channel click could be heard and the image of King Henry in desert camouflage and beret appeared, a television news clip replaying the earlier lines, "No king of England, if not king of France!" (2.2.193). The video contrast between the youthful Prince Hal and the wartime monarch underscored the white racial standards embedded in concepts of national authority. Penlington articulates the ramifications of this staging, "...the removal of the dreadlocks could be read as a character decision to renounce a signifier of black (specifically, Jamaican) culture in order for him to succeed as King in a predominantly white England" (179). Thanks to this decision, the production staged the king's ascendency as a move from the margins to the white hegemonic center, one in which stereotypic markers of non-whiteness were neutralized. Instead of a Jamaican patois and dreadlocks, Lester's King Henry channeled the posh, white, public-school demeanor of a Tony Blair both in the cabinet room and on the battlefield.

A similarly blind-yet-not-blind approach to casting transpired with Noble's Hostess Quickly and her Isabel, Queen of France. Like Lester's Prince Hal, she first identified as part of the Caribbean diasporic community associated with the Boar's Head Tavern, but then as the black wife of the white King of France, Charles VI (Ian Hogg), she functioned in the ostensibly "race-neutral" world of the French court—though, of course, that was simply whiteness masquerading as neutral. In the transition, she traded her pink top, denim skirt, and pink suede boots for a restrained blue crepe skirt, jacket, and matching court shoes. The wardrobe switch and the discreet disappearance of her braids operated to underscore "playing" white as normative and "race-neutral"—a guise Noble assumed though clearly performing Queen Isabel as a black woman whose daughter (Félicité du Jeu) bore no skin-color resemblance to her. Penlington reports that Reynolds and White describe as "colour-blind" the casting of Noble as wife to the white King Charles VI (178); however, since the production clearly capitalized on her blackness to create the Caribbean ethos of the

Boar's Head Tavern, something more complex and troubling was transpiring. Though it might easily be argued that Noble's costume change marked economic and class status differences more than ethnic or race difference, the shift worked together with the disappearance of Quickly's braids to suggest that the production was not consistently blind nor fully mindful of its racial semiotics. With both Lester and Noble, the shift to higher status came with a removal of hair and clothing signs of blackness on the assumption that the two actors would read as more authoritative, dare one say "white," simply through costuming and demeanor alterations. These adjustments eerily echo elements of New Labour's Social Exclusion policies as both Lester and Noble rendered themselves suitable to centers of power by abandoning the racial and cultural markers previously setting them apart—once again placing the onus for inclusion not on necessary changes to systems of institutional racism but rather on the individual "outsider."

Audiences *were* asked to "see" blackness explicitly, though briefly, in Act Four during the night before Agincourt; as with the previous examples, the moment traded in black racial stereotypes. Michael Dobson summarizes the moment in his review for *Shakespeare Survey*: "Pistol was played by another of the cast's black actors, Jude Akuwudike, so that Henry's announcement of his alias 'Le Roy' occasioned a gleeful, spurious moment of hand-slapping bonding when Pistol brightly repeated it as 'Leeroy!'" (282). Dobson appears to deem necessary, "another of the cast's black actors," so that the reader will "get" the "Leeroy" joke. The reviewer's comment illustrates the mixed messages of colorblind casting—don't see but, occasionally, see race—and the assumption that unless otherwise noted, actors performing Shakespeare will be white. On stage, this passing detail was played for laughs (interspersed clapping erupted on the archived video) in a production that tended to restrain the text's humor given the action's resonance with current events in the Middle East. Worryingly, the "Leeroy" reference allowed audiences to break into race to reinforce and laugh at stereotyped aspects of black urban culture—specifically its naming and speech patterns. This direct invocation of black culture also threatened to confirm white normativity, conceiving of whiteness as a non-raced neutrality enacted by Lester's Henry V and ruptured only briefly as in the case of Pistol's "Leeroy."

At the same time that the singularity of the moment reinforced black stereotypes and elevated whiteness as normative, the detail simultaneously offered a more complex display of race performativity. Indeed, this dangerously stereotypic moment could also be seen to spotlight race as an ideological construct rather than a biologically inscribed ontological category. The moment of recognition with Pistol suggested that for much of the production Lester was "playing" white in his performance of Henry V—a fact that in many ways might confirm white supremacist ideology. But the moment also pressured the one-way directionality of such racism by insisting that the same must then also be true of Akuwudike. In that way, Akuwudike's blackness was similarly performative rather than essential—particularly in light of the rehearsal diary's indication that the Jamaican accent emerged from rehearsal room directions. The casual greeting between the two actors of color on stage then could be seen to underscore the performative nature of racial identities. Indeed, as cultural critic, Touré, points out,

> The ability to maneuver within white society—and how high you can rise within white power structures—is often tied to your ability to modulate. Black success requires Black *multi-linguality*—the ability to know how and when to move among the different languages of Blackness.
>
> (11)

Margo Hendricks's work on blackness in the early modern period and the Shakespearean stage informs such a rereading of the Hytner production. She explains:

> Like class, race as a performative act is founded upon behavior, bio-physicality, and spectacle. In this context, passing becomes a useful theoretical framework for reflections on race, performance, and Shakespeare. Race in Shakespeare's plays is always located in the performative register: whether it is Prince Hal "passing" as an ordinary soldier or Portia "passing" as a man or Othello "passing" as a Venetian. To consider the performance of race in Shakespeare in this light is to recognize the instability of "whiteness" as a centrifugal force for racial identity, let alone "blackness" as a signifier for people of African ancestry.
>
> (524)

Just as this scene exposed the fact that Lester was "playing" white for much of the production, so the viewer should also be compelled to recognize Akuwudike's Caribbean blackness as performative.

In addition, Pistol's "mispronunciation" marked Lester's blackness and, perhaps inadvertently, demonstrated how colorblind casting often isolates non-white performers from one another and alienates those actors from a significant aspect of their identities—what playwright Winsome Pinnock has described as "cut[ting] the black body from its own history" (qtd. in Akbar, "Winsome Pinnock"). The moment of mutual, racial recognition broke the diegetic illusion, asking audience members to notice how rarely non-white actors are allowed to "play" with one another or "see" and "be seen" as black. In an interview about performing as Salieri in Peter Shaffer's *Amadeus* at the National Theatre in 2018, Lucian Msamati insists,

> I don't come into anything unaware of who or what I am and what it represents: my skin-colour and my heritage is mine and I carry it everywhere I go. Whenever someone talks about "colour-blindness" I say "I want you to see my colour."
>
> (qtd. in Akbar, "Lucian")

In *Henry V*, the "Leeroy" exclamation broke into the theatrical status quo that Msamati describes as endemic to colorblind practices: "somewhere underneath it is the tacit understanding that 'we are allowing you to have that which is ours'" (qtd. in Akbar, "Lucian"). Here the "Leeroy" burst into the possibilities of seeing blackness, pushing signification in multiple directions, allowing audiences to acknowledge, through laughter, the cognitive disconnect often required in colorblind casting and one that also highlighted the homogenizing impact of RP on the nation and its figures of authority.[25]

As a release valve, the "Leeroy" exclamation freed audiences from having to pretend that skin color difference was both invisible and insignificant. Facilitating a collective sigh of relief that the perceptible difference was real and carried meaning (even if a contested and problematic one), this break into racialized identities could offer a way forward for multicultural productions of the history plays—though preferably not to reify existing race stereotypes or to reinforce whiteness as normative. Crucially, such breaks must confront the constructed, performed, and strictly policed nature of whiteness itself as a putatively non-raced category.[26] As Richard Dyer insists, seeing whiteness and "analysing white racial imagery" expose the unearned privileges rooted in the visibility/invisibility of whiteness (9):

> ...this then is why it is important to come to see whiteness. For those in power in the West, as long as whiteness is felt to be the human condition, then it alone both defines normality and fully inhabits it.
>
> (9)

In Hytner's production, the movement between diasporic Caribbean identities and "unmarked" European royalty by Lester and Noble and the very explicitly performed blackness of Akuwudike's Pistol could be turned to a more complex questioning of racial categorization in general and, specifically, of the too-long unchallenged race-neutrality of whiteness: "...whiteness claims for itself a racial exceptionalism even as it does racial work, even as it works arduously to prove black bodies to be of no matter and white ones to be *race-free*" (Little Jr. 95). In such a model, actors and creatives would be empowered to consider the text and its possibilities, puncturing the smoothly performed diegesis with an exploration of the intersection between the four-hundred-year-old text and contemporary understandings of race and identity in the United Kingdom. Such clarity that humans do bear visible markers of color difference corrects the pathological avoidance of race matters inherent in colorblind practices. This kind of dramaturgical business, when deployed more frequently and intentionally, could deepen the race work of non-traditional casting by helping audiences acknowledge the performed and mythologized nature of race identities, both in the present as well as historically, especially during the English Renaissance in which, as Virginia Mason Vaughan explains, "...the black body, however marginalized, functions as a crucial building block in the construction of a white norm for early modern England" (92). Deliberate race breaks in performance can guide audiences to recognize such white self-identification strategies not just as historical but also as contemporary: "At the level of representation, whites remain, for all their transcending superiority, dependent on non-whites for their sense of self, just as they are materially in so many imperial and post-imperial, physical and domestic labour circumstances" (Dyer 24). Rather than intensifying complicity with white racial supremacism by encouraging audiences to "ignore" skin color difference, these breaches in the diegesis could invite viewers into dialogue concerning how we see race, construct it, perform it, and, all too often, rely upon its categorizations to determine in- and out-groups in the nation. Not only would such breaches help challenge racial stereotypes as constructs rather than biological *a priori* givens, but also such elements could shatter the prevailing belief in whiteness as the non-raced, neutral position on stage and in the nation's history.[27]

Who Tells Your Story?

Though rare, details like Pistol's "Leeroy" possessed the power to expose the performed nature of race—both black *and* white—and in so doing, to demonstrate the constructed and arbitrary nature of whiteness as authoritative. While Hytner's production did not expand such moments into a more prominent pattern, its approach to historiography did reveal the dubious, mythologizing narratives that become the authoritative story of the past and the nation's identity. As many have noted, Hytner capitalized on the relevance of *Henry V* to a nation at war; the National Theatre archive materials include a sheaf of newspaper clippings about soldiers in Afghanistan and Iraq that inspired the production's interest in the mediatization of conflict. These clippings guided stage design and costuming choices and also keyed into the production's repeated interest in how news is created and transferred over time as a rough-draft version of history-making. Clippings featured articles on the Royal Marines, photographs of two female US soldiers napping, a *Daily Telegraph* headline from 18 March 2003 reading, "The Coming of War: A Special Report," with a soldier in desert fatigues on the cover. Another caption read, "Brothers in arms: Eight pairs of siblings are serving together in the 2nd Royal Tank Regiment as it waits in the Kuwait desert for orders to head into Iraq." Two other pieces showed Iraqis in Prisoner of War camps, one of the men hooded (an image that would come to carry more critical meaning once news of the torture and abuse at Abu Ghraib prison surfaced in June of 2003—though photos did not emerge until April 2004 in US media). Following the inspiration of these clippings and translating the original play text's historiographical preoccupations—embodied particularly in the Folio version's addition of the Chorus—Hytner established conventions of 24-hour news outlets as a recurring motif for stage business and thus spotlighted the role of news reportage as a first-pass at historiographic work.

The production cleverly adapted play text material to highlight how the act of framing, recording, and glossing military action transforms raw events into history and a nation's identity.[28] The modern-dress costuming allowed Hytner to take full advantage of his contemporary context and to draw a range of parallels to the war unfolding in Iraq and on television screens across the world. The audience in the National consumed material in multiple forms—enacted on the stage, simultaneously filmed and projected, and then recirculated as video in scenes that followed: "The small television screens placed around the stage not only emphasized the importance of public opinion and propaganda but helped to fill the vast, difficult space of the Olivier Theatre" (Potter, "English" 453). Set design (Tim Hatley) created a grid-like video screen across the backstage and pressed the action forward towards the audience, reminding viewers of the reproducibility and recirculation of nation-defining images. Television cameras appeared as onstage props, and video footage replayed through multiple scenes with sound-bite excerpts of the monarch's words. Repeatedly, scenes included camera "set ups," with Henry V on film delivering addresses such as the threat before Harfleur, a speech recirculated and subtitled in subsequent scenes at the French court. When material wasn't camera-ready or brand-image-suitable, such as the threats of sexual violation and brutality outside Harfleur, King Henry signaled for the feed to be cut. The French King was also seen in a makeup bib, likewise, preparing for his own on-camera moment. This thoroughly developed media motif stressed the control exerted by the powerful over the narratives that are disseminated and reinforced through repetition; King Henry's "cut" signal to the camera neatly telegraphed the way that those who control historiography seek to eliminate stories and data disruptive of the dominant narrative.

At the same time that the production offered a study in how narrative control dictates the arc and content of history, much stage business replicated the resistance possible in the face of hegemonic myth-making. Control of video images throughout the performance emanated from multiple sources—the monarch, his courtly "team," those watching the footage (Pistol and Nell or Katherine, for example) who could "click" off the video, and, of course, the audience in the theater (opting to look at the screen or at the actors on stage). Other details stressed the leveling of import that accompanies media circulation thanks to viewer choice and selectivity. In the transition from Act One to Act Two, for example, King Henry's speech replayed on the large video screen:

> Therefore let our proportions for these wars
> Be soon collected, and all things thought upon
> That may with reasonable swiftness add
> More feathers to our wings; for, God before,
> We'll chide this Dauphin at his father's door.
> Therefore, let every man now task his thought,
> That this fair action may on foot be brought.
> (1.2.304–10)

The Boar's Head Tavern denizens channel surfed, quickly clicking off of the king's bellicose determination through images (according to the promptbook) of darts, the archbishop, and finally snooker. These elements highlighted the stubbornness of reception itself; audiences, such as those at the Boar's Head Tavern, make choices to listen or not; camera footage may be curated, but other "versions" still compete as alternative narratives.

The production presented its most pointed critique of this form of reportage and history-making in a promotional video that "aired" after Agincourt. The large screen revealed a video with a waving Union Jack background, titled "The Battle of Agincourt." As light pop music played for underscoring, the video cut between slow motion images of King Henry and his triumphant soldiers. A text crawl at the bottom of the video declared headlines such as "A Royal fellowship of death," and "God thy arm was here." In answer to the text's call from the monarch, "Let there be sung *Non nobis* and *Te Deum*" (4.8.123), the video featured an all-male choir intoning a "Deo Gratias" over the pop song beat. To increase the jingoistic volume, a bass voice began a sung refrain, "We want to thank you Lord" and "We thank you Lord for victory" before reaching a conclusion with the word "Victory" superimposed over the Union Jack flag. The video's kinship with declarations such as George W. Bush's infamous "Mission Accomplished" assertion on May 1, 2003, aboard the aircraft carrier USS Abraham Lincoln could not be ignored. Relying on the Biblical language of good and evil and the workings of providential protection, the video matched pitch-perfectly much of Bush's language: "In this battle, we have fought for the cause of liberty and for the peace of the world....Your courage, your willingness to face danger for your country and for each other made this day possible. Because of you our nation is more secure. Because of you the tyrant has fallen and Iraq is free." Bush hailed the moral righteousness of the coalition forces: "And wherever you go, you carry a message of hope, a message that is ancient and ever new. In the words of the prophet Isaiah, 'To the captives, come out; and to those in darkness, be free'" ("Bush makes"). Opening just five days after Bush's staged victory lap, Hytner's *Henry V* and its laudatory video mimicked the hollowness of Bush's claims. Indeed, the dissonance between Bush's statement and the grinding continuation of the conflict in Iraq intensified over the summer months and confirmed such propaganda to be more wishful thinking than reality.

In the production's costuming, staging, and approach to mediatized historiography, the Iraq war was very much present and yet, in the absence of persons of Arab descent, the war was very clearly *not present.* Despite its provocation to conceive of the national hero, Henry V, in new skin, the production occluded the Arab ethnic minority of the UK, a group heavily impacted by the nation's post-9/11 military and security policies.[29] Engy Abdelkader's comparative study of European countries and rates of Islamophobia states that by 2011 (ten years into the War on Terror), "approximately 75 percent of Britons selected Islam as most violent" in a comparison of world religions (34). More specifically, "43 percent of Britons saw Muslims as fanatical while 32 percent saw the Muslims as violent" (34). The Association of Chief Police Officers confirms that "fifty to sixty percent of all reported hate crimes in Great Britain are perpetrated against Muslims" (Abdelkader 51). It is unfortunate that Hytner's timely production, while delivering a searing, contemporary portrayal of the lies that justify war, sidestepped too overt a representation of that very conflict by not including persons who might read as of Arab descent. In her careful discussion of the NT's archive and the program book for *Henry V*, Silverstone observes a similar silence in the paratextual materials; she notes that though other images of historic warfare appeared in the program, none from the recent Middle Eastern campaign were included; she considers this omission from the program book—to which I would add the failure to represent Arab identity in the cast—as an ethical violation. Silverstone argues that the contemporary context renders Shakespeare persistently relevant even while silencing the people whose blood and treasure were being violated in Afghanistan and Iraq: "Performance can thus be used to uphold essentialist narratives about Shakespeare's relevance and universalism that can work to occlude difference and, on occasions, to perform further violence on individuals and groups" (134). Though perhaps unintentional, the omission of Arab identities from the performance and the published paratextual materials illustrates the selection and deletion process central to the historiographical enterprise, a reminder that even progressive, well-intentioned attempts at telling history will not escape all the blind spots created by centuries-old structures of nation and race.

Hytner's interest in the mythologizing transmission of history emerged more deliberately and amelioratively through the production's casting and staging of the Chorus. The performance's treatment of the Chorus re-enacted history's development from the rough draft of reportage to the narrative shaped and refined by the hands of an academic. Assigning the dubious authority of the Chorus to a female, Penny Downie, the production explored, through her performance, the shifting relationship the historian or biographer develops with and to her subject. Early ideas for Downie's Chorus included imagining her as "'being a war correspondent', delivering bulletins from the war room, embarkation camp and frontline;" however, that initial concept gave way to a vision of the Chorus as university "lecturer" (Rosenthal 695). From her first entrance, Downie's Chorus reminded viewers of the historiographic task by carrying in a stack of books and gesturing to them throughout her invocation to the muse and conjuration of the legendary monarch. Hytner explains that the production aimed to chronicle a transformation in the historiographer's perspective—from enthusiastic advocate to rueful critic by play's end. He recalls:

> Penny started the play committed to the official version of the invasion of France. Act by act, she became more and more aware of the limitations of her vision, because the action she introduced was at odds with her description of it. In a play that's so concerned with presentation, she struggled to impose her narrative on the truth. At the end, foreseeing the disaster of the Wars of the Roses, you felt she'd lost faith in her whole story.
>
> (Hytner 56)

Hytner perfectly captures, in his description of Downie's Chorus, the gaps of historiography as described by Michel de Certeau—the ill-fitting remainders that survive (albeit on the margins) the decision-making processes of history-telling (4).

Hytner's choice of Downie also defied the overwhelmingly masculine voice of history, though reactions to her performance illustrated how reviewers interpreted the fact of her sex in highly stereotypical fashion, approaches that undermined her authority on the grounds of gender.[30] For example, Dobson's discussion of the Chorus began by cataloguing aspects of her physical appearance and attire—"wearing her hair imperfectly tied up and the sort of clothes in which a female academic might choose to face a television camera (right down to costly red shoes)" (279). While reviewer attention to detail assists in creating the written archive concerning this production, sexism lurks in the phrasing, inviting readers to picture an academic—whose anomalous status as "female" must be underlined—lacking fashion sense but thrown into the spotlight and eager to splash out on bright red heels (these ones purchased from the High Street store, Hobbs, according to the costume bible—hardly a high-fashion super-brand such as Jimmy Choo). Dobson elaborates on what he deems a problematic intersection between sexist stereotypes and the role of the Chorus:

> Casting such a woman as the Chorus, interestingly if a little worryingly, placed her attitude to Henry under suspicion from the first: there was little risk of the audience taking this cloistered presenter's gushing enthusiasm for the king as an authoritative statement of what either the play or the production would be seeking to show us.
>
> (279–80)

Glancing at an imagined sexual inexperience of Downie's "cloistered" Chorus, Dobson seems to imply that her attraction to the monarch made it obvious from the start that the audience should question the authoritative nature of the Chorus's pronouncements—an interrogative stance, Dobson assumes, should be gradually revealed. One might suggest that the problem here lies with the reviewer's set of gender stereotypes rather than with the production's casting and costuming choices. Another reviewer, Patricia Tatspaugh, also slotted the Chorus into an easily accessible gender stereotype: "Penny Downie's earnest, school-marmish Chorus seems to counter on-the-spot reporting with the long view of history" (103). Sexist stereotype aside, Tatspaugh's review rightly characterizes how the production relied on Downie's performance of the Chorus to contrast the rough draft of reporting with the considered, "long view" reflections of historiography. Downie's gender—rather than opening up a ludicrously stereotypic meditation on her potential sexual attraction to Henry V—should have underscored to viewers how rarely the historian's voice is imagined as female. As she walked in and out of scenes, shuffling through her archive of documents, Downie's Chorus—her skirt and sweater insisting she be gendered female—wielded the authority of historiography. Even as Shakespeare's text certainly draws attention to the gap that opens between historic action and the narration of those events, Hytner's choice to represent the Chorus in the body of a woman insisted that viewers recognize how infrequently stories of past and nation—flawed though they may be—take shape through the voicing of female memory.

Working in sympathy with this shift in the gender of the historiographer was a production emphasis on the exploitative dynastic traffic in women. In its approach to representing the role women fulfill in nation-building, Hytner's production stressed the high price paid by women to cement the bonds of men. The imperiled female bodies invoked in Henry's threat outside the gates of Harfleur transformed explicitly into the Princess Katherine. As Henry's charge to the governor of Harfleur was being recorded, at "And the flesh'd soldier....mowing like grass / Your fresh fair virgins and your flow'ring infants," the king mimed the "cut" sign across his neck to prevent such details from circulating digitally. Nonetheless, the lines did recirculate on a video seen by Alice and Katherine who visibly flinched at "mowing like grass / Your fresh fair virgins" (3.3.13–14). Most notably, the Hytner production refused to comply with the play text's attempt at a comedic ending in Act Five's marriage, though laughter on the archived video suggests the audience craved release. (Most laughter occurred when Henry insisted he loved France so much that he would not "part with a village of it.") For most of Act Five, Scene Two, Katherine and King Henry stood on opposite sides of the stage, and her imperviousness to Henry's blandishments never relented: "the whole interview, was just a sort of diplomatic rape" (Dobson 283). Dobson observes, "...there was no pretence that Félicité du Jeu's Princess Catherine was in any way pleased to be getting married off to her country's conqueror" (283). In an awkward yet powerful gesture, Katherine refused to take the outstretched hand of Henry V as the treaty-couple walked offstage, bravely defying the audience's desire for cathartic reconciliation.[31] In contrast to the sexism rippling through the Boyd *Henry VI* productions, Hytner's *Henry V* consciously offered an empathic recognition that nation-building historically has relied upon the objectification of women and their function as instruments of exchange. By highlighting the agency available to Katherine—that of refusal and visible non-compliance—the production recovered fragments of female agency from the historic past. Hytner's production amplified this effort at recovery by granting the authoritative voice of historiography to a female as Downie's rueful Chorus uttered the concluding words of the play. Indeed, this final tableau of history as told by a woman suggested that such a history might compute the cost-benefit analysis of territorial expansion quite differently and rather more skeptically.

In several ways, the Hytner production from 2003 offered a number of lessons regarding how Shakespearean history might be extended to help third-millennium Britain articulate its complex and multicultural identity. Representing the diverse communities of Britain, not just in minor roles but through the casting of the iconic monarch exerted pressure on a whites-only historic memory. However, when those non-white bodies operated functionally "as white" (with white established as normative by the performance), this severely limited the instructive possibilities of the casting. Break-out moments that invited viewers to see very acutely how racial identities were performed and stereotyped could have provided ways of adapting the plays to its multicultural cast, audience, and nation, but the avoidance of Arab voices and the fullest possibilities of the contemporary context predict in some ways the cautiousness of the televised histories that follow. Nonetheless, Hytner's casting of a female Chorus did put pressure on the masculinist work of historiography and heightened sympathy with Katherine's frustrated agency in more progressive ways than subsequent televised adaptations such as *The Hollow Crown*. Without exception, the major Shakespearean histories funded by the largest televisual outlets in the United Kingdom would rely exclusively on heritage-style, period costuming and medieval *mise-en-scène* and would fail to follow even the imperfect experiments of Hytner's *Henry V*. The director's own turn two years later, in 2005, when the war in the Middle East continued, to a faux medieval setting signaled a retreat from the possibilities of a reinvigorated adaptational approach to Shakespearean history.

Evasions: *I* and *II Henry IV* in 2005

In 2005, Hytner returned to the matter of Shakespearean history with the two parts of *Henry IV*. These productions, staged in the late spring just prior to the 7/7 attacks in London, lacked the contemporary intervention into history that characterized the earlier *Henry V*. Indeed, this suite defanged history of its political purchase and withdrew from the fuller possibilities of retelling Shakespeare's medieval chronicles. Rather than deploy modern dress as a means to examine the modes of history-telling manifested through the ongoing wars in Iraq and Afghanistan, the two plays resided in a medieval-light *mise-en-scène* that neutralized such opportunities; despite wearing jeans and leather jackets, the actors functioned within what Silverstone describes as, "a medieval dress aesthetic and setting" (Silverstone 127). Thinning out contemporary particularity, Hytner's *I* and *II Henry IV* productions predicted the further confinement of televised Shakespearean history in the third millennium within the straight-jacket of period design and costuming. This formula would make a thoroughgoing interrogation of these stories much more difficult because authenticity became both the rule and a distracting preoccupation, one that often invoked an elegiac craving for a bygone era. That very tone of loss and wistful nostalgia would, indeed, provide the key in which *The Hollow Crown* rendered history in 2012, retreating to the palisade of authentic historical recreation to the accompaniment of diversity tokenism. In 2005, Hytner's *Henry IV* productions circumvented the potential for social critique inherent in Shakespeare's polyvocal histories and neutered the meaning of race through a conservative adoption of colorblind casting that left the fourth wall intact and did not invite attention to the performance of race.

Of the roughly thirty members comprising the cast of the two parts of *Henry IV,* only three performers were BAME: the father and son, Northumberland (Jeffery Kissoon) and Hotspur (David Harewood), and Darren Hart who played the drawer, Francis, in *I Henry IV* and the conscript Thomas Wart in the second play. This meant that, in contrast to both the Boyd *Henry VI* cycle and Hytner's *Henry V*, persons of color did not reach the highest levels of power and that two of the three persons of color were confined to one aristocratic household. James N. Loehlin notes regarding the casting of Hotspur and his father:

> Hytner's casting just hinted at the possibility of ethnic conflict in the Percy rebellion, in that both Hotspur and his father, Northumberland (Jeffery Kissoon) were played by actors of African descent; but the production didn't highlight this, and none of the reviewers commented on it.
>
> (*Henry IV* 174)

The reach, then, of multicultural Britain was restricted in ways contrasted with the Boyd productions which distributed persons of color across households and affinities, or Hytner's *Henry V* where BAME performers acted on both sides of the England/France divide. As with the Boyd productions, no women of color appeared in the *Henry IV* productions (unlike *Henry V*). Stage business in the *Henry IV* plays generally ignored the skin color of the three BAME performers and encouraged the audience to do so as well; no "break" into race identities occurred in quite the way dictated by Lester's dreadlocks in *Henry V* or Pistol's "Leeroy" exclamation. However, this does not mean that the production was devoid of problematic racial representation; in fact, as would be expected, the isolation of Hart, in particular, as a player of two lower-class parts led to pernicious racial and social class stereotype intersections and racist tableaux.

In *I Henry IV*, Hart's race rendered even more problematic the way Hal (Matthew Macfadyen) and Ned Poins (Adrian Scarborough) plague Francis the drawer (2.4), exploiting the serving-man's inability to converse with Hal while Poins continually calls, "Francis" from within. In Costume Designer Mark Thompson's digital files, the entry for Hart as Francis reads, "Francis: youngest member of the gang. Low class, artisan apprentice; black youth, pub boy." These thumbnail notes, designed to guide costuming choice, imply a set of unspoken assumptions embedded in the phrase, "black youth," particularly when combined with the term, "gang," to describe Hal, Falstaff, and their compatriots. More importantly, the descriptor offers further evidence that creative teams are by no means colorblind and do consider, however insufficiently, the shorthand characterizations possible given the semiotic combination of an actor's race, his part, and his costuming.[32] In this case, the interpretive option for an audience easily to categorize Francis as a certain kind of lower-class "black youth" was matter-of-factly recognized rather than troubled. Worryingly, as Francis, Hart delivered lines at a slower pace and with a lower-class accent, details that would not have mattered if the large cast had included a total of more than three persons of color across a range of roles.[33] As dictated by the script, Francis cleared tavern tables on house right during Act Two, Scene Four, moving steadily towards the seated Hal as he endeavored to answer the prince's questions. However, Ned's offstage calls repeatedly flummoxed the young man, turning Hart's Francis round and round as the calls from the prince and Ned gathered rapidity. The result was a tableau which left Francis, the black youth, as the butt of two white men having a bit of fun—a racist trope from the canon of white supremacism that ended with the white Vintner finally beating Francis off stage for supposed dereliction of duty.

In *II Henry IV*, Hart's Thomas Wart accumulated a similar number of racist tropes through the course of the conscription scene (3.2). Costuming suited the scarecrow nature of Falstaff's conscripts but replicated stereotypes about race, class status, and intelligence. Indeed, much like his role as Francis, Hart's performance of the conscript Thomas Wart keyed into the racist stereotype of the ineffective and dim-witted Jim Crow, the "slow-thinking, slow-moving" black who, "wore tatters and rags and a battered hat" (Lemons 102). Wearing cut-off patched trousers and a cap with strings dangling (much like a jester's cap), Hart walked pigeon-toed and stood during the assessment of his battle-worthiness with an empty broad smile, hands held close to his chest, and idly turning his torso back and forth compulsively. The costuming and performance choices combined to create of Hart's Thomas Wart a simpleton, but the degrading and racist innuendo extended beyond those details. Falstaff's callous pocket-lining at the expense of soldiers ill-equipped for combat took on painful white supremacist overtones when, in particular, he appraised Wart's worth by standing beside him, and tapping him in the stomach with a cane, as if to evaluate physical strength, replicating the history of slave auctions in his gestures. The lack of company diversity meant that, indeed, the rest of Falstaff's rag-tag, would-be army were played by white actors who suffered similarly as the objects of class-based disdain. Nonetheless, the scene assumed unforgiveable racist implications added to the classism inherent in the characterization of Thomas Wart and his unwilling compatriots. It might be tempting to overlook this passing but deeply troubling characterization of Francis and Wart that borrowed from the white supremacist vocabulary of American Minstrelsy, especially in light of the casting of Harewood and Kissoon. However, Harewood's performance as the higher status Hotspur, alongside the Afro-British Kissoon as his father Northumberland, simply could not be expected to bear all the weight of the race work necessary to correct the multiple problematic roles Hart assumed under Hytner's direction. In the two parts of *Henry IV*, Hytner may have retreated from the pressing topicality of his *Henry V*, but that retreat maintained an all-too-current (for the early 2000s) liberal obliviousness regarding the representation of multiethnic British historicity.

In his memoir, Hytner acknowledges that this suite of performances sidestepped direct engagement with the political context of 2005 and the gender and racial diversity of third-millennium Britain. He writes, explaining the production's avoidance of contemporary context:

> But loving the *Henry IV* plays too much, I felt more constrained by them than I did by *Henry V*. I was wary of bringing too much of the present to them. I wasn't convinced that a narrative about civil war in England, the consequences of regicide, and the stricken conscience of the usurper would make much sense if the plays were presented, as they were in the 1590s, in a modern context.
>
> (156)

Explaining that he saw the two parts of *Henry IV* as too remotely steeped in an inaccessible "Tudor terror" regarding "the chaos of the Wars of the Roses," Hytner admits his miscalculation:

> Writing now, in 2016, that terror feels much closer. Town and country are divided, and so are North and South, Scotland and England. There is nothing remote about Hotspur's rage, on behalf of the neglected North, at the "jeering and disdained contempt" of the proud king. Falstaff milking Gloucestershire for money and "continual laughter", is the incarnation of London's contempt for Middle England. I overestimated the stability of our body politic and I wish I could have another go at tapping into folk memories of civil strife.
>
> (156)

Though the memoir does not account directly for the flawed racial representation of the *Henry IV* productions, Hytner does acknowledge how little political purchase the performances granted women:

> Had I included more women in the *Henry IV* company, I would have forced myself to be less anodyne. I would have had to create a stage world where women were part of the political power structure, or a world less confined by the literal representation of power.
>
> (Hytner 159)

More pointedly when discussing the silencing of women's voices in the Henriad and his own productions' failure to correct that omission in a contemporary context, Hytner asks a crucial question:

> What kind of incomparable panorama of England leaves out half of its population? And what kind of production makes no amends for what may be an acknowledgement of historical reality, but feels hard to defend in the context of the age-old insistence that Shakespeare is for all time?
>
> (158)

To Hytner's self-interrogation, I would add, what kind of "panorama of England" fails to account for a nation comprised, both historically and presently, of multiethnic peoples? Indeed, in the notion of "amends," and the responsibility of contemporary performance to do just that—atone for past omissions and misrepresentations—Hytner's comments should as readily be applied to the embodiment of multiethnic identities.[34] However, short-sightedness persists about how his own productions have not always made amends and about the degree of audience comfort with diversified representation of Shakespearean history:

> If we claim him [Shakespeare] as our national playwright, we could start by allowing in the entire nation. Nobody now seriously thinks that skin colour should preclude actors from taking part in the performance of Shakespeare's plays, any more than I should be precluded from directing them because I am a third-generation Jewish immigrant. They belong to all of us: to Adrian Lester as Henry V and David Harewood as Hotspur as much as to (Irish) Michael Gambon as Falstaff. Audiences had no problem with any of them, and will soon have no problem with equal representation of women in the companies who perform his plays.
>
> (159)

Lingering in his own laudable initial assertion, "we could start by allowing in the entire nation," remains an obliviousness to how his own productions have not always used the power of Shakespearean history to recast the collective ownership of the national story. Furthermore, by insisting, "Nobody now seriously thinks that skin colour should preclude actors" from playing Shakespeare, Hytner's blithe optimism actually makes it more difficult to combat the deepening hostilities roiling beneath his characterization, only two paragraphs earlier in his memoir, of a deep national divide.

What's Past is Prologue

For centuries, Shakespearean history has provided the foundation upon which "fortress Britain" was built; John of Gaunt's "This England" and Henry V's "Band of Brothers" conjure an in-group exclusivity and remembered corporate achievement that operate as sustaining myths of an all-white nation. Though Shakespeare's history plays body forth incipient British nationhood *and* predict the fissures that render illusory a unified national monoculture, four hundred years of performing these words in the bodies and voices of white actors have muted those resistant possibilities in the texts. Turning such stories to new purpose—especially in order to expand the representation of who belongs on the island—requires deliberate, self-conscious, and articulate intervention. Correcting the problem by quietly replacing Laurence Olivier or Kenneth Branagh with Adrian Lester proves insufficient; the white supremacism and prejudices encoded in these performed works and clinging to their audiences demand a much more intentional reflection on the creative choices necessary to render a hospitable definition of the nation and its history.

These notable productions at the start of the third millennium could have been trend-setters, could have established practices to be refined, reconsidered, and improved upon to craft truly fresh appropriations of Shakespeare for a multicultural Britain. Imperfect and inconsistent in their depiction of multiple lines of marginalization, these productions and their attempts at representational equity failed to push third-millennial television in a more progressive direction; indeed, their fledgling efforts at cast diversity were all but abandoned by the televisual adaptors that followed. Much like the recommendations of the FMEB report so thoroughly undermined by the press firestorm and New Labour's rapid retreat from its policy suggestions, these important productions of the history plays starring persons of African descent did not lead to the renovation of adaptational assumptions regarding Shakespearean history and the British nation his plays helped shape. Instead, they instantiated what would be typical of the raft of small-screen approaches to come—continued and limited colorblind casting and an unwavering determination to silence the painful, ongoing conversation about social justice and equality. As Afua Hirsch observes:

> Britain is not unique in these problems, Western European nations have all been changed by people from their former colonies, alongside the ideology of racial superiority that had those people as colonial subjects in the first place.... But what *is* unique about Britain is the convoluted lengths we are willing to go to, to avoid confronting the problem. We will not name it, we avoid discussing it and, increasingly, we say we can't see it. We want to be post-racial, without having ever admitted how racial a society we have been.
>
> (125)

While, on the one hand, these stage productions imaginatively represented the metahistorical understanding of Shakespeare's history plays, they failed to turn a sustained eye on the underlying racism embedded in the techniques by which the powerful deploy constructions of history to delimit the nation.

To varying degrees, the Boyd and Hytner productions utilized stage business, design, and costume to signal the "constructedness" inherent in Shakespeare's take on history. Unfortunately, these productions did not reason overtly from Shakespeare's dramatization of the decision-making and fiction-building of historiography to the exclusionary nations such myth-making comes to form and the victims—women, persons of color, and the lower classes—at whose expense the nation emerges. As de Certeau reminds us, constructions of the past operate on an in- and out-group formulary that ostracizes women, persons of color, and the lower classes (3). Productions like Boyd's and Hytner's that highlighted the historiographic sophistication of Shakespeare's plays—their mindfulness about who tells the stories of a people and which stories survive and come to dominate—should have offered a richer meditation on the plight of the marginalized. In doing so even more overtly, they might have made a lasting impact on the way in which Shakespeare's history translated to the small screen in an era that became more and more preoccupied with the question of who truly counted as "British."

Notes

1 In addition to provoking adjustments in production choices, political shifts, according to Stephen Purcell, influence alterations in how theater audiences respond to performance: "Changes in language, dramatic conventions, theatregoing habits, living conditions, national and global politics, and much more are surely influential in shaping the ways in which audiences form their responses to Shakespeare's drama" (71).

2 Americans will find a rough equivalent to the assumptions and policies of Social Exclusion in the colorblind racism described by Eduardo Bonilla-Silva and manifested in the post-civil rights era United States, a brand of racism whose "major themes are (1) the extension of the principles of liberalism to racial matters in an abstract manner, (2) cultural rather than biological explanation of minorities' inferior standing and performance in labor and educational markets, (3) naturalization of racial phenomena such as residential and school segregation, and (4) the claim that discrimination has all but disappeared" (42).

3 *The Future of Multi-Ethnic Britain* report levels criticism at New Labour's Social Exclusion unit's approach: "But if a focus on the margins and boundaries means that there is no pressure for change at the centre, or in society's principal power relationships and hierarchies, the benefits of inclusion may be slight" (79). Furthermore, the report notes that, "it is unfortunate that the concept of social exclusion displaces and deemphasises concerns about inequality and relative poverty," arguing that the essentially "colour-blind and culture-blind" policies fail to recognize, "that poverty affects certain communities disproportionately," and that the same "anti-poverty measures" will not work effectively across different racial and ethnic populations (82).

4 For a fuller discussion of the report's release, see Chapter One.

5 Straw's assertions accord with those of Tony Blair several years prior to the release of the *FMEB* report: "…Tony Blair, stated in 1997 that he valued and honoured British history enormously and considered that the British Empire should neither elicit 'apology nor hand-wringing' and that it should be deployed to enhance Britain's global influence" (El-Enany 213). Both politicians thus ignore the pressure of so many postcolonial voices who declare, "that no one colonizes innocently, that no one colonizes with impunity either; that a nation which colonizes, that a civilization which justifies colonization—and therefore force—is already a sick civilization, a civilization which is morally diseased" (Césaire 39).

6 In numerous interviews, Oyelowo describes the racism he and his family, "a regional royal family" from Nigeria, experienced over the years as residents of the UK. In an interview in late 2020, he recalls statements hurled at his father during Oyelowo's youth, "Go back to where you came from," and compares that with his brother's far more recent encounters post-Brexit: "My brother, who is a healthcare professional in the UK, was on the train not long after the Brexit decision and that exact phrase was used to him on the tube. 'Go back to where you came from.' So no one can tell me Brexit wasn't at least in part about race'" (Hattenstone).

7 See, as discussed in the first chapter, Leslie Odom Jr.'s (Aaron Burr) remark, "But this show [*Hamilton*] has been such a gift to me in that way because I feel that it's my history, too, for the first time ever" (qtd. in Lurie). The impact of such casting extends to audience members as well, who, as Amy Cook notes, must reconsider race-based assumptions about identity and history: "…Lin-Manuel Miranda's *Hamilton* altered the story of the founding of America and also invited its spectators to expand their categories of what political leadership looks like" (13).

8 Another audience member, an "angry letter writer," "insisted that casting Oyelowo as the historical Henry VI was an 'obvious untruth' and a 'distracting irritation throughout the performance'" (qtd. in Steigerwalt 426).

9 This tracks with theorizations focused on the roles women have been assigned historically in nation-building. For example, Elleke Boehmer argues that while woman as mother may serve the nation as metaphor, this does not elevate her sex to positions of historical and national agency: "Gender always already gives nationalism its legitimating symbols, its self-validating show" (30); "Cast as originator or progenitress, a role authorised by her national sons, she herself, however, is positioned *outside* the central script of national self-emergence" (29).

10 As Parekh explains: "Social identity has a gender dimension. In most societies, women have available to them a narrower range of identities than have men. And since they are generally seen as transmitters of the society's culture, their social identities are more heavily scripted" (*A New Politics* 16). Similarly, Benhabib writes: "Women and their bodies are the symbolic cultural site upon which human societies inscript their moral order. In virtue of their capacity for sexual reproduction, women mediate between nature and culture, between the animal species to which we all belong and the symbolic order that makes us into cultural beings" (*The Claims* 84). The Boyd production in many ways simply assumed as status quo the traffic in women explained by Gayle Rubin: "If it is women who are being transacted, then it is the men who give and take them who are linked, the woman being a conduit of a relationship rather than a partner to it....If women are the gifts, then it is men who are the exchange partners. And it is the partners, not the presents, upon whom reciprocal exchange confers its quasi-mystical power of social linkage. The relations of such a system are such that women are in no position to realize the benefits of their own circulation" (174).

11 Carol Chillington Rutter describes the misogynist ways in which Joan's prowess is habitually constructed: "There is no way for a woman to act (as patriot or freedom fighter, for example) except sexually, and, by definition, any action marks her as sexual transgressor, therefore impudent and demonised, a monster. Thus, power in a woman has one single source, darkness, with two names, sexuality and witchcraft" (191).

12 I cite this video recording evidence acknowledging what Purcell spots as an interpretive limitation: "Archive recordings allow researchers to identify communal responses such as laughter and applause, but this rarely allows for an analysis of individual reasons" (153).

13 The play's multicultural cast in which non-white players acted on both sides of the "good" and "bad" moral face-off should have made the fair/black binary resonate differently, particularly, when the cycle's embodiment of Christian piety, Henry VI, was played by a person of color. On stage, such lines became throw-away business as usual given the blocking and performative strategies.

14 Instructions in the promptbook read, "puts dagger to throat then at crotch."

15 Viewed years later in the confines of an archive carrel, such deconstruction of historiography's oppositional schema can be detected in the repeated use of the trap as Henry V's grave *and* Joan's pyre but in the moment of performance, it should be noted that distinction, not commonality, still garnered enthusiastic affirmation in the form of audience response throughout most of the scenes involving Joan. One wonders, was the response a nervous tic provoked by the woman-on-top disorder of a military operative like Joan or a comforting resort to familiar, deep-seated prejudices against the country's current EU partner?

16 Ralph Berry articulates the signification of such doubling: "But subterranean linkage between characters, and with it the experimental possibility of doubling, is inherent in Shakespearean drama" (15); it encourages an actor to find affinities between parts as it "exploits likeness" (Berry 19, 22).

17 In contrast, Bell mentions rehearsing Joan "in 'RP' for the first few days, but I didn't think it worked" (164).

18 Hampton-Reeves and Rutter interpret this accent choice in the context of devolution: "Fiona Bell brought out Joan's proletarian character by playing her in her native working-class Scots accent—another aspect of the cycle's 'devolution' of national culture, but also an indication of class that placed this shrieking, spitting, indecent monster within the frame of York's own extreme fantasies" (199).

19 "In Shakespeare's most extensive representation of a plebeian insurrection, English commoners, led by Jack Cade, rise up against the learned, rich, and powerful men whom they see as their oppressors" (Howard and Rackin 66). Stephen Greenblatt parses the anti-intellectual resentments activated by Shakespeare's rebel leader: "The poor whose passions Cade is arousing feel excluded, despised, and vaguely ashamed. They have been left out of an economy that increasingly demands possession of a once-esoteric technology: literacy. They do not imagine that they can master this new skill, nor does their leader propose that they undertake any education. It would hardly suit his purposes if they did so. What he does instead is manipulate their resentment of the educated" (*Tyrant* 40).

20 In opposition to the aristocratic dismissal of the lower classes found throughout *II Henry VI*, Richard Helgerson argues that the Cade rebellion articulates a "strong counter discourse, a discourse of popular protest and popular power" (206).

21 Rokison-Woodall's comment inadvertently reveals an assumption complicating non-traditional casting of the history plays; her statement overinvests in the single distinguishing feature of skin color when establishing who might look like the historic Henry V. The statement that Lester would "look nothing like the real Henry V" assumes that skin color negates any other phenotypical or human likeness that Lester might share with the few images that exist of the fifteenth-century English monarch and implies the unspoken corollary that by virtue of their whiteness alone somehow Laurence Olivier or Kenneth Branagh more authentically resemble Henry V.

22 The night before *Henry V* rehearsals commenced, George Bush and Tony Blair confirmed their plans to invade Iraq (Rosenthal 694–95).

23 Rosenthal writes: "The Iraq conflict which determined the on-off-on-again sponsorship of the Travelex season was the predominant influence on Hytner's *Henry V*" (694). In an interview with Julian Curry, Lester notes that Hytner selected modern dress only after the invasion began, "Suddenly the country went to war, as we were in rehearsal. We responded to the situation."

24 Writing in 1987, Gilroy predicts the shift of the left towards a "law and order" ethos targeting black criminality in order to recapture disaffected working-class white voters. He displays a prescient insight when describing the roots of what would become the reemergent far-right nationalism of the post-9/11 era: "The racial connotations of these images [of black criminality] and their concrete attachments to the languages, aims and organizations of overtly racist groups will not simply evaporate while socialists struggle to hitch the law and order issue to their own political purposes. They are more likely to remain and drag the political energies of the white working class down into the depths of racism and reaction" (*There* 142).

25 Penlington reasons from these "break-outs" of race and the return to RP in *Henry V* to the larger problems of colorblind casting: "…despite casting actors of different ethnic origins, references to other cultures (both in appearance and voice) are reduced and 'neutralized' in the service of the dominant English discourse (whose accent is located as middle-class home counties)" (179).

26 Arthur L. Little Jr. explains the way in which white race neutrality depends upon the performance of blackness: "Notwithstanding, one of the very important aspects of these performances of blackness, and one of the very real ways in which whiteness works, is their performance of the non-performative nature of a whiteness that lies beneath the paint or mask. Crucially, this is not just a 'whiteness' of the skin but a whiteness within that underwrites and provides the authority for these black impersonations: it's whiteness qua featurelessness, *ideologically*" (90–91).

27 Francesca T. Royster describes the staging of constructed whiteness in Edward Hall's *Rose Rage* (Chicago Shakespeare Theater, 2003) that other productions of the history plays should more consistently and self-consciously develop: "The play asks us to rethink the ways that 'colorblindness' works as a default category of performing whiteness. We are made to think about how and why we read bodies as 'white.' And it asks us to rethink our assumption of early modern English history as a story of stable white identity" (230).

28 Hytner explained that the production would confront "'the way contemporary media spin is involved in the waging of war nowadays'" (qtd. in Rokison-Woodall 109).

29 For a discussion of the history and shifting meaning of the term "Islamophobia," see Fernando Bravo López who argues that, "Islamophobia can effectively be confounded with a form of racism or cultural racism because it occasionally targets minorities that are effectively racialized. But it is the perception of Islam as a threat that engenders the racialization of the Islamic identity. It is the need to identify the threat, to identify the Islam incarnate in Muslims, that causes the Islamic identity to be transformed into an involuntary identity: the Muslim will be identified not on the basis of his beliefs but rather on the basis of his origin, his ancestry and a series of ethno-cultural traits" (569). For this reason, what López regards as often religious intolerance or cultural racism transmutes into racism, particularly in post-9/11 Europe.

30 As Diana E. Henderson reminds us, the Chorus was played by a woman in the guise of "Clio, the Muse of History" when Charles Kean cast his wife in that role in 1859 (241), a practice that persisted as late as the 1930s when Sybil Thorndike also took the role (242).

31 On the night I attended the performance, Katherine's refusal to comply provoked extended, even stunned, silence from the audience.

32 A line deletion from this scene also gave the lie to an insistence on colorblindness since the script did edit out a reference to the drink, "brown bastard."

33 Of the twenty-seven actors, three were persons of color in *1 Henry IV*, and two were persons of color in *II Henry IV*.

34 In "Resisting History and Atoning for Racial Privilege," I contend that mindful and multiethnic recirculation of Shakespeare's Henriad creates a context in which, "a privileged audience participates in recuperative acts that can begin to atone for how Shakespearean history, even when it contains disruptive shards of the past, has still been employed to perpetuate cultural racism and profound inequities" (380).

3 Shakespeare and the Cultural Olympiad

Gender, Race, and the British Nation in the BBC's *Hollow Crown*, Series One

"And Crispin Crispian shall ne'er go by,
From this day to the ending of the world,
But we in it shall be remember'd;
We few, we happy few, we band of brothers."
(*Henry V*)

Much as the Nicholas Hytner productions of 2005 slipped into a backward-looking wistfulness very different from the modern-dress geopolitical indictments of the director's 2003 *Henry V*, the BBC's adaptations of Shakespearean history in 2012 resorted to the comfortable verities of heritage drama to sidestep contemporary multiculturalism and postcolonial inheritances. As part of the 2012 Cultural Olympiad celebrating both the Queen's Diamond Jubilee and the London Olympics, the BBC launched a season of programs entitled, "Shakespeare Unlocked." To boost cultural capital, the BBC partnered with the Royal Shakespeare Company and its World Shakespeare Festival as well as the British Museum (*Shakespeare Unlocked*). The season featured a range of programming, including a documentary hosted by Simon Schama, scene performances and analysis by members of the Royal Shakespeare Company, and freshly produced, full-length adaptations. Described on the BBC's companion website as "a season exploring how one man captured so much about what it means to be human," "Shakespeare Unlocked" most notably presented *The Hollow Crown,* the plays of the second tetralogy (1595–99) in four feature-length adaptations that aired in June and July of 2012 prior to the opening of the London Olympic Games.[1] Just as the postmodern United Kingdom made its own history in 2012, the BBC turned to a cycle of plays that constitute "a long, sustained and extra-ordinarily innovative dramatic meditation on the nature of history" (Holderness, *Shakespeare* 8). In a year marking the jubilee celebrations of a female monarch whose name conjures the "Golden Age" of another ruling Elizabeth—its literary achievements, voyages of discovery, religious reform, and incipient colonialism—the BBC chose to commission Shakespeare's relentlessly masculinist plays that dramatize the mechanisms by which a nation forms identity and incurs losses endemic to that process.[2] Executive produced by Sam Mendes and Pippa Harris of Neal Street Productions, *The*

DOI: 10.4324/9781003043065-3

Hollow Crown developed in the shadow of another British icon—James Bond. The Bond series marked its fiftieth anniversary with the Mendes-directed *Skyfall* (2012), a film that increasingly demanded Mendes's attention and left oversight of the Shakespearean adaptation to Harris (Davies). Though Neal Street Productions also helms the long-running melodrama, *Call the Midwife* (2012–present), its adaptation of Shakespearean history manifests a closer kinship with the toxic white masculinity of the Bond series than with the lightly multiethnic feminism of its East End serial. By limiting the agential role of women and marginalizing the voices of Britain's non-white citizens, Series One of *The Hollow Crown* enrolls Shakespearean historiography in service to the nation's submerged but persistent patriarchal white supremacy.

While the legacy of Shakespeare appeared across the celebrations of the London Olympic Games and the Queen's Diamond Jubilee year, of particular interest is the curious way in which the pastiche artistry of Director Danny Boyle's opening ceremony referenced the national playwright. A display selectively remembering history—much like Ernest Renan's nation that has "forgotten many things" (45)—"Isles of Wonder" shared a number of problems with the BBC's *Hollow Crown* and its compromised deployment of Shakespearean history to promote a vision of the equitable, integrated, and welcoming nation in 2012. Danny Boyle's London Olympic Games opening ceremony staged post-imperial Great Britain as a raucous collage of icons as varied as Mr. Bean, James Bond, J.K. Rowling, William Shakespeare, and Mary Poppins on a set referencing both J. R. R. Tolkien's idyllic Shire and the soot-covered industrialized city of a Charles Dickens novel. While Britain no longer ruled the world, Boyle's spectacle celebrated the sceptred isle's cultural heritage and social welfare leadership. Charlotte Higgins, chief arts writer for *The Guardian*, explains: "it was Boyle's impassioned poem of praise to the country he would most like to believe in. One that is tolerant, multicultural, fair and gay friendly and holds the principles of the welfare state stoutly at its heart." Higgins articulates the fantasy central to the mythos of the ceremony—a cultured and compassionate Britain as Boyle would like it to be rather than as it exists. Boyle's ceremony featured a choreographed celebration of the National Health Service and asserted a vision of the Good Society that takes care of its own.[3] In its whimsical, generous-minded excess, Boyle's program catalogued Britain's global reach and cultural legacies—from children's literature to popular music to the invention of the Internet. However, absent from the evening's sequences was a direct acknowledgment of Great Britain's imperial past and colonial crimes. Perhaps unsurprisingly, imperial history and the postcolonial present collided when the ceremony referenced the nation's Shakespearean heritage, replicating problems also visible in the adaptations of *The Hollow Crown.*

Shakespeare the Harbinger of Progress and a History of Evasion

Knitting together the four home nations of Great Britain, the opening moments of Boyle's exuberant display set in motion a loosely chronological representation of the nation's history—one that both cast William Shakespeare as a technocrat industrialist and failed to remember Britain's slave trade and colonial rule. While a young boy sang, "Jerusalem," opening scenes in the London Stadium rendered literal both this "green and pleasant land" and the "dark Satanic mills" of the William Blake and Hubert Parry English anthem. Designed in a patchwork of crofts and cottages and dotted with straw bales and wild flowers, the early bucolic scenes featured women tossing and gathering apples, men bee-keeping, teams playing football and cricket on a grassy pitch, and still more villagers dancing round a maypole. This pastoral idyll was intercut with a video of children's choirs from Northern Ireland, Scotland, and Wales, insisting on the shared status of the United Kingdom's constituent nations as hosts of the games. However, agrarian pleasures soon gave way to the thrumming advances of manufacturing, a shift triggered by the evening's notable Shakespearean "appearing." Costumed inexplicably as the British engineer and railway pioneer, Isambard Kingdom Brunel, Sir Kenneth Branagh signaled this sea-change and the Industrial Revolution's transformation of human relationships to land, time, labor, and one another. Providing the source text for the night's "Isles of Wonder" theme, the newly knighted actor, film adaptor, and impresario declaimed Caliban's well-known lines from *The Tempest* (1611), standing at the foot of a replica Glastonbury Tor, crying out:

> Be not afeard; the isle is full of noises,
> Sounds and sweet airs, that give delight and hurt not.
> Sometimes a thousand twangling instruments
> Will hum about mine ears; and sometime voices,
> That if I then had waked after long sleep,
> Will make me sleep again, and then in dreaming,
> The clouds methought would open, and show riches
> Ready to drop upon me, that when I wak'd
> I cried to dream again.
>
> (3.2.135–143)

Branagh-Brunel's words heralded an army of costumed laborers who removed the green turf to reveal a black and gray hard surface while smokestacks and water mills slowly rose across the once verdant pastureland. Counterintuitively, Caliban's lyrical description of the island's natural wonders and magical properties operated to usher in the mechanical devices spreading across the stadium's floor—giving new meaning to the passage's, "thousand twangling instruments."

In addition to the strange overlay of Branagh, Brunel, and Shakespeare, the multiple and echoing referents occluded the resonance of Caliban's lines and his indigenous opposition to colonial rule.[4] Reciting lines assigned originally to one of the most significant voices of proto-colonial resistance in the Shakespearean canon, the Northern Irish Branagh did so framed visually and aurally by a confounding accretion of "British" hegemonic identifiers: Glastonbury's mythic King Arthur, the Bard from Avon, British industrialism, and Edward Elgar's "Nimrod" variation (which played majestically as underscoring).

Branagh's own ambivalent status as a Northern Irish immigrant to England as well as an interpretive tradition in which Caliban embodies the subaltern Irish only magnified the contradictory strains of Boyle's Shakespearean referencing.[5] Where was Shakespeare in all this over-signification, and what kind of Shakespeare emerged from the histrionics of spectacle? The abundance of heart-thumping metonyms for Britain threatened to render Caliban's lines nothing more than a buoyant welcome to the world at the start of a commercialized athletics competition and thus gloss over any disruptive undercurrents in the Shakespearean quotation.

Why then connect Shakespeare metonymically to the ruptures of industrialization, unless to position the poet as a herald of progress and innovation? Periodic shots of Branagh looking on with pride and ownership presented him as Brunel observing with satisfaction the thing he had wrought—a fully mechanized land. But what kind of progress was implied? The passage chosen and its Shakespearean character, Caliban—the native-born islander oppressed by an Occidental colonizer, Prospero—might have offered a glancing acknowledgment of an industrial age operating hand-in-glove with global settler colonialism. Furthermore, the indirect referencing might have gestured towards the well-known institutional service Shakespeare performed as British export through colonial educational systems.[6] However, most likely, these subterranean *nostra culpa* remained deeply buried and, instead, this Shakespearean appearing associated the poet with a forward-looking Britain, one open to change even when such transformation threatens drastically to alter the natural terrain or to obscure the nation's vexed history.

Indeed, the omissions in the ceremony's history-telling were as curious as the strange reverberations of the Branagh-Brunel-Caliban overlay. Ostensibly re-enacting highlights of British history from roughly the late eighteenth century to the twentieth, the opening ceremony spotlighted the Suffragette Votes for Women protests, the losses of World War I, and the HMT Empire Windrush arrival of West Indian Commonwealth citizens after World War II. The replica Windrush vessel and its swaggering, luggage-carrying black passengers (predominantly male) remained visible on the television transmission only briefly. Ironically, only a few months later in October of 2012, Theresa May's Home Office instituted the Hostile Environment Policy, a strategy designed to make the UK as unwelcoming as possible to "illegal immigrants," provoking them to leave "voluntarily" (Griffiths and Yeo 6–8). By creating a vast and diffuse system to enforce reporting of suspected illegal immigrants through the banking, educational, policing, and health sectors, the Hostile Environment Policy would make those very Windrush immigrant-citizens illegal aliens in their own country, causing loss of access to medical care, shelter, and, in some cases, even triggering deportation to island nations that had not been their home for decades (Griffiths and Yeo 17).[7] But this brief and unqualified reference to the non-white colonial citizens who immigrated to Britain in the wake of World War II was not the most egregious element of the evening's historiography.

Boyle's jaunt through the past quietly omitted substantial history that transpired between the pastoral idyll and the twentieth century, ignoring material that would have confirmed the socio-political and humanitarian costs of British colonial authority for the empire's subject peoples. The "historic" segment of the ceremony jumped in its tableau from pre-industrialization to the Industrial Revolution without obvious visual reference to the steady expansion of the empire or its substantial enmeshment in the transatlantic slave trade. Of course, such a historiographic omission is not unusual, according to David Olusoga who assesses the privileged place industrialization enjoys in the national story; the Industrial Revolution "is constantly replayed in our national imagination as a history of coal and iron, of factory towns and mines, and has rightly become a central feature of our national self-image" (25). However, Olusoga notes a crucial narrative lacuna—the expropriated labor of plantation slaves in the United States who supplied the British empire's manufacturers: "In the first half of the nineteenth century it was possible for slaves in the Southern states to spend most of their stolen lives producing the cotton that stoked Britain's Industrial Revolution" (26). Olusoga indicts such silences in the narrative of British industrial progress: "Yet this is a history that is usually silent about the source of the cotton that was processed in Lancashire's 4,500 mills" (25). Furthermore, as Robert Miles and Annie Phizacklea argue, profit from sugar plantations in the British Caribbean islands "was accumulated to finance the so-called industrial revolution" (17). Boyle's opening historical montage bore no signs of that history nor anything of the global reach of the country's colonial-imperial military and administrative incursions. Indeed, Gargi Bhattacharyya et al observe, "British nationalism necessarily relies on the structured and purposeful forgetting of the violence and domination that characterized empire" (59), as made abundantly clear by Boyle's pastiche of history. Boyle's omissions tracked precisely with the efforts to turn patriotism to liberal ends or "progressive patriotism" as characterized by Bhattacharyya et al: "Whereas right-wing nationalism practices an imperial nostalgia, progressive nationalism appears to depend on imperial aphasia—a deliberate forgetting of a colonial past" (72). Such was the case as Boyle's ceremony moved rapidly onward to celebrate the multicultural present, heedless of the narrative omissions troubling the viability of a multicultural British polity.

After the well-remembered dance commemoration of the NHS, the ceremony transitioned to a catalogue of British pop music and more contemporary cultural exports, a segment that traded on an unapologetic and confident multicultural national identity. These segments noticeably cast the nation in optimistically integrated and diverse terms without acknowledging the British Empire's abuses and the more recent, contentious history of 1990s race violence typified by the Stephen Lawrence case (whose mother, activist Doreen Lawrence, was one of the honored guests carrying in the Olympic flag). Indeed, two of Lawrence's 1993 murderers, Gary Dobson and David Norris, had only just been convicted and sentenced to life imprisonment a few months prior to Boyle's production in January of 2012—a quest for justice that took twenty years and a formal inquiry (the Macpherson Report) to achieve. Obscuring that painfully recent history of racist violence, the British pop music sequence centered on a "meet cute" encounter catalyzed by the return of a lost cell phone and foregrounded advances in technology impacting human culture in ways that echoed the earlier advent of the factory. Notably, that narrative opened by representing in domestic situation-comedy-style film, a visibly multiracial family—depicting the British nation as hybrid and joyously multicultural (as evidenced by the elaborate dance party that constituted the majority of the episode). A final dance sequence made more overtly visible the former British empire through the artistry of Akram Khan (a British choreographer of Bangladeshi heritage) and Emeli Sandé (Zambian-British). Just prior to the entrance of the athletes, Kahn led a number featuring the red, yellow, and orange color palette often visually associated with Britain's former southeast Asian colonies. Dancing to Sandé's version of "Abide with Me," Kahn and his troupe offered an extended visualization of the kind of cultural enrichment the ceremony appeared to posit as part of a robust, confident and healthy multicultural nation. "Abide with Me" (lyrics by Henry Francis Lyte and "Eventide" tune by William Henry Monk) also embedded a slant reference to the imperial past since it is typically sung on Anzac Day, memorializing those Australians and New Zealanders who fought in the empire's global conflicts. The piece earned its position in the ceremony by virtue of the fact that, for decades, it has been sung before the FA Cup finals as well as the Rugby League Challenge Cup final. Thus, though these later segments declared an assured and integrated contemporary United Kingdom, the amnesiac representations of the evening's earlier historiography revealed the thinness of such unearned, blithe multiculturalism.

Some might deem it churlish to expect that the rhetoric of an Olympic Games opening ceremony might admit room for historical and cultural self-doubt and self-reflection. However, in the context of third-millennial politics, the breezy affirmation of a healthy multicultural nation comes at the expense of sustained and rigorous self-examination and typifies a liberal myopia insufficiently aware of unfinished historical business. Just such inattention would blind liberal voters and advocates to the far-right nationalism brewing, thanks to the War on Terror and the 2008 financial crisis and manifesting fully a few years later as the migrant crisis hit a peak. Viewed in terms of the ongoing problems with representing the nation through the framework of Shakespearean history, the Boyle display confirms that, regardless of mimetic modality, ignoring the uneasy past proves a habit hard to break. In productions of the history plays, the degree of "authenticity" associated with its narratives functions as a barrier to inclusive casting and a reimagination of the nation's past; however, the Boyle ceremony's pastiche approach need not have been fettered by the facts of Shakespeare's medieval history, and yet, that same cultural avoidance of fissures within the record persisted. Instead, the opening ceremony offered the world a curated history anchored in a vision of the nation's benevolent inclusiveness and positioned its icons of literature from Shakespeare to Barrie to Rowling as progressive, universal humanitarians.

Reading *The Hollow Crown* in the context of the Queen's Diamond Jubilee and the London Olympic Games spotlights Shakespeare's continuing centrality to the epistemologies of nationhood vying for ascendency in post-imperial Britain. Though vastly different in aesthetic, *The Hollow Crown*, much like Boyle's opening ceremony, advances a British nationalism too often deaf to the casualties—primarily women and ethnic minorities—incurred over the course of Britain's self-formation and acts of self-defining.[8] Furthermore, by relying on a naturalistic aesthetic and heritage style filming, *The Hollow Crown* asserts its vision of Shakespeare and British heritage as "true" and "real," obscuring the means by which a people names the nation.[9] Bowing under the weight of a celebratory and patriotic agenda, the inherent conservatism of a naturalistic aesthetic, and the traditionalism that Shakespeare's authority provokes, Series One of *The Hollow Crown* reifies the sexual vulnerability (typified by Katherine Valois's marriage to Henry V) and domestic limitations of females (exemplified by Hotspur's Kate) without adequate effort to ironize or question that status.[10] While the adaptation of *Richard II* most notably strives to preserve a complex understanding of woman's role in British history, both parts of *Henry IV* and *Henry V* sacrifice such depiction to the manifest destiny of Henry V's apotheosis. Constrained by the naturalism of its heritage style, the first series of *The Hollow Crown* similarly fails to represent with any complexity the multicultural makeup of the nation in 2012, opting instead to keep Britain's Shakespearean history predominantly white with only a very few exceptions. *Richard II* presents the most integrated cast of the four films, but its bookend, Sharrock's *Henry V*, troublingly replays the racist trope of the magical negro even as it expands the Duke of York's role for a performance by the Afro-British Paterson Joseph. Thus, in its representation of both gender and race, the first *Hollow Crown* series falters much like Boyle's "Isles of Wonder," despite their very different artistic modalities. These 2012 Olympic Shakespearean instances demonstrate that realistic, heritage aesthetics may be an archivally authenticated justification for historically sidelining women and persons of color, but when the same omissions occur in the fantasy landscape of Boyle's production, we must seek for other answers as to why the difficulties of history go unaddressed, and, sadly, white privilege seems a ready answer.

The BBC's Shakespeare for an Inclusive Britain

Over the course of its history, the BBC's appropriations of Shakespeare have repeatedly intertwined the corporation's own status and security with the cultural resonance of Britain's Bard. The BBC's history of Shakespeare adaptation has been thoroughly explored with particular attention paid to *The Shakespeare Plays* (1978–1985), the project designed to create a video library of the complete dramas performed to reach a broad popular audience.[11] The BBC adaptations following in the wake of *The Shakespeare Plays* have been smaller in scope and distanced from the aesthetic limitations of the previous work, but the same reliance upon Shakespeare to heighten the BBC's status and affirm its use-value characterizes those smaller-scale projects and pushes them to the social and political right. One such example, *Shakespeare Retold* (2005/06), adopts a modern and distinctly televisual filming style marketed to update and renovate the schoolroom classics but persists in crafting female agency within the recognizable constraints of romantic comedy film and televisual idiom (Pittman, *Authorizing* 135). Both Olwen Terris and Margaret Jane Kidnie have identified the new millennium battles over the BBC's licence fee as context for the production of *Shakespeare Retold.*[12]

Just as in the case of *Shakespeare Retold, The Hollow Crown* broadcast coincided with another licence fee and charter re-negotiation. The BBC initiated its own review of services in July of 2009, anticipating that the next fee settlement would, "be tough irrespective of the complexion of the Government" (*Putting* 1). At first offering a two-year fee freeze, the BBC eventually negotiated with the government an extended freeze until 2017 in exchange for "BBC security of funding, but at a reduced level," requiring a budget trim of 16% for the overall organization (*Putting* 1, 13). In December 2010, the BBC published a mission document, *Putting Quality First* with the informing subtitle, "Getting the best out of the BBC for licence fee payers," as part of its response to criticisms leveled during the negotiation process.[13] A number of initiatives followed from this mission document—an investigation into the portrayal of gays and lesbians on the BBC and a diversity strategy addressing inequities both in content portrayal and in organizational hiring.

The BBC's Diversity Strategy 2011–15, developed as part of the *Putting Quality First* initiative, states as one of the media corporation's objectives the delivery of "high quality programming which reflects modern Britain accurately and authentically" (*The BBC's Diversity* 1).[14] The document cites a study by the Cultural Diversity Network cataloguing portrayals on UK television in 2009: it noted that "Men occupy double the screen time versus women"; and "Black and minority ethnic people represented 10% of the TV population compared with nearly 13% of England's population" (*The BBC's Diversity* 7). The strategy statement prioritizes improving representation on screen—diversity of gender, ethnicity, sexual orientation, age, and mental and physical ability—not just in numbers but also in quality:

> And this is our audiences' minimum expectation. Not just more portrayal, but a balanced portrayal that reflects their experience in a way that is accurate, authentic and non-stereotypical, across a range of programme genres, and where "difference" is sometimes incidental and not always the primary point to a story we are telling.
>
> (*The BBC's Diversity* 6)

Adaptations of Shakespeare's plays—long a site for the theatrical practice of colorblind casting—might well be ideally suited to the goal of increasing diversity where "difference" is not necessarily the point of the story. Such a venture would simply cast persons from a wide range of ethnic backgrounds to signal quite visibly that Britain's poet belongs to all its twenty-first-century citizens. However, just as the strategy document explains the law mandating better diversity—the Equality Act 2010, the Public Sector Equality Duty—it notes a small caveat that renders the BBC exempt from certain provisions that might threaten "editorial independence." One of those "exempt" areas identified is casting—the single most visible means by which the media institution may improve upon its representation of the UK populace (*The BBC's Diversity* 5). Since the diversity strategy acknowledges the continuing disparity in representation of women, it also seems natural to expect that attention to when and how women are portrayed might govern artistic choices. However, this assumption proves faulty when, as Ramona Wray points out, "most contemporary television drama" is a "collaborative venture" that involves multiple funding agencies and production companies ("Shakespeare" 3), rendering thornier the BBC's oversight of its own diversity initiatives in the area of dramatic output.

Following *The Hollow Crown* money trail underscores the practical difficulties inherent in operationalizing a diversity vision when the production of content is distributed across multiple entities and funding sources. In July 2012, when BBC director general, Mark Thompson, hosted a gala launch for Thea Sharrock's *Henry V* (starring Tom Hiddleston) at the British Museum, series producer Mendes chose to reveal that BBC Worldwide, the broadcaster's "commercial arm," had refused a year and a half earlier to fund the nine million pounds in costs associated with *The Hollow Crown*. Licence fees supported a portion of the production under the BBC2 budgetary umbrella (approximately 25% of costs), but Mendes won the remaining funds from NBC Universal (Mag. Brown).[15] The BBC Worldwide spokesperson explained: "We have to balance every investment against commercial returns including projections from our international sales team" (quoted in Mag. Brown). Though the negotiations that resulted in BBC Worldwide's refusal to finance fully *The Hollow Crown* took place in January of 2011, Mendes only spoke out at the time of the British Museum launch, perhaps resenting the BBC's decision to capitalize on what it now recognized as a going concern thanks to Hiddleston's film stardom. In addition, the press reported yet another way in which *The Hollow Crown* became oddly entangled with power-jockeying at the very height of BBC governance. BBC Trust chair, Lord Patten, announced in July 2012 that George Entwistle would soon replace Mark Thompson as BBC director general; apparently at the time of Entwistle's final interview for the position (June 2012), *The Hollow Crown*'s *Richard II* had just aired (Lister). Lord Patten hailed the film as evidence of Entwistle's suitability to lead the BBC since the then-head of BBC TV had originally commissioned the series: "'As reviewers have said, it was probably the best televised Shakespeare there has ever been'" (qtd. in Lister). Of course, Entwistle's disastrous fifty-four-day tenure as director general might suggest that the Shakespearean litmus test Lord Patten deployed was not a fail-safe deliberative method. Lord Patten's comment also demonstrates the duty to fulfill a British heritage cultural remit still persistent at the highest levels of the corporation's decision-making even as the broadcaster seeks to bring its human resources and artistic content into better alignment with contemporary Britain's shifting demographics.

The BBC's reluctance to risk resources on the Neal Street Productions enterprise it originally commissioned highlights competing instincts at the media giant—both a desire to appropriate Shakespearean prestige value as its own and a bottom-line-driven and familiar anxiety: "Will Shakespeare sell?"[16] Not just a one-off event associated with the year-long celebration of British nationhood, *The Hollow Crown* must generate revenue beyond 2012 through international broadcast, DVD sales, and digital streaming much as its older sibling, *The Shakespeare Plays*, did. The finance fracas demonstrates a significant barrier to the BBC's diversity agenda and one characteristic of the distributed way in which television programming develops. Money remains the prime mechanism of influence over production content and casting, but as the BBC limits its actual investment in programming development, the influence it can wield over content branded as its own through airing diminishes. Furthermore, since the Parliamentary directive regarding equality of representation excludes casting (for reasons of aesthetic freedom) as an area of enforcement, even legislation can lend no real teeth to the diversity policy at the BBC. If the BBC does not pay the full bill, how then can it enact its stated commitment to inclusiveness and non-stereotyped portrayal of minority ethnicities and women? The sheer cost of television production necessitates reliance upon outside entities which receive only a portion of their actual funding from the BBC, and yet, by airing programs such as the externally produced *The Hollow Crown*, creating a website tie-in, and positioning the series as the crown jewel of its Shakespeare Unlocked season of programming, the BBC claims the films as representative of its brand and mission. Even performers involved in the production cloud the distinction between production company and BBC brand; on the DVD bonus featurette, "*The Hollow Crown*: The Making of a King," Jeremy Irons (who plays Henry IV) declares: "The fact that these four plays are being done by the BBC in this Olympic year, I think, makes them slightly iconic." Here Irons parses no distinction between the Neal Street Productions and NBC Universal corporate cultures that primarily financed the films and the BBC that provided partial funding as well as a paratextual context, broadcast event, and airing platform for the series.

By airing, packaging, and promoting the four film adaptations of Shakespeare's second tetralogy as a sequential unit, the BBC follows a distinctly twentieth-century performance tradition that imbricates the broadcast corporation and its brand within British cultural history and acts of self-definition. No evidence indicates that the history plays were ever performed as a cycle in Shakespeare's lifetime; Scott McMillin points out, "Nothing from the Elizabethan theatre suggests that the better part of a week of a busy commercial repertory would have been given over to a series of plays in one vein" (5).[17] The BBC's cycle packaging harkens instead to another epochal moment for Britain—World War II. Director Anthony Quayle's 1951 cycle production of the second tetralogy (the Shakespeare Memorial Theatre Company) staged E. M. W. Tillyard's reading of the chronicle plays as a grand narrative of Britain and established a post-war trend that appropriated the history plays to assert

English cultural dominance after the long battering by Nazi Germany (McMillin 10, 35–36). Though *The Hollow Crown* relies upon three different directors, production coordination of the four films places them firmly within the post-war cycle tradition and prompts analysis of them as interrelated artworks. The bookend films, *Richard II* and *Henry V*, were directed by Rupert Goold and Thea Sharrock respectively, and the two parts of *Henry IV* were helmed by Richard Eyre but share cast members with Sharrock's *Henry V*. On the DVD bonus featurette, "*The Hollow Crown*: The Making of a King," Neal Street Productions' Harris likewise explains that the directors consulted across the four films to establish continuity, agreeing to the period scene design and visiting one another's sets to establish overall cohesiveness.[18] In addition, the four films share an on-location naturalism associated with the Branagh canon of Shakespeare on film. Positioned at a moment of corporate crisis and waning national support for the BBC, *The Hollow Crown* Henriad cycle thus reaches back to multiple sources of cultural authority—both the Golden Age of Elizabeth I and William Shakespeare and the moral high ground of the beleaguered but triumphant World War II Britain. Such traditionalism may well run counter to the progressive politics of a new millennium BBC determined to improve its record on diversity and inclusion.

The Gender Politics of the Henriad and *The Hollow Crown*

At first glance, the Henriad may not promise much fruitful ground for the BBC's commitment to diversity of representation, particularly its under-representation of females, but recent critical debate has prompted second-look re-evaluations of such received wisdom. On the one hand, Jean E. Howard and Phyllis Rackin argue that the second tetralogy steadily sidelines women from the stage of history-making and nation-building; the plays' focus on masculine maturation and performative power embodied in the transformation of the laddish Prince Hal into King Henry V necessarily relegates women to positions of lesser significance. Howard and Rackin elaborate on the Henriad's progress towards a masculine pre-eminence achieved at the expense of female agency:

> By the time we get to *Henry V*, even the French women are safely contained at home. The gendered distinction between hearth and battlefield is now fully in place, and no woman appears—or is mentioned as appearing—in any army. Entirely confined to domestic settings and domestic roles, female characters serve only as the objects of male protection and the occasions for masculine competition.
>
> (206)

On the other hand, Anna Kamaralli argues: "The dominance of masculinity in these plays need not render what female presence there is an inconvenience or an irrelevance" (174). She continues:

> Shakespeare's history plays show a man's world more unequivocally, more inescapably, more impenetrably than his comedies or Romances, perhaps even more than most of his tragedies. Yet when women appear in these plays they are rarely presented as mere victims of the system, or of individual men, but as having agency. Sometimes that agency even extends to become power.
>
> (172)

Melissa E. Sanchez likewise offers a recuperative reading of women in the history cycle, focusing on *Richard II* where women demonstrate the impossibility and inadvisability of divorcing the affective from the political (96); she points out in contradistinction to Howard and Rackin that the women of *Richard II*, rather than instantiate a powerless domesticated subjectivity, actually further early modern debate regarding absolutist and constitutionalist monarchy (99). Such critical reassessments of women in the history plays might thus render the Henriad an ideal place in which to pursue the BBC diversity mandate—forcing viewers to think again about the role women have played in history and the narratives told about those roles. As Sanchez observes in the conclusion to her searching discussion,

> Instead of telling only sad stories of women's progressive and seemingly inevitable marginalization, I propose that we also attend to the ways that women *have* mattered to the stories through which we reconstruct the politics of the past—and imagine those of the future.
>
> (112)

Unfortunately, this call to mindful reconsideration of gender and the nation in the history plays remains largely unheard by the production team responsible for *The Hollow Crown* with one exception. The most aesthetically experimental of the four films, Goold's *Richard II*, interpolates multiple scenes of mimetic reproduction depicting an artist in the act of creation—most frequently a painter in the process of producing a portrait. This meta-narrative leitmotif directs viewer attention to the constructed stories that build a nation and coincides with a more complex exploration of female agency within the confines of the early modern play. However, the other two directors fall into patterns of gender representation that still regard knowing and naming the nation as predominantly masculine enterprises. Three crucial scenes from the adaptations by Goold, Eyre, and Sharrock stage varying degrees of female participation in history-making and instantiate the BBC's fledgling and not consistently successful attempts to strengthen gender diversity through nuanced and non-stereotyped portrayals.

Director Goold's *Richard II* maintains the space for female agency identified in the play text with little teleplay trimming of Richard's Queen Isabella and by preserving Act Five's family crisis over Aumerle's loyalty to Henry IV. While the film excises reference to the murder of the Duke of Gloucester and thus the crucial intercessory scene in which his widow pleads with John of Gaunt to pursue vengeance (1.2), Goold's adaptation utilizes the camera to stress the influence of female agents on history. This is best demonstrated in the Duchess of York's defense of her son. Lindsay Duncan's Duchess of York battles with husband and king for her son's life and does so with the aid and support of the camerawork to emerge as a prime agent—moving literally in the film's imagery from the hearth to the court. The scene begins with traditional gender roles underscored by the Duke of York who has returned home to recount to his wife the deposition of Richard II. Despite the disparity in knowledge that grants the husband power, the two begin the scene in visual equilibrium, both seated and framed symmetrically on either side of a blazing hearth while the Duke of York (David Suchet) narrates the suffering of deposed Richard.[19] Once Aumerle (Tom Hughes) arrives and the Duke of York springs into action to expose his son's proposed treason, Duncan's Duchess abandons the hearth to plead with her husband as he prepares for departure to court. She moves closely into her husband's space and pins him against the vestibule wall. Close-ups on her face from a low angle stress her capacity to act and heighten her power, and Duncan controls her voice to a contralto that avoids the too-ready stereotype of shrieking wife. The camera records the frenetic power of the Duchess by contrasting it with a dumbfounded Aumerle who must be goaded into self-preserving action as the scene rushes to a close with all family members heading to court.

In Act Five, Scene Three, the camera tracks with the Duchess as she strides into the king's presence to intercede at full volume for her son's life. When she kneels to make her case to her monarch-nephew (Rory Kinnear), the camera moves to eye-level rather than adopting the high angle point of view on her that would be the standing Henry IV's actual viewpoint. For much of her speech to the king, though she kneels next to her husband arguing against his demands for strict justice, the camera cuts the Duke of York from the frame. After the Duchess has won her case for mercy and the life of her son, Goold even allows a strain of moral superiority to emerge in the mother's parting words addressed to Aumerle: "I pray God make thee new" (5.3.146). The composition of the scene, which places Aumerle on a bench while Duncan remains standing over him, implies that though she may have saved her son's life, the Duchess of York does not condone his treasonous conspiring. Perhaps one of the most striking aspects of the scene is that it resists the temptation to mock the Duchess of York and make of her a figure of fun, the silly woman implied by Henry IV's denigrating comment upon her arrival, "Our scene is alt'red from a serious thing, / And now chang'd to 'The Beggar and the King'" (5.3.79–80).[20] Though the play text itself offers in Henry's derision an avenue for treating the Duchess of York with amused diminishment, Goold instead films her intercession with consistent dignity and imagines a woman's domestic role extending to the halls of power.[21] Of the four films comprising *The Hollow Crown*, Goold's *Richard II* works most strenuously to recognize the active role women play in weaving and preserving the fabric of national identity.

In addition, though reliant upon the same richness of on-location setting as the other three films—an approach that unites the four installments—Goold tempers the tendency of such verisimilitude to assert an epistemological conclusiveness. Of the series films, *Richard II* deploys the most visually estranging techniques, ones that remind the viewer of the representation's fictionality: sharply tilted camera angles, extreme close-ups, repeated zip zooms, handheld shots, and the previously mentioned recurring motifs of mimesis. Peter Kirwan notes in a blog posting responding to the original airing that Goold's production "was the most inventive". Goold establishes his meta-narrative perspective with such a stylized initial tableau that the viewer at first imagines that Richard II, rather than hold court in Act One, poses stiffly for a portrait (one reminiscent of the panel image in Westminster Abbey). Ben Whishaw delivers an interpolated voice-over of Richard's lament, "Let's talk of graves, of worms, and epitaphs," and continues, "let us sit upon the ground / And tell sad stories of the death of kings" (3.2.145, 155–156). During the voice-over, the camera pans down from the rafters of St. Davids Cathedral (the Welsh cathedral selected by the film crew as location site in place of the text's Windsor Castle) to the great rood and then to the throne canopy and Richard himself, robed, crowned, and holding orb and scepter with regal self-satisfaction. Wray's careful close reading of this initial sequence stresses the "quality television" idiom of the entire *Hollow Crown* series, self-conscious about mimesis and attempting a "strategic *recreation*" of the Westminster portrait ("Shakespeare" 9). Just as Richard's words invoke the artifice of storytelling, so the visual scene stresses the constructed nature of art; Whishaw sits with absolute stillness and his white, fur-trimmed cloak has been carefully composed for symmetry just as have the golden draperies that create the throne's enclosure mirroring the folds of the cloak.[22] Tomas Elliott astutely notes that the non-diegetic insertion of Whishaw's voice-over as film prologue accompanying the staged vision of the monarch enthroned, "serves to draw our attention to the constructedness of the televised drama, immediately undermining the so-called historical reality of its opening shot" in St. Davids (74). In addition, Goold transforms Shakespeare's Bushy into a painter, first seen depicting St. Sebastian while Richard observes. The camera closes in on the partially completed image of St. Sebastian and then widens to reveal the model to whom a series of thin leather cords affix into position the requisite wounds and arrow shafts for the martyr's portrait. In case the mechanics of representational art have been missed, the camera closes again, this time on Richard's finger as he scrapes the model's "wound" and discovers the "blood" to be paint. A later moment in which Queen Isabella (Clémence Poésy) poses for her portrait again includes close-up images that display the means of mimesis—bowls, brushes, palette, egg yolk, pigment, and water. Such filmic choices stress the mediating role of art—whether it be the paint palette or the camera—and signal that the making of art does not simply create an image but a truth, and, in the case of history, a narrative that knows and names the nation.

In contrast, Richard Eyre's adaptation of *I Henry IV* delivers an epistemology of nationhood that struggles to validate female agency in the manner achieved by Goold's more self-aware tactics. Eyre's filmic naturalism renders the means of creation nearly invisible as the realistic details of Eastcheap lade exactness and accuracy onto the storytelling and assert the absolute truthfulness of a narrative in which women make little impact upon English history. With the tempting comedy found in Mistress Quickly's malapropisms and the sexual eagerness of Doll Tearsheet (a character imported into *I Henry IV* and whose exposed backside serves as her introduction to the viewing audience), the film succumbs to stereotypes of the tavern wench. This leaves Lady Percy, another of Shakespeare's shrewish "Kates," to articulate a counterpoint to the masculine imperatives of history-making. Eyre's approach to the confrontation (2.3) between a combative Kate and her husband, the rebel Hotspur, represents the claustrophobic narrowness of a woman's world and the masculine prerogatives that confine the female would-be agent of history. In contrast to the Duchess of York's sway at court, Lady Percy wrangles for influence in the marginal worlds of her Northumberland castle and, later, of Wales—never at court or on the battlefield of the play.[23]

Reading literally Kate's reference to "Harry's bed," the *Hollow Crown* scene takes place in Kate's bedchamber and the corridors adjoining it. Cutting back and forth between Hotspur's (Joe Armstrong) agitated letter reading and Kate's (Michelle Dockery of *Downton Abbey* fame) overhearing, the filming critiques Hotspur's temper by recording Lady Percy's reactions. Though stage directions as old as the quarto editions insist that Hotspur enters "*solus*," Eyre's film qualifies focus on the rebel by cutting to Kate for an unspoken commentary. In fact, much of Hotspur's speech is muffled by the filming choice that focuses on the seated Kate with head in hand silently listening to and judging her husband whose voice we barely overhear at times. When he at last enters the chamber, he sits on the bed beside the naked Kate who covers herself with bedclothes. She urges confession from him and, by clasping his face in her hands, holds him in two-shot until Hotspur calls for the servant. While Hotspur and the servant speak, she sidles to the edge of the bed just barely in shot and shrugs into a dressing gown; the fact of her sexual appeal is underscored by two moments in which the servant's eyes deliberately travel to the bed where the naked back and side of Kate are just visible. At the servant's exit, Kate again demands Hotspur's confidence by standing and asking, "What is it carries you away" (2.3.75); she communicates a sparring yet affectionate tone to the relationship by repeatedly hitting him to prompt his attention.

The filming marks the two as equals, though Kate's influence appears circumscribed by the bedchamber; however, the stridency of masculine dominance emerges in several details—the first a harsh move by which Hotspur flings Kate on the bed and the second a deliberate and physical silencing of her. For a total of thirty seconds, Hotspur's hand entirely covers Kate's mouth as he recounts the old saw of female garrulousness. Despite his aggression, the two kiss and fall onto the bed one last time before Hotspur's departure. While much of the scene endeavors to display Kate's determined, even pugilistic, agency and to reveal an unvarnished depiction of how masculinist strategies rely upon the closeting and silencing of women, the confrontation of patriarchal ideology diminishes at scene's end when a stringed orchestra sweetly provides romantic underscoring to Lord and Lady Percy's amorous farewell. In combination with the insistent sexualizing of Kate by means of costume (or lack thereof) and the gaze of the male servant, this romanticized close mutes critique. Furthermore, as will be seen in *Henry V*, forceful containment of female agency may be attributed to an antagonist and northern outlier like Hotspur but cannot be displayed for subversive interrogation in the champion of the Henriad, Henry V himself.

As a result, Thea Sharrock's *Henry V* presents the Lancastrian monarch's wooing of Katherine Valois not as chilling act of conquest—such as that depicted in the Hytner staging in 2003 (National Theatre)—but as the gentle postures of a charming young man desiring mutual affection. While some may read Henry V's unnecessary wooing of a woman already won by conquest and treaty as a mark of his benevolent instinct towards consensus-building, the scene more cynically typifies the Machiavellian monarch's inclination to close off resistance.[24] As Howard and Rackin have pointed out, Branagh's film version featuring Emma Thompson as "Kate" to the director's "Henry," telegraphs a romantic reading of that troubling scene: "...many viewers knew that the French princess was played by Emma Thompson, who married Branagh that same year. Thompson's appearance as Katherine encouraged the notion that Henry's love for her was to be 'real'" (8).[25] Such is also the case in the portrayal by Branagh's young protégé, Hiddleston, although his Henry lacks an actor of the strength and presence of Thompson in Katherine's place.[26] Melanie Thierry plays Katherine as timid and demure virgin innocent—seated with hands in her lap for much of the eight-minute scene and rarely meeting the gaze of Henry or reaching the eye-level of the camera. Hiddleston's halting delivery as the scene commences conveys romantic uncertainty and inexperience, a fact belied by the previous films which show him sampling with gusto the sexual favors of Doll Tearsheet. Hiddleston echoes the boyish charm exemplified by his off-camera mentor Branagh, and a soundtrack of romantic clichés defangs a moment of undeniable domination. The camera is complicit with Henry's act of colonization repeatedly, almost never allowing Katherine the power of the gaze but always placing her as its object. For 33% of the scene, the camera films Henry in isolation while Katherine enjoys only 12% of the scene in solo command of the camera's frame. While a rhythm of shot-reaction-shot often brings Katherine back in the frame, she is frequently minded by the watchful nurse to her right. When all three figures are in the frame, the camera is positioned so that Hiddleston's entire body just fills the full vertical; as a result, Thierry's Katherine appears even more diminished. Furthermore, rack focus keeps Henry in focus and blurs Katherine who stands in the foreground, a common visual tactic that insists viewers regard men as the makers of history.[27]

In addition, by crafting an interpolated bookend, Sharrock posits the fruitful union of the couple and further softens what could be a more strident look at the traffic in women, long the *modus operandi* of dynastic power. Sharrock's film adaptation actually begins with the funeral of Henry V and a voice-over of the Chorus's invocation of the muse while a visibly distressed and mourning Katherine stands at her husband's coffin. At the film's end, the final shot of Act Five dissolves from Henry and Katherine holding hands and gazing into each other's eyes to a high angle shot of the widowed Katherine. As she turns from her dead husband, she takes up their child, Henry VI, and embodies the primarily procreative function of women within monarchy; Dan Leberg argues that this additional scene, "naturalizes Katherine's complicity in her own conquest, over-determining the ambivalent complexities of her broken-English responses to Henry V's romantic advances" (39). In contrast to Goold's interrogative estrangements, Sharrock's bookend does not invite the same critique of the ways in which modes of telling dictate truth. The film circumvents the untidier ideological implications of its Madonna and Child image and bookended funeral with the plaintive soundtrack tune that scores an elegy for lost chivalry. With soft-focus romanticism and wistful soundtrack, Sharrock's framing strikes a note of nostalgia that rather longs for the lost hero than questions the stories that create the chivalric paragon.

Sharrock repurposes another of Shakespeare's metahistorical elements—the Chorus—to craft a filmic revelation that drifts towards sentiment rather than historical interrogation. Taking inspiration from the final Chorus's rueful reminder that Henry VI and his counselors, "lost France, and made his England bleed," *The Hollow Crown* reveals in its closing shots that the Chorus (John Hurt) is a previously seen boy from the Agincourt battlefield who carries with him into adulthood a bloody token, "the talismanic flag stained with York's blood" (Wray, "*Henry V*" 10). Standing by an empty throne, Hurt's Chorus utters the film's final lines while strings, woodwinds, and brass mute the self-annihilating recursivity of monarchy that the words stress. The visibly aged Hurt turns to the camera after kissing tenderly his relic and asks, "for their sake, / In your fair minds let this acceptance take" (Epi. 13–14); the insistent pulling of sentimental heartstrings neuters the critical dissonance of those parting lines. Furthermore, by at last rendering the disembodied choric voice-over a living and breathing veteran of the wars (not to mention British stage, film, and television), *The Hollow Crown* invests the editorial voice of the Chorus with the personal subjectivity, affect, and "realness" of Henry's surviving "band of brothers."[28] Thus, Sharrock's conclusion both references and silences the latent ambivalence found in the "hollow crown" series title, which derives from Richard II's famous deconstruction of monarchical pomp: "For within the hollow crown / That rounds the mortal temples of a king / Keeps Death his court" (3.2.160–162). Richard's *memento mori* to kingship paired with the final Chorus of *Henry V* articulate the limits of power, though such self-reflection loses teeth in the context—a BBC series of specials under the Shakespeare Unlocked umbrella designed to celebrate the humanity and insight of the country's greatest poet and featuring many of England's most beloved stage, film, and television actors.[29] The screenplay quietly omits from the Chorus's final sonnet a phrase perhaps deemed inappropriate for film given its direct reference to stage performance: "Which oft our stage hath shown" (Epi. 13). But such trimming undermines the meta-theatricality of *Henry V* and signals a preference for naturalism that effaces the intruding voice of the teller of stories and the maker of national myths.

Relying on a naturalistic, heritage aesthetic, *The Hollow Crown* cloaks its artifice in a visual realism to life, thanks to the high-definition quality and the on-location settings, running the risk of a troubling epistemological ascendency. The naturalism of *The Hollow Crown* produces a narratological opacity similar to that which Sarah Hatchuel investigates in the Branagh film *oeuvre*. She asks of this naturalistic style, "Does filmic narration conceal the act of enunciation and forbid any exposing of illusion? Or, can the mechanisms of artistry still be apparent?" Hatchuel asserts that such style, "is shaped to provide the impression of a natural and real world, and the enunciative discourse is drowned into that universe." Such naturalistic techniques disguise the artifice of the constructed world; the mud-spattered soldiers, the oily-haired denizens of Eastcheap, and the black-toothed tavern-goer at the Boar's Head testify to the "truthfulness" of the film's history, which silences the struggle of women to play a meaningful and agential role in shaping the British nation.[30] The insistent veracity of such visual detail threatens to deny a dissenting perspective on English history.[31]

Henry V and Racial Representation

In addition to its vexed treatment of female agency, a problem neutered by the nostalgia of the final film's conclusion, the series' inadequate ethnic diversity deserves parallel examination. Of the four films, *Richard II* makes most effort to craft a multihued cast. Crowd shots include persons of non-Caucasian skin color, and several minor speaking roles such as the gardener's assistant and the queen's lady are taken by persons of color. One notable and more significant speaking part goes to the Afro-British actor, Lucian Msamati, who plays the Bishop of Carlisle. However, both parts of *Henry IV* include no persons of color, and *Henry V* assigns only one part, that of York, to an Afro-British actor (Paterson Joseph). By heightening the Duke of York's role in *Henry V* but leaving him very noticeably isolated as an actor of color, Sharrock's film recycles the magical negro trope in a failure of colorblind casting that perpetuates the blind spots exposed in Boyle's opening ceremony.[32]

As discussed in Chapter One, Ayanna Thompson calls Shakespeare scholars, theater practitioners, and filmmakers to account more precisely for the semiotic overflow of race in performance. In her well-known assessment of colorblind casting's inherent problematics, Thompson reflects:

> The practice reveals the hauntingly unspoken question that hovers behind the arras of every Shakespearean production in which colorblind casting is

> employed: What constitutes a blindness to race? If old fears and stereotypes continue to be perpetuated in productions that employ colorblind casting, how "blind" is the approach? The specter of racism in these instances whispers in the ear that blindness may never be possible.
>
> ("Practicing" 11)[33]

Nor, indeed, should blindness be the goal as the missteps of the Sharrock film demonstrate. Quietly and inexplicably, the race of *Richard II*'s Aumerle changes by the time of *Henry V*'s action; played in the first film by the Caucasian Tom Hughes, under his inherited title as the Duke of York, Aumerle transforms into the Afro-British Joseph. Though this shift goes utterly unacknowledged in the naturalistic style of the series, Joseph's biography should inform the racial problematics of the final film in Series One. In his memoir, Joseph identifies his parents as Caribbean immigrants from St Lucia who met in London as part of the Windrush generation. Joseph recalls growing up aware of his visible otherness in Britain:

> As an immigrant, your radar is very sharply attuned. You listen for language signals in a heightened way. How else can you keep yourself safe in a potentially hostile environment, if you aren't aware of the meanings and interpretations of words? It is the immigrant's best armour.
>
> (3–4)

Published in 2018, Joseph's memoir utilizes the loaded phrase, "hostile environment," to characterize the context of his immigrant childhood but, in doing so, he also pointedly references much more recent history—the Conservative Government's Hostile Environment policy designed to render as difficult as possible routine access to a range of services for refugees and migrants not to mention its own non-white citizens such as Joseph's Windrush parents. Though the series does nothing to recognize Joseph's heritage or to acknowledge that the Duke of York's race has altered, the actor's own biography could trigger a more complicated exploration of the British nation, if only such an adaptation of Shakespeare's history possessed the courage to rethink its aesthetic approaches in order to provoke self-critical reflection upon Britain's past and multicultural future.

On the one hand, *The Hollow Crown* casting of Joseph as the Duke of York might exemplify the best intentions of colorblind casting and an improved commitment to diversity in BBC programming. The series' production team creatively expands the impact of Joseph's Duke of York on the film's main arc, the rise of a triumphant warrior-king, Henry V. Textually, the Duke of York plays an invisible role save for the moment when he volunteers to lead the "vaward" (4.3.131) in Shakespeare's culminating battle at Agincourt. The *dramatis personae* lists him as present in only one (4.3) out of twenty-three scenes in the five acts of the play, and in that scene, he speaks only two lines.[34] In much the way that Henry V's uncle, the Duke of Exeter, can function in performance as a mentor figure, Sharrock's adaptation presents York as a younger version of the trusted advisor.[35] Through reassigned lines, placement of Joseph within the camera frame in all councilor scenes, and edits to reaction shots of Joseph, the film positions the Duke of York as a companion to the lead character.[36] A count of shots that include Exeter and York within the frame illustrates how thoroughly Sharrock elevates York's influence as a parallel force to that of Exeter. For example, Act One, Scene Two uses editing to signal the influence of Exeter (with edits to midshots or close-ups of Anton Lesser's Exeter twenty-three times in under ten minutes). Though not listed in the players for the scene, Joseph's York stands in close proximity to Exeter and the camera reveals his reactions thirteen times. Furthermore, Ben Power's teleplay reassigns Westmerland's lines (1.2.124–29) to York so that he contributes verbally to the war council. Similarly, in the Battle of Harfleur, the film cuts to shots of York eleven times—those cuts capturing him reacting to Henry's "Once more unto the breach, dear friends" charge and later presenting the defeated governor of the town to the conquering Henry. In Act Three, Scene Six, when Henry must make a crucial disciplinary decision that severs his ties with the companions of his youth, York again emerges as the prime goad to that next step in monarchical ascendency. (The Duke of York rather than Exeter is blamed for Bardolph's arrest in the teleplay, and the film includes York within the frame throughout the interpolated representation of Bardolph hanged.) Throughout Henry's night of self-doubt before the Battle of Agincourt, York assumes singular importance. He appears in thirteen separate shots giving positive eye contact, comforting nods, and other forms of non-verbal affirmation to the king in the hours before battle commences.

Another alteration—this an omission—likewise heightens the significance of York's role in the young king's rise. The Sharrock *Henry V* entirely omits Act Two, Scene Two in which the king orchestrates the exposure of his would-be assassins.[37] This particular deletion contains overtly homoerotic material and reveals a rival friendship to the heteronormative brothers-in-arms affinity scripted for the Duke of York and the king in the BBC adaptation. Lord Scroop, identified by Exeter as the king's "bedfellow," suffers the most affective recrimination from the wronged monarch in this scene of traitors exposed:

> Thou that didst bear the key of all my counsels,
> That knew'st the very bottom of my soul,
> That (almost) mightst have coin'd me into gold,
> Wouldst thou have practic'd on me, for thy use?
> (2.2.96–99)

The king's lament over loyalty and confidence betrayed for financial gain takes on erotically charged significance in the Branagh adaptation where claustrophobic camera proximity recreates the intimacy of the bedchamber. Branagh's King Henry at one point lies on top of Lord Scroop (Stephen Simms) and caresses the once-dear face (seen in tight profile). The BBC film makes no room in *Henry V* for another form of minority identity nor will it entertain a closeness of affection that might interfere with the heteronormativity of Hiddleston's Henry V, especially when, as Elizabeth Kolkovich has argued, a homoerotic "intimate relationship" with Poins in the *Henry IV* films has been sacrificed already as part of Hal's transformation into King Henry (645, 650). In Sharrock's *Henry V*, a competing narrative of friendship and/or desire disappears and makes even neater the elevation of the Duke of York as Henry's prime contemporary, confidant, and advisor. Read most sympathetically, these examples illustrate the pervasiveness of York's presence throughout the film and may demonstrate the good faith effort of the BBC's programming to alter the representation of British history in light of multicultural policy and its own diversity statements.

On the other hand, Joseph's enactment of the expanded York role takes on vexed resonances when read in light of the tropes associated with black masculinity in popular film. Since the production team cast the only non-Caucasian as the Duke of York, the character who will die as one of the few Englishmen of "name" at Agincourt, York transforms from an example of responsive multicultural television practice into the expendable "black best friend" of film. More specifically, *The Hollow Crown* York embodies aspects of the magical negro stereotype, the black man who nurtures white masculinity and then willingly departs the scene once his healing power has worked its magic. Teleplay writer Power shapes York's ending so that the black man's plot exit supports an apotheosis of Henry's warrior identity. While the magical negro develops as a distinct feature of American racial history, its roots in eighteenth- and nineteenth-century fetishizing of the "Noble Savage" (Hughey 564) render it part of a Western European vocabulary of race as well.[38] Matthew W. Hughey summarizes the magical negro stereotype as

> a stock character that often appears as a lower class, uneducated black person who possesses supernatural or magical powers. These powers are used to save and transform disheveled, uncultured, lost, or broken whites (almost exclusively white men) into competent, successful, and content people.
>
> (544)

Though not of the lower-class origins typical of the magical negro as in, for example, *The Green Mile* (Dir. Frank Darabont, 1999), the Duke of York is of lower social status in comparison with the young monarch. Similarly, Henry V is still only recently shedding his identity as under-achieving heir apparent more content to cavort with thieves, pickpockets, and confidence men than submit to sober mentorship by his father's courtly advisors—a prime candidate for the salvific medicine of a magical negro.

In his martial prowess at Agincourt, York epitomizes the supplementary role the magical negro plays to white male self-actualization, and several additions to the teleplay amplify this function. When the French unhorse Henry, his sword falls to the ground in slow motion effect, and the king must resort to defending himself with an inadequately short dagger. Once York notices, he throws his long sword to the king, giving the monarch one last knowing and reassuring nod as if to say, "You've got this!" Minutes later, York's death manifests the perfidy of the French who stab him in the back while he rests from battle. York meets death while once again fostering the growth to maturation of another white male—the Boy who will become the play's narrator and Chorus by film's end. In this case, York places a reassuring hand on the Boy, who observes the battle from the woods; the two make eye contact and exchange wry smiles just seconds before the sound of an unseen dagger, slipped into flesh, punctures the intersubjective moment. York's death then serves as the needed motivator for and explanation of the famous crux, King Henry's order to kill the surrendered French prisoners. The order and the executions occur in the aftermath of York's death in Sharrock's adaptation and as a demonstration of Henry's abiding affection for his friend and brother-in-arms.

While the teleplay maintains some of the description of York's death narrated by Exeter, it quickly conflates and omits play text material in order to justify in the crucible of male friendship Henry's order to kill all surrendered French prisoners. This must, however, be friendship of a certain kind as signified by another omission. Just as in the earlier deleted reference to the king's intimate, Lord Scroop, so in Exeter's description of York's death, the teleplay evades homoerotic material:

> The noble Earl of Suffolk also lies.
> Suffolk first died, and York, all haggled over,
> Comes to him where in gore he lay insteeped,
> And takes him by the beard, kisses the gashes
> That bodily did yawn upon his face.
>
> (4.6.10–14)

Rather than a "testament of noble-ending love" between men as richly imagined by the play text's "kisses the gashes," the film scripts a closing act for York that confirms him in the heteronormative and supplemental role of the magical negro. In death, York facilitates the full actualization of Henry V's character, a monarch deeply loyal to his people who willingly risks his life for his nation. The killing of the prisoners appears no longer a morally dubious act but rather a sacrifice in atonement for the loss of his precious companion, the Duke of York. Joseph's Duke of York thus fulfills Thompson's description of the magical negro, "a figure who helps to save a white protagonist: a kind of *negro ex machina*" (*Passing* 78), who can be dispensed with once those lessons in self-actualization have been internalized by the white male. Furthermore, as the inspiration for the Boy-turned-Chorus, Joseph's York actually catalyzes the hegemonic voice of history that will deny non-Caucasians and non-English a more fully agential role in the national story—a black sacrifice underpinning white history.

Rackin characterizes a throughline of intensified self-scrutiny in Shakespeare's history plays, culminating in *Henry V*: "the plays become increasingly self-reflexive, encouraging their audiences to meditate on the process of historical representation rather than attempting to beguile them into an uncritical acceptance of the represented action as a true mimesis of past events" (*Stages* 29). However, the play text's preoccupation with how disparate entities become a unified nation through the act of telling and performing history has been curiously silenced by this most recent televisual adaptation. Perhaps for reasons of discomfort (given the spirit of Olympic unity) or narrative streamlining, Shakespeare's categorization of soldiers in *Henry V* by nationality (English, Irish, Scottish, and Welsh) has been all but erased by the Sharrock film (a fact more rich in meaning given the Scottish Independence Referendum that took place two years later in September of 2014).[39] In *The Hollow Crown*, all that remains of the playwright's multinational voicing is the Welsh character Fluellen (Owen Teale).[40] The film's quiet removal of these elements from the play text exhibits uneasiness with Shakespeare's own interest in the mechanisms of nation-building by means of multiethnic identities. Certainly, in a moment when the concept of "Britishness" and its emblem in the Union Jack were advanced as lucrative brands of the 2012 London Olympic Games, shining a spotlight on the historic and contemporary fractures within Great Britain might not have seemed advantageous. Those elements of Shakespeare's play carry in them a painful history of English jingoism and expose the failure of warfare to paper over internal dissent.[41] A more thoughtful representation of the multiple countries and ethnicities that came to form Great Britain and of the many nationalities who have migrated to its lands could account for a heritage costly to multiethnic human value.[42] As Ruben Espinosa points out, "Englishness in *Henry V*… is still being wrought, and its interconnection with otherness—be it with the French, Irish, Scots, Welsh, and even Turks—reveals the influence and importance of the foreigner in understanding the self" ("Fluellen's" 74). Sadly, the tokenism of Joseph's casting appears symptomatic of a British multicultural policy that demands further reflection and reform.[43] A better artistic solution would rely upon greater variety in multiethnic casting to distribute representation across character types, genders, and class status, demonstrating that the words of Shakespeare belong to British people of all backgrounds and take on new meaning when voiced by non-traditional agents.

Such a correction requires a deliberate corporate approach and structure. In the case of Sharrock's *Henry V*, the magical negro motif seems so noticeable in the Caucasian racial landscape of the film that one suspects institutional silence as the culprit. Who then is responsible in 2012 for a production marked by myopia regarding the performance of ethnic identity? In short, who made the series of artistic decisions resulting in the magical negro of the BBC's *Henry V*? The collaborative nature of the televisual artistic enterprise challenges any effort to satisfactorily untangle the web of agencies. Television production in many ways dilutes personalized agency even as its finished artifact represents an accretion of numerous individual choices. In the process of creating *Henry V*, many team-members made decisions or defaulted to certain practices that resulted in the magical negro echoes. The elevation of York began with Powers's teleplay, but the casting director, the producers, the director herself, and the editor all had opportunities to intervene as the white complexion of the overall cast and the knock-on effects of Joseph's casting became evident in production. This decision-making web mirrors the phenomenology of lived agentive power as explained by Albert Bandura: freedom of individual agency does not function unalloyed and unimpeded by other constraining agents. Bandura provides the label of "collective" agency to account for this reality: "Most human pursuits involve other participating agents, so there is no absolute agency. Individuals have to accommodate their self-interests if they are to achieve unity of effort within diversity....Effective group performance is guided by collective intentionality" ("Toward" 164). In another study, Bandura explains that no output of such collective agency, "operates independently of the beliefs and actions of the individuals who make up a social system" ("Exercise" 76). In the case of the BBC's *The Hollow Crown*, individual artistic choices took place in the context of other agentive moves and, more importantly, within the structural frameworks or "social systems" of Neal Street Productions and the BBC. Thus, in answer to the question of responsibility, individual, collective, and systemic factors must be reckoned.

With executive representation so lopsidedly Caucasian, institutionalized white privilege at a production company and at a media giant like the BBC may well be the primary culprit for what happens in Sharrock's *Henry V*. Characterized by Peggy McIntosh "as an invisible package of unearned assets" (1) and "invisible systems conferring unsought racial dominance" (McIntosh 4), white privilege dangerously operates through omission and inattention and relies upon "structures of privilege that organize society as a whole" according to Allan G. Johnson (12). McIntosh argues that privileges derive from sets of "interlocking oppressions"—"social class, economic class, race, religion, sex, and ethnic identity"—and that these "take both active forms, which we can see, and embedded forms, which as a member of the dominant group one is taught not to see" (4). This is not to excuse individual agents under the blanket of white privilege but rather to point out its pervasive capacity to blind any given individual to the representational problems inherent in "gifting" one speaking part to a person of color. Indeed, casting Joseph as York and appreciably elevating his presence throughout the film might well have assuaged any latent guilt over failures of systemic power-sharing. Ugandan-British actor, Sheila Atim, rightly identifies the problem as one in which not enough creative power-sharing with diverse perspectives takes place at the decision-making levels of theater companies and production teams. In an interview, she explains,

> It is not just the representation on stage. The reality is until you get to the top level you are the last person—as the actor—to come on board a project. In terms of how the shots are called and before we get to the casting process, we need to look at shifting the culture of that group.
>
> (Woodward)

As intertextual and historical reference points expand exponentially through digital distribution, dialogue at the production level becomes more and more essential.[44] No team can ever possibly anticipate the full range of intertextualities or racial semiotics provoked by any given mimetic act; however, conversation and institutional self-scrutiny regarding entrenched racial and economic privileges could prove ameliorative. Discussions about the racial discourses, intentional and unintentional, emerging throughout a production's creative process might well lead to adjustments in casting, teleplay writing, and editing—alterations all the more necessary to a broadly multiethnic and global audience of digital consumers.[45]

Coda: Selective Memory

Ultimately, *The Hollow Crown* stakes British identity on a persistently white, masculinist monarchy even as questions arise about its necessity and even when the prime example of that institution is a female in her Diamond Jubilee year. The gender and race trouble of *Henry V* seem even more unaccountable given the fact that the film was led by Sharrock, a female director laboring and creating in a male-dominated industry and who also had first-hand experience of Britain's postcolonial economic and diplomatic alliances thanks to a youth spent living in Kenya (E. Brown). Rather than wrestle with a Britishness inflected by the complexities of gender and racial identities, the series resorts to a tabloidism of the male gaze and a racist character trope that contravene the mission statement and commitment to diversity established in the BBC's licence fee agreement. For the state and its citizens, confronting how national identity forms, who the victims of that process are, and what to make of that history when looking backward and forward invites real creative imagination and bravery. The Henriad dates from the moment when Britain began to take a recognizably modern form through the writing and re-writing of chronicle histories, the production of maps and chorographies, and the legislative, military, and bureaucratic consolidation of its power in England, Ireland, Scotland, and Wales (Helgerson 2–3; Rackin, *Stages* 24). Shakespeare's plays expose the fictionalizing and frequently brutalizing processes that make national identity possible even as they find room to celebrate that very identity: in a famous example of this tension, Shakespeare assigns his hero of Agincourt, Henry V, both the brotherhood-of-Englishmen Crispin's Day speech *and* the order to kill the French prisoners without provocation.[46] Furthermore, these history plays dramatize women both as agents and victims of an emergent British identity. Too complacent with and/or protective of the received authority of the Shakespearean text and the BBC's own institutional status, *The Hollow Crown* fails to fulfill the media corporation's diversity mandate and neglects the ambivalent questioning of the plays, wedding Shakespearean authority yet again to traditional definitions of who writes, speaks, acts, and shapes British history.

Like the Shakespeare festivals, historical sites, and cultural tourism so ably scrutinized by Graham Holderness, Barbara Hodgdon, Dennis Kennedy, and

Douglas Lanier, the 2012 Cultural Olympiad and the BBC's Shakespeare Unlocked season attempt to conjure an "authentic Shakespeare" and a concomitantly idealized English national history and identity. Shakespeare festivals and tourism promise an escape from the fragmented technologies of self and nation in the postmodern era; however, that act of reaching back always reveals in its very nature the artificiality of the gesture. In his genealogy of arts festivals, Kennedy explains:

> Like the restored Olympics at the turn of the century, the arts festivals laid claim to a connection with the quasi-religious festivals of ancient Greece, which for the theatre were idealized as arenas of political, social, and spiritual integration.
>
> (176)

Lanier articulates, "the imagining of cultural or national community" as central to the festival and historic site ethos (*Shakespeare* 146); he continues,

> Shakespeare offers a symbolic alternative to—and thus potentially a critique of—the alienation and fragmentation characteristic of postmodern life, while at the same time his image and work are drawn into the very processes of reproduction, mediatization, and commodification from which Shakespeare seems to promise escape.
>
> (145)

In her reading of Stratford as tourist site and a return to origins, Hodgdon dissects the ways in which curating the material remnants of Shakespeare confirms his centrality to "national history" (*The Shakespeare* 195). Likewise, Holderness exposes the necessary fictions grounding the bankside Globe reconstruction—that project yet another harkening after fantasized national heritage at the expense of archaeological fact (*Cultural* 89). The films of *The Hollow Crown* become "heritage sites" of their own digital variety—offering access to the cultural iconicity of William Shakespeare and to "then," a Golden Age of early modern English expansion and adventure. As a result, Leberg argues, the combination of Shakespeare's cultural capital with the authenticist visual vocabulary of *The Hollow Crown* neuters the political purchase of the history plays:

> One of the consequences of this veneer of literary authenticity, however, is the normalization of politics that contemporary audiences may read as only Elizabethan, which negates any meaningful analysis of how these politically-charged plays reflect on their moment of production.
>
> (36)

No amount of on-location filming or scenic and costuming detail should occlude the reality that this is represented history shaped and formed by the technologies and ideological cravings of the "now," crafting and fictionalizing the very "then" that is sought.

As related manifestations of heritage fantasy, the London Olympics opening ceremony and *The Hollow Crown* construct understandings of British nationhood imbricated in technologies of communication—one a referential and metonymic variety that selectively recounts the past and the other reliant upon an aesthetic vocabulary that affirms authenticity. However, the juxtaposition of the two national representations illustrates that the omissions of historiography are no respecter of mimetic mode. Both Olympic moments fundamentally fail to conceive of the nation in gendered and racially complex ways. Furthermore, they both continue to trade in racist literary troping. Here I return to a final example from Boyle's pastiche celebration. In the segment staging Britain's contribution to the world of children's literature—a portion of the evening simultaneously spotlighting the humane triumph of the NHS—Boyle metonymically invoked the books through their villains and initiated the segment with a reading from J. M. Barrie by J. K. Rowling. The episode highlighted the work of Great Ormond Street Hospital for Children (GOSH), the institution that benefited in Barrie's will from the gift of the Peter Pan book rights and the controversial extension of those rights after 1987 when the original copyright expired (Laskow). The racist depictions of indigenous peoples in Barrie's work have been difficult for adaptors to correct over the years, in part, because of the gate-keeping role GOSH has played as holder of the copyright—a fact vexing the carefree multiculturalism of the ceremony's staged nurses and patients. In Boyle's ceremony, the fictional villains and their minions haunted the children and their GOSH caregivers. While Voldemort, Cruella de Vil, and Captain Hook towered over the stadium, a large host of human-sized monsters threatened the children (a case of late-night bedtime reading transformed into nightmare). But, as demonstrated by the carelessness of *The Hollow Crown*, once again a racist trope featured as part of the ceremony sequence—for, unbelievably, the literary monsters thronging the stage were clearly humans in blackface (with minstrel-style makeup—green instead of the typical white—outlining the eyes) and wearing dark wooly costumes.[47] Though vastly different in quality from the ceremony's earlier sins of historical omission, the blackface monsters, sins of racist commission, manifest from the same privileged reluctance to acknowledge the nation's colonial-imperial past and to account for its exclusionary practices of self-definition.

Despite the glaring evidence, all was not right in Boyle's merry pastiche, reviewers consistently interpret his spectacle as a progressive condemnation of David Cameron's Conservative-Liberal Democratic coalition government, reflecting the director's "not-so-hidden left-leaning politics" (Abrams and Parker-Starbuck 20). Owen Hatherley similarly characterizes the ceremony as a left-wing "version of austerity nostalgia" (43).[48] This impression that Boyle successfully harnessed the patriotic energies of nationalism to advocate for a progressive, plural society endured in the liberal imagination in the years that followed 2012. In an opinion piece for *The Guardian* six years later, Zoe Williams drew on Boyle's vision to defend a progressive, "good nationalism," arguing, "Good nationalism is a certain specific solidarity based on the things you have created together, as a nation, and the things you aspire to create: you could call it, for short, Danny Boyle nationalism, and it takes in the NHS, the industrial revolution, the internet, as well as other less cinematic things, such as the sewage system." However, such an effort to embrace even the seemingly benign and inclusive nationalism on offer in Boyle's imagination fails to take seriously the foundational exclusions mobilized more effectively by the far-right to justify an authoritarian, anti-immigrant and racist national chauvinism.[49] The London Olympic Games opening ceremony sadly typified a self-congratulatory liberalism oblivious to its own failures. Much as in the case with *Henry V*'s magical negro, creative-team white privilege blind spots explain why such an obvious and despicable racist image as Boyle's blackface literary monsters made its way from conception to embodied performance just as Britain welcomed the world's many peoples of all hues, who arrived hoping *not* to be othered yet again by the white imaginary.

When I first wrote about *The Hollow Crown* in the context of the London Olympics and Boyle's opening ceremony, I could not access the full recording of the ceremony—not yet publicly archived and thus locked as it was behind the NBC proprietary wall in the United States. As a result, I wrote from my memory, my notes, and from shorter YouTube clips, especially of Branagh's performance, and argued that Boyle, by representing Britain through metonymy and pastiche, not as a unified whole, avoided the perils of heritage filming that plagued *The Hollow Crown*. Returning to the production in 2021 when the whole of the Boyle spectacle is now freely accessible digitally, I write deeply troubled by its careless optimism, unapologetic omissions, and outright racist details—elements that would erupt only a few years later during the 2015 migrant crisis and the 2016 Brexit referendum into a terrifying wave of xenophobic, racist nationalism. I had originally argued that the metonymic artistry of Boyle put in problematic relief the authenticist historical stylings of *The Hollow Crown*'s aesthetics. What appears all too clear with the benefit of hindsight is that regardless of representational mode, sexism and racism adhere like unrelenting and unforgiveable burrs in the telling of Shakespeare's history. We cannot even begin to grapple with those problems when a refusal to tell history aright governs decision-making across all aesthetic approaches. As Jan Assmann notes, "Through its cultural heritage a society becomes visible to itself and to others. Which past becomes evident in that heritage and which values emerge in its identificatory appropriation tells us much about the constitution and tendencies of a society" (133). The Shakespeare that emerged through the London Olympic Games opening ceremony and the films of *The Hollow Crown* tells of a nation not yet acknowledging its misogynist and racist histories and thus dangerously underprepared to support a healthy multicultural nation grounded on principles of equality.

Notes

1 In the United States, the BBC's partners at PBS host a website tie-in to the "Shakespeare Unlocked" programs titled for American airing as "Shakespeare Uncovered" that includes teacher viewing helps and discussion guides. PBS originally aired *The Hollow Crown* as part of the 40th anniversary season of Great Performances on four consecutive Friday nights starting 20 September and concluding 11 October 2013.

2 Executive Producer Pippa Harris recognizes no potential irony in the choice of plays, enthusing, "The plays seemed particularly fitting for this particular year, with the Olympics but also the jubilee. They are about monarchy, they are about England. They are about British history" (qtd. in Davies).

3 I am grateful to Marcella Myers who pointed out that Boyle's sunny vision of British healthcare does not quite match the parlous state in which the NHS now stands with so much of its functionality parceled out to private and for-profit entities (See Flinders; S. Smith).

4 Caliban's relationship to *The Tempest*'s Prospero "echoes the interpersonal power dynamics underpinning the colonial project across nations: the coloniser's objectification of the colonised" (Pittman, Corredera, Denslow and Bailey 91). As Kim F. Hall explains, "Caliban embodies the contradiction and contest characteristic of border spaces, and in that position he contests Prospero's imperial visions" (152).

5 In *Shakespeare Remains*, Courtney Lehmann parses with meticulous care the specter of Irish identity in Branagh's career, demonstrating how the actor-director has relied upon Shakespeare as the mechanism to "subvert his own Irish heritage" (170).

6 Numerous postcolonial engagements with the canon have exposed "the complex ways in which Shakespeare's writing was entangled from the beginning with the projects of nation-building, Empire and colonization" (Neill 168). For example, Gauri Viswanathan, Martin Orkin, and David Johnson explain the specifically curricular means by which the Shakespearean text served to shore up British imperial authority in colonial territories.

7 Gargi Bhattacharyya et al argue that, "What should have been learnt from the 'Windrush scandal'—from the illegalisation and expulsion of long-settled Commonwealth citizens—was that racist discrimination persists across a range of state institutions and practices, and that this takes new forms as punitive, everyday borders proliferate" (28).

8 I do not aim to establish a direct line of influence between the London Olympic Games opening ceremony, the Cultural Olympiad, and the BBC Shakespeare Unlocked programing/*Hollow Crown* productions; however, without doubt, these manifestations of the London Olympic moment were interconnected and bureaucratically linked. The London Organising Committee of the Olympic and Paralympic Games (LOCOG) reported directly to the International Olympic Committee (IOC) and oversaw most aspects of the London Olympic Games, including the opening ceremony. The IOC's report on the London Olympic Games explains that, "In 2010 a Cultural Olympiad Board was formed as a committee of the LOCOG Board" and chaired by LOCOG member Lord Hall of Birkenhead CBE (*Final Report* 37). LOCOG provided financing and procured additional exterior funding to support the aims of the Cultural Olympiad, an extra-sport display designed "to showcase the culture of the host nation" (*Final Report* 37). In addition, Bill Morris, Director of Culture, Ceremonies and Education for LOCOG, served as a member of the Cultural Olympiad Board as did the BBC Director-General, Mark Thompson. The BBC played a crucial role in the visibility of the Cultural Olympiad; its media promotional materials catalogue the range of televisual, radio, and live events under its umbrella, including the alliance with the Royal Shakespeare Company that produced Shakespeare Unlocked ("London 2012"). The Cultural Olympiad

enjoyed "over 165 hours of BBC coverage of London 2012 Festival programming (excluding news)" (*Reflections on the Cultural Olympiad* 22). Thus in governance hierarchy, financial interconnection, and human resources, Boyle's opening ceremony, the Cultural Olympiad, and the BBC Shakespeare Unlocked/*Hollow Crown* productions shared a significant network of influence that shaped the epistemologies of British nationhood emergent in 2012.

9 Philip Auslander's careful work with the phenomenon of "mediatization" identifies the profound ways in which performances transmitted "on television, as audio or video recordings, and in other forms based in technologies of reproduction," strongly influence knowing by "shaping the sensory norm" (4, 37). For Auslander, the technical reproduction of mediatization and the liveness of performance have so thoroughly interpenetrated as to be inseparable from each other and have impacted audience perceptions of the knowable and the real. Auslander's identification of mediatized knowing should prompt not only skeptical examination of the "real" Britain communicated by both Boyle's spectacle and *The Hollow Crown* but also a critical exploration of the modes of narration that construct nationhood in the two broadcasts.

10 Indeed, this tendency of the BBC series to downplay the significance of women in the Henriad corresponds to what Lehmann identifies in her *Shakespeare Quarterly* article as a "distinctly cinematic backlash against women in recent Renaissance-period films and Shakespeare adaptations featuring transgressive female characters" ("Crouching" 260).

11 Holderness explains that the democratizing possibilities of televisual Shakespeare represented by the BBC's filming of the Shakespeare canon, "are in practice systematically blocked, suppressed or marginalised by the conservatism of the dominant cultural institutions" ("Radical" 223), and Olwen Terris argues that the BBC series "conflated the superiority of Shakespeare with its own tradition and created the canon in its own image–conservative, culturally authoritative, durable and necessary" (207). Despite these ideological limitations, the authoritative completeness of the BBC series proved a commercial success as Susan Willis indicates: "By 1982, the series had paid for itself and was even making a profit due to foreign sales" (8).

12 Terris suggests that, "mindful of the fact that its charter was up for renewal and the licence fee might have to be re-negotiated, the BBC once again looked to classic literature to fulfil a cultural remit" (210). Kidnie elaborates on this context and identifies a White Paper "released in the Spring of 2006" which assigned the BBC the task of "Building Digital Britain" by 2012 as another reason for the series (131); Kidnie reasons that the BBC could draw upon the cultural status of Shakespeare as emblem of national continuity even as the BBC transitioned to new millennium modes of broadcast transmission. In his review of *The Hollow Crown* for *The Guardian,* Mark Lawson also points out the BBC's tendency to resort to Shakespeare during "licence fee renegotiation." Repeatedly, in times of institutional and fiscal vulnerability, the BBC turns to Shakespeare to reaffirm its cultural significance. This need gained urgency in 2012 not only because of the post-2008 recession but also because of the distributed and proliferated nature of media access now so decidedly decentralized on the one hand and on the other hand dominated by an oligarchy of media giants controlling so much television, internet, and radio content.

13 *Putting Quality First* articulates four objectives designed to provide value in exchange for the guaranteed fees: "Increase the distinctiveness and quality of its output"; "Improve the value for money it provides to licence fee payers"; "Set new standards of openness and transparency"; and "Do more to serve all audiences" (3).

14 According to the strategy document, the network of BBC outlets reaches 97% of UK "television viewers, audio listeners and web users every week." The BBC recognizes that it must better reflect the increased diversity of that audience: "Quite

simply, our determination to visibly increase our diversity on and off air is part of our fundamental commitment to serve all our audiences" (*Diversity* 2).

15 Wray specifies that "the BBC, NBC Universal, Neal Street Productions, and WNET Thirteen" collaborated in the production of *The Hollow Crown* ("Shakespeare" 3).

16 In his standard history of cinematic Shakespeare, Kenneth S. Rothwell traces the profit anxiety across the oeuvre of the poet's filmed drama.

17 The first recorded staging of the Henriad as a cycle of plays actually dates from nineteenth-century Munich and the direction of Franz Dingelstedt (McMillin 3).

18 Harris elaborates on the production vision and directorial working relationship for the cycle of plays: "We wanted to give each director as much freedom as possible within their own film so that they could choose their own teams—we weren't imposing people on them—but then to be able to link the films together so that as an audience you can watch from start to finish, and it feels like a cohesive whole. All the directors have bought into the fact that this is part of a bigger picture. You know, Thea [Sharrock] has been out on set to see what Rupert [Goold] was filming on *Richard II* so that she could get a sense of his approach, and, you know, we've been cross-casting across *Henry IV* and *Henry V*, which meant that Thea and Richard [Eyre] have been working together on that. So, I think it's a very satisfying blend of the whole lot working together as a cohesive serial" ("*The Hollow Crown*: The Making of a King").

19 While the husband and wife face each other seated at the hearth, the camera most frequently records their symmetrical positions from the hearth point of view with the interior's large window (opposite the fire) as the central focal point of shots presenting the two in colloquy (the Duke and Duchess of York on the left and right sides of the frame respectively).

20 Comparison with another recent production of *Richard II* (Dir. Gregory Doran for the Royal Shakespeare Company, 2013) underscores the significance of Goold's choices in adapting 5.2 and 5.3. Doran's *Richard II* exploits the humorous potentiality of the confrontation and in so doing mutes the Duchess of York's impact on history-making. For example, the exasperated, eye-rolling reactions of all three men (Nigel Lindsay's Henry IV, Oliver Ford Davies's Duke of York, and Oliver Rix's Aumerle) when the Duchess of York (Marty Cruickshank) arrives at court undermine her status as a molder of history. With her skirt bustled awkwardly in front from her hasty gallop, the Duchess of York uses her riding crop to silence her husband in a slapstick gesture that elicits chuckles from the Stratford-upon-Avon audience. In addition, when Cruickshank outstretches her arms to intensify her supplication, the Duke of York mimics the gesture with an exaggeration that makes light of his wife's demands (and draws robust audience laughter and even applause). In contrast, Goold's filming choices silence these elements of humorous absurdity to honor the Duchess's intervention in history.

21 Rackin points out that the shift from "dignified blank verse" to "doggerel rhymed couplets" upon the Duchess's arrival at court signals a "generic debasement" that highlights the "indecorousness" of her actions ("Women's Roles" 75). Goold's filming strikingly elevates the Duchess's plea against both the grain of the play text and the tendencies of the sibling films in *The Hollow Crown* cycle.

22 Wray summarizes the captivating preoccupation with aesthetics established by the film's incipit: "there is sensual satisfaction to be had in the extent to which the sequence materialises the past at the level of warm colours, eye-appealing patterns, sinuous forms, carved structures, and medieval artistry" ("Shakespeare" 8).

23 None of the quarto texts nor the 1623 Folio establish the scene location; this fact relies upon the eighteenth-century editor Edward Capell. Following Capell, the studious realism of *The Hollow Crown* filming style establishes Kate's marginality by placing her in the visually remote landscape of a northern castle.

24 Such readings exemplify Norman Rabkin's well-known assertion that *Henry V*, "points in two opposite directions, virtually daring us to choose one of the two opposed interpretations it requires of us" (279).

25 In his performance history of *Henry V*, James N. Loehlin similarly notes that the biographical details of the Branagh-Thompson marriage in combination with a "warmly lit and closely shot" *mise-en-scène* underscore "the inevitability of their union" (*Henry V* 144–145).

26 Branagh and Hiddleston have worked together on several projects, and reporter Serena Davies characterizes Hiddleston as "something of a protégé to Ken Branagh." Hiddleston played a supporting role to Branagh in the first two seasons of the BBC drama, *Wallander* (2008, 2010), a series executive produced by Branagh, and Hiddleston took the part of Loki in Branagh's box-office hit, *Thor* (2011).

27 This filmic convention by which the male figure absorbs prime camera focus at the expense of female agency has, of course, a long history even at the BBC; Reynolds notes that in the BBC's *Complete Shakespeare* adaptation of *Hamlet* (1980), film angle and focus in the Nunnery Scene of Rodney Bennett's production repeatedly sideline Ophelia so that Hamlet remains the "active, dynamic force" and Ophelia "is presented as passive" (198). Reynolds continues: "The scene thus constructed becomes almost exclusively a further extension of Hamlet's narrative, his crisis, his betrayal, whilst those of Ophelia are marginalized" (198–199). Despite the gap of thirty-two years, the BBC Shakespeare still relies on modes of visual communication that downplay female agency.

28 While the interpolation of Henry V's funeral might seem designed to expand Katherine's limited presence in the film, Leberg asserts the primacy of Hurt's reveal: "Hurt's visual cameo appearance in the final minute of *H5* ultimately carries greater televisual weight than the addition of Katherine's grief; even in a modern production, the women of Shakespeare's histories exist at the convenience of English men" (39).

29 In contrast to the sentimentalized vision of chivalric monarchy in *The Hollow Crown*'s conclusion, Barbara Hodgdon argues that the generic divisions and multiple endings of *Henry V* actually "question the ideology that supports kingship" (*The End* 186).

30 Kirwan, too, acknowledges the visual splendor of the series but simultaneously laments the films' tendency to be "conservative in their readings": "The films are beautiful, but smack to me of Shakespeare to be seen and appreciated rather than to be engaged with or provoke conversation. While they are in many ways a resounding success, creating a Shakespeare that will reach the broadest possible audience and latch onto public mood broadly celebratory of individual achievement and ideas of the home nation in an Olympic year, it's perhaps also a missed opportunity for the exact same reasons."

31 Linda Nochlin's discussion of Orientalism in the visual arts bears upon the aesthetic of *The Hollow Crown*. Nochlin articulates the danger of hyper-naturalism in works such as the paintings of Jean-Leon Gerome: "A 'naturalist' or 'authenticist' artist like Gerome tries to make us forget that his art is really art, both by concealing the evidence of his touch, and, at the same time, by insisting on a plethora of authenticating details, especially on what might be called unnecessary ones" (38). Much as Gerome crowds the picture plane with evidences of his truth-telling that deny the artifice of his vision, so the makers of *The Hollow Crown*, especially the directors of the final three films, achieve compelling sensory authority.

32 Regarding the tension between the historical authenticity of the series and its timid multiethnic casting, Kinga Földváry reflects: "In general, the kind of colour-blindness that characterises *The Hollow Crown* seems to me a rather cautious, or even cowardly solution" (113).

33 Deborah Cartmell observes just such an example of this possibility in a much earlier film, Kenneth Branagh's *Much Ado About Nothing* (1993), when Emma Thompson's Beatrice refuses the proposal of Denzel Washington's Don Pedro; Cartmell points out the denial "is more noticeable and problematic than it would be if the two actors were the same colour. Beatrice's refusal, no doubt accidentally, can be interpreted as racist" (7).

34 In the quarto text, York only speaks the lines slightly modified by the Folio edition: "My gracious Lord, upon my knee I crave, / The leading of the vaward" (E3r). The 1623 Folio marks York's entrance with, "Enter Yorke," immediately before he offers: "My Lord, most humbly on my knee I begge / The leading of the Vaward" (87).

35 As is well known, the Adrian Noble Royal Shakespeare Company production of *Henry V* (1984) and the Branagh film both cast Brian Blessed as the Duke of Exeter, "the young king's guide and protector" (Crowl 28). In the Noble production, Blessed's "bear-like Exeter....provided a useful foil for Branagh's sensitive King, doing the dirty work and liking it while Henry looked on, pained but resolute" (Loehlin, *Henry V* 90). Though, as Peter Orford notes, Sharrock strives to differentiate her film from the precedents of Olivier and Branagh (243), in her expansion of the Duke of York as a peer-companion and guide to King Henry, Sharrock echoes the pattern previously set by the Noble and Branagh treatment of Exeter.

36 Kirwan similarly notes the prominence of York "as a particularly close friend of Henry V" in the Sharrock adaptation.

37 Interested in how the play's polyvocality diminishes in film adaptation and results in a more jingoistic narrative, David Livingstone argues that *The Hollow Crown*'s, "omission [of 2.2] only further imbalances the plot as additional dissident voices are left unheard" (91).

38 The global interpenetration of film markets makes it unsurprising that traces of the magical negro might surface in a British television film; it does also seem somewhat naïve not to anticipate the ways in which an international audience exposed to popular film tropes might "read" York's function.

39 Ruth Morse argues that, "Taking out the scene of the four captains was a solution to allowing it to hijack the whole play, which it so often does. We get, instead, something complex and balanced....The nations are contextualized to comprehend the regions; the three regions are subsumed in a larger whole" (18). Rather than rescuing the play from jingoistic appropriation, such deletions thwart engagement with the exclusionary mechanisms underpinning nation-formation and chronicle history.

40 Wray's reading of the film in light of Iraq War cinematic tropes explains, "The infamous question – 'What ish my nation?' (3.3.66) – becomes untenable in a production where relations between men take precedence over national affiliation" ("*Henry V*" 10).

41 Isabel Karremann argues convincingly that *Henry V* stages moments of memorialization that often enact simultaneously the processes of forgetting or "nationalist oblivion" necessary to nation-building (125). Through its omissions, conflations, and silences, Sharrock's adaptation performs "nationalist oblivion," neutering crucial components of the play text that underscore the ideological freight of such action.

42 Rosemary Gaby notes in the baleful tones of the series' medievalism a "sense of regret haunting" the "representation of British history" (238); that ambivalence about the past might have taken on greater precision had the production company preserved some of the entrenched people group differences that trace back to the play text.

43 In his examination of the BBC *Shakespeare Retold* adaptation of *Macbeth*, Maurizio Calbi suggests that the blame placed on two Serbians for the death of Duncan

telegraphs similar discomfort with the steady "inflow of refugees or migrants" and Britain's uneasy multiculturalism (174, n. 22).

44 Though statistics on SVOD (Streaming or Subscription Video on Demand) usage can be closely guarded corporate secrets, reports each year highlight an ever increasing population of streaming consumers. In April 2016, *The New York Times* reported that Netflix boasts a worldwide subscription of over 75 million members (Wingfield). Amazon Prime's subscribers range from 57 to 61 million (Wingfield), with a new monthly enrollment option positioned to deepen Amazon's competitive inroads against Netflix. Nielsen's *The Total Audience Report* for the first quarter of 2016 indicates that 50% of TV households (in the United States) now have access to SVOD programming and DVR (Digital Video Recorder). Nielsen also calculates that Q1 2016 saw 158 million time-shifted DVR adult viewers. 162 million adult viewers utilized the Internet on a PC, and 191 million users accessed content via an application or the web on a smartphone; another 106 million utilized a tablet. Lastly, 61 million viewers relied on a game console, and 60 million on another multimedia device (such as Roku or Apple TV).

45 For additional discussion of digital streaming and interpretive approaches to Shakespeare and race in adaptation, see my "Colour-Conscious Casting and Multicultural Britain in the BBC *Henry V* (2012): Historicizing Adaptation in an Age of Digital Placelessness."

46 As scholars have repeatedly demonstrated, Shakespeare's history plays contain both celebration and critique of monarchy, not just in the second tetralogy but also in the first cycle as Leah S. Marcus has so convincingly shown in *I Henry VI*'s elision of Joan La Pucelle with Elizabeth I. If capitalized upon in adaptation, this textual richness and nuance could prove well suited to a postmodern assessment of British history and nationhood.

47 Boyle's blackface villains mirrored deeply inscribed racist patterns typical of children's and young adult fantasy in which, "Darkness is personified, embodied, and most assuredly racialized" (Thomas 20). Ebony Elizabeth Thomas explains: "…in the Anglo-American fantastic tradition, the Dark Other is the spectacle, the monstrous Thing.…The Dark Other is the present-absence that lingers at the edges of every fairy tale" (23).

48 Hatherley writes: "Compared to the imperial pageantry expected at such occasions, it was taken as a vivid and timely reminder of the radical institutions that the Coalition government were, at that point, busy dismantling"; however, he quickly points out that "austerity nostalgia" remains largely and more successfully, "a right-wing phenomenon" (44).

49 Bhattacharyya et al characterize as both dangerous and oxymoronic a "progressive patriotism": "The problem for progressive nationalists is that the right (and worse, the far-right) have obtained a political monopoly on its use and thus fill it with regressive or conservative content.…The right's nationalism is problematic for the progressive nationalist because it is used to articulate nativism, racism, jingoism, xenophobia, etc." (70).

4 *Hollow* Refuge

The BBC's *The Wars of the Roses* and This Fortress Built by Nature

> "Let's whip these stragglers o'er the seas again;
> Lash hence these overweening rags of France,
> These famish'd beggars weary of their lives."
> (*Richard III*)

In 2016, Neal Street Productions returned once again to the material of Shakespearean history for a planned Series Two adapting the plays of the first tetralogy. Just as Series One coincided with the Cultural Olympiad, Queen's Diamond Jubilee, and 2012 London Olympic Games, so Neal Street Productions crafted Series Two as part of the rolling celebrations marking major national milestones—the 400th anniversary of Shakespeare's death and the ninetieth birthday of Queen Elizabeth II. BBC Four even re-aired Series One of *The Hollow Crown* in April 2016 for its Shakespeare Festival. Casting choices, textual edits, and publicity interviews associated with Series Two all signal that *The Wars of the Roses* commemorated not just the great dramatic poet and longest-reigning monarch but also Great Britain's role as cultural custodian, particularly of Shakespeare's global longevity. The series gathered together an impressive troupe of well-known British actors who represent Brand Britain to the far-flung digital viewing audience. At the same time that the series marketed the enduring cultural capital of Britain, *The Wars of the Roses* premiered under less salubrious circumstances on three consecutive Saturdays (7, 14, and 21 May) just as the final campaign to leave the European Union raged hotly in the run-up to the Brexit vote on 23 June. Indeed, Kinga Földváry describes the broadcast as "dominated by a haunting sense of an internally divided kingdom, ruled by manipulative and monstrous monarchs" that coincided with "the Brexit referendum, when British identity and the country's relationship to Europe was at its most uncertain" (108). While *The Hollow Crown: The Wars of the Roses* reinforced the cultural capital of Shakespeare's homeland, voters and pundits debated issues threatening Britain's geopolitical stability and economic capital.

The Neal Street Productions' enterprise (led by Pippa Harris and Sam Mendes) celebrates British heritage, both theatrical (through its well-known cast) and architectural (in the form of heritage-style, on-location settings). The

DOI: 10.4324/9781003043065-4

series' producers and creators all mention the quality of the assembled cast as a factor driving decision-making. Edits to the scripts and the shape of the three-film adaptation of the four plays were determined by how best to tell the story of Benedict Cumberbatch as Richard III: "Just as the twisted shape of Richard III looms large over Shakespeare's first tetralogy of English history plays, so too Benedict Cumberbatch's performance as Richard casts a shadow over the second series" (Gerzic 188). Betting on the high-profile status of Cumberbatch, the creative team members reveal that the entire series grew out of the decision to secure the *Sherlock* star for the part of Shakespeare's tyrant. Unsurprisingly, this casting decision governed approaches to cutting the *Henry VI* texts, "the most marginal and least seen of all Shakespeare's plays" (Hampton-Reeves and Rutter 1). Director Dominic Cooke's explanation of the singular focus on the step-by-step progress towards Richard's ascendency demonstrates how casting dictates thematic and interpretive focus:

> We have to condense the story down, so we started with, "What logic do we use to make our cuts and to shape the stories?" The question we said was, "How many bad decisions does it take to put up a psychopath in power?" So we started from the very beginning with that and anything that didn't relate to that we got rid of.
>
> ("The Making of *The Hollow Crown*")

On the DVD bonus film, producer Mendes similarly conceives of the series as a means to gather and archive performances by great British stars: "We were blessed with an incredible cast. It's been a wonderful thing to watch what has been effectively a multigenerational festival of British actors" ("The Making of *The Hollow Crown*"). Teleplay author Ben Power similarly remarks on the quality of actors enlisted for the productions:

> One of the great treats of *The Hollow Crown* is that you can put the greatest of our actors in parts that are small but hugely significant. Judi Dench playing Cecily, Duchess of Gloucester [sic, York], not a part which always on the stage really has a huge amount of impact, but as Richard III's mother was essential to our story."
>
> ("The Making of *The Hollow Crown*")

Though presented as a laudable element of the series, the cast make-up also bears the imprint of Brexit's shadow, inadvertently replicating the increasing insularity evident in the months preceding the referendum vote. The resolutely "British" nature of the cast can be detected in the disappearance of European continental actors, what Anna Blackwell describes as, "the effacement of the plays' internationalism" (173). Whereas Series One casts numerous French actors (e.g. Clémence Poésy, Jérémie Covillault, Mélanie Thierry, Edward Akrout, Lambert Wilson, Stanley Weber), Series Two relies exclusively upon British and Irish nationals, a shift sadly predictive of the little island's narrowing future.

In addition to the heritage of British theater and film acting, Mendes's Series Two commentary confirms a general commitment to the historical properties of the nation in its "authenticity" of location: "One of the conditions right at the beginning was we want to film these plays in location, and what came out of that was something really dynamic and exciting and very visual" ("The Making of *The Hollow Crown*"). On the same bonus film, Director Cooke explains that such on-location filming necessitates a level of visual verisimilitude contrary to the representational styles of the stage: "If you're doing Shakespeare on stage, you're in a world that is artificial, clearly artificial. And once you get into film and in our production, real location, there's a level of realism and naturalism that you also have to observe." Even Cumberbatch weighs in on the meaning of place within the vocabulary of the films: "One of the joys of the job was this extraordinary heritage tour of Great Britain. It was remarkable and, you know, a real honor for all of us to have access to these incredible parts of our history" ("The Making of *The Hollow Crown*"). As the white male lead and key component of the series's marketability, Cumberbatch easily speaks for the cast and crew and asserts ownership of a national history through the plural possessive pronoun, "our," even though exactly who that "our" encompasses in the United Kingdom was hotly debated in 2015 and 2016. Sidestepping that knotty issue, the series offers viewers a tour of two different forms of an ostensibly shared British heritage: its respected and highly trained actors and its conserved great houses, castles, and cathedrals.

Where the descendants of more recent, often non-white immigrants to Great Britain (primarily from the sundered empire) fit into the heritage-style tour of cathedrals and country homes remains unclear. As in Series One, the second installment of *The Hollow Crown* treads cautiously into the terrain of colorblind casting. With the exception of York in *Henry V*, actors of color fill predominantly marginal roles throughout the first series, and, in fact, no visibly non-Caucasian actors participate in the two parts of *Henry IV*. The same inhibitions that limited multicultural casting in the earlier series—particularly a commitment to visual verisimilitude and "authentic" history-telling—most certainly influenced choices made for the adaptations of Series Two. In *The Wars of the Roses* trilogy, Sophie Okonedo, a Londoner of Jewish and Nigerian descent, is the most prominent person of color, taking on the role of Margaret of Anjou. Over the three films of the second series, the list of non-Caucasians is quite small: Paul Bazely (Catesby) is South Asian; Ivanno Jeremiah (Blunt) is Ugandan-British, and Jude Owusu (Messenger) immigrated to England at seven years of age from Ghana. Bazely, Jeremiah, and Owusu only appear in *Richard III*, so Okonedo is the only person of color with a speaking part in the first two films. During the English battles against France in *Henry VI, Part I*, only white extras populate the English army, but two extras of African descent appear on the French side. At one point, a close-up on one of the black extras provides an affective reaction shot during Joan de Pucelle's rallying cry outside Rouen. The two black extras reappear in a French crowd shot just before the English burn Joan at the stake later in the same episode. Furthermore, Okonedo's

Margaret arrives in England with no persons of color in her retinue, and the series makes no effort to re-color the English court she rules. Shots of the English court when Margaret assumes the throne never include other persons of color. Thus, it appears that in the first two films of *The Wars of the Roses*, only the French side features multiethnic cast members and extras, and only very thinly so at that. In the context of Brexit, these choices reinforce dangerously, if inadvertently, myths of British white racial purity and the fear that darker-skinned contamination comes by means of a continental invasion. Once again, the series fails to place multiple persons of non-Caucasian background in larger roles, and, as with *Henry V*, this results in tremendous pressure on the one major figure of darker skin tone, Okonedo, and on her performance of Margaret, who becomes in Jennie M. Votava's words, "a figure of both the power and the disempowerment of gendered and racial alterity writ large" (174).

Though commissioned and filmed prior to Prime Minister David Cameron's referendum call (20 February 2016), Series Two of *The Hollow Crown* adapts Shakespearean history in ways that dramatize anxiety over the threat to national inviolability posed by refugees and darker-skinned minorities. The heavily documented xenophobia of the Leave campaign provides a complicating intertextual reference point for *The Hollow Crown*'s interpolated prologue to *I Henry VI* and the ensuing episodes' representation of female power. Already othered in the plotting as Henry VI's dowerless French queen, Okonedo's visually anomalous status as the only prominent person of color replicates the racist fears roiling under the surface of the Brexit vote, fears that the non-white intruder would undermine national sovereignty and economic independence. In the Trojan invasion myth signifying throughout the texture of the *Henry VI* plays and *The Wars of the Roses*, Okonedo's Queen Margaret operates as another Helen of Troy whose bodily race and gender combine to disrupt order and "right"/white hierarchy. In *Richard III*, Margaret briefly "belongs," when her occult access to Nemesis proves of use to the aggrieved Yorkist women. In a move that endeavors to distance the production from the racism of the refugee debate, the film stresses analogues between the Vote Leave rhetoric and Richard's increasingly paranoid insularity; however, the tableau of order established by Henry VII's Tudor dynasty at film's end returns to white racial uniformity and leaves the Afro-British Margaret an outcast in company with the dead of Bosworth. Lastly, through its avoidance of the first tetralogy's Jack Cade-led peasant's rebellion, *The Wars of the Roses* also silences the conflicts and disaffections over class inequalities articulated by many of the Vote Leave electorate. In these ways, Series Two of *The Hollow Crown* spotlights Shakespeare's function as a barometer of 2016's resurgent English nationalism.

"Take Back Control": Brexit and Race-Baiting

While fear over a largescale influx of displaced Middle Easterners stoked the Vote Leave fires, the Pew Research Center reports that in 2015, of the 1.3 million refugees entering the European Union, Norway and Switzerland, "more than half of asylum seeker applications" were submitted to just three countries, Germany, Hungary, and Sweden. The UK experienced a 0.2% change in foreign-born population while in Sweden the jump was a dramatic 1.5% (16.8% to 18.3%) (Connor and Krogstad). Despite these facts, the Brexit campaign's tendency to tap into deep-seated racisms and animosities towards those seeking refuge manifested in its print and video advertising. Sivamohan Valluvan's research confirms the fears underlying the vote: "it is apparent that the assortment of more overtly xenophobic, race-baiting themes was 'wot won the referendum'. Themes relating to immigration, refugees, Muslims, the spectre of Turkey, the Roma" ("Defining" 232). On 23 May just when Series Two of *The Hollow Crown* first aired, a Vote Leave print advertisement baldly captured the racist heart of the movement. The controversial image in which footprints trekked towards a widely open UK passport doubling as a door stoked fears that Turkey and its "population 76 million" might soon join the EU and thus find a doorway into Britain (Boffey and Helm). Campaigners, justice secretary Michael Gove chief amongst them, argued this would lead to an inundation of Britain with brown-skinned Turks, secret Islamic State sympathizers, and a population of immigrants whose fertility rates far outstripped British citizens. Gove and others drew the disingenuous conclusion that this migration posed both a very real security risk in the fight against terrorism and an economic threat to the over-burdened National Health Service (Boffey and Helm). These fallacious claims drank deeply from centuries-old Orientalist stereotypes of the sexually rapacious and fecund East.

In the final month of campaigning, Vote Leave propaganda continued to stress the threat of invasion from disorderly, brown-skinned outsiders. On 16 June 2016, Nigel Farage unveiled an especially pernicious print ad labeled "Breaking Point." The advertisement featured a Getty Images photographic taken by Jeff Mitchell on 15 October 2015 and depicting Middle Eastern refugees queuing to cross the border between Croatia and Slovenia (Stewart and Mason). As Heather Stewart and Rowena Mason observe in their *Guardian* report, a text box covered the only white face in the flow of humans on foot so that the message of the poster caption, "The EU has failed us all," threatened that a horde of brown, non-British people would soon be flooding the nation. Reporters and commentators on Twitter quickly pointed out the similarity between the "Breaking Point" imagery and that of Nazi anti-Semitic propaganda.

A similarly egregious video again focused on the possibility of Turkey's admission to the EU and not-too-subtly characterized the Turkish people as unruly and destructive ("Brexit: 10 Most"). To demonstrate the danger of what it constructed as Cameron's shifting position on Turkey, a video of an altercation in the Turkish parliament (labeled on screen "Ankara, May 2016") ran throughout most of the Vote Leave advertisement. For much of the ad, the Ankara video rolled in split screen with the recording of Cameron's policy speech, printing selected text from the speech over the image of the parliamentary fracas. In particular, the creators accompanied Cameron's phrase,

"Together, I want us to pave the road from Ankara to Brussels," with an overlay graphic of Europe. The graphic's animated red arrows moved from Turkey, to other EU member countries, and ultimately across the channel to the United Kingdom. Further editing created the illusion of the Turkish parliamentary video pushing Cameron off screen as the voiceover concluded, "We are giving £2 billion to Macedonia, Serbia, Albania, Montenegro and Turkey to join the EU."[1] The map of Europe accompanying the closing voiceover highlighted the UK in blue but disproportionally enlarged a bright red and unnamed Turkey whose neighbors, Syria and Iraq, were threateningly labeled. The map's oversized £-sign arrow pointed towards Turkey and a similarly dominant arrow of people headed towards the UK reinforced fears about lost resources and the incursion of unruly foreigners set to sully the pristine nation. Declaring the familiar slogan, "Let's take back control," the ad reached a conclusion with the Turkish parliamentary uproar rolling until the very end, visible through the semi-transparent graphic overlay of the Vote Leave icon ("Brexit: 10 Most"). The video advertisement typified what Nadine El-Enany describes as the race-baiting strategies of the Vote Leave campaign:

> The Leave campaign constructed migrants, a category that operated as a catch-all for anyone not considered white and British, as unjustly enriched and undeserving of access to territory and resources. Britain was presented as belonging to white British people, illustrated by the rhetoric of "taking back control."
>
> (31)

Thus, despite claims that the Brexit vote hinged primarily on working-class economic alienation, these images confirm the persuasive role played by race in catalyzing voters.[2] The context of Brexit's heightened atavistic nationalism inevitably directs attention towards the depiction of race and foreignness in *The Wars of the Roses* as the series adapts Shakespearean historiography and nation-building for twenty-first-century viewers.

Aliens at the Border

In light of this poisonous rhetoric, *The Wars of the Roses* frames its trilogy of films with an opening prologue that inadvertently reinforces the white supremacist ethos of Vote Leave campaigning. For its broadcast of the first tetralogy, the creators opt to compress the three *Henry VI* dramas into two televised films, resulting in understandable truncation of the plot and lacunae in action. Despite those cuts and omissions, the production makes the evocative addition of a prologue staging the iconic geography of Britain as island nation. The series opens with a traveling overhead shot of the English Channel and a Judi Dench voiceover taken not from *I Henry VI* but from Ulysses's doctrine of degree in *Troilus and Cressida*. Stripped of their context and presented in conjunction with the powerful symbolism of the white cliffs, the transplanted lines wed national "degree, priority, and place" (1.3.86) to a geography that holds intruders at bay and parses no distinction between refugee and invader. Indeed, the threat of "what discord follows" (1.3.110) combines with the on-rushing camera to shorthand anxieties about the "invasion" of displaced persons and refugees crossing the seas at peril and moving across Europe to seek asylum during 2015 and 2016.[3] Aired just at the moment that the British electorate voted to sever EU ties and tighten borders, the series prologue situates its Shakespearean history within an isolationist national self-conception that does not heed the "strangers' case" (*Sir Thomas More* Add.2.6.155).

This incipit follows a pattern established by Series One, which commences with a Richard II voiceover by Ben Whishaw, but in this case, the lines Dench intones import a complicated and contradictory intertext for the series' meditation on internecine conflict:

> The heavens themselves, the planets, and this earth [replaced "centre"]
> Observe degree, priority, and place,
> Office, and custom, in all line of order;
> Take but degree away, untune that string,
> And hark what discord follows.
>
> (1.3.85–86, 88, 109–110)

At "Office, and custom," the camera tilts upwards while continuing its forward movement to reveal the chalky cliffs, Albion's "fortress built by Nature." The *Hollow Crown* series creators may not expect audience members to question the source of Dench's lines as anything other than the denoted play, *Henry VI, Part I*, but, of course, this opening performs a quotational sleight of hand. The Series Two prologue borrows Ulysses's doctrine of degree from *Troilus and Cressida* and imports the Greek politician's language of *a priori* natural hierarchies.[4] Shakespeare's Ulysses deems such hierarchies (the familiar God-ordained Great Chain of Being) essential to social order as his well-known speech anachronistically deploys medieval Christianity in ancient Troy and moves from the example of the heavens to patriarchal society to diagnose what has gone amiss in the Greek camp. Stripped of their context in Shakespeare's problem play and presented in conjunction with the powerful symbolism of what Paul Gilroy describes as "the nation-defining ramparts of the white cliffs" (*Postcolonial* 14), this transplanted speech fuses claims of right order with British national identity—a nation bounded by the seas, protected by its terrain, and ordered by nature itself.

Setting in motion the resonant semiotics of the cliffs, the film's opening implies a natural order of things in which England's island breed reigns superior to outsiders who dare cross her forbidding border. The delivery of this passage troublingly posits the enduring ontology of nationhood predicated by the land rather than constructed by the powerful and adjusted over time and at the expense of others, Benedict Anderson's "imagined political community" (6). The prologue conducts a further substitution whereby the affectively expanding visual imagery, rising orchestral scoring, and fluid camera movement supplant the Dench quote and harken to John of Gaunt's familiar panegyric in *Richard II*. Indeed, by replacing "this centre" in Ulysses's statement with "this earth," the script directs viewers to supply the well-remembered lines long associated with "an insular vision of a total and sovereign England" (Maley and Tudeau-Clayton 10):

> This fortress built by Nature for herself
> Against infection and the hand of war,
> This happy breed of men, this little world,
> This precious stone set in the silver sea,
> Which serves it in the office of a wall,
> Or as a moat defensive to a house,
> Against the envy of less happier lands;
> This blessed plot, this earth, this realm, this England.
> (2.1.43–50)

Both the explicitly quoted passage from *Troilus and Cressida* and the ghosted lines from *Richard II* appear in dramatic contexts that undermine the sureness of those virtues and the assertion that a Providential natural order guides and protects the British nation. John of Gaunt's idealized country falters in the face of overpowering social disease; protection of the nation might well prove pointless when the land "hath made a shameful conquest of itself" (2.1.66). Invoked just at the moment that the British electorate voted to sever its ties with the EU, the cliffs locate this particular strain of Shakespearean history within an isolationist national self-conception.[5] The camera rushing over the channel in view of the cliffs shorthands anxieties about a very real "invasion" of displaced persons and refugees crossing the seas at peril and trudging across Europe to seek asylum during 2015 and 2016 when the series was made and aired. Such imagery conjures the threat of pollution from outside and obfuscates Britain's own invasionary strategies in the second Iraq War, incursions that dominoed into the refugee crisis a decade later.[6]

The out-sized rhetoric and fear-mongering of the Brexit campaign muted such facts, but a resistant reading of the *Troilus and Cressida* quotation also troubles the national and racial self-protection implied by the cliffs. The tangled referentiality of this opening unspools into contradictory strands that expose problems inherent within nation-making. The prologue points the alert viewer to Shakespeare's adaptation of the Trojan War myth—a conflict that could be described as the urtext of East/West violence, a constitutive binary central to the final propaganda push in the run-up to the Brexit referendum. Furthermore, in an irony perhaps unintended, the passage's speaker, Ulysses, and his Greek compatriots do not defend a well-ordered homeland but rather have invaded and will destroy Troy, the civilization from which mythic Britain claimed lineage as sons and daughters of Aeneas's descendent Brut. In that context, the quoted passage's praise of order rings hollow since it frames Ulysses's destructive plans for Troy and confuses where sympathies should lie—with the Greek invaders or the Trojan defenders. In addition, when Ulysses claims at the end of this homily, "Troy in our weakness stands, not in her strength" (1.3.137), he not only directs attention to the fictional and fluctuating binaries that justify conflict but also to the schisms within national groups that complicate shared goals. That these foundational myths and binary oppositions only thinly paper over an all-too-common human tendency to self-destruction is underscored by the status of the fallen Troy as mythic origin point for Britain.[7] Given the vexed role played by Troy's modern-day homeland, Turkey, in the Vote Leave propaganda, *The Hollow Crown* deployment of Ulysses's speech offers both conservative bulwark reinforcement (beware disorder from outside) *and* resistant deconstruction (beware of internal self-harm and bigotry).

The persuasive aural and visual language of the incipit, however, cuts short those contrary reverberations. Despite the hermeneutical instability of the quoted lines, the camera movement in the episode's opening and the cliffs themselves persist in labeling pollution from the outside as the great national threat. The confused referentiality of *I Henry VI, Troilus and Cressida*, and *Richard II* speaks through the problematic signification of the cliffs. Their whiteness codes dangerously as metonym for concepts of racial purity, what Ali Rattansi has called Britain's "mythical white-island-race self-image" (119). As representations of inviolability, the cliffs embody an impenetrability that reads as sexual purity. The heated Brexit campaigning intensified debate over the very things traditionally emblematized by these images and underscored the non-neutrality of geography, especially when the porousness of such iconic landscape was the very thing contested by Vote Leave. In this context, *The Wars of the Roses* mobilizes the persistent icon of British isolation and national purity, the White Cliffs of Dover, and weds that imagery to the national poet.

The Hollow Crown: The Wars of the Roses concludes its interpolated prologue by implying a causal question as relevant in the twenty-first century as when Shakespeare first wrote. The episode opts to edit the *Troilus and Cressida* quotation to finish with, "untune that string, / And hark what discord follows." Thus, *Henry VI, Part I* begs the question, "Who 'untunes' the string?" Is it the child-king Henry VI, his chief advisor and uncle, the Duke of Gloucester, the French Joan de Pucelle, the immigrant Queen Margaret, or the rebellious Richard Plantagenet, Duke of York? In partial answer to that question, the prologue's camera follows a medieval messenger on horseback as he jumps a rosebush hedge of red and white flowers while the orchestral music crescendos and the title appears, *The Hollow Crown, The Wars of the Roses, Henry VI Part I.* Not until the Act One, Scene One funeral of Henry V concludes does the viewer learn that the galloping messenger atop the cliffs brings news of England's losses on the European mainland. Thus, the question implied by the opening gathers precision: who, then, bears responsibility for the territorial losses on the European continent? Given the pressure of the looming Brexit vote, the play's reference to lost European territories reverberates with the possibility of reduced economic influence and status in the wake of a Vote Leave success. Though Shakespeare's *Henry VI* plays offer up as explanation external forces—the French—who might "untune" the English national hymn, those same plays illustrate repeatedly that internal strife, jealousies, and power disequilibriums catalyze the York and Lancaster wars. The lessons of Shakespearean history applied to the Brexit context would suggest that self-sabotaging racism targeting darker-skinned refugees compelled a vote harmful to national and individual self-interest while the root causes of unrest and political dissatisfaction could be found within internecine conflict and untended economic and social policy failures. Though the series that follows points to internal strife as culpable for England's wounds, the opening simultaneously accesses a raft of references similar to those unleashed and operationalized by the Vote Leave campaign. The nation's fortress mentality, the very thing highlighted with nostalgia by the series prologue, could very well spell the further waning of a post-imperial Britain.

Margaret of Anjou, Refugee and Alien Invader

Nonetheless, *The Hollow Crown*'s casting and treatment of Margaret of Anjou offers an escape route to avoid the rigorous self-correction demanded by the Brexit moment. The *Wars of the Roses* conflation of the *Henry VI* plays first characterizes Margaret of Anjou as frightened war refugee and at-risk object of violent desires, but over the course of the narrative, she transforms into the civilization-destroying Helen of Troy alluded to by the play's intertextual references. In its portrayal of Margaret, the series toggles between sympathy for her as a displaced person and fear of her disruptive potentiality within white England; as the plotting advances, her status as black female and alien outsider cancels out occasional glimmers of humane fellow-feeling. Shakespeare's drama invites comparison between Helen of Troy and Margaret of Anjou, and the BBC performance replicates the ambiguity of the ancient woman's representation as both victim of larger forces that exceed her control and a culpable manipulator of the power dynamics. Mihoko Suzuki characterizes the Homeric Helen's doubleness as both "goddesslike beauty and scourge of war" (16) for the soldiers gathered in Ilium. Subsequent "translations" of the Homeric figure oscillate between those poles, often blaming Helen for masculine patterns of "self-generating and self-sustaining war":

> Homer thus reveals the process through which men make sense of the divisions of experience and affirm community among themselves (even across battlelines) by scapegoating Helen, the female Other, and by reducing her to an emblem to which they assign a double meaning.
>
> (16)

Jean E. Howard and Phyllis Rackin stress that, like Helen, Shakespeare's Margaret serves as a scapegoat for social and political disorder, "the first tetralogy's most sustained example of the danger which ambitious and sexual women pose to English manhood and to English monarchy" (82). As Suzuki has shown,

Homer's literary heirs, including Shakespeare, have recycled Helen's doubleness in their own narratives of imperial power.

The plays of Henry VI craft Margaret not only to echo Homer's Helen but also her literary descendants, particularly Vergil's Dido and Juno. At one point when chiding her husband, Henry VI, Margaret compares herself to Dido listening to the tales of Aeneas as reported by Ascanius:

> How often have I tempted Suffolk's tongue
> (The agent of thy foul inconstancy)
> To sit and [witch] me, as Ascanius did
> When he to madding Dido would unfold
> His father's acts commenc'd in burning Troy!
> (*II Henry VI* 3.2.114–118)

In Dido, Margaret figures herself as another refugee, Vergil's Phoenician who seeks shelter in North Africa and undertakes rule over Carthage. Of course, the Vergilian reference goes wrong in a number of ways. Though the entirety of this particular speech aims to berate Henry VI for heedless undervaluing of Margaret's devoted love, in truth, the phrase, "I tempted Suffolk's tongue," also alludes to the hidden desires at work between her and the courtier. Furthermore, her description of the "madding Dido" reminds the audience that the Queen of Carthage's civilizing efforts at order and justice give way to chaos once she is consumed with passion for Aeneas: "The towers she started do not rise. The young men / No longer drill or build defending ramparts / Or ports. The work stalls, halfway done" (Vergil 4.85–87). A threat to order on multiple levels, Margaret-as-Dido operates both as refugee and failed ruler who bodes ruin for her own people and who thwarts masculine imperial destiny writ large with her curses. As such, Margaret-Dido also assumes the role of Juno, the ireful goddess aiming to stall the Trojan's divine destiny to found the Roman empire. Though many of the Homeric and Trojan War references do not survive the teleplay's substantial compression, the series' interpolated *Troilus and Cressida* prologue invites intertextual reverberations that transform the representation of Margaret into a warning about the dangers of harboring darker-skinned immigrants and refugees. In *The Wars of the Roses*, depictions of Margaret replicate the doubled portrayal of Helen and her literary descendants—dramatizing both the refugee's powerlessness and the vengeful scourge of war.

As the anomalous black woman of the series, Okonedo's Margaret knits to these ancient misogynist tropes multiple racist stereotypes. The pattern of scapegoating inheres in the mythic constructions from Homer and Vergil recycled in the *Henry VI* plays; however, by casting Margaret as the only woman of color, the BBC adaptation interleaves stereotypes of black women as sexually promiscuous and implacably angry with the ancient motifs. In the context of African-American history and white supremacy in the United States, Patricia Hill Collins identifies "controlling images" or stereotypes of black women that "are designed to make racism, sexism, poverty, and the other forms of social injustice appear to be natural, normal, and inevitable parts of everyday life" (77). Though her examples derive from the particularities of black female oppression in the United States, Collins insists that, "since the images themselves are dynamic and changing, each provides a starting point for examining new forms of control that emerge in a transnational context, one where selling images has increased in importance in the global marketplace" (79). Collins argues that stereotypes of black women travel internationally and appear in media artifacts beyond American borders—an assertion confirmed regarding stereotypes of black men in the previous chapter's discussion of the magical negro image circulating through Thea Sharrock's *Henry V*. In the case of *The Hollow Crown*'s Queen Margaret, she too easily fills the controlling image Collins identifies as the "Jezebel," "a woman whose sexual appetites are at best inappropriate and, at worst, insatiable" (91). Melissa V. Harris-Perry traces these stereotypes of black women to the racist pseudo-science of the eighteenth and nineteenth centuries that fueled the transatlantic slave trade and justified the sexual exploitation of black females in British slave-owning colonies and on the plantations of the American South: "sexual lasciviousness was a deliberate characterization that excused both profit-driven and casual sexual exploitation of black women" (56). Discussing the case of Saartjie Baartman, the so-called "Hottentot Venus" exhibited in Piccadilly Circus, Harris-Perry explains the "scientific discourse," that "Black women were seen as physiologically and anatomically different. Their rampant sexuality was easily discerned in their misshapen and exaggerated sexual organs" (58). This preserved white women as the vessels of racial and sexual purity and exonerated white men for their sexual exploitation of black women: "The myth of black women as lascivious, seductive, and insatiable was a way of reconciling the forced public exposure and commoditization of black women's bodies with the Victorian ideals of women's modesty and fragility" (55). Though predatory white masculinity so obviously violated the integrity of slave family units, the myth of the hypersexual black female recast that dynamic into one where the rapacious desires of black women were incendiary to white domesticity. In the BBC production, a second dominant stereotype of black women, the "Sapphire," is mobilized by the casting of Okonedo as Margaret, "one that characterizes them as shrill, loud, argumentative, irrationally angry, and verbally abusive" (Harris-Perry 87).[8] Harris-Perry demonstrates the long-lasting imprint of these constructs on social policy and in popular culture well into the twenty-first century. Set up from her first textual characterization as a disrupter of English continuity, Margaret of Anjou, played by a woman of color in an otherwise almost entirely white cast, triggers these familiar racial stereotypes and becomes in the context of 2015 and 2016 English paranoia, a black war refugee turned vengeance-seeking destroyer of hearth and home.

Margaret's first appearance on camera during a night-time attack on Angiers establishes visual motifs to be repeated and embellished as her representation unfolds over the three films, ones that rotate between Margaret as powerless victim of war and as knowing threat to peaceful English domesticity. The series immediately aligns her visually with the English enemy, Joan de Pucelle (Laura Frances-Morgan), by crosscutting between the capture of Joan, attired in white nightdress, and Margaret (similarly clothed in white shift with one shoulder exposed) who cowers as the English soldiers invade her father's keep.[9] The crosscutting and wardrobe choices twin these two disruptive Frenchwomen, as in so many productions (including the previously discussed Michael Boyd cycle for the Royal Shakespeare Company), and predict that, despite Joan's imminent demise, Margaret will continue the shepherd-maid's loyal advocacy for French sovereignty and defiance of English rule. While battle is waged in the castle bailey, Shakespeare's Suffolk, renamed in the films as "Somerset" (Ben Miles), proceeds down an interior corridor, bloody sword forward, approaching his, as yet, unseen quarry. Before revealing Margaret to her soon-to-be paramour, Somerset, the camera displays her upraised dagger; underlining her association with the bellicose Joan, this initial approach to Margaret depicts her as disembodied instrument of violence. After Somerset easily deflects the dagger, the camera then reveals Margaret with long, loosely curled hair down, her body bathed in overhead, bluish-white light and positioned at the end of Somerset's extended sword. Despite severe edits to the "seduction" scene of Shakespeare's text (*I Henry VI* 5.3), the teleplay preserves Somerset's twice-repeated description of Okonedo's Margaret as "fair." A more self-reflective script might have adjusted that racially coded term of physical beauty to language of praise not so steeped in the subtext of white supremacy. As Kim F. Hall establishes, the fair/dark binary in the early modern period, "not only served aesthetic purposes but supported an ideology that still continues to serve the interests of white supremacy and male hegemony" (4). Hall points out that the early modern discourses of fairness also "most often refer to the appearance or moral states of women," and thus the teleplay's maintenance of the epithet, despite hundreds of lines deleted and archaic words substituted, taps into that deeply racialized moral rubric (9). Nonetheless, the production casts a multi-ethnic actor with little thought to how the text's racist language should be reconsidered as it resonates through the semiotics of a non-white body on screen.[10] Thus, from her first moments in the episode, Okonedo's Margaret signifies as disempowered war prize and as latent, immoral threat to "right" order.[11] As Harris-Perry explains, the black woman is always already both—at-risk, disempowered property and tempting but destructive sexual agent. Repeatedly in the series, Margaret's vulnerability as outsider is strongly overtaken by her status as threat. Certainly, the play text scripts these competing and contradictory aspects of Margaret's characterization, but they acquire problematic overtones when enacted by a singular woman of color and in the context of a twenty-first-century Europe riven by the debate over non-white asylum-seekers and war refugees.

In the adaptation of *I Henry VI,* set dressing, background action, and shot selection combine to gesture towards the trade in women older than Homeric storytelling, and, as the skin color of Okonedo may silently remind viewers, typical of the exploitation of African women. After the castle invasion ends successfully for the English, the scene that unfolds depicts the winning soldiers gathering plunder for transport. A long shot shows Margaret's father, the defeated and guarded Reignier, Duke of Anjou (David Troughton), not on the walls of the castle as indicated in many modern editions (stage directions dating from the 1623 folio) but rather seated at a table littered with broken crockery and disordered linens. A midshot foregrounds a pile of plate and candles, and films the two white men—Somerset and Anjou—bargaining over Margaret's body as she stands between them, eyes cast down; her nightdress falls even further down her left arm and chest than in the previous scene—stressing her bodily vulnerability. Because even her father is cast as white, the optics of the scene harken to the long history in which the bodies of darker-skinned women constitute a trade in flesh between white men. As Emily MacLeod rightly observes regarding this scene and its visual framing, "The image of a woman of colour being haggled over as an object of sale is disturbing," (158) and results, in part, from what, "the film-makers want to leave untheorised, namely the racial identity of the actors" (155). MacLeod continues,

> The camera connects our "looking" at Okonedo with the objects surrounding her, emphasising her status as an object as well. The choreography of these objects…the spoils of war, links them prosthetically to the black, female body that they are deliberately placed beside.
>
> (158)

The similitude between Margaret and the material booty of war is visually and aurally stressed throughout the scene thanks to the continual clanking of the soldiers who amass war prizes in the richly decorated space. That she, like the ancient Helen, functions as the *time* forming male identity and power emerges in Suffolk's gloating reflections at the close of Shakespeare's *1 Henry VI* text:

> Thus Suffolk hath prevail'd, and thus he goes,
> As did the youthful Paris once to Greece,
> With hope to find the like event in love,
> But prosper better than the Troyan did.
> Margaret shall now be Queen, and rule the King;
> But I will rule both her, the King, and realm.
>
> (5.5.103–108)

As a new Paris, Suffolk ignores the ill omen he invokes, aiming to "prosper better" even as he deploys the tactics of theft and seizure so fateful to the Trojans. Shakespeare's Margaret will transmute this humiliating moment into a goad to consolidate power and seek vengeance, a causal connection the adaptations underscore by repeating filmic motifs from this initial scene. This early representation of Margaret as refugee from war and patriarchal pawn creates sympathy for the vulnerable woman. However, the arc of the series transforms this trauma into motivation for her monomaniacal revenge.

To stress the threat posed by Margaret's bloody instincts, the film first establishes the York nuclear family as an admirable model of unified interdependencies, loyalty, and affection contrary to the woman-on-top dynamic of Henry VI's marriage to Margaret. The casting also makes this contrast into one which elevates the racial purity of the Yorks against the dysfunction of the interracial marriage between Okonedo's Margaret and the white Henry VI played by Tom Sturridge who is also seventeen years younger than his on-screen wife (this despite the fact that the historical Henry VI was approximately nine years older than Margaret of Anjou). As the Duke of York (Adrian Dunbar) nurses grievances and ambitions, the film reassigns portions of his deliberative soliloquy (*II Henry VI* 1.1.214–59) to his wife Cecily (who does not appear in the Shakespearean text at this plot juncture). In the film, the husband and wife sit side-by-side at the hearth of the castle's hall, debating action and watching two of their sons practice sword play. On the one hand, the decision to introduce Cecily (Lucy Robinson) endeavors to mitigate the relentless masculinity of these plays, what Phyllis Rackin has described as the genre "least hospitable to women" ("Women's" 73). On the other hand, this York model of idealized and domesticated femininity simultaneously advances an instructive contrast to the disruptive power of Margaret. Cecily functions as a trusted partner, assuming some of the duties of the Kingmaker Warwick, as she "advises" her husband. The politics of gender representation come into even sharper focus when the film cuts from this depiction of home life to a torchlit castle corridor in which Somerset and Margaret flirt in the shadows. The disruptive passions of Margaret in contrast to Cecily soon find further reinforcement in a series of crosscut scenes that shuttle between the murder of Henry VI's Lord Protector, Gloucester (played by the *Downton Abbey* favorite, Hugh Bonneville), and Queen Margaret's adulterous liaison in Somerset's bed. This editing choice silently telegraphs the murderous repercussions of Margaret's hypersexuality and ratchets up the moral peril since the target of her dangerous desires is the beloved patriarch, the Earl of Grantham of the six-season ITV series. Episode one of *The Wars of the Roses* concludes with Act Five, Scene One of *II Henry VI* in which York presents himself for the throne with, "Here is a hand to hold a sceptre up" (5.1.102). For its closing images, the film cuts from court to York's arrival home, joyously calling out, "Cecily," and hailing his four sons before the screen fades to black. Thus, the first episode's parting image closes on a domestic stronghold ruled over by a mother and father who boast an abundance of children, all devoted to their singular cause. This image juxtaposes with the dysfunctions of the interracial marriage of Henry VI and Queen Margaret in which the hawkish and promiscuous French queen overmatches the weak and youthful monarch. Bookended with episode one's prolegomenon from *Troilus and Cressida*, these contrasting family units posit the non-white Okonedo's Margaret as the dissonant agent who untunes the "string" from which discord follows.

The Trojan War reference manifests again in *The Wars of the Roses: Henry VI, Part Two* staging of the Duke of York's demise, which invokes Vergil's depiction of Helen in the flaming city and harkens back to the heroism of valiant Hector. A crucial description of York's death excised for the teleplay may nonetheless have provoked the setting and lighting choices that transform the deaths of York and his youngest son Rutland into a Night of Troy re-enactment. The text's post-hoc description of York's death imagines the would-be claimant to the throne as a Hector of his people: "Environed he was with many foes, / And stood against them, as the hope of Troy / Against the Greeks that would have ent'red Troy" (*III Henry VI* 2.1.50–52). The description continues, "By many hands your father was subdu'd, / But only slaught'red by the ireful arm / Of unrelenting Clifford and the queen" (*III Henry VI* 2.1.56–58). In the "hope of Troy," the passage borrows language associated with Homer's Hector, and in "ireful arm," the speaker glances at both Homer's raging Achilles and Vergil's implacable Dido and Juno. The *Hollow Crown* adaptation deletes this particularly freighted literary embellishment of York as doomed hero defending his homeland but opts to literalize the references to the Night of Troy in profoundly vexed ways, revisiting the initial presentation of Margaret defeated and captive in her own home. The series creatives retool the written text and craft a *mise-en-scène* to replay anxieties of invasion in strongly affective detail, amplifying episode one's rushing camera movement across the English Channel and up the cliffs. Historically, York and Rutland both die at the Battle of Wakefield, but as *The Wars of the Roses* expands the play text's embedded Trojan references, they perish in a night-time assault on their home, Sandal Castle (filmed at Haddon Hall). This invasion involves color-coding not just because of the roiling Brexit controversies but also due to the complexion of Okonedo's Queen Margaret—the darker-skinned Helen whose "beauty, terrible beauty" brings down a civilization.

Through Okonedo's costuming in this scene, the series once again triggers a reference to the third-millennial debate over British multiculturalism, integration, and, specifically, Muslim religious and cultural practices. In previous scenes (in the throne room, for example), Queen Margaret wears a peaked, medieval *hennin* swathed in gauzy fabric. However, as the scene unfolds at the York home, Margaret has traded her *hennin* for a black, crown-topped and tightly fitting veil that looks suspiciously like a *hijab*—the emblem of Muslim faith profoundly contested in the so-called liberal West. The well-known "*l'affaire foulard*" in France, for example, saw "public officials and institutions that supposedly champion women's emancipation" oppose Muslim communities of faith by "suppressing the practice of veiling" in schoolgirls (Benhabib, *The Claims* 94). Seyla Benhabib explains that the range of clothing items worn by Muslim women—*chador, burqa, hijab, niqab*—are conflated in the Western eye, "assum[ing] the function of crucial symbols of complex negotiations between Muslim religious and cultural identities and Western cultures" (*The Claims* 95). Valluvan's critique of resurgent nationalism in the UK highlights the role played by a disingenuous white European outcry over Muslim misogyny, "in affirming the non-integrated status of the minority ethnic subject" (*The Clamour* 74).[12] Margaret's highly charged headwear, the *hijab*, aligns her visually with the Muslim minority in the UK and appears just at the pivotal moment in the episode when the outsider-queen commits an act of domestic terrorism—invading the York home and murdering two of its male members.

To heighten the affective impact of Margaret's aggression, the Night of Troy sequence begins with a return to the York nuclear family as an idealized gendered and racialized hierarchy from which all order flows. Set at the half-light of dinner, the textual material of *III Henry VI,* Act One, Scene Two takes place primarily in the hall of a medieval castle featuring a centrally positioned dining table, a setting that should remind viewers of the flame-lit hall in which Reignier bargained away Margaret in episode one. In the York home, behind the patriarchal head of table hangs a large tapestry of the house emblem, an embroidered white rose. The textual material in which York's sons conspire with their father occurs at the table with all the family members seated and the Duchess Cecily positioned opposite her husband. An overhead shot reveals the careful symmetry of the table with parents at either end and four siblings seated opposite one another (two on each side) in a warm, candlelit ambience. Edits to the text of this scene stress the righteous position of a father who will not heed his sons' urging to violate his solemn word and seize the throne. The mother, Cecily, who cannot speak as she has no lines in the original Shakespearean text, communicates with her soup spoon; the spoon reacts (stopping midair) to her son Richard's suggested oath-breaking at "Then seeing 'twas he that made you to depose, / Your oath, my lord, is vain and frivolous" (1.2.26–27). In response, York shouts (punctuated by the clunk of a goblet on the table), "Richard, enough," thus establishing a moral rectitude not necessarily in keeping with the remainder of the text; lines omitted from the film but present in Shakespeare's text reveal York consolidating support in order to pursue actively the crown: "While you are thus employ'd, what resteth more, / But that I seek occasion how to rise" (*III Henry VI* 1.2.44–45). In the televisual film, immediately after York chastises Richard, a servant enters to alert the family that Queen Margaret "intends here to besiege you in your house." To underscore that the domestic world is under assault, the teleplay has replaced the text's "besiege you in your castle" with the more evocative phrase, "besiege you in your house." In the text, when York hears the news, he replies, "She shall not need, we'll meet her in the field" (1.2.65) and proceeds to exit in order to assemble his troops. However, *The Wars of the Roses* opts to stage the conflict within the home. The York family members cluster at one of the leaded windows to assess the invasion force and "pose" for a last portrait of the domestic unit about to be robbed of its oldest and youngest members: the father occupies the foreground with all four sons around him and his deeply shadowed wife hovers in the background with her arm around her youngest, Rutland. This not only heightens the stakes for an audience unfamiliar with the history or play text, but also links the moment to Margaret's earlier scene of humiliation and thus implicitly motivates her vengeance. Significantly, the fact of her skin color renders Queen Margaret the non-white woman who demolishes the sacred and racially pure York family.

The Wars of the Roses hastens the arrival of the Queen and her men so that when the messenger reports, "She is hard by," this translates into an almost immediate attack, one that echoes Margaret's initial representation as refugee from the violence that devastates domestic safety. The family gathered at its board in the great hall visually revisits the earlier scene in which the defeated Reignier sits at the hall table and sells off his daughter to Somerset and the English monarch; just as Margaret experienced the violation of a night-time raid of her home, so now she rains down terror on the domestic world of her political rivals. Choosing to film both scenes at night and within the halls of two great homes, *The Wars of the Roses* builds a causal link explaining the refugee-turned-avenger. But for *The Hollow Crown* Margaret, suffering and vulnerability have not fueled sympathy for others who also endure violence; instead, that earlier scene, visually echoed in the York home, justifies her revenge. This representation again corresponds with aspects of the angry black woman stereotype described by Harris-Perry, "The brash, independent, hostile black woman rarely shows vulnerability or empathy" (88). By presenting the original violation of Margaret's home at night, the series establishes a visual vocabulary for invasion repeated and avenged in the second episode's depiction of York's death. His death thus becomes the consequence of the benevolent welcome given the penniless Margaret of Anjou—skin color difference intensifies this oblique component of the filming and immediate airing context.

The only person of color in this sequence, Okonedo's fierce medieval queen becomes the brown-skinned violator of a visually fetishized white family in the sacred space of home. Where once she arrived as a refugee and benefited from offered shelter, now she wields unexpected power, disruptive to white families as surely as the stereotyped hypersexual and pathologically angry black woman of Harris-Perry's analysis. Thinking first of saving his family from such rage, York shouts urgent extra-textual instructions, "Richard and Edmund with thy mother fly," and "Go Richard, look to thy mother," while Duchess Cecily presses, "Come son," though she will ride away without any of her offspring. As the York men defend their home, Margaret strides with torch aloft through the melee and into the hall to the accompaniment of minor key low brasses, drums, and agitated violins in recurring arpeggios. Enraged, she hurls from the table the remains of the dinner—cloth, service wear, and food, the symbols of York aristocratic hospitality. When Margaret approaches the Yorkist white rose tapestry, the camera angle cuts to overhead. This overhead shot looks down on the chaos engineered by the warrior Margaret just as that same shot angle looked down moments previously on the symmetry of the York family meal observed with "degree, priority, and place… in all line of order." The repeated angles and juxtaposed moments form a heavily moralizing pair that tap into the white/black, good/evil binary, a binary already presented in the play text's language and further heightened by Margaret's characterization.[13] Closeups of the white rose tapestry fringe catching alight and the face of a satisfied Queen Margaret connect the Queen's pyromancy to the city of Troy set ablaze on the night of its destruction. *The Wars of the Roses* crosscuts this emblematic moment with the death of Rutland at Clifford's hands; like Helen of Troy, Margaret not only wreaks havoc on the city but also cuts short the promise of a younger generation. The semiotic overflow gathers substantial moral weight as the references reach back to Homer and Vergil and to Christianity's codification of black and white as emblems of purity and pollution. These freighted echoes culminate in the Death of York which weds the ancient, Christian, and racist tropes vilifying Margaret throughout the series.

In his final moments, York telegraphs the imperiled Priam as well as the sacrificed Christ defeated by the adulterous, enraged, and evil Margaret. A cornered Duke of York watches with tears in his eyes as his battlements flame and the cruciform body of his dead son Rutland lies before him. His dehumanizing epithet for Margaret and his moral assessment emerge in this final confrontation with Queen Margaret:

> Thou art as opposite to every good
> As the antipodes are unto us,
> Or as the south to the septentrion.
> O tiger's heart wrapp'd in a woman's hide!
> (*III Henry VI* 1.4.134–137)

Here York attaches a good and evil moral rubric to his contest for political ascendency, one that ignores his own plotting against a divinely ordained king of England. Both the moral assessment, "opposite to every good," and the bestial language of "tiger's heart" resonate problematically when addressed to Okonedo's Margaret, the lone black female appearing in all three films of the second series. The adaptation intensifies the moral contrast by replacing the famous paper crown which Queen Margaret presents to York with one made of thorns fashioned from a conveniently proximate white rose bush. She sadistically shoves the crown of thorns on York who groans in Christ-like agony. Just as she stabs York, *The Hollow Crown* makes another textual adjustment that returns to black female sexual stereotypes; Margaret whispers, "Here's for beloved Somerset," instead of the text's, "And here's to right our gentle-hearted king" (1.4.176). The teleplay substitutes for the king's name, that of Margaret's beheaded lover, and also distances her from a justifiably moral cause—defending her monarch and husband. By deleting the infinitive "to right" and replacing it with the preposition "for," the teleplay Margaret dedicates York's death to her lover rather than frames it as an act of moral correction. The celebrity intertext associated with Dunbar's York reinforces Margaret's perfidy; just as she earlier colluded in the killing of *Downton Abbey*'s patriarch, here she executes the upright anti-corruption investigator, Dunbar's Superintendent Ted Hastings, of the BBC's long-running crime procedural, *Line of Duty* (2012–2021). In the death of the York patriarch, the various myths, moral rubrics, and stereotypes circulating through the play text, teleplay, and black body of Okonedo come into sharpest relief.

The Outsider's Timely Utility

The Wars of the Roses: Richard III similarly unleashes troubling racial stereotypes as suited to Margaret's marginalized position in a world ruled by the Yorkist heir Edward IV, stereotypes unacknowledged or inadequately managed by the creative team. However, at the same time, the anxieties about the external threat to white hegemonic power centered on Margaret take a strategic turn and moral reversal in the third film. As Margaret becomes essential to plotting revenge against the usurping Richard of Gloucester, the film shifts its dynamic of "in" and "out" onto Richard III who adopts the Brexit-like rhetoric of fortress Britain; by the time of Bosworth, he has become the mouthpiece of English insularity and isolation with a young Richmond the flag-bearer of national multiculturalism. However, this vilification of the Vote Leave ethos by association with the policies and rhetoric of Richard III does not last once Richmond accedes as Henry VII and peaceful coexistence includes a white populace only. As her instrumentality reaches an end, Okonedo's Margaret returns to her outsider position, ruling as Queen Death over the corpse-strewn field of Bosworth, a parting image that, sadly, telegraphs persistent unease with Britain's non-white citizenry and immigrants.

Racial troping established by the first two films of *The Wars of the Roses* continues with Margaret's first appearance in *Richard III*. Literally haunting the ascendant Yorks as a prophet-seer (1.3), the visibly aged Margaret confronts Keeley Hawes's mysteriously ageless Queen Elizabeth and courtiers in a room filled exclusively by Caucasian actors. As conduit to the unseen world of vengeance, Shakespeare's Margaret already functions within the *Richard III* play text as liminal—operating between the worlds of the living and the dead; the film further isolates her by virtue of skin color, costuming, and hair and make-up treatment. Positioned as the disruptive and aggrieved antagonist to the Yorks, she appears with hair disheveled, skin mottled, and clothes distressed to prophesy the short-lived triumph of Edward IV's reign. As Margaret proceeds from one enemy to the next, uttering maledictions and "showing" the future in her magical mirror (which the editor intercuts to reveal), musical scoring renders her powers other-worldly. The intercut analeptic and proleptic shots seen through Margaret's mirror appear as female voices hum an ominously suspended single note that occasionally wavers up a step on the scale, punctuated by portentous bell-ringing. The sustained note increases in volume, palpably hanging in the air, when Margaret holds the mirror in front of a given target. Both televisual strategies—the interpolations in the mirror and the soundtrack—reinforce the text's positioning of Margaret as capable of harnessing threatening unseen powers. Once again, the visual outsider, the black woman, promises to disrupt the sanctum of white power. Indeed, as filmed for the series, this confrontation takes place immediately outside the sickroom of a dying King Edward IV. Here the visible fact of Okonedo's racial identity reinforces her provocative otherness, which the episode fails to counterbalance with more thorough-going diversification of parts. When the mourning mother confronts her enemies with the image of her dead son Edward, Margaret raises a wooden plaque worn around her neck to reveal a visibly pale-faced young man; thus, even when she invokes the kin of her own body, his skin color alienates her from visible belonging.

Much as, historically, white feminism only shoulders the burdens of black and brown women when it might prove expedient, so thanks to the color-casting in *Richard III,* the white York women appear to gravitate to Margaret's numinous strength only in a moment of political and familial loss.[14] When Richard's crimes push the former queen, Elizabeth, to the margins along with her grieving mother-in-law (Judi Dench), the two Yorkist women require access to the occult powers of their enemy Margaret, transforming the black ex-queen into a thing of convenient use for the two white women and offering her, briefly, a new circle of belonging. The film transplants Margaret's lessons in cursing (4.4) to the pathos-laden graveside of the two princes, making shot selection and editing choices that highlight the use to which Margaret will, for a time, be put. A rich symphonic chordal progression in minor key mourns the dead princes and their twin cross-marked mounds. As Elizabeth declares, "Ah, who hath any cause to mourn but we" (4.4.34), this music gives way, and the crack of a twig signals the approach of the physically distressed Margaret. Elizabeth's self-pitying and exclusionary phrase rings dissonantly as it coincides with the appearance of the black and bereaved Margaret, inadvertently reminding the acute viewer of the ways in which white feminism has often ignored the struggles of black women in its quest for equality with white men.[15] Despite the self-absorbed insensitivity of Elizabeth's lament, Margaret kneels at the graves with feeling and what might telegraph as empathy and a qualified "belonging" as the suspended notes of the earlier female chorus return with her.

Both substantial reordering and deletion of the scene's lines and shot selection work to soften Margaret's *schadenfreude* and build a temporary alliance between the wronged women. For example, the teleplay quietly deletes the vindictive, early asides: "Hover about her; say that right for right / Hath dimm'd your infant morn to aged night" (4.4.15–16); "Plantagenet doth quit Plantagenet, / Edward for Edward pays a dying debt" (4.4.20–21). Her condemnation of the Duchess of York as bearer into the world of Richard III likewise is substantially reduced so that especially harsh passages, such as the following, disappear:

> O upright, just, and true-disposing God,
> How do I thank thee that this carnal cur
> Preys on the issue of his mother's body,
> And makes her pew-fellow with others' moan!
> (4.4.55–58)

The teleplay heavily trims other lengthier vaunts so that particularly pointed lines are deleted such as Margaret's accusation of Queen Elizabeth: "Thou didst usurp my place, and dost thou not / Usurp the just proportion of my sorrow? / Now thy proud neck bears half my burthen'd yoke" (4.4.109–111). Such line deletion necessarily occurs when four plays become three televisual films with a stated thematic focus on Richard III's rise to power. More than simply expedient, however, the cuts to Act Four, Scene Four suggest a deeper empathy might just be possible between the three women all suffering at the hand of Richard. These adjustments assuredly rescue Margaret temporarily from the entrenched stereotype of the angry, unfeeling black woman incapable of compassion—a welcome adjustment to the dominant notes of her characterization in the series. This short-lived affinity between York and Lancastrian women does also facilitate an extra-diegetic feature of the series as showcase of great British stars—it centrally positions Dench's Cecily, Duchess of York as benevolent moral agent—a fact stressed by shot selection and editing.

Shot selection underscores the shifting affinities between the three women and temporarily endeavors to erase the dangerous otherness of Margaret through alignment with the Yorkist women and Dench's matriarch in particular. The camera cuts five times to long shots that behold the three women in careful spatial relationship to one another; filmed from a slightly lower angle, the long shot first shows the two York women on the extreme left and Margaret on the extreme right in a tableau that typifies their continuing antipathy, an opposition stressed by the vertical lines of the trees quite literally dividing the visual space between the women. Edits to this tableau chart their changing relationships and interdependencies over the scene. As Dench's Duchess of York pleads, "O Harry's wife, triumph not in my woes!" (4.4.59–60), she moves closer to the ex-queen so that the next long shot tableau positions Dench dead center, her significance reinforced by the tree that ascends vertically immediately behind her and up through the middle of the shot. This titan of English stage and film thus moves to serve as a bridge uniting the women—Hawes and Okonedo still opposing one another at the extreme left and right of the frame as the lesson in cursing begins. At last, exerting the force of her matriarchal role both within and outside of the play text, Dench's Duchess reaches out to Elizabeth, who takes her hand, and then, with firm resolution, to Margaret who pauses briefly with hands clenched. The camera cuts to a close-up that shows Margaret opening her right hand and slowly reaching to the Duchess's immediately followed by her left hand's movement to Elizabeth as they close the scene in a circle of mourning and malediction. The suspended vocalizations increase in volume to link these curses to the earlier moment, but only Margaret closes her eyes and tilts her head upward in a trance-like manner—she remains the vital conduit for these women to the powers of the unseen world and serves an essential function in their pursuit of vengeance.

To stress this coalition of aggrieved women, the adaptation opts to include Margaret in Act Four, Scene Four's confrontation of King Richard. In the film's variation, the three women wait, like *Macbeth*'s weird sisters, to intercept Richard on his way to battle, with the Duchess foremost followed by Elizabeth and then Margaret. Though she has no lines in Shakespeare's text, Margaret joins in with "A husband and a son, thou owest me," as the three, led by the Duchess, call the king to account for his misdeeds. The hovering curse soundscape associated with Margaret transfers in this scene (with added orchestral underscoring) to the Duchess as she confronts her criminal son,

Richard. This united resistance constitutes the affinity apex for the three women. Unfortunately, this bond is steadily undone by the remainder of the film which repositions Margaret as disconsolate outsider by its close. A tainted minister of retribution, she haunts the film's concluding scenes but never again operates as part of a coalition but rather as a liminal figure poised between life and death. The white bodies of Elizabeth and her young daughter can be incorporated into the newly reformed state but not that of the black Margaret.

While Margaret temporarily finds affinity with the York women and briefly belongs to their alliance of revenge, the film strategically problematizes anxieties over the alien outsider by locating those concerns in the play's titular villain in contrast to the open-armed Richmond. Reckoning with the textual Richard's isolationist rhetoric, the film attaches to the usurping and tyrannical king a Vote Leave, bunker mentality of white hegemonic power under threat. In the severely edited script, notable lines retained voice King Richard's disdain for the so-called mongrel make-up of Richmond's host:

> Remember whom you are to cope withal:
> A sort of vagabonds, rascals, and runaways,
> A scum of [Bretons] and base lackey peasants.
> (5.3.315–317)

Like Farage stirring up a Vote Leave crowd, Richard exhorts his soldiers, "Let's whip these stragglers o'er the seas again" (5.3.327), and hectors in call-and-response format: "Shall we let them enjoy our lands? Lie with our wives? Ravage our daughters" (edited from 5.3.336–337), pausing after each incendiary interrogative for loud "nays" from the soldiers. Richard's last-ditch effort to hold the throne by emphasizing the precarity of diminishing resources—"Shall we let them enjoy our lands?"—echoes strongly through the Leave campaign's claim that EU membership imperiled the financial security of the NHS at a weekly cost of the infamously fabricated £350 million. The previously discussed "Breaking Point" image of an immigrating horde full of darker-skinned men also allusively conjured the sexual violation of white women embedded in "Ravage our daughters." Of course, the Vote Leave rhetoric of Richard III's oration contrasts with the ameliorative tenor of Richmond's familiar exhortation and visibly (though lightly) multicultural army, distancing the film, its Tudor hero, the play, and Shakespeare from the nation's longstanding fortress mindset, white supremacism, and exclusionary violence.

Such vilification of the pro-Brexit tropes runs counter to the spotlighting of Margaret's threat throughout the first two films, but the thinness of this corrective move can be detected in contrasting scenes that close the series. Richmond's army features Ugandan-British actor, Ivanno Jeremiah, as Sir James Blunt, who operates as a visually prominent second to Richmond much as previously seen in the Series One *Henry V* with Paterson Joseph's York. However, this gloss of multiculturalism vanishes all too quickly in the final scenes. Though Blunt's stab unseats Richard III and provokes his final cry, "A horse, a horse!" (5.4.13), Blunt's vital service does not earn him a position in the crowd of courtiers at Richmond's coronation as Henry VII, nor does the episode script a filmed death that would easily explain his absence. Indeed, much as Margaret has provided essential access to the avenger's invisible world for the Duchess and Queen Elizabeth, Jeremiah's Blunt serves his purpose but then disappears, not to be incorporated into the gathering of white bodies celebrated by the film's penultimate scene. Though Richmond's army had included faces of color in its ranks as well as Blunt's substantial mid-range and close-up on-camera presence, not a single person of color rejoices in the union of House Lancaster and House York at the coronation inside what is meant to be the sacral space of the nation's cathedral, Westminster Abbey. As King Henry VII and Queen Elizabeth process through the nave (Hawes's dowager Queen Elizabeth now once again at the center of power looking on from the raised dais), the camera pans through the assembled crowd to show the faces of an exclusively white citizenry. Even as Richmond utters his lamentation over internecine violence that could, likewise, telegraph analogically to the contention over Brexit, civil harmony comes visibly at the price of the exclusion of non-whites.

To the credit of the series creatives, *The Wars of the Roses* does not leave this brightly lit, golden-hued celebration unalloyed. Instead, the episode cuts once again to the desaturated palette of a Bosworth Field littered with the dead and ruled over by the haggard Margaret. Once she no longer serves the York matriarch's needs, Margaret has returned to the lonely work of haunting. In contrast to Shakespeare's text, the teleplay positions Okonedo's Margaret as agent of Richard's nightmares and as a grim Queen Death at battle's end. On the eve of Bosworth, Margaret manifests as necromancer during Richard's night of troubled sleep. She startles him awake and holds forth the mirror in which appear Richard's victims, beginning with King Henry VI. Color desaturation and distortions at the edges of the picture plane that create a fish-eye effect reinforce Margaret's uncanny access to Richard's unconscious and command of the cohort of the dead she ostensibly has conjured. The final shots of Bosworth Field reinforce Margaret's role as Queen Death as the camera booms up and over Margaret centrally positioned and surrounded by corpses in a Hieronymus Bosch-like circle of death. Thus, the two actors of African descent fulfill crucial roles in the ouster of Richard but find no lasting home within the circles of white British power—Jeremiah's Blunt silently "disappeared" from Richmond's side and Okonedo's Margaret confined to the scene of carnage—highlighting the disingenuousness of Richmond's multicultural band and of the film's ever-so-light critique of Vote Leave racism by association with Richard's battleground rhetoric.

Conclusion: What Is Forgotten

But the representational problematics of *The Wars of the Roses* do not end with the question of Okonedo's race and gender as a short excursus on social class and the Brexit vote contextualizes. Sociologists have tracked the steady gutting of the British welfare state across Conservative and Labour governments alike, a strategy of defunding, privatization, and budget cuts only rendered more painful by the austerity measures that resulted from the 2008 global financial crisis. In her ethnographic examination of class and the Brexit vote, sociologist, Lisa Mckenzie, recounts the ways in which class relations were framed by Margaret Thatcher's government of the 1980s and then recalibrated by New Labour in the 1990s. The Thatcher government, "attempted to dilute class meaning with what was called 'a home owning democracy,'" just as policies targeted and undermined the community-building influence of the trade unions (S266). New Labour opted to downplay structural and institutional inequalities to shift blame directly onto those members of the working class who self-excluded from new opportunities (S270). These differing approaches, according to Mckenzie, share a similar result—alienating the working class hit hardest by deindustrialization and suffering strongly from a sense of being "left behind" in the global goods and labor markets. Mckenzie critiques dismissive attitudes towards the working classes following the EU referendum results: "The cosmopolitan middle-class reaction of shock and outrage as regards working-class Brexit voting patterns risks contributing to narratives of a 'feckless poor' that will only exacerbate further social exclusion, and class distinction" (S271S–272). Though she may discount too strongly race and xenophobia as Vote Leave factors, Mckenzie makes a case for the way in which class inequalities transcended traditional party distinctions to motivate many typically Labour-voting individuals to cast a ballot for Vote Leave, doing so as an act of defiance—"a howl of anger" (S278)—towards those in both parties who had too long neglected class inequities and, in fact, had increased income inequality through systematic policy-making and austerity measures. She admits, "Although there was an undeniable fear in these communities about 'outsiders' coming and taking what little was left, these views were directly connected to a sense of abandonment, financial struggle and political remoteness" (S276). Mckenzie closes her study with a call to "expose deep structural inequalities that are hiding in plain sight behind the cultural distinction of class prejudice" (S278). More recent data corrects aspects of the "left-behind" voter thesis since, "The proportion of people who voted Leave in the lowest social classes was just 24 per cent," and white middle-class voters in the South of England largely determined the referendum outcome (El-Enany 215).

Gargi Bhattacharyya and her co-authors offer an elaboration on these dynamics that better accounts for the interconnection between austerity economics and racism in working-class Brexit voting patterns. Cataloguing the impact of governmental neglect over decades, they explain:

> Britain has seen a massive rolling back of state spending more broadly. In particular, services administered through local government have been slashed, with an extreme impact on libraries, children's centres, youth services and support for the vulnerable, including notable cuts to services relating to domestic violence, mental health and disability support.
>
> (Bhattacharyya et al 7)

After a long period of neglect and abandonment by the welfare state, those dispossessed by such economic policies crave government action—even of the dangerously authoritarian variety:

> the moment of English nationalism that finds form through Brexit takes the disruption and disappointment of state neglect and rearticulates it as an outcome of national decline. In an echo of other English and British nationalisms, this iteration of nationalism includes a strange amalgamation of anti-elitism with a longing for authoritarianism.
>
> (61)

The well-documented neoliberal failure to reckon with the alienating impact of extreme wealth inequality on traditional Labour adherents left such voters susceptible to the alluring poison of Vote Leave's rhetoric and carefully curated bogeymen—the immigrant, the migrant, the asylum seeker, and the multi-ethnic residents already calling the small island "home."

Given the intersecting class and race struggles roiling during the years of the refugee crisis, one *Wars of the Roses* omission from the *Henry VI* plays is rather surprising. Much like Remainer strategists oblivious to the corrosive impact of economic austerity on traditional voting blocks, the adaptors of *The Wars of the Roses* opt to quietly ignore the fractious matter of social class struggle by removing from the teleplay all traces of the peasant's rebellion led by Jack Cade in *II Henry VI*. Shakespeare's depiction of the Jack Cade rebellion provides dramatic material for a consideration of class rooted in Britain's long history of resistance and protest. The tendency to scapegoat perceived others as the cause of poverty, to crave authoritarian rule as a solution to governmental neglect, and to reject intellectual elitism are all catalogued as component features of resistance in the drama. Admittedly, deleting the Jack Cade rebellion handily eliminates some chaotic absurdities embedded in the original play text but it also instantiates a pathological forgetfulness—seen previously in regards to the colonial-imperial past—once again characteristic of British nationalism. Bhattacharyya et al explain the dynamics culminating in 2016 in ways that could as easily characterize the Cade rebellion imagined four-hundred years earlier, material that, if adapted, could have spoken so pointedly to the deprivations provoking the Brexit vote:

> In the context of inequality and precarity, austerity without end, and when the state has nothing to offer except the impossible promise of security, the figures of the "gangster", the "immigrant" and the "terrorist" work their perverse magic, distorting democratic possibilities and licensing the worst kinds of authoritarianism.
>
> (13)

But rather than take time to examine Britain's history of working-class unrest and the aristocratic manipulation of that class, the series excises the rebellion entirely. Given the stated rubric determining textual cuts—that all components of plotting must center on Richard III's road to tyranny—the elimination of the Cade plot makes streamlining sense. However, as an invitation to a considered self-examination of an internally riven polity, the Cade material matters to the historiography Shakespeare crafts and constitutes. Instead, the filming repeatedly imagines the threat of external invasion as the cause of national distress, and even when, briefly, invasion in the guise of Richmond proves restorative it soon receives the golden-hued gloss that transforms an outsider and interloper into God's rightfully ordained monarch taking once again, "this long-usurped royalty" (5.5.4).

The Wars of the Roses concludes with a visually othered threat—the abject Queen Margaret who had invaded the isle's sacrosanct halls of power as a refugee-cum-terrorist—impotent and isolated among the dead. By casting Okonedo as Margaret, the Neal Street Production and BBC-branded series endeavored to improve its representation of multiethnic British people even as the definition of "British" was being dangerously narrowed by the Brexit Referendum vote. As usual, the BBC took some amount of pushback for its casting choice but not necessarily for the reasons outlined here. The usual flutter of detractors waving the flag of historical accuracy objected in print to Okonedo's enactment of the Frenchwoman's role.[16] But the solution is not to return to a mode of "genetic realism" but rather to a more thorough-going representation of the many peoples that now make up the United Kingdom (Steigerwalt 426). In a provocative reading of *King Lear* "as a discursive intervention into Brexit," Stephen O'Neill identifies ways in which,

> Shakespeare becomes a conceptual space on to which we project our desires, or through which we address ideological contradictions and the dynamics of power in our own times, or indeed find a means to efface or sublimate them in the (re)turn to the historical past.
>
> (121, 122)

O'Neill catalogues the frequency with which Gloucester's blind "leap" from the Cliffs of Dover served as a metaphor for the Brexit vote. Beyond such analogies, O'Neill calls for an exploration of how Shakespeare's play reimagined in our own historical moment "could be used more progressively through its exploration of 'unaccommodated' humans as a reminder of human rights in Europe" (O'Neill 134). Likewise, the second series of *The Hollow Crown* could have revisited Shakespearean history mindful of how its narration might serve as a more progressive "conceptual space." Unfortunately, Series Two of *The Hollow Crown* squanders an opportunity to utilize Shakespearean historiography to assert full historical subjectivity and rights of citizenship across race, gender, and class identities without reinforcing the country's tendencies to xenophobia and isolationism.

Notes

1 According to Charlie Cooper, the advertisement was "doctored" to include the sound of a woman screaming and glass breaking.
2 Leonardo Scuira stresses the falsity of the Leave Campaign's opportunistic approach: "Taking advantage of people's nationalist propensity, government representatives and eurosceptic plutocrats from private entities sought to nurture a xenophobic sentiment in the population by saying that foreigners were stealing their jobs. Although these smear allegations are an effective way of getting people to balk at EU rules, they do not reflect the reality of the situation. On the contrary, recent figures actually indicate a steady slump in the unemployment rate ever since Gordon Brown departed from Number 10 Downing Street" (113–114).
3 Votava's reading also locates the series prologue within the context of fraught Anglo-French relations as manifested throughout the history plays: "The opening visual reference to the English Channel calls attention to the ongoing Anglo-French conflict and connects it directly to the titular Wars of the Roses. The disorienting camerawork provides a kinesthetic and visceral reminder of how, in his histories, Shakespeare consistently treats Frenchness as otherness" (174).
4 This same passage appears under striking circumstances in another recent British series. In "Misadventure," (Season Two, Episode One) of the Netflix heritage drama, *The Crown*, Antony Eden (Jeremy Northam) and Harold Macmillan (Anton Lesser) debate the merits of military action in response to the Suez Canal Crisis. The scene begins with Eden remembering his *Hamlet* and uttering, "I'm afraid that when sorrows come, they come not single spies," which Macmillan finishes with, "but in battalions." Shakespeare functions as a shorthand between the two politicians—a language they share that asserts their fitness to govern and the cultural superiority of their country. Moments later in the conversation, Macmillan deploys Shakespeare's *Troilus and Cressida* as international policy: "Take but degree away, untune that string," and this time, Eden completes the thought, "and hark what discord follows." As in the case of *The Hollow Crown* series two reference, here in *The Crown*, this passage from *Troilus and Cressida* operates within a context of postcolonial unrest and upended authority.
5 Sarah Grandage confirms that John of Gaunt's speech, "carries an implicit undertone of insularity, of inward-looking and suspicion of the outsider, in the need for defence against the envy of the less fortunate" (131–132). Her study of newspaper article appropriations illustrates that the imagery corresponds with contemporary "fears of invasion and attack, in the form of immigration, bird flu or terrorism" (145).
6 Seyla Benhabib and others have noted the moral failure of culpable nations: "The United States, the United Kingdom, France are countries who are still actively militarily involved in these regions in some way or another, and they have a responsibility towards the refugee problem" (qtd. in Sierakowski).
7 Indeed, Heather James argues that Shakespeare's appropriations of the Trojan myth in his *oeuvre*, "doubt the ideological ground on which the Tudors had based their myths of political origin" (33).
8 Named the "Sapphire" after the nagging wife of the 1930s radio program and 1950s television series, *Amos 'n' Andy*, this domestic image tropes black marital discord, dramatizing the black wife's anger over her husband, "whose lack of integrity, and use of cunning and trickery provides her with an opportunity to emasculate him through her use of verbal put-downs" (Jewell 32). Though the Sapphire stereotype typically targets black men, in *The Wars of the Roses*, the inept and white Henry VI becomes an easy domestic and political object of the Sapphire-Margaret's disgust as she seeks to fire her king-husband in shared hostility towards the York family.

9 James and others have well established that Vergil's *Aeneid* signifies in the background of these early history plays. This moment in which *The Wars of the Roses* presents Margaret cowering in fright at invasion reflects Aeneas's scornful representation of Helen in his own account of the Night of Troy: "Now I was all alone there—no, I saw / Through Vesta's doorway, quiet, skulking, hidden, / Tyndareus' daughter in the glare that flames / Shed for my ranging feet and searching eyes" (2.567–570).

10 Votava notes a similar problem in the way the episode establishes the linkage between Joan and Margaret by means of the white nightdress—an emblem of their "gendered fragility" (176). Votava argues: "the episode exposes a pitfall of remaining blind to racial difference. In presenting white as a symbol of female innocence, the dressing gown engages the implicitly racialized meanings of the standard Western black/white binary," but then fails to consider how that binary shapes an understanding of the black Margaret (177).

11 Despite the filmic choices that limit her autonomy, Okonedo plays Margaret with a steely skepticism (eyes narrowed, sarcasm in her clipped words, and the occasional side-eye glance) as she gradually understands Somerset's political and sexual interest in her and discovers her own.

12 Valluvan identifies the "centrality of a putatively liberal feminist symbolism in the determining of renewed European nationalisms, a symbolism that writes itself upon the colonial script that Spivak memorialised as the project of 'white men saving brown women from brown men'" (*The Clamour* 74).

13 Anthony Barthelemy traces this binary to early Christianity: "In the Christian tradition, whiteness is desired, blackness is condemned. White is the color of the regenerated, of the saved; black is the color of the damned, the lost. This allegorical reading of white and black finds repeated expression from the earliest of Christian exegeses to the present" (3).

14 Perhaps most famously, Audre Lorde chastises the error, both moral and tactical, of white feminists who do not integrate the burdens of non-white, lesbian, and poor women into political and social reform agenda: "The failure of academic feminists to recognize difference as a crucial strength is a failure to reach beyond the first patriarchal lesson. In our world, divide and conquer must become define and empower" (42).

15 In his discussion of the complicities of white women and feminists with white supremacism, Ruben Espinosa summarizes: "If there are battles being fought and won where women's rights are concerned, those who are fighting these battles are also perpetuating anti-Blackness" (*Shakespeare* 78).

16 Földváry recounts: "As it appears from viewer comments, what most people found at odds with their general perception of the series as a whole was the historical inaccuracy of employing any coloured actor to play medieval English nobility" (111). Votava also demonstrates the inability of viewers to reconcile the authenticist medieval *mise-en-scène* with the "colorblind" casting of Okonedo, citing an unsurprising public objection from a member of UKIP: "several public commentators perceived Okonedo's casting as a deviation from the norm. Most notorious was the following tweet by UK Independence Party Councillor Christopher Wood: 'So the @BBC has given up on any kind of historical accuracy. How can Margaret of Anjou be played by Sophie Okonedo?'" (171).

5 The Disappearing Moor

Race, Authenticity, and the Nation's History in *Wolf Hall* and *Bring Up the Bodies*

"Think ye see
The very persons of our noble story
As they were living."

(*Henry VIII*)

In the "Author's Note" concluding *Wolf Hall* (2009), Hilary Mantel recognizes George Cavendish's, *Thomas Wolsey, Late Cardinal, His Life and Death* (1554–1558), as a powerful affective source both for her novel and the drama of William Shakespeare. She writes: "Its influence on Shakespeare is clear." This conviction locates Mantel's novel in an adaptative genealogy—Cavendish-Shakespeare-Mantel—and reveals her own substantial knowledge of *Henry VIII* or *All is True* (1613), Shakespeare and John Fletcher's co-authored play (though Fletcher's authorship goes unacknowledged in Mantel's note). Indebted to the history plays in their intertextual descent from *Henry VIII*, Mantel's novels acquire their own generic status as staged history in their adaptation by Mike Poulton into a two-play suite for the Royal Shakespeare Company (first produced in 2013).[1] The BBC televisual adaptation of Mantel's novels (*Wolf Hall* and *Bring up the Bodies*, 2012)—Peter Kosminsky (director) and Peter Straughan (teleplay author)—aired on BBC Two (January 2015) and on PBS in the United States (April-May 2015). Notable for its effort to maintain Mantel's deft non-linear movement across time, the series likewise displays faithfulness to a particular brand of visual and aural verisimilitude associated with the heritage film genre.[2] Though the original novels' disruption of time may undermine filmic naturalism, the series' mimetic techniques strive for significant levels of "authenticity" in on-location filming, naturally-lit interior cinematography, period-precise costuming, and musical scoring akin to that of *The Hollow Crown*, Series One and Two. Produced with scrupulous attention to the ornamental details of its Renaissance interior spaces and a determination to film at night by candlelight alone, the BBC's *Wolf Hall* jeopardized the safety of its actors and equipment in order to present a "truer" representation of lived experience in Renaissance England.

The BBC series exploits naturalistic techniques as an authorizing representational gesture and brand distinctiveness rooted in authentic history-telling even

DOI: 10.4324/9781003043065-5

though such effort at verisimilitude runs contrary to the mechanisms of omission and dilation found in Shakespeare and Fletcher's play and Mantel's own highly positional narrative of Thomas Cromwell's rise. A tension thus develops between the claims to veracity in film technique and the insistent destabilizing of historical certainty found in both the seventeenth-century play and its twenty-first century novelistic transformation by Mantel. Furthermore, in their reliance upon the history play and heritage film as authorizing stylistic guides, the BBC adaptations twin the racial codes embedded in those two genres to reinforce an exclusively white story of the English nation. The creative migration of Mantel's Cromwell narratives from novel, to stage, to televisual series reveals persistent problems with casting and racial representation in staged history and heritage filmmaking. While a troubling reference to blacking up for a masque in *Bring Up the Bodies* appears in the novel and staged adaptation, the BBC series quietly deletes that detail though it preserves other "theatricalized" masque performances from the novels and stage plays. Tracing the sanitized fate of this reference to blacking up—the disappearing moor—illustrates the BBC's recognition of racially problematic tropes but also exposes the limits of its creative imagination when conjuring an "authentic" English past. In its representational choices, the BBC adaptation denies the impact made by persons of color on the emergent English nation and insists on a dubious historical authenticity.

Ghostly echoes of and references to the institutionalized Shakespeare industry create a parallel authenticity language in the *Wolf Hall* franchise and knit its representational complexities to the traditions of Shakespearean history and performance. Interconnectivities include the author's own acknowledged intertextuality with Shakespeare, the informing shadow of the RSC productions, the Globe Theatre's first Artistic Director, Mark Rylance, playing the lead role of Cromwell in the BBC series, the Globe's Director of Theatre Music, Claire van Kampen, overseeing the period music soundtrack for the series, and the stage and film Shakespeare performance record of other actors such as Damian Lewis (Henry VIII) and Anton Lesser (Thomas More).[3] Indeed Shakespeare—the playwright, the dramatic *oeuvre*, and the performance traditions—threads through much of Mantel's novels and the BBC's televisual adaptation. Early reviews of Mantel's first Cromwell novel pinpoint her indebtedness to Shakespeare. Joan Acocella's *New Yorker* review links Mantel's prose style to the dramatist: "She has read Shakespeare closely." Stephen Greenblatt's lengthier assessment for *The New York Review of Books* places Mantel's endeavor in the context of historical fiction-writing and identifies Shakespeare as an originary source for many tropes of the genre. Greenblatt observes the following: "In English literature it was Shakespeare who invented much of what we expect to find in historical novels." His review expands:

> Indeed one of his last plays, *Henry VIII*, takes up precisely the events that lie at the heart of *Wolf Hall*. (The contemporary title of this play, *All Is True*, gets at something that the historical novel wishes to get at.) It is

> striking that Shakespeare relies on one of the historical sources upon which Mantel draws heavily, George Cavendish's *The Life and Death of Cardinal Wolsey*, and still more striking that his play ends at almost the same moment as Mantel's novel.

By directing reader attention to the alternate title of the Shakespeare and Fletcher play, *All is True*, Greenblatt predicts the epistemological complexities regarding history found in the BBC adaptation.

Although Greenblatt's reference to *All is True* opens up questions of veracity and knowability, the historical costume drama trades in a vocabulary that often ignores the inherent uncertainties associated with the historiographic task and attempts to grasp the past. Such epistemic confidence, often characterized as "authenticity" in historical drama, relies upon external signifiers of the past—the well-made costume, the carefully selected location, the precisely dressed interior, and the correctly chosen period music. Those signifiers assume the existence of an identifiable beginning and the knowability of the past—a past recuperated through expert study and the archive. The OED defines authentic "as possessing original or inherent authority," and its Greek derivation implies "of first-hand authority, original," an etymology that links the authenticity project in film and television to a notion of authority. In heritage film, the "correct" building, attire, and period *mise-en-scène* function as the means by which a viewer accesses an originary moment; these material details vouch for the authorized truth claims of the narration.[4] Andrew Higson explains that heritage films, "seem to articulate a version of the national heritage that contributes to a core English identity" (*English Heritage* 6), though he acknowledges that such films do also allow for critique of that version. Heritage film nonetheless is "a selective preoccupation with the past" (Higson, *English Heritage* 50), relying on an overwhelming visual richness that strongly asserts authenticity. For Patrick Wright, national heritage's production of the past (especially at National Trust stately home sites but also within the filmed versions of those spaces), "engages hopes, dissatisfactions, feelings of tradition and freedom, but it tends to do so in a way that diverts these potentially disruptive energies into the separate and regulated spaces of stately display" (74). He concludes more pointedly: "Where there was active historicity there is now decoration and display; in the place of memory, amnesia swaggers out in historical fancy dress" (74). Such methods of historical verity find a parallel in the way in which restoration projects like Shakespeare's Globe and aspects of the Shakespeare commercial tourism industry articulate authenticity and paper over the highly contingent nature of any reconstruction (as discussed previously in Chapter Three).[5] Stephen Orgel's notion of an "authenticity topos" in much performed Shakespeare points out a craving for the humanly "real" also at the heart of the BBC's approach to Renaissance history. Orgel writes:

> What is authentic…is something that is not in the text; it is something behind it and beyond it that the text is presumed to represent: the real life

> of the characters, the actual history of which the action is a part, the playwright's imagination, or the hand of the master, the authentic witness of Shakespeare's own history.
>
> (24)

As I have argued elsewhere, "What becomes clear in critical practice is, of course, how essentially inaccessible that originary essence is" (Pittman, *Authorizing* 3). Indeed, the hand of the shaping present will always intervene in efforts to access the past: "The relation of memory and the past is therefore not simply one of storage and retrieval but of a reconstruction of the past under conditions and constraints determined by the present" (Karremann 8). The BBC's authenticity topos paradoxically strives to recreate that illusive essence even as patterns of visual and aural technique imply the impossibility of the project.

Mantel's Historiography

In many ways, the BBC's care with the look, sound, and texture of sixteenth-century life not only creates a rich sensory experience but also quite precisely echoes Mantel's splendid instinct for period-specific material detail. Through remarkable attention to the minutiae of Tudor quotidian habits, Mantel crafts a highly particularized depiction of early modern England. At the same time, she questions the existence of and our contemporary access to anything remotely like a complete and unified history. Indeed, perhaps her scrupulous care with furnishings, food, and social customs misleads adaptors who mistake such detail for certainty and monolithic understanding. For in truth, Mantel's Booker Prize-winning novels disrupt such assertions by means of their most noticeably disorienting device, point of view. In *Wolf Hall*, Mantel's novel self-consciously invites the reader to regard the Henrician court from the exclusive point of view of Cromwell, the uniquely unsympathetic bureaucrat of many other tellings. Readers move through time as Cromwell weaves the narrative of his life and ambitions; characters develop only through the eyes of Cromwell, and readers experience events as Mantel's third-person limited point of view dictates. Her trick of predominantly using the third-person masculine pronouns "he, him, his" to refer to Cromwell almost exclusively makes for challenging interpretive work at times, but it also continually reminds readers of the limits of knowledge and the restriction to Cromwell's point of view imposed by this version of history.[6] As others have noted, her especially unflattering portrayal of Sir Thomas More highlights the constructedness of history and throws into doubt the verities in earlier books, novels, plays, and films (depictions that have transformed over time into commonly accepted historical "fact").[7] Mantel radically undermines the long tradition of portraying More as humanist and Catholic saint and martyr—a recalibration derived directly from the controlling narrative perspective of Cromwell.

Mantel's alterations and reinterpretations have not gone unnoticed by practicing historians. Simon Schama writes, "Try dropping the words *Wolf Hall* into a room full of historians these days and you'll find out pretty quickly what they think of historical fiction." For example, the now-discredited David Starkey's very public critique when interviewed by *The Telegraph* insists on a hard-line stance against such literary inventiveness: "It [Mantel's novel] is based on a deliberate perversion of fact" (qtd. in Furness).[8] Though less strident in his language, Tudor historian, John Guy, ruefully laments at the Hay literary festival in Wales that prospective undergraduate students interviewing "to study history at Cambridge," "imagine Hilary Mantel's novels are fact" (qtd. in Mark Brown). Schama's self-described, more "relaxed" response to Mantel's portrayals of Cromwell and More still cautions that such characterizations simply do not match the archival record. Schama elaborates: "I don't much mind that historical novels and films take liberties with the facts, commit sins of omission or make imaginative interpolations provided they do not pretend to claim the same kind of authority in telling you how it really was as accounts based on documented fact seek to do." Even Schama's more generous response to Mantel remains confident in the authority of "documented fact," an allegiance that obfuscates what Michel-Rolph Trouillot has observed—that the selection processes and techniques of archival practice leave "documented fact" an, at times, misleading rubric for historical truth.[9]

In interviews and public lectures, Mantel advances, in part as a response to her critics, a nuanced and often knowingly contradictory stance on the authority and authenticity of her craft. In a series of five BBC Reith Lectures (Summer 2017), Mantel presents a sustained reflection on historiography, historical fiction, and adaptation. In the first Reith lecture, she describes a "contract" between the author of historical fiction and her audience along the lines Schama stipulates:

> But I argue, a reader knows the nature of the contract. When you choose a novel to tell you about the past, you are putting in brackets the historical accounts—which may or may not agree with each other—and actively requesting a subjective interpretation. You're not buying a replica, or even a faithful photographic reproduction—you are buying a painting with the brush strokes left in.
>
> ("The Day" 5)

Mantel's visible brushstrokes constitute a self-consciously reflective historiography—a meditation on what it means to access and narrate the past. At the close of her first lecture, Mantel admits: "it is impossible now to write an intelligent historical novel that is not also a historiographical novel, one which considers its own workings" ("The Day" 7). As such, she asks readers never to forget that they consume art, *not* reality. The highly visible nature of her narratological techniques continually and, for her, ethically, remind viewers that her telling of history remains subjective. She jettisons strategies (such as the reliable omniscient narrator) that would render her telling transparent and that would, so to speak, conceal the brushstrokes to achieve a "photographic reproduction." For Mantel, historical fiction, "if well written, doesn't betray history, but opens up its essential nature to inspection" ("Adaptation" 2). In her fiction, Mantel avoids betraying history through erroneous plot contrivances that would make the known arc of the past impossible; instead, she professes to adapt distinctive interpretive approaches to the facts and thus to provoke self-aware engagement with the nature of history.

Mantel advocates for an approach to history and to historical fiction that resides in the fissures and gaps of the record while acknowledging the factual boundaries established by that record. For example, in the opening lecture, "The Day is for the Living," she summarizes:

> We need to pass on the stories, but also impart the skills to hack the stories apart and make new ones. To retrieve history we need rigour, integrity, unsparing devotion and an impulse to scepticism. To retrieve the past, we require all those virtues—and something more. If we want added value—to imagine not just how the person was, but what it felt like, from the inside—we pick up a novel.
>
> (7)[10]

Even as *Wolf Hall* and *Bring up the Bodies* "hack" away at received Tudor history, Mantel maintains some informing factual allegiances that assert her credibility and integrity as a re-embodier of historical narrative. Indicting some works of historical fiction for violation of major facts, Mantel insists on the accuracy of the world she recreates and on the plausibility of her distinctive interpretation of the evidence. Multiple times she has taken the television series, *The Tudors*, to task as, "historical drama from less skilled and scrupulous hands," adding, "We're all allowed to laugh at *The Tudors*, aren't we? Isn't that what it was for?" (qtd. in Perry). In her lecture, she cites *The Tudors* as negative exemplum:

> Most historical fiction is, I like to think, in dialogue with the past. *The Tudors* was not holding a conversation—just stamping, whistling and making faces. It offered a strange blend of the ploddingly literal and the violently implausible. In trying to spare the viewer the effort of thought, the writers declared war on the laws of time and space.
>
> ("Can these" 5)

She jeers at a basic inattention to period detail (such as sixteenth-century characters traveling in eighteenth-century conveyances). More significantly, she ridicules *The Tudors* for the cause-effect problems created by conflating and carelessly interleaving the lives of two historical figures—Henry VIII's sisters Margaret and Mary. Arguing, "The writers have eaten the future," Mantel observes that the whole of Tudor monarchical inheritance evaporates when Margaret Tudor no longer marries the king of Scotland, James IV ("Can these" 5).[11] In contrast, she anchors her own integrity in care with these verifiable details, allowing more latitude for the positional and perspectival inventiveness of her approach.

This loyalty to a certain form of historical accuracy despite interpretive latitude with archival evidence may explain the limits of both Mantel's and the BBC's approach to casting Tudor history. In her Reith lecture dismissal of *The Tudors*, her opening laugh-line, "You may remember from ten years back the spectacular TV series, *The Tudors* in which Henry VIII was played by a very small Irishman," inadvertently reveals buried assumptions concerning representation in fictionalized accounts of history ("Can these"). Though she proceeds to make the cogent cause-effect case for the deficits of *The Tudors*' reckless history-telling as explained above, her cavalier line, "in which Henry VIII was played by a very small Irishman," bears examination. Eliciting in-group laughter from the recorded audience, the sentence builds to the punchline that the six-foot and two inches English monarch was played by the five-foot and ten inches Irish actor, Jonathan Rhys Meyers. One wonders, is the joke here the difference of four inches or the nationality of Rhys Meyers? In the first lecture of the series, Mantel describes her own Irish great-grandmother's life, and the title of the first lecture derives from a phrase attributed to her Irish ancestor, "The Day is for the Living." But surely, Mantel's punchline is in part about the Irishness of the actor rather than simply his height (and girth) deficiencies. Despite following her own call to "hack" away at received stories, Mantel remains faithful to particularized details including, it would appear, physical and national identities as demonstrated in her derision of casting in *The Tudors*. This intransigent and stubborn allegiance to certain facts despite considerable flexibility with other aspects of the historical record explains the slow pace at which racial representation has adjusted to multicultural Britain within historical fiction and the heritage genre.

Adapting Mantel and Asserting Authenticity

The BBC *Wolf Hall* demonstrates the compelling power of authenticity to contravene even those projects of historical narration rooted in self-aware and self-critical source material. In part, the significance of the Mantel novels stems from a break with the way elements of the English Renaissance and Reformation have been narrated previously for the popular audience. The BBC team embraced the project of adapting Mantel's novels precisely for that reason—the radical freshness of perspective and point of view. At the same time, the BBC series brandishes historical authenticity as a badge of honor, even when aspects of the series quietly reveal the thinness of that very claim and the concomitant impossibility of reclaiming the absence of history. Indeed, the series balances within paradox. That absence of the historical past grasped by means of chronicles, archives, material goods, and architectural remains can never be reconstituted or repossessed in a fully authentic manner. Furthermore, in a familiar story like that of Henry VIII, his wives, and the English Reformation, an audience cannot un-know the ending of the story. An alternative point of view, such as the one Mantel crafts through the eyes of Cromwell, never changes the fact that an audience anticipates the birth of Princess Elizabeth, the execution of Anne Boleyn, and even the death of Cromwell no matter how well told or expertly performed the story.

The filmmakers of *Wolf Hall* do not escape that fact either, for as scenes unfold in painterly perfection, they are peppered with visual and aural cues that take the viewer out of the immediate diegetic moment. These rifts trigger a mindfulness of history and its absence much as Shakespeare and Fletcher evoke when they write, "Think ye see / The very persons of our noble story / As they were living." (Prologue.25–27). Here the playwrights acknowledge that history requires an "as if" imaginative recreation—readers and viewers must "think" and "see" the presence that is not. The pattern of extra-diegetic disruption in the series echoes the habits of intervention found in the history play canon of the English Renaissance as Brian Walsh explains:

> The living, breathing body on stage disrupts rather than effects continuity and thus highlights how the temporality of drama forces audiences into awareness that the actual past is always irrecoverable and so there is always the need for conscious—and constant—acts of performance for it to exist. (26)

Such interconnectivity between the loss of the past and the efforts of the present to unearth and re-vivify those absences forms the subject matter of the Mantel novels and their televisual adaptation. Thus, throughout the series, although the surface of authenticity dominates the visual and aural texture, a pattern of flashback and foreshadowing ruptures the narration of a past and throws into doubt the prospect that when it comes to chronicling history, "All is True."[12] The BBC series oscillates between competing historiographical positions—on the one hand asserting a strong degree of authenticity and on the other hand puncturing that representation to reveal the artificiality of any endeavor to recount the past.

In some ways, the BBC's truth claims run counter to the iconoclastic work Mantel does to destabilize long-held historical certainties regarding the reign of Henry VIII and the deaths of Wolsey, More, and Anne Boleyn. Even as her novels strive to sympathize with the frequently villainized Cromwell in ways that should insist on the highly positional nature of historical "fact," the BBC series that beautifully and creatively reworks her novels deploys a raft of techniques shoring up traditional notions of historical authenticity.[13] Much of the publicity material—DVD and Blu-ray extras, website tie-in blogs, and video interviews—trumpet the loving attention to historical time and place characteristic of the series' high production values. Director Kosminsky describes the truth-telling aims and corresponding filming techniques relied upon in the BBC's *Wolf Hall*:

> What we tried to do was shoot it in as naturalistic and realistic a way as possible. The performances are not really heightened in any way, and this,

> for us, was doing service to the style that Hilary herself had talked about in relation to her books as wanting to feel you were there in the moment with the characters.
>
> ("*Wolf Hall*: The People & The Politics")

Kosminsky elaborates on this notion in a panel interview for the British Film Institute (12 Jan. 2015) in which he explains the exclusive use of handheld cameras, often positioned just behind Cromwell's shoulder: "You shoot it like a documentary. You don't get ahead of it. You try to make the audience/the viewer feel that they are experiencing events with Cromwell as they happen—not stood back…." ("Wolf Hall Q&A"). This telling comparison to documentary filmmaking highlights a true-to-life quality sought by the entire film team.

The website tie-in materials on both PBS.org and BBC.org celebrate the capacity of on-location filming to heighten the "realness" of the series. The PBS Masterpiece site catalogues major locations and indicates which scenes were filmed at each site. The Masterpiece "Locations of Wolf Hall" pages reveal the patchwork artistry and illusion necessary to create "authentic" Tudor sites—photographic captions frankly list the multiple historical locations represented by one filming site. In spite of the illusion, those same photographic captions also echo the assertions of authenticity repeatedly voiced by cast and crew. For example, the Penshurst Place note includes this comment from director Kosminsky:

> We know because [Penshurst] was near where Anne Boleyn grew up that Henry VIII visited there on a number of occasions while he was paying suit to Anne Boleyn. And there's a gallery…where we know Henry VIII and Anne Boleyn walked while Henry was romancing her. And to be able to stand in that room…It was magical.
>
> ("The Locations of Wolf Hall")

Because an actual royal visit to Penshurst is not scripted in the series teleplay or the source novels, the function of this authentic location shifts. The filmed Penshurst, instead, stands in for Whitehall, Anne's London residence throughout the series—a form of "slant" authenticity. Locations like Gloucester Cathedral provide exteriors and interiors of multiple and very different locations—the court of Henry VIII, Blackfriars, and Calais Castle. In addition, Lacock Abbey is both interior and exterior of the Seymour's Wolf Hall and the interior of Calais Castle ("The Locations of Wolf Hall"). In "*Wolf Hall:* Filming on Location," a Masterpiece website video, Kosminsky reflects:

> So the actors are standing in a building that existed 500 years ago, lit by candlelight exclusively just as that building was designed to be lit at night, and they're wearing costumes that look and are put together and designed exactly in the way that costumes of that period were. And when you put all these things together it becomes more like real life.

In that same video promotion, Executive Producer Colin Callender explains:

> One of the central characters in the drama is actually England and England's country houses and the palaces of England. The fact that we were able to shoot on the real locations had a profound effect on the actors and their performances and the sense of reality.[14]

At the same time, Blu-ray extra interviews of Gavin Finney (Director of Photography) and David Johnson (Locations Manager) reveal the care with which differing exteriors and interiors were knit together to create the illusion of "reality." Finney explains that the team aimed for a "unity of style" across the locations—a euphemism for the photography and editing craft required to make the interiors and exteriors appear seamlessly connected and accurately representative of the early sixteenth century ("*Wolf Hall*: History and Design"). Yet in spite of this construction, the language of BBC production team members insists repeatedly on an elision between historically accurate and the humanly "real."

The series team likewise curates and composes an aural landscape to accompany the visual locations that also signifies historical accuracy. Director of Theatre Music for Shakespeare's Globe, Claire van Kampen (Rylance's partner), sourced and arranged all Tudor music utilized as part of *Wolf Hall* and collaborated with Debbie Wiseman who composed contemporary musical scoring. For the period music, van Kampen relied upon her work at Shakespeare's Globe and on musicians from the Globe. A *Wall Street Journal* article reporting the popularity of the two soundtrack releases—van Kampen's period selections and Wiseman's score—quotes van Kampen: "The music is authentic... to the extent that is knowable. I did faithfully try to use the music [Henry] would have heard as much as I could" (qtd. in Ramey). Corinne Ramey cites one example of the series' historical care with music choices: "the vocal work 'Te Deum,' by 16th-century composer John Taverner, is played for Anne Boleyn's coronation in *Wolf Hall*, because Ms. van Kampen's research found that it was likely played in Westminster Abbey on that date." Not just in selection of music but also in performance, the team practiced authenticity: "Even the filming process had aspects of the authentic. 'The musicians were filmed live playing in the gallery where Henry actually walked with Anne Boleyn,' says Ms. van Kampen. 'We all had goosebumps'" (Ramey). Again, the scholarly care driving authentic representation promises an affective frisson—the thrill of touching the past and approaching the lived experience of Henry VIII, Anne Boleyn, and their Tudor courtiers.[15] The *Wolf Hall* team relishes these moments in which the past and the present coincide by means of a corporate effort at historical accuracy even as those claims are often accompanied by a sideways acknowledgment that representation might not be as authentic as desired.

The visual and aural landscape of the series thus underscores a naturalistic approach to storytelling in conflict with the more radical perspectivism of Mantel's novels. In a Blu-ray extra, Executive Producer Callender describes Mantel's novels as a "missile" thrown into the traditions of historical fiction

("*Wolf Hall*: Bringing it to the Screen"). Inspired by the source material, Callender insists that the series aims to unsettle tropes of historical fiction and filmmaking: "We wanted to blow the cobwebs out of historical drama and tell something much meatier, much more muscular, much more visceral and really show this world that we think we know from a perspective that we haven't seen before" ("*Wolf Hall*: Bringing it to the Screen"). The language deployed by Callender telegraphs a gendered derision aimed at a literary form—historical fiction—associated with predominantly female authors and audiences; the BBC promises *Wolf Hall* will be "meatier" and "more muscular" than the typical costume drama fare.[16] Despite that understanding of Mantel's ballistic impact on not just the received "truths" of Tudor history but also the genre of historical fiction, the BBC's *Wolf Hall* stands in a paradoxical relationship to its source material. By constraining point of view to a single perspective, Mantel accurately reflects how humans experience the places, times, and events that come to constitute history. Redirecting twenty-first-century readers to the unique point of view of Cromwell avoids the strident truth claims of institutionalized history-telling. However, the medium of film necessarily broadens point of view; even if the camera repeatedly sits just behind Rylance's shoulder as he walks through Tudor sites, the heritage film style will always include establishing shots, long shots, and medium shots that frustrate an exclusively singular point of view. In what Higson calls the "pictorialism" of heritage films,

> There is also a preference for long takes and deep focus, and for long and medium shots, rather than for close-ups and rapid cutting. The camera is characteristically fluid, but camera movement is dictated less by a desire to follow the movement of characters than by a desire to offer the spectator a more aesthetic angle on the period setting and the objects that fill it.
> ("Re-presenting" 117)

If the series intends to conform to the traits of historical drama and heritage filmmaking with their strong traditions of pictorialism, then the singularity of perspective achieved in the novels cannot be maintained without significant estrangement. The extreme narrowness of vision required to limit film exclusively to Cromwell's point of view would no longer allow the series to meet expectations of historical drama—a painterly representation of locations, peoples, clothing, and interiors. Despite the dust-clearing and coded sexism implicit in the producer's claims about the adaptation, the gestures to authenticity manifest a lurking fantasy of fidelity to historical accuracy.

This oscillation between understandings of history as coherently unified and authentically represented or history as perspectival and only fragmentarily visible informs the style of the televisual *Wolf Hall*. Just as a range of techniques strives for authenticity of representation, so a cluster of devices stresses the impossibility of thorough-going historical accuracy.[17] Analepsis and prolepsis occur repeatedly throughout the series to embody the intervening hand that represents the past. Though the series commences with Cardinal Wolsey's

(Jonathan Pryce) ouster from power, it rapidly flashes back to moments from his ascendency—for example, cutting from his expulsion from York Place to an earlier encounter in which the Cardinal buffets Thomas Boleyn (David Robb) for his daughter's wayward interest in Harry Percy (Harry Lloyd). Similarly, as Cromwell rounds up Anne Boleyn's (Claire Foy) lovers, analepsis again reminds viewers that these young men partook in a scornful dramatization at the fallen Cardinal's expense—thus implying loyalty to and vengeance for the now-dead prelate as motivation for Cromwell's action against the queen and her courtiers.

The film also utilizes music to disrupt the smoothly linear narration of historical time—particularly by generating anxiety about the future for the characters depicted on screen. Just as period-specific music confirms the authenticity ethos of the film, so music proleptically functions to voice the opposing impulse—recognition that the present and its knowingness always interfere in narration of the past. Wiseman's fresh-composed score complements the period music collected by van Kampen but also warns listeners of the story still to come. Most notably in this regard, Wiseman deploys a half-step, two-note motif reminiscent of the *Jaws* theme made famous by John Williams as a caution to viewers that the unseen shark approaches. Frequently played during moments of transition, the *Wolf Hall* two-note motif establishes a mood of melancholy reticence consistent with the series' softer portrayal of Cromwell. In addition to tone setting, the half-step passages create unease about the present, an unrest that reinforces a viewer's knowledge of the future still to unfold for Queen Anne, Henry VIII, and Cromwell himself.

Visual imagery combines with these habits of diegesis and scoring to disrupt the possibility that a true history exists if only the right tools were at hand to facilitate access. In episode three "Anna Regina," the filming of Anne at her coronation—though staged with characteristic attention to the authentic surfaces of the past—also proleptically references her death. Interior space, costuming, and period music combine to body forth history. But even that surface authenticity of the cathedral space is not strictly accurate since the coronation is filmed at Bristol Cathedral not Westminster Abbey. More importantly, the photographic and framing choices rupture the "now" of the represented past and import the situatedness of a present viewer who cannot unknow historical ends. Anne's prostration before Archbishop Cranmer (Will Keen) demonstrates the proleptic technique. With great care, the pregnant Anne first kneels, then with arms outstretched in cruciform formation, is gently lowered to the cathedral floor. The film cuts to a close-up shot viewing Anne from above as she turns her head to be fully prostrate on the ground, a move that predicts her later preparation for the executioner. Thus, the filming collapses into one moment the apogee and the nadir of Anne's power and demonstrates the way in which the present destabilizes any telling of the past.

In *Henry VIII*, Shakespeare and Fletcher impose the epistemic advantage of hindsight onto the closing moments of the play—illustrating plainly the impact of the present on historiography. Shakespeare and Fletcher's *Henry VIII* closes with the christening of Anne's daughter and Cranmer's prophecy of Elizabethan prosperity and Jacobean continuity. The Archbishop's vatic wisdom airbrushes the complications of Tudor succession with a providentialist gift for omission; the disgrace and execution of Queen Anne, the restoration of Catholic rites under Mary I, Cranmer's martyrdom, and Elizabeth's own reluctance to admit her cousin James I as heir go unacknowledged and unspoken in the Archbishop's fervency. Beginning with, "Let me speak, sir, / For heaven now bids me; and the words I utter / Let none think flattery, for they'll find 'em truth," Cranmer proceeds to silence substantial details of the historical record and crafts a selective truth that makes possible a providential view of English monarchy (5.4.14–16). The play then concludes with a dubious example of historiography, one open to the easy critique of contemporary seventeenth-century viewers. Ivo Kamps points to the asynchrony of Cranmer's prophecy in the context of the drama's competing historiographic modes: "*Henry VIII* draws our attention to the operations by means of which historiography produces a past and the ways in which historiography and historians mystify those operations by sanctifying them" (197). Likewise, the BBC's *Wolf Hall* sets in motion conflicting historiographic attitudes; as the series revisits the Renaissance, the production strains towards an authentic representation of history even while utilizing techniques that undermine the effort. The series captures the potent craving for an accurately represented past and the simultaneous recognition that no such uniform and recuperable past exists.

The Disappearing Moor

The BBC's visual and aural attention to the surfaces of authenticity sidesteps pressing questions about history and nation in Mantel's recursions to Britain's storied past. Perhaps in the name of authenticity and as a result, once again, of white privilege blind spots (illustrated repeatedly in the third-millennial performances of the history plays addressed in the previous chapters), both Mantel's novels and their adaptations leave unchallenged certain historical verities that demand reconsideration—in particular, the complexion of the past and the myths of cultural homogeneity that fuel white racial nostalgias. This nostalgia, accessed in 2016 by the Vote Leave slogan, "Take back control," fueled the Brexit debate and emerged several times during Mantel's 2017 Reith lecture tour. For example, during the questions following Mantel's lecture, "The Iron Maiden," historian Diarmaid MacCulloch asks: "Over the last twelve months, I've become increasingly irritated by the analogy between the English reformation and Brexit. Now, do you share my irritation?" The author responds,

> Yes. I have also been distressed by what's a very simplistic analogy. First, let me say that in the ten years beforehand we broke with Rome, Europe had been reconfigured because you had the rise of the protestant states in Germany, within the Holy Roman Empire, but states becoming either Lutheran or non-aligned. You had the Scandinavian monarchies, the Swiss cities breaking with Rome, becoming Lutheran. What foreign policy in

> the 1530's was trying to do was not come out of Europe but go into a new kind of Europe. It's unhistorical and I think unhelpful to compare the Reformation with Brexit.
>
> ("The Iron Maiden" 7–8)

In her response to MacCulloch, Mantel argues that a complex understanding of history does not reinforce twenty-first-century isolationism but rather a more selectively networked participation in the geo-political landscape of Europe. To another audience member in Antwerp who raises Brexit, she answers:

> There has been a gigantic failure on the part of the voting public in Britain to know their history, to examine the evidence that was put before them, and a giant failure of imagination. I think the whole thing is shameful, regrettable and I think—time will prove how destructive it may be. All nations have a fantasy of a golden age, but I would say ours was to come. I'm not so sure, now.
>
> ("Silence Grips" 8–9)

Here Mantel links a people's failure to "know their history" to the catastrophic decision to exit the European Union. Mantel does not elaborate on what specific gaps in knowledge might have motivated the vote, though her answer to MacCulloch's question indicates at the least she refers to Britain's long interdependency with the nations and peoples on the European continent.

The additional informing yet forgotten history of white supremacy that Mantel herself might be guilty of ignoring certainly also shares blame for Vote Leave. Taking up Mantel's assertion that a failure to know history led to the referendum results, one might argue that the overwhelming xenophobia driving the Vote Leave camp may well demonstrate cultural amnesia regarding the many contributions that immigrants and multiethnic communities have made to British culture and identity over hundreds of years. The infamous Vote Leave slogan, "Take back control," accesses a pseudo-heritage of unspoken white supremacy, a mystified time when the white male human subject did not answer to others, did not account for his unearned privilege, and enjoyed unquestioned pre-eminence. In fact, the silenced history of resistances—gendered, ethnic, class, and racial—suggests that the long arc of white supremacy has not gone unquestioned over time, and furthermore, that the implied cultural and national homogeneity of such nostalgias does not survive a freshly vigorous study of the archives.[18] Though her comments criticize the epistemic inadequacies informing the colossal mistake of the Vote Leave decision, Mantel's own novels and their adaptations participate in a whites-only historical representation of early modern England—what Onyeka Nubia summarizes as characteristic of period film depictions, "so Christian, so white and so happy" (10)—that indirectly contributes to misunderstandings about the multiethnic and multiracial peoples who shaped English history, even that of the treasured Tudor past. Indeed, Mantel's narratives elide a "national rebranding" in which "Whiteness affixed to power...accommodated the rise of an English colonial and imperial imaginary," incipient during the very years covered by the Cromwell novels (Smith, *Race and Rhetoric* 6).

Meticulous scholarship, most notably by Imtiaz Habib, dismantles many of the assumptions about the complexion of an "authentic" early modern past. Relying on a total of 448 records (13), Habib reconstructs the lived presence of persons of color in early modern England and Scotland. The breadth of occupations and roles suggests a wider impact than most historical accounts and heritage films have previously represented. Habib's work establishes the presence of a black population "in early modern England, in considerable plurality, range of locations, and periodic continuity, that together demonstrate black people to be a known even if denied ethnic group rather than stray individuals encountered by few or none" (14). The records of aristocratic houses, civic archives, royal households, legal and tax rolls, and parishes all reveal a significant black history; documentary evidence confirms that blacks practiced varied occupations—for example, musician, entertainer, laundress, servant, soldier, and metal worker (2–4). Habib points out that the alliance between the Tudor King Henry VII and the Spanish monarchs, Ferdinand and Isabella, "connected England with a country that has a large black population in it" (21). When their daughter, Catherine of Aragon, arrived in England (1501), her retinue included blacks, a fact prompting Thomas More's epistolary jibe, "'you would have thought they were refugees from hell'" (qtd. in Habib 24).[19] More's reaction illustrates the elision between black skin and evil fueled by the representational habits of medieval mystery plays. As Greg Bak explains, "Demons and sinners in late medieval iconography and popular drama were often represented" in blackface (206). Habib's archival work gestures beyond that crude symbolic and racial mimicry to the factual presence of persons of color in London in circles that would necessarily have overlapped with those of Cromwell both at court and in commercial venues. The presence of a black servant in a merchant household ("'Dyego Negro servaunt with Thomas Bowyer'") demonstrates an avenue by which blacks arrived in London; Habib suggests that Dyego Negro was, "probably the procurement of a merchant trading in the Iberian peninsula" (45). In addition, the black trumpeter, John Blanke, participated in celebrations for the short-lived son of Henry VIII and Catherine in 1511 (Habib 40), and his marriage record signals further social integration into England. David Olusoga explains that

> ...Blanke's place within the Tudor court may well have been a reflection of the studied modernity to which the Tudors and the English aristocracy aspired, as by the early sixteenth century Africans had become a recognized feature of the international, outward-looking cultures of Renaissance court life and pageantry.
>
> (60)

Though not yet substantial in number, these individual references suggest a pattern of black presence coinciding with the arrival of Catherine of Aragon that would expand over the following decades.

Mantel does not populate Cromwell's mercantile London with the persons of African descent who would, indeed, have appeared in trading households given the prominence of Iberian peninsula alliances, nor does her court of Henry VIII include blacks in Catherine's entourage. She does, however, invoke the masquing traditions in which blackened white bodies impersonate "moors." In *Bring Up the Bodies*, Mantel describes Christmas season revels (1535) in the context of ambassadorial visits from France and Spain.[20] In the novel, the courtier Henry Norris explains to Cromwell his exit from the gathering, "I have to dress up as a Moor. Will you excuse me, Mr Secretary?" (125). When Norris reappears in costume and blocks Cromwell's free movement, the novel focuses on Cromwell's frustration that he cannot follow the king and Charles V's imperial ambassador, Eustache Chapuys, into private conference. As Norris answers Cromwell's questions, Mantel describes him, "He [Norris] pushes back his woolly wig to reveal his noble forehead" (126), a detail that directs attention both to the representational props employed to mime African identities and the physiognomic features that code racial differences.[21] Writing from Cromwell's point of view, Mantel repeatedly refers to Norris as "The Moor" in this short episode: "the Moor beseeches" (126); "The Moor giggles" (127). When the courtier, William Brereton, joins the scene and jokes with Norris about Queen Anne's rumored over-familiarity with the anatomy of her gentlemen favorites, Cromwell observes, "Norris blushes easily, for a Moor" (127). Norris's "playful" intervention in Cromwell's effort to follow Ambassador Chapuys and King Henry behind closed doors angers Cromwell, and in Mantel's sleight-of-hand pronouns, Norris's blush blurs into the Secretary's point of view:

> But here is Norris blocking his path. In his Moorish drapery, his face blacked, he is playful, smiling, but still vigilant. Prime Christmas game: let's fuck about with Cromwell. He is about to spin away Norris by his silken shoulder, when a small dragon comes waggling along.
>
> (126)

Here Mantel's estranging and often disorienting approach to naming and pronoun usage may explain the series of paragraphs in which Norris becomes "the Moor."

This stylistic detail also capitalizes upon hierarchies of status and skin color difference embedded in the term, "moor"—a racial reference with its own confused and ethically vexed function throughout the early modern period.[22] In this case, the repetition of "the Moor" creates of Norris a thing to be jostled and maneuvered in the great game of Cromwell's courtly influence. Cromwell's iteration deploys the noun as one more linguistic technique—an epithet—by which he affectively distances himself from and dominates the power players at Henry's court. Indeed, this moment instantiates how epithets like "the Moor" have been deployed to thingify non-whites for centuries, and Mantel's casual usage to channel Cromwell's strategies seems a tactical and ethical blunder on the novelist's part. Furthermore, the authenticity defense that moors did, indeed, operate as stock figures in court masquing provides insufficient justification for the detail's inclusion; if historical particularity warrants the blacking-up detail, then the same resort to period authority would dictate that Cromwell's world include non-whites in other trade and courtly capacities.

Despite ethical problematics, Mantel's selection of this particular masquing detail actually underscores her own credentials as a scrupulous student of literary traditions and crafter of authentic historical fiction. Indeed, scholars confirm that, "In 1510, King Henry VIII and the Earl of Essex dressed themselves 'after Turkey fashion', their torchbearers and six ladies covering themselves with fine black lawn to appear 'like Moreskoes' or 'black Mores'" (Loomba 17). Mantel thus illustrates the quality of her research with this particularly obscure detail of Henrician court history, though her Moorish impersonation occurs in 1535 not 1510. She likewise reveals familiarity with the tendency to use blacking up in medieval miracle and mystery plays to signify Satan and his devils:

> The association of blackness with evil has a long history on the English stage as well. There the tradition goes back at least to early medieval drama. In many medieval miracle plays, the souls of the damned were represented by actors painted black or in black costumes.
>
> (Barthelemy 4)

In *Wolf Hall*, Mantel actually refers to this precise religio-dramatic practice in a masque entitled, "The Cardinal's Descent into Hell" (245). That masque (repeated in the BBC adaptation as a leitmotif explaining Cromwell's long-brewing vengeance) depicts Cardinal Wolsey dragged to Hell by devils, two of whom are played by Norris and Brereton. In her description of the *Wolf Hall* interlude, Mantel indicates that the courtiers reveling in Wolsey's fall wear masks rather than blackface, but she also uses language that again links the scene to techniques of racial impersonation: "The cardinal rolls across the floor, kicking out at the demons, but they harry him, in their wooly suits of black" (246). That earlier masque operates as unspoken backstory to Norris-as-Moor in *Bring Up the Bodies* by means of Mantel's direct reference to "the Moor" and because the same courtiers participate in both scenes. Their reappearance in *Bring Up the Bodies* at a moment of blacking up, gestures to the representational traditions Mantel appears to know well in which black signifies evil; as Geraldine Heng expresses it in her magisterial study of race in the Middle Ages, "Black is damned, white is saved. Black, of course, is the color of devils and demons, a color that sometimes extends to bodies demonically possessed…" (16). The earlier masque in *Wolf Hall* informs Norris's Moor in *Bring Up the Bodies*—not just in the reference to the "woolly" props but also in the moral judgments the black face or mask invites from the English courtly audience. Thus, Norris-as-Moor in *Bring Up the Bodies* enacts the thingification of non-white Others and replicates a racist moral rubric by echoing the earlier masque and medieval alignment of black with devilry.

Poulton's stage version of *Bring Up the Bodies* adapts with light adjustment Mantel's Christmas revels scene from the year preceding Anne's death. In Poulton's staging, Norris passes through the conversational cluster of Cromwell, Chapuys, and King Henry. As he bustles across the stage, Norris addresses Cromwell, "Will you excuse me? I have to dress up as a Moor" (198). After a difficult exchange between King Henry and Chapuys over whether or not the king will allow his daughter Mary to visit the dying Katherine, Norris reappears, and the stage directions indicate, "NORRIS, *dressed as a Moor, intercepts him* [Cromwell]. *A dragon hurries past*" (199).[23] As in the novel, the scene centers attention on the awkward diplomatic relations at the end of Queen Katherine's life, and Norris's role in the Christmas festivities seems merely period window-dressing. Just as in the novel, once Norris reappears with Brereton, the joking turns ribald. Stage directions that follow Brereton's, "I do believe you're blushing, Norris" (200), draw attention to the racialized moment, "NORRIS *puts his hand to his blacked-up face*" (200). While the first stage directions regarding attire simply describe Norris "dressed as a Moor," this second statement confirms that in Poulton's adaptation of Mantel, Norris's face has been artificially darkened. In fact, the "joke" about his blushing depends upon the fact that he cannot be seen to blush in his costume and make-up—a racially charged joke rendered more acute in staged performance than on the page of a novel because of the white body playing the role and donning the blackface make-up before a live audience. On the archived RSC recording of the play (Dir. Jeremy Herrin), Norris (John Ramm) clearly wears a light layer of blackface make-up on his cheeks and chin which accompanies the Moorish flowing gown and headdress he wears. Thus, Mantel's period-specific reference to masquing travels from her novel to the stage production without editing of the racist content, nor in the transition from the page to the stage does a reconsideration occur regarding which non-white ethnic groups might be represented in the creative casting of certain roles. Headshots of the full cast in Stratford-upon-Avon, London, and New York quickly confirm an entirely Caucasian company.

Though the RSC has expanded its multiethnic casting in both its Shakespearean and non-Shakespearean productions since the start of the third millennium, the runs of *Wolf Hall* and *Bring Up the Bodies* do not contribute to that trend.[24] Hannah Miller, Head of RSC Casting, explains the company's colorblind casting policy:

> It is our ambition at the RSC to try to ensure that the demographic of Britain today is reflected on our stages. I will always assume that I am bringing in the best actors for a particular role regardless of their cultural background or ethnicity, unless I have had a discussion with the director to the contrary.
>
> (qtd. in Rogers and Thorpe 486)

In the case of Poulton's adaptations, the claims to historical authenticity appear to have influenced the decision to exempt the production from the patterns of multiethnic casting found in many other RSC productions where ratios typically number "10%–20% ethnic minority actors to 80%–90% white performers" (Rogers 426). The stage adaptations of the two novels experience special treatment that exempts them from the multiethnic casting conventions now associated with Shakespearean history, as if Mantel's and Poulton's work meets a higher standard of historical veracity necessitating what Jenna Steigerwalt terms, "genetic realism" (426). As has been noted, Mantel's novels replicate Shakespeare's own highly perspectival approach to history telling, making it surprising that similar casting strategies were not applied to staging the Poulton adaptations of her novels. Shakespeare's example as a teller of history recurs several times throughout Mantel's Reith lectures. When introducing the last of Mantel's lectures, "Adaptation," delivered at the Arts House in Stratford-upon-Avon, presenter Sue Lawley articulates the connection again:

> Resurrecting the dead is arguably, of course, what Shakespeare did with his history plays from King John to Henry VIII, 200 years of royal power struggles. Those plays, of course, are works of Shakespeare's imagination based fairly loosely on the historical figures themselves. Nevertheless, says Hilary Mantel, historical fiction whether a novel, a play or a film brings the dead to life.
>
> ("Adaptation" 1)

Lawley draws express parallels between the historical resuscitation conducted by both Shakespeare and Mantel, but the parallels do not extend to contemporary policies of casting at the RSC. This wrong-headedness on the part of the novels and their adaptations actually contradicts Mantel's own stated goals as a writer seeking to hack apart received history. One particularly potent way to do just that would be to revisit the assumed whiteness of Britain's Tudor Age, acknowledging, as archivists have carefully pinpointed, the active presence of non-whites, refugees, immigrants, and non-English in Cromwell's thriving commercial London. Instead, both Mantel's and Poulton's works deploy the representational habits of racial impersonation that thingify non-whites and deny historical subjectivity to Britain's multiethnic peoples.

While Mantel's moor migrates from novel to stage, Norris's impersonation does not travel to the BBC's televisual version, a silent omission that illuminates persistent corporate and artistic blind spots concerning racial identity and English history. Apparently, a reference to blacking up may appear in a novel, its significance lost in the brevity of the moment or its impact neutered by the limits of a reader's imagination and/or attention. That same reference may also transfer to a stage performance, playing to smaller, affluent, often predominantly Caucasian, audiences (Poulton's plays were staged as a costly two-drama suite). However, in 2015 and in light of its well-publicized corporate commitment to diversity and equality of representation, the BBC miniseries quite rightly opts to delete Norris-as-Moor from its visual spectacle. That decision may seem innocuous and simply wise at first glance, but the choice reveals a fascinating degree of awareness about diversity of representation. The disappearing moor of the BBC version demonstrates that creative teams can "see" race and, most certainly, can identify a controversial representation (the blacked-up white man) well worth omitting from a teleplay. But even as egregious representations can be seen and eschewed, that same production team cannot "see" the more subtle racisms of its own heritage filmmaking—the relentless whiteness of British history-telling—and thus correct those blind spots. Though the caricature of blacking up disappears, the even more significant step wherein an all-white cast could be adjusted to better recreate London as a cosmopolitan hub of England in the sixteenth century is not taken by the production team. This trio of versions undermines any plausible deniability for the BBC—the possibility that production teams simply do not notice their racist storytelling habits. The disappearing moor demonstrates that creative teams can "see" inappropriate representations of blackness but choose not to "see" the intransigent heritage film practices that continue to imagine the British past as the exclusive domain of whiteness. Indeed, as Romano Mullin notes, "In depictions of early modern England, the disappeared stories are often those of women, the poor, the disabled, and those of differing sexualities and ethnicities" (99). Higson also observes, heritage films, "often seem to insist on the purity and distinctiveness of a traditional Englishness and eschew the particular type of cross-cultural inter-textuality that is such a strong feature of contemporary aesthetics" (*English Heritage* 6). In the case of the Mantel televisual adaptations, an awareness of racial coding in its source material still does not prompt the BBC to reconsider the complexion of the history it claims "authentically" to replicate. In this, the BBC manifests a selective authenticity; its commitment to historical verisimilitude is belied by the willingness to silently disappear the moor without then enhancing multiethnic representations in other ways.

The problems unpacked here derive, in part, from genre limitations—the failures a result of the heritage film tropes informing the BBC's adaptations of material from Mantel and Poulton. Too often, heritage film's attention to the particularized surfaces of the past creates a set of viewer expectations that make the "sudden" appearance of multiethnic cast members a supposed distraction from the immersive mimesis. With the insistence of its representation, heritage drama reinforces homogeneous versions of national identity: "The discourse of heritage ensures that the national community is bounded both temporally, by traditional historical narratives, and spatially, by the geographical vision of the nation. Heritage cinema plays a crucial role in this process of imagining English nationhood" (Higson, *English Heritage* 50). Indeed, the conventions of heritage drama determine the stubborn whiteness of the BBC's adaptation. In many ways, since whiteness has been encoded in the practices of heritage film, multiethnic casting threatens to puncture the representational illusion. In the "great man" narrative underpinning the BBC *Wolf Hall*'s treatment of Thomas Cromwell, persons of color might disrupt viewer attention. Even with an adapted text the BBC touts as a "ballistic" rewriting of Tudor history, only certain recalibrations of the past prove acceptable—rethinking the characters of

Cromwell and More may be permissible but not reimagining the complexion of the Henrician court.[25]

The Inauthenticity of White History

In a novel, careful research translated into words on the page creates the historical *mise-en-scène*. The novel then relies upon reader imagination to conjure the world crafted through language. Thus, the artistic rendering of realism within the novel cannot be fully transparent—the creative hand remains visible in the black letters on the page. On stage something similar happens. Though more available tools can support immersion in a replicated real time and place—costuming and the occasional piece of set furnishing and design—much must still be imaginatively supplied by the theater audience. Even when a theater production strives for considerable historical realism, the physical limits of the playing space itself will thwart such efforts since the ghost of the previous scene hovers on the very boards trod upon as plotting continually moves forward. In addition to the dimensional limits of theater, the practice of doubling, in which the actor playing multiple parts never fully disappears, similarly disrupts the illusion of a "really real" historical recreation. However, on screen the degree of verisimilitude can be at such an overpowering photographic level as to make the "brushstrokes" disappear within the richly realized visual field, achieving what Hayden White names, "historiophoty" (1193). When that replicated world has traditionally been cast as white, any cross-ethnic casting threatens to dismantle narrative coherence.

But just such disruption is precisely what is required—not simply the elimination of racist practices such as "blacking up" but rather a thorough-going reimagination of what a cosmopolitan sixteenth-century London looks like and thus who belongs to and owns British history today. Systematically reworking the most accessible forms of historiography, the dramas of television and film, to incorporate non-whites, immigrants, and refugees could begin to correct inauthentic and falsely homogenous understandings of British history. Indeed, as Mantel herself notes, the Vote Leave campaign and the coded racisms of "Take Back Control" found a foothold because of a failure rightly to know the past. In *Wolf Hall*, Mantel writes, "Beneath every history, another history" (61), but, sadly, she does not seem to reference here the long-buried and silenced history of Britain's multicultural peoples. Until representations of the past "see" race—both white and non-white—imagining a national identity that accords equal status to all citizens will be difficult. History operates as a validation of national and political subjectivity and can also function as an ameliorative tool when used to recognize the heterogeneous stories of the past. Since, as Paul Gilroy argues, blacks in Britain have been "expel[led] from historical being altogether," the anti-racist project must "respond by revealing and restoring the historical dimensions of black life in this country" (*There Ain't* 18). Doing so should, most certainly, address the moment, the English Renaissance, when that very process of historical exclusion was being invented.[26]

In a landmark issue of *Shakespeare Quarterly*, Ian Smith rejects the "fetishizing" of "historical accuracy" (120) that mutes race dialogue; he urges a commitment to "'speaking about' race" that locates "whiteness in relation to other social identities and classes, exchanging exceptionality for the collective solidarity of coalition building" ("We are Othello" 123). Mantel, Poulton, and the BBC creative team fail to acknowledge, let alone correct, the way in which whiteness has defined the past and its "authentic" heritage representations. Though not an adaptation per se of Shakespearean history, Mantel's Cromwell novels and their adaptations participate within Douglas Lanier's "Shakespearean rhizomatics," which encompasses Shakespeare's texts but also "includes faithful and unfaithful adaptations, and adaptations of them, and adaptations of *them*" ("Shakespearean Rhizomatics" 30). The Mantel novels and their RSC and BBC versions trade on the prestige value of Shakespeare and his historiography, and yet are not necessarily constrained by the playwright's authorizing imprimatur in quite the same way as the films of *The Hollow Crown* series. Nonetheless, they demonstrate how the preserve of Shakespearean history—whether on stage, on screen as "faithful" adaptations, or as rhizomatic "cousins" staged and filmed—only reinforces a long-standing belief in British history as a "whites-only" affair—a dangerous nostalgia fueling the crises of 2016. In her Reith lecture, "The Iron Maiden," Mantel critiques the heritage industry as promulgator of indulgent fantasies: "The heritage industry is built on confusion, a yearning for a past which is sordid and gorgeous, both together. Purer than our age, also more corrupt. There's a certain kind of historical fiction [that] feeds collective fantasy…to save us from our humiliating ordinariness and whisk us into fairytale." Mantel differentiates her own craft as historical novelist from such escapism, eschewing the nostalgia that often accompanies the heritage journey into a collective past: "So what can historical fiction bring to the table? It doesn't need to flatter. It can challenge and discomfort. If it's done honestly, it doesn't say, 'believe this' – it says 'consider this.'" Unfortunately, her innovative and deeply self-aware Cromwell series whether on page, stage, or screen does not dispel the fantasy of a monoethnic British history nor compel readers or viewers to "consider" white history as inauthentic history.

Notes

1 Poulton's two-part stage adaptations of Mantel's novels began performance life with the Royal Shakespeare Company and ran in Stratford-upon-Avon (11 December 2013–20 March 2014) at the Swan Theatre, transferring to London's Aldwych Theatre in 2014 for a limited run, and then to New York's Winter Garden Theatre from 9 April 2015 to 5 July 2015. Thus, the stage adaptations ran simultaneously in the United States with the airing on PBS of the BBC six-part series.

2 Andrew Higson's definition of heritage film and its service to nationhood informs the chapter that follows: "The discourse of heritage ensures that the national community is bounded both temporally, by traditional historical narratives, and spatially, by the geographical vision of the nation" (*English* 50).

3 Both veterans of the Royal Shakespeare Company, Damian Lewis has played Posthumus and Laertes on stage, and Anton Lesser's long career includes performances as Troilus, Petruchio, Hamlet, Romeo, Henry IV, Brutus, Leontes, and Richard III.

4 Sarah Cardwell catalogues those authenticating features observable in one subgenre of heritage film—literary adaptation: "Close attention is paid by the makers of these adaptations to what is often called 'authenticity' (period accuracy): costumes, hairstyles, buildings, landscapes, furnishings, modes of travel, behaviour and speech are usually presented as being faithful not only (or not even) to the source text, but to the era with which the source text was concerned" (114).

5 Terence Hawkes connects such striving after origins to a de-politicized fantasy: "The potential of 'origin' as an agent of affirmation, confirmation and limitation makes it a powerful ideological tool. If we can persuade ourselves that in some way origins generate authenticity, determine, establish and reinforce essentials, then we can forget about change and about the history and politics which produce it" (142).

6 Greenblatt elaborates on the purpose of this technique: "The point is not to create an insoluble puzzle but to make you, the reader, do a little work in order to orient yourself. And orienting yourself in this novel always means returning to Cromwell, who has, we are told, a special gift for orienting himself" ("How It Must").

7 Eric Sandberg identifies such strategies as essential to Mantel's distinctiveness: "Mantel's unconventional use of the historic present, her controversial reevaluation of the Thomas More-Thomas Cromwell relationship, and her emphasis on the depiction of internal subjectivity are comparable strategies of differentiation" (58).

8 On June 30, 2020, while speaking on a conservative podcast, Starkey discounted slavery as genocide: "Slavery was not genocide, otherwise there wouldn't be so many damn blacks in Africa or in Britain would there? You know, an awful lot of them survived" (qtd. in Siddique). Though he walked back the comments, many rallied to condemn this, only the most recent, example of Starkey's racism; repercussions include the HarperCollins decision to cancel his book contracts and the loss of several UK university positions (Flood).

9 "Silences enter the process of historical production at four crucial moments: the moment of fact creation (the making of *sources*); the moment of fact assembly (the making of *archives*); the moment of fact retrieval (the making of *narratives*); and the moment of retrospective significance (the making of *history* in the final instance)" (Trouillot 26).

10 Mantel's distinction between the recuperation of *history* versus the *past* echoes Cardwell's definition of these terms in her study of classic novel adaptations on television. Cardwell defines history as "the attempt to record, evaluate and narrativise details of the events, people and places of the past," while "the past" represents a "far more abstract concept than that of history," one with which the audience of heritage films desires numinous connection (116–117).

11 Ramona Wray offers a more sympathetic take on the history-telling of *The Tudors*, arguing that its "depiction of the Renaissance is revisionist," abandoning "an expected 'golden age' heritage-based template to move into as yet untested arenas"; "In *The Tudors*, no single version of history is ultimately privileged: the events and transactions of the past alternately appear as assimilation, imitation, and bricolage" ("Henry's" 40).

12 Indeed, Annabel Patterson argues that the *All is True* title of the Shakespeare and Fletcher play functions as a critique of historical objectivity: "I suggest that Shakespeare was not only mocking such claims, but selecting a subject that helped to explain, in historical terms, why historical objectivity was (both tragically and comically) hard to come by: that is to say, the coming of the Reformation to England" (149).

13 Thomas S. Freeman's assessment of the Tudor and Stuart periods on film asserts the basic premise that, "all films…suffer from inherent limitations which prevent them from accurately representing the past….the authenticity in recreating sets and costumes, in which filmmakers take such pride, is an illusion" (20).

14 The English landscape and country house setting almost did not happen for the series. Initially *Wolf Hall* (like its historical-fiction television cousin, *The White Queen*) was to be filmed in Belgium; however, producer Callender explained, "that thanks to the recent television tax breaks, they had been able to film in various National Trust houses" (Perry).
15 Mantel herself delighted in the visual quality of the adaptation, declaring, "Every face seems to me one that Holbein would recognize, even if he didn't paint it" (qtd. in Ellis-Petersen).
16 Allison Machlis Meyer discusses the perception of historical fiction as a female genre in her work on the novels of Philippa Gregory (262).
17 Tom Betteridge's thoughtful exploration of Henry VIII on film rightly critiques three other treatments of this familiar story—*A Man for All Seasons* (1966), *The Six Wives of Henry VIII* (1970) and *The Tudors* (series 2, 2008)—for their assumptions about the certainty of a historical truth. Though the two earlier treatments take opposing methods to the postmodern film techniques of the more recent *The Tudors*, Betteridge argues that all three works assume the existence of a stable historical narrative: "The hangings and crowds, the confusion and noise that fill the screen in *The Tudors* create the illusion that without them it would be possible to approach to the truth of history, that Wyatt and the viewer would be able to see and hear what is going on. But the transparency of *The Six Wives of Henry VIII* is as flawed and partial as the opaqueness of *The Tudors*; neither can deliver the historical accuracy and truth that they both so desperately desire" (216).
18 For example, Trouillot introduces his recovered narrative of the Haitian Revolution by observing, "…any historical narrative is a particular bundle of silences, the result of a unique process, and the operation required to deconstruct these silences will vary accordingly" (27).
19 Habib continues: "that this negative marking of black people comes from someone [who] will become one of England's most famous Humanist philosophers is starkly indicative of how even European high philosophy will be complicit in the marking down of black people and the negative interpretation of blackness in early modern Anglo-European political and cultural history" (25).
20 It is worth noting that when references to blackness occur here, they do so in connection with Spain and its ambassador, capitalizing on English fears about Spain's contaminating affiliation with North Africa and Arabs.
21 Here Mantel's language confirms the depth of her historical research and her engagement with modes of racial representation in the early modern period. The woolly wig as stage prop is referenced in *Henslowe's Diary*, and multiple physiognomic texts reference the forehead as a key site for divining identity and prognosticating the future (Corredera, "Faces and Figures").
22 Anthony Gerard Barthelemy concisely traces the confused signification of "moor" and concludes: "*Moor* can mean, then, non-black Muslim, black Christian, or black Muslim. The only certainty a reader has when he sees the word is that the person referred to is not a European Christian" (7).
23 Mantel's novels and Poulton's play adaptations utilize the spelling "Katherine."
24 Improvements in multiethnic representation at the RSC must be applauded with caution, as Jami Rogers argues, given that the uptick takes place in the context of steadily shrinking overall cast size: "The twenty-first century has seen the ratio of black/Asian/mixed race to white actors at the RSC tick upwards as cast sizes have continued to shrink, with the total number of actors in productions in the vicinity of 20 performers per play between 2000–2012. The percentage of white to black/Asian/mixed race actors has shifted very little, however, which is an indication of the presence of a glass ceiling when it comes to employing black and Asian actors" (Rogers 420).

25 As the UK slowly emerged from the COVID-19 pandemic in the summer of 2021, the RSC website announced its upcoming stage adaptation of Mantel's final Cromwell novel, *The Mirror and the Light* (2020) and posted photos of the cast. While certain roles will be reprised, notably Ben Miles's Cromwell and Nathaniel Parker's Henry VIII, BAME (Black, Asian, Minority Ethnic) actors have been cast as characters ranging from Richard Riche to Elizabeth Seymour with the most diversity centered on Cromwell's household (Paul Adeyefa as Christophe, Terique Jarrett as Gregory Cromwell, and Jordan Kouamé as Rafe Sadler). Time will reveal what casting strategies the BBC may opt to take in filming the long-awaited final television episodes of the series.

26 Trouillot describes, "the emergence of a new symbolic order" during the early modern period that gave rise to a conceptualization of "The West" essential to the European colonial-imperial project of the ensuing centuries: "The West was created somewhere at the beginning of the sixteenth century in the midst of a global wave of material and symbolic transformations. The definitive expulsion of the Muslims from Europe, the so-called voyages of exploration, the first developments of merchant colonialism, and the maturation of the absolutist state set the stage for the rulers and merchants of Western Christendom to conquer Europe and the rest of the world" (74).

6 The Trouble with History

Intersections of Nation, Race, and Gender in *King Charles III*

"Past and to come seems best; things present worst."
(*II Henry IV*)

To anyone who has lived through the first twenty years of the third millennium, it will come as no surprise when I suggest that much of the frankly progressive optimism and promise of 2000 has withered, particularly between 2016 and 2020, crushed by despicable increases in racist police brutality, continued conflict in the Middle East, a rapidly warming planet, a horrific global pandemic, and the anti-immigrant nationalist projects in two of the world's leading English-speaking democracies, the United Kingdom and the United States. What, exactly, does the telling of history have to do with these crises? Why does the representational strategy of performed Shakespearean history still matter at this moment of peril? In Michel-Rolph Trouillot's clear-sighted articulation, "History is the fruit of power, but power itself is never so transparent that its analysis becomes superfluous. The ultimate mark of power may be its invisibility; the ultimate challenge, the exposition of its roots" (xxiii). Such excavation involves revisiting received historical narratives and seeking for the erasures, omissions, and silences—Michel de Certeau's shards of the historiographically left-behind. These "silences" transpire, as Trouillot catalogues, at each stage of the historiographical enterprise—from event, to record, to archive, to narrativization: "Silences are inherent in history because any single event enters history with some of its constituting parts missing. Something is always left out while something else is recorded" (49). Because "Inequalities experienced by the actors lead to uneven historical power in the inscription of traces," historical records build, "upon these traces" and "privilege some events over others," necessitating the resistant work of recovery described by de Certeau and Trouillot (48). The election of Donald J. Trump in the United States and the Brexit Vote in the United Kingdom illustrate the dangerous potency of historical narratives that define the nation as exclusively white. In response, performances of Shakespeare's polyvocal history plays can enlist the iconicity of the Bard of Avon to puncture such nation-defining narratives.

The performance approaches to Shakespearean history chronicled in this book underscore the limited achievement between 2000 and 2016 in re-

DOI: 10.4324/9781003043065-6

presenting the history canon to reflect third-millennium, multicultural Britain. Too often, treatments of this material have reinforced received and inaccurate conceptualizations of British identity: "The plays of Shakespeare can be conflated into an illusion that Tudor England was mono-ethnically white and that therefore the rest of early modern society was too" (Nubia 11). Though certainly not without their blind spots—especially to do with intersecting marginalized identities—the remarkable history play productions helmed by Michael Boyd at the Royal Shakespeare Theatre (2000) and Nicholas Hytner at the National Theatre (2003)—the subject of Chapter Two—did not act as catalyzers of representational change. They did not spark a departure from the naturalistic heritage styles in the televised histories that appeared in the first twenty years of the third millennium, a time period that saw televised Shakespearean history dominated by a nostalgic, period-focused verisimilitude. Even, as in the case of *Wolf Hall*, when the Shakespearean historiographic reference point is proximate and adjacent rather than directly lineal, the aesthetic drive towards authenticity dictates a monoethnic depiction of the Tudor era and its nation-defining history.

Though colorblind, color-conscious, nontraditional, or gender-blind casting have made substantial, but certainly not uncontested, inroads in performed Shakespeare, the history plays remain relatively resistant to racial and gender reimagination on stage and screen. Angela C. Pao explains that, "The relationship between representation and reality associated with a particular genre is instrumental in determining how readily and productively the conventions of realistic illusionism can be breached by nontraditional casting" (34). In the case of Shakespeare's ten history plays, the claims to historical facticity—that these dramas represent real human beings from the substantial historical record and written and visual archive who were verifiably white—have often been cited to justify all-white productions of these texts. For example, Trevor Nunn defended his all-white 2015 *Wars of the Roses* by indicating that he had "made an 'artistic decision' to cast according to 'historical verisimilitude'" (Owen). Nunn asserted that the complex aristocratic lineages of the compressed tetralogy demanded, according to casting director Ginny Schiller, a "colour aware" naturalism (qtd. in Owen). Writing unencumbered by the verities of the historiographic record, Mike Bartlett can make no such defense for *King Charles III: A Future History Play* (2014). Bartlett self-consciously appropriates the Shakespearean history play to create a "future-history," but despite writing with the freedom of a futuristic frame, Bartlett's text and the stage and televisual productions that followed appear as straitjacketed by the conventions of a whites-only British history as any of Shakespeare's medieval narratives.

By means of five-act structure, iambic pentameter verse, and title and subtitle, Bartlett deliberately positions his *King Charles III* in the tradition of Shakespearean history. Reviewers of the Almeida Theatre (2014) stage production and the BBC filmed adaptation (2017)—both directed by Rupert Goold—repeatedly note echoes of *Richard II* and *I Henry IV* in particular.[1] In addition, the speculative subject matter of the drama's plotting echoes concerns central to Shakespearean history as demonstrated by a brief summary. *King Charles III* imagines a constitutional and monarchical crisis triggered by disagreement over how best to preserve Great Britain as a liberal democracy. Beginning with the death of Queen Elizabeth II and the accession to the throne of the Prince of Wales, the play explores the new monarch's efforts to wield his authority with integrity—though to many his attempts look suspiciously like a hyper-privileged, "father-knows-best" paternalism. When asked to sign a bill ostensibly designed to protect his subjects' privacy, King Charles recognizes this as a violation of the freedom of the press.[2] His refusal to sign the bill and his dissolution of parliament create an opportunity for the Duke and Duchess of Cambridge to usurp the throne, bypassing King Charles in the interest of preserving the institution of monarchy and pacifying an outraged populace.

Through such plotting, Bartlett employs Shakespearean history as a vehicle to reflect on the state of the British nation in the twenty-first century and the role monarchy should or should not play in its contested future. As Bartlett explains in an interview,

> The idea for *King Charles III* arrived in my imagination with the form and content very clear, and inextricably linked....An epic royal family drama, dealing with power and national constitution, was the content, and therefore the form had surely to be Shakespearean.
>
> (Bartlett, "How I wrote")

Accessing Shakespearean form for his reflection on the British nation, Bartlett takes on material (both past and present) deeply imbricated in Britain's history of white supremacism.

Untethered from the "truth claims" of history that have held back, rightly or wrongly, more inclusive casting experimentation, the speculative material of *King Charles III* offers a framework in which to correct the omissions of historiography. However, at the most basic level of casting, the adjustments seem unforgivably light. The 2014 Almeida stage production lists only one person of color (Nyasha Hatendi who played three minor characters, Sir Gordon, Nick, and Spencer), though photographs suggest that a crucial part, that of a kebab van owner, was also performed by Hatendi. In the transition to the 2017 BBC televisual version, the cast gained slightly more ethnic and gender diversity—with the leader of the opposition (Priyanga Burford), an all-night café owner (Hatendi), and Prince Harry's girlfriend (Tamara Lawrance) all played by persons of color. In crowd shots, multiethnic Londoners repeatedly feature as well.[3] Unfortunately, rather than substantially recalibrating racialized definitions of the nation as received through Shakespearean history on the page, stage, and screen, Bartlett's conjuration of a future recycles atavistic nationalism, illustrating the race trouble that persists when it comes to adapting the matter of Shakespearean history. A "lost opportunity for reimagining race," as Joyce Green MacDonald has noted (167), *King Charles III* fails to envision a future history of Great Britain that accounts for its multicultural citizens; instead, the play transforms a person of color into a mouthpiece of old-fashioned yet resurgent imperialist nostalgia. Similarly, although Bartlett clearly strives to correct the marginalized representation of women in Shakespearean history, inattentive colorblind casting once again draws a distinction between the historical agencies of white women and those of color. By failing to confront the racism and sexism long embedded in the narration of history, *King Charles III* cannot body forth sufficiently the very Britain it ostensibly seeks to underprop—an inclusive, welcoming liberal democracy comprised of many cultures and ethnicities, each member enjoying full subjectivity and historicity.

For too long, European historiography has erased persons of color, and Shakespearean history has reinforced that erasure through performed enactment. Enlisted repeatedly to bolster British identity and providential destiny, the history plays have operated as a tool for white supremacism by denying "an authentic kind of historic being" (Gilroy, *Postcolonial* 32) to persons of color. As discussed in Chapter Two, not until 2000 did a person of color take a lead role in a major British production of Shakespeare's history—David Oyelowo as the eponymous monarch in Michael Boyd's *Henry VI* cycle (2000) for the Royal Shakespeare Company. In *Postcolonial Melancholia*, Paul Gilroy insists, "...we cannot avoid consideration of the relationships between race thinking, historiography, historicality and the sometimes evasive, normative codes of white supremacism" (32–33). And this is where a reinvigorated historiography (one filtered through the authoritative imprimatur of Shakespearean history) can be enlisted for ethical service—artworks as "objects and instruments of action," and more importantly, "responsible actions" (Wolterstorff 78). Too often, postmodern reflections on British nationhood such as Bartlett's revert to an elegiac longing for an imagined, monolithic greatness. Indeed, Gilroy identifies regret over Britain's faded global ascendency and a concomitant increase in racist fortress mentality as symptoms of what he diagnoses as "postcolonial melancholia" (*Postcolonial* 12). In *King Charles III*, Bartlett cloaks these familiar trappings of imperial nostalgia in a faux multiculturalism that sidesteps an opportunity to participate in the "oppositional reflection" on historiography and white supremacism Gilroy urges.[4] An interrogation of such faux multiculturalism must then extend beyond Bartlett's single play text to the broader challenges of seeing and representing race, gender, and nation in the performance of Shakespearean history.

"That England, that was wont to conquer others"

Writing at the end of the twentieth century, Edward Said finds in the discourse addressing "the residue of imperialism" a pattern of forgetfulness and "unappreciated magnanimity" (21), which is closely related to Gilroy's "postcolonial melancholia":

> Dismissed or forgotten were the ravaged colonial peoples who for centuries endured summary justice, unending economic oppression, distortion

> of their social and intimate lives, and a recourseless submission that was the function of unchanging European superiority. Only to keep in mind the millions of Africans who were supplied to the slave trade is to acknowledge the unimaginable cost of maintaining that superiority. Yet dismissed most often are precisely the infinite number of traces in the immensely detailed, violent history of colonial intervention.
>
> (Said 22)

As he characterizes postcolonial amnesia, Said catalogues the oft-ignored crimes of the past still informing and defining colonial-imperial nations like Great Britain, which have translated their reduced dominance into new forms of geopolitical and economic power-brokering and influence.[5] Gilroy's diagnosis of "postcolonial melancholia" stresses that a corollary to the erasure of a distasteful past is an attendant mourning for the unified whole said to have faded away but which, truly, never existed. Gilroy also links together a lamentation for the loss of British global ascendency with an increase in racist fortress mentality:

> ...the core of British particularity is deemed to be under disastrous attack from three different directions: Americanization, Europeanization, and a nonspecific subsumption by immigrants, settlers, and invaders of both colonial and postcolonial varieties. Behind these multiple anxieties lies the great transformation that quickly reduced the world's preeminent power to a political and economic operation of more modest dimensions.
>
> (*Postcolonial* 12)

Four hundred years earlier, Shakespeare anticipates this in the context of incipient early modern nationalism in John of Gaunt's "This England" lamentation. As Willy Maley rightly argues:

> Of course, there's never been an England in the sense suggested by John of Gaunt....When England was not a colony of Rome or France, it held colonies itself—Ireland from the twelfth century, Wales from the thirteenth—and was thus always something more or less than self-contained, never quite at home.
>
> (17)

Even as John of Gaunt elevates "This precious stone set in the silver sea" and mythologizes Albion's geographic virtues, his reflections spotlight an already-squandered reality in which those assets have been indiscriminately wasted. Furthermore, this oft-cited passage, serving as a portmanteau for vague yet potent nation-defining assertions, includes a passing bit of casual racism quietly deleted or conveniently ignored but all too typical of the *oeuvre* and the era—"in stubborn Jewry"—that should remind readers of nationalism's reliance upon an objectified other. As Sivamohan Valluvan notes, "...nationalist sway at any given historical moment requires a particular kind of racial othering" ("Defining" 238). John of Gaunt's elegy thus endeavors to conjure into existence the unified nation and does so through memory and the differentiating categories of "us" and "them" / "in" and "out." However, as has been thoroughly noted by many scholars, the dying Lancastrian patriarch does so assuming that the nation's shining moment remains always-already in the past.

In *King Charles III*, Bartlett opts to ventriloquize "postcolonial melancholia" in an extended meditation on British nationhood articulated by a person of color—a speech that revisits John of Gaunt's "sceptred isle" elegy.[6] At the center of the play text, Bartlett features a kebab van owner who reflects on the state of the nation to a wandering and lost Prince Harry. In the published play text, in playbills, and on the Almeida Theatre's archived website, this part goes uncredited. The playbill for the Almeida production that transferred to London and Broadway shows one person of color in the cast, Zimbabwean-British actor Nyasha Hatendi, who is credited as playing the three minor characters, Spencer, Nick, and Sir Gordon. Production photographs of the kebab van scene show Hatendi also playing a fourth part, that of the kebab vender, identified in the text as "Paul." This quiet assignment of a "minority" role to the only person of color telegraphs representational carelessness and a deeply troubling elision of racial difference on the part of the production. Required to code-switch between Spencer (a laddish companion to Harry), Nick (the Prime Minister's Communications Adviser), and Sir Gordon (Chief of the Defence Staff), Hatendi then also appears to be deemed the only cast member "appropriate" for the kebab seller part. While audiences are expected to "see" but "not see" Hatendi's race in the first three roles, they most certainly are invited to note his identity as a person of color and access handy, though faulty, stereotypes (particularly of non-white immigrants) when Hatendi plays the kebab van owner. Otherwise, why not give the part to another white member of the cast less burdened by doubling? In the BBC adaptation, scripted by Bartlett and also directed by Goold, Hatendi plays and receives credit for performing the kebab vender now transformed into an all-night café manager-owner, again named Paul (though as would be expected for a televised version, he does not double any other parts).

Multiple racial problematics emerge from Paul's articulation of the British nation through the voice and body of a non-white citizen and the food heritage of an immigrant culture; first, his reflections ventriloquize New Nationalist attitudes in ways that confound racial equity. In the play text, the kebab vender begins his John of Gaunt-style ruminations with the death of the queen:

> You know since she died. World's gone mad. I swear. Every night, people have this look. Bit like you—They come here, they want a kebab, a Coke, and it's like they're terrified. And I think I know why. They don't know where they live. They don't know what Britain is any more.
>
> (73)

Viewed most sympathetically, Paul's sacral elevation of the monarch as locus for national meaning-making seems designed to demonstrate the successful assimilation of immigrants from the former empire. As if anticipating multicultural naysayers, Bartlett might be seen to counter assertions that non-white British people lack loyalty to the nation through the character of Paul. For example, David Goodhart suggests that an emphasis on diversity has disrupted the "solidarity" needed for a thriving welfare state, "We need to be reassured that strangers, especially those from other countries, have the same idea of reciprocity as we do. Absorbing outsiders into a community worthy of the name takes time." In contrast to this waning national unity, he critiques the enclave-style separatism of immigrant communities: "The 'thickest' solidarities are now often found among ethnic minority groups themselves in response to real or perceived discrimination." Paul's sense that the monarchy provides national cohesion for *all*—both native inhabitant and immigrant alike—might signal the playwright's rejection of anti-multicultural polemic.

At the same time, the speech carries within it a number of striking ironies that make Paul a mouthpiece for the thinly veiled racisms of New Nationalism, which hinge on constructions of key figures of fear—the migrant and the black male (Valluvan, "Defining" 233). When Paul observes, "They don't know where they live. They don't know what Britain is any more," he echoes statements made by white middle-class and working-class voters who describe "not recognizing" their neighborhoods as immigrants have moved in, bought homes, entered schools, established businesses, and built mosques. Asserting both spatial and ideological dislocation, Paul's comment would seem right at home in the mouth of a white citizen ruefully noting that the complexion of the country has so altered as to render Britain unrecognizable. Indeed, Paul's words troublingly repurpose key elements of Enoch Powell's infamous, "Rivers of Blood," speech in Birmingham which, "helped to reinvigorate English racism and fascism" (Bhattacharyya et al 63). Bhattacharyya et al contend that "Powellism," though in muted notes throughout the governments of Tony Blair and David Cameron, "remained an implicit anchor, but one which could remain submerged except at crisis points, such as the 7/7 bombings or the 2011 riots" (Bhattacharyya et al 66). This long-standing theme of aggrieved whiteness transformed once again into the rhetoric of New Nationalism during the 2015 migrant crisis and run-up to the Brexit vote. Richard Dyer likewise confirms:

> The theme of outnumbering has been a mainstay of white racial politics, becoming the organising principle of British post-war debate, moving from discussion of "overcrowding" (especially in relation to housing) to the language of "flooding" and "swamping" used respectively by Enoch Powell and Margaret Thatcher.
>
> (26)

In his 1968 address to a Conservative Association meeting, Powell's invective vilified immigrants and focused sympathy on beleaguered and besieged white Englishmen:

> But while, to the immigrant, entry to this country was admission to privileges and opportunities eagerly sought, the impact upon the existing population was very different. For reasons which they could not comprehend, and in pursuance of a decision by default, on which they were never consulted, they found themselves made strangers in their own country.
>
> (Powell)

Voicing a racial and ethnic estrangement experienced by lawful and rightful [white] citizens, Powell deployed incendiary imagery designed to coalesce anti-immigrant sentiment: "They ["decent" and "ordinary" Englishmen] found their wives unable to obtain hospital beds in childbirth, their children unable to obtain school places, their homes and neighbourhoods changed beyond recognition, their plans and prospects for the future defeated" (Powell). These words—"their homes and neighbourhoods changed beyond recognition"—recycled in the third millennium and (dis)located in the mouth of a person of color—acquire a vagueness that neuters and "purifies" the implied and unspoken racism of "They don't know where they live."

Paul's ventriloquism here also suggests that the way a person of color "belongs" is by adopting the in-group's exclusionary discourse and thus effacing the distinct situatedness of that particular Briton's lived identities. Bartlett's scripting of this scene and the casting of Hatendi combine to obscure the racism of New Nationalism, to thin out the precise racial identity of Paul, and to set the price of belonging as adoption of the very exclusionary language that could well be deployed to disenfranchise a non-white business owner like the character of Paul, especially given the fact that, "…the exclusionary principle that the nation hinges on not only 'inferiorises' those who are defined as not belonging but also renders the excluded Other the overdetermined and outsized object of political discourse" (Valluvan, *The Clamour* 35). Bartlett's, "This England" moment offers plausible deniability concerning the racist implications of nationalist rhetoric—because how could a line like, "They don't know where they live," even be racist if a person of color laments the very same thing? Such slipperiness of signification renders doubly challenging the effort to combat the range of coded and overt racisms in New Nationalism.

Furthermore, Paul's, "They don't know what Britain is any more," recirculates postcolonial nostalgia—the question of what Britain *is* once the sun has set on its empire. To answer that question, Paul imports a metaphor obviously inspired by the context of the late-night comfort food he serves:

> Slice by slice, Britain's less and less. You cut the army, that's one bit gone, squeeze the NHS, the Post Office closed, the pubs shut. Devolution. Less and less. Smaller all the time and when does Britain get so cut down, that it's not Britain any more?
>
> (73)

Here the NHS, pubs, and devolved empire all appear leveled in significance and similarly essential to a faded concept of the nation. In his wistful language,

Paul manifests "a conservative cultural nostalgia and the thinly veiled imperial mythology that accompanies it….a nostalgic formation that remembers a homely greatness and the genteel whiteness redolent of that greatness" (Valluvan, "New Nationalism"). Bartlett's Paul concludes his reflections by suggesting that the queen's recent death further diminishes coherent national identity: "Well the Queen's dead. If you take enough layers away, what have you got left, underneath, know what I mean? Maybe she was what held it together" (73). Here the kebab metaphor becomes clear as Paul uses it to characterize the cutting away or thinning out of an essential British identity. In this crucial passage, Bartlett appropriates a relatively recent import to British food culture—the kebab's "marinated slices of lean meat and minced meat on a vertical spit" (Sirkeci 146)—to visualize the multicultural nation, a whole made from discrete parts. And, in the teleplay, Bartlett makes the Queen's role absolutely analogous to the kebab's steel rod: "Like this meat here. It's not one thing. Different pieces, different slices, collected around one core piece of steel. But you take that away, it all falls apart. Maybe she is what held it all together."[7] However, even as the image strains for a new vocabulary to describe the multicultural present of the United Kingdom, it implies insufficiency, depletion, scarcity, and continued dependence upon the ancient institution of monarchy as embodied by Queen Elizabeth II.

In addition to its ventriloquized New Nationalism and postcolonial melancholy, the speech departicularizes the racial specifics of the kebab and the shop owners who popularized it in Britain. Indeed, the play's dates of production (2014 on stage and 2017 on television), straddling the years of the refugee crisis in Europe and the Brexit vote, actually highlight a crucial evasion by Bartlett, Goold, and the television production, that of the Turkish immigrants largely responsible for the increased availability of the kebab in Britain. Variously known as shawarma (Arabic) and as "döner kebab" (Turkish for "rotating" and "roast meat") and related to another Mediterranean iteration, the Greek gyro (which also means "turning" or "rotating"), the kebab took root in UK food life with the influx of Turkish immigrants (Sirkeci 144–145). Ibrahim Sirkeci explains that early immigrants were Turkish Cypriots in the 1950s, and that during the 1990s and 2000s, Kurdish asylum seekers "dominated the inflows." According to Sirkeci, kebab shops hit new popularity peaks in the 2010s (154). Between 1980 and 2016, "At least 41,224 Turkish citizens applied for asylum in the UK" (148). Since employer prejudice often forces immigrants into small business ownership, the number of kebab shops in the UK has tracked steadily with the rise in Turkish immigrants; Sirkeci's data identifies, "a parallel between the growth of the diaspora population and the number of kebab businesses" (149). One mark of the established place the kebab now occupies in the UK is the existence since 2011 of the British Kebab Awards, attended or praised by politicians from across the spectrum—Labour's Ed Miliband and Jeremy Corbyn, the Liberal Democrat, Nick Clegg, and former Prime Minister and Leader of the Conservative Party, David Cameron, who asserted when endorsing the British Kebab Awards, "The kebab industry has made a very significant contribution towards the UK economy and shows entrepreneurial aptitude through each and every successful small business venture. Kebabs have become part of our food heritage, alongside fish and chips and curry" (qtd. in Sirkeci 152). Tory Boris Johnson also described the awards as, "appropriate recognition of the cultural and economic contribution of the humble kebab to the British economy" (qtd. in Sirkeci 152). Little need be said about the empty opportunism of Johnson's comment given his complicity with the Vote Leave campaign's vilification of Turkey and the immigrants traveling from Turkey to escape conflict in the Middle East.

A number of now-infamous print and video Vote Leave advertisements threatened "this seat of Mars" with an unregulated influx of Middle Eastern refugees moving into Europe from Turkey. Well-remembered print ads (discussed in Chapter Four) graphically fueled fears that just as brown refugees would be flooding the borders, substantial funding essential to social welfare services such as the NHS would flow outwards to the EU. Other related "Vote Leave" strategies preyed upon fears that Turkey might join the EU and thus create the open door for refugees to overwhelm Britain. In this context, then, the choice of the Goold stage production and the BBC filmed adaptation to cast the kebab vender as Afro-British sidesteps the reality that the majority of such food establishments are overwhelmingly owned by Turkish-Kurdish refugees—individuals who do not generally look of African descent as Hatendi does. Ignoring particularities of ethnic identity, the casting choice assumes one ethnic minority is much like another, eliding differences at a moment when Turkey resonated so powerfully and negatively in voters' imaginations.

This then gives the lie to the deployment of the kebab as Bartlett's metaphor for multicultural Britain. The cone of piled meat slices seasoned, gathered around a spit, and rotisserie roasted appears at first an apt representation of the diverse people groups who make up the nation—their unique ontologies preserved in the image of the discrete slices and the nation's non-coercive embrace signified by the cone's structural formation and reliance upon the central steel rod. However, in the hands of Bartlett and the production teams at the Almeida and the BBC, the image drives towards insistent homogenization. The unexamined whiteness of history-telling and, too often, of production teams themselves lead to this faux multiculturalism, one in which the Motherland appears generously to adopt as its own emblem an immigrant food import; but implicit in this very image is the suggestion at best of depletion and at worst of appropriation.[8] Shave the meat off, serve it in pieces, and the distinctiveness disappears. This misguided metaphor epitomizes a deeply troubling view of Britain's multiethnic peoples as grudgingly admitted citizens but also as threats to the integrity of a fondly fantasized national unity.

"I ask no less than power": Gender Intersections

Even as the imagery of the kebab instantiates a privileged inattention to British multiculturalism and the power dynamics implicit in cultural appropriation,

Bartlett nevertheless does endeavor to better acknowledge, through the female characters of *King Charles III*, the constrained yet vital role played by women in nation-building. In doing so, Bartlett addresses quite self-consciously (by means of textual echoes and character analogues) the lacunae of Shakespearean history regarding the subjectivity and agency of women. For example, his Princess Diana (Katie Brayben) haunts her former husband, Charles, as a malevolent presence—part martyred wife and part Hamlet Senior's Ghost—while Catherine, the Duchess of Cambridge (Charlotte Riley), manifests a Lady Macbeth-style political keenness and ambition.[9] Through the Duchess of Cambridge, Bartlett most directly confronts outmoded conceptualizations of women as mere vessels for alliance-building and lineage longevity. But as has been seen in several of the productions addressed previously, the limits of imagination are met when it comes to intersectional identities such as Prince Harry's black girlfriend, Jess (Afro-British Tamara Lawrance). Her character's exclusion from the final coronation scene of the film replicates the treatment of Sophie Okonedo's Queen Margaret in *The Hollow Crown*; both recent televisual treatments of Shakespearean history confirm that black women have no place in British narratives of identity, reinforcing the fact that, "Race and gender are interconnected categories" for difference-making in the nation (Orkin and Joubin 201). As illustrated by the kebab scene's racial and ethnic sleight of hand, the gender politics of *King Charles III* reinforce the trouble with history—even when that genre undergoes radical reformulation as "future history."

As part of the project to expand the field of agential influence for women in Shakespearean history, Bartlett crafts his Duchess of Cambridge in direct contradistinction to the image of Kate famously and very publicly articulated by Hilary Mantel. In her 2013 provocation for the *London Review of Books*, "Royal Bodies," Mantel describes Catherine Middleton:

> I saw Kate becoming a jointed doll on which certain rags are hung. In those days she was a shop-window mannequin, with no personality of her own, entirely defined by what she wore. These days she is a mother-to-be, and draped in another set of threadbare attributions. Once she gets over being sick, the press will find that she is radiant. They will find that this young woman's life until now was nothing, her only point and purpose being to give birth.

Mantel's essay details the carnivorous consumption of royal bodies by the subject who gazes—characterizing patterns of objectification that trace from Princess Diana back to Marie Antoinette and the Tudor queens Mantel revivifies in her Thomas Cromwell fictions. Though cautioning readers about the tendency to ogle royals as if on a tour of Bedlam, Mantel's ungenerous description of Kate attributes a blankness and unflattering lack of individual character to the Duchess. Locating the Duchess of Cambridge within a genealogy of female consorts, Mantel argues, "Kate Middleton, as she was, appeared to have been designed by a committee and built by craftsmen, with a perfect plastic smile and the spindles of her limbs hand-turned and gloss-varnished." Mantel elaborates: "Kate seems to have been selected for her role of princess because she was irreproachable: as painfully thin as anyone could wish, without quirks, without oddities, without the risk of the emergence of character." Reduced to her physical appearance and biological necessity to the Crown, Mantel's Kate recedes as human into type in much the way Dyer describes the instrumental passivity of white women modeled on the Virgin Mary archetype, "a pure vessel for reproduction" (29) ensuring that "possessions are passed on to those who should properly inherit them" (26).

In *King Charles III*, Bartlett shapes the character of Kate to confront dismissals of the Duchess much like that in Mantel's essay. Indeed, Bartlett invites associations with Shakespeare's powerful women of tragedy through slant quotations from both *Macbeth* and *King Lear*. For example, Prince William concedes to Kate, "Then if it's done, it's done at once" (96), and Kate comments to her husband, "For nothing comes of nothing said" (47). To highlight the difference in his Kate, Bartlett first invokes nay-saying depictions through King Charles's comments to her at the funeral of Elizabeth II:

> You're radiant, despite the grave
> Restrictions of the mourning dress. It is
> Your gift my dear, it's what you've brought to us.
> A sense of fashion, better hair as well.
> (12)

Here King Charles specifically locates the Duchess of Cambridge, now Princess of Wales, within the surface-level assets Mantel also catalogues. In lines that judge—the implied inappropriateness of radiance at the gravesite—Charles also confines Kate's role to the ornamental demands of brand monarchy.

But Bartlett's adaptation of Kate directly counters the characterization advanced both by Mantel and the fictionalized Charles III by positioning her as instigator and co-conspirator in a bid to seize the monarchy from her father-in-law. Bartlett's Kate delivers a soliloquy that takes aim directly at the plastic doll constructions of the Duchess of Cambridge, and in the film version, visual and auditory techniques accompanying the soliloquy underscore the ascendant agency of this Kate who intends to shape history and the nation. As civil unrest erupts over the king's resistance to Parliament and the Prime Minister, Kate watches reports of the disturbances on her iPhone, seated in the luxury of the palace in the easeful attire of the wealthy—starched white shirt and designer jeans. However, she is no passive object of the nation's consuming gaze. Without musical scoring and in deadly stillness, the scene begins as Riley's Kate tilts her head to the left towards the camera and observes, "You're looking at me," making eye contact down the camera lens with the follow-up, rhetorical query, "aren't you?" Very deliberately she moves from the indirect and unaware side-view "portrait" pose to the confrontational self-composure of the portrait sitter who "looks back" at the unseen audience.

But I know nothing, just a plastic doll
Designed I'm told to stand embodying
A male-created bland and standard wife,
Whose only job is prettying the Prince, and then
If possible, get pregnant with the royal
And noble bump, to there produce an heir.
And spare.
But being underestimated so
Does mean I can observe and plan and learn
the way to rule.

Kate's soliloquy abstracts the key elements of Mantel's dismissal before insisting that such underestimations work to her advantage. Gradually, the camera reveals that this soliloquy occurs with the nanny and children in close proximity—the Duchess nods to them at "an heir. / And spare"; however, this diegetic audience does not react, heightening the aesthetic space in which Kate's words live and her ambitions unfold. Strategically, string orchestral scoring begins only as Kate's rising aims become clear: "But if I must put up with taunts, and make / So public everything I am, then I / Demand things for myself" (92). Fully regal underscoring asserts her right to "ask no less than power," as she strides (in the center of the camera's frame) through the palace corridors, the movement of both her body and the camera stressing her agential role in the making of nation and history. Here the television filming borrows from the vocabulary of political thrillers and dramas where the characteristic walk-and-talk creates transitions between scenes and conveys the sense that busy and powerful people cannot afford to waste a moment of time, a technique utilized extensively by Aaron Sorkin in *The West Wing* (1999–2006). From this pivotal moment onward, Kate acts as prime mover in Bartlett's Shakespearean history, creating alliances and exerting the pressure that will force Charles to abdicate and William to accede.

Admittedly, the obvious Lady Macbeth analogue might trouble this understanding of Kate as agent and of *King Charles III* as a corrective to the many Shakespearean history plays in which women are ultimately sidelined in favor of patriarchal authority. Since Bartlett's Kate more self-consciously engages the audience and articulates a direct critique of patriarchal power—"These little rooms of power are stocked full / With white, and southern, likely Oxbridge men" (91)—she constitutes not only a response to Mantel's aspersions but also an expansion of the cloistered "Kates" in Shakespeare's history, for example Hotspur's wife, Kate, and Henry V's Katherine of Valois. Nonetheless, it is fair to wonder whether or not Bartlett's Kate constitutes an appreciable improvement upon Joan de Pucelle or Queen Margaret, both of whom inscribe their names in history relying on morally questionable methods and strategies that the play texts often discount when wielded atypically by women. Furthermore, with Charles III performed on stage and screen by the aging acting legend, Tim Pigott-Smith, who died between filming and broadcast, Bartlett's drama takes on rather melancholic tones and garners sympathy for the hapless and principled Charles. Pigott-Smith delivers a gently towering performance as a wronged Lear in his right, if naïve, mind and as a champion of the fourth estate. When cornered by the Cambridges and other allied political operatives, Pigott-Smith's Charles plays the loving husband and father desperately giving way to his children because, "I cannot live alone" (116). His behavior may well leave the audience with questions about the ethics of Kate and William's political maneuverings to "save" the monarchy at Charles's expense. But, even in light of these questions about moral rectitude, the film version of *King Charles III* admits Catherine as a co-equal agent who largely determines the nation's ruling monarch.

Such is not the case with Prince Harry's girlfriend, the art student, Jess. In much the way that the play elides particularities of identity in the broad strokes of the kebab vender casting, so the film adaptation evades opportunities to reflect on the distinct experience of being black and female in the United Kingdom. Played on stage originally by the white actor, Tafline Steen, Jess is performed by the British-Jamaican, Tamara Lawrance, in the BBC filmed version but with little alteration to the script—as if one working class art student can be replaced with another but without an exploration of what it means more minutely to be a black woman in Britain. While Bartlett obviously made changes from the play script to the teleplay, one wonders why an effort to shape the script to meditate on the unique historical positionality of black British people wasn't at least attempted, especially when the original play and its film adaptation include a humiliation of Jess centered on the publication of nude photos. This particular plot device gathers more complex semiotic resonance when the sexualized female body in question becomes the black body of Lawrance, triggering the too-familiar stereotype of the Jezebel "as lascivious, seductive, and insatiable" (Harris-Perry 55, discussed in relationship to Queen Margaret in Chapter Four).[10] Nonetheless, Jess's role in the BBC adaptation remains largely unchanged from that in the play text, her political voice confined to criticism of class difference and wealth inequality, grievances she catalogues for the privileged Prince Harry. This half-hearted attempt to improve multicultural representation by replacing Steen with Lawrance, combined with a failure to recalibrate the text, appear as the all-too-familiar feint in which social class difference overshadows any effort to address systemic racism in Great Britain.

Initially, Jess enters the play wielding a confident freedom of agency not unlike Bartlett's reimagined Kate; however, plotting and filmic discourses steadily marginalize and minimize her distinct and full subjectivity in contradistinction to that of the Duchess of Cambridge. Harry (Richard Goulding) first meets Jess in a nightclub where she pulls no punches, perceptively diagnosing the Prince's resentment of his inherited public role. The camera stresses her significance in the scene by locating her centrally within shots, visible within the wider context of the club and the circle of Harry's mates in middle-distance shots. As her words provoke and entice Harry, the film signals a turn to the romantic with violin underscoring and a shift from midrange to shot-reverse-shot closeups of the two would-be lovers. Bartlett's Prince Harry makes clear that Jess's appeal begins with her truth-telling agency and the door she opens for him to escape the family business. Nonetheless, filmic and literary choices soon mark the difference between Kate and Jess as historical agents—a difference too easily explained by race. First, the film presentation of the two women differs substantially in the degree of access to interiority offered by the adaptation. While Kate enjoys the extended camera intimacy of a soliloquy as described above, Jess's motives and her character remain relatively opaque to the viewer. Rarely in scenes alone or unaccompanied for long, Jess does not function independently of Prince Harry nor does she shape political strategy in the way Kate does. While in the play text Jess and Kate exchange half a dozen lines (43–44) about their shared upbringing in the vicinity of Reading, the film deletes that conversation and limits Jess as an appendage to Harry and outlet for his desire to emancipate from the cage of royal life. In addition, the fact that Jess speaks very little poetry in the blank verse play could well be a class-driven artistic choice that tracks with Shakespearean conventions and might not attract much comment when played by the white Steen. However, when the filmed adaptation shifts the race of Jess, the explanation of her prosaic speech can too easily be her blackness. Just as the teleplay deletes Jess's friendly interchange with Kate, so it substantially trims her lines in scene after scene. While in the printed version Jess spars with James Reiss, Charles's press secretary, over an ex-boyfriend's attempted sale of nude selfies, the film Reiss (Tim McMullan) flatly refuses to aid Jess in countering the blackmail, leaving her visually isolated and minimized by the hard surfaces and cement structure of a Brutalist undercroft. In contrast with the walk-and-talk traveling shots of Kate, here the forward movement of the film's editing abandons Jess and foreshadows her ultimate exclusion.

The scene depicting Harry's declaration of independence from the Crown and desire for union with Jess enacts a further silencing of this isolated woman of color. The published photos do not dissuade Harry who insists instead on an audience with King Charles and Camilla (Margot Leicester), defending Jess as well as his own wish to "live a life of normalcy" by renouncing his public roles (90). In this scene, Bartlett's play text allows Jess five lines of iambic pentameter in which to explain to Charles her joint future with Harry; however, the film version deletes even this minimal participation. Throughout the scene in which Harry seeks to "Cast off the princely burden," Jess stands mute, distraught, talked about by a total of four white characters in the room—Harry, Charles, Camilla, and Reiss. In addition, the blocking places Jess in front of a large and brightly illuminated exterior window, making her the only person in the scene to be severely backlit for a high percentage of shots; doing so seriously compromises the HD video quality of her image, an insensitivity to lighting darker-skinned actors that Pascale Aebischer has traced in several filmed staged performances.[11] Even though King Charles does not regard the publication of the nude photos as a barrier to Harry's relationship, MacDonald observes that in the BBC's adaptation, "a black Jess' front-page nudity…points us to the ambient desire and derision surrounding black women and their bodies in popular culture, and to how this complex response can frame and ground white fictions of probity and order" (172). Jess experiences further alienation through dialogue that *does* survive the transfer from stage to screen. Charles accedes to Harry's request and muses, uncomfortably now given Jess's visible racial identity, "dissimilarity it seems does make a match"; he utters lines originally intended to stress class difference but that now very obviously also spotlight skin color difference. In a final patriarchal move framed by the camera, Charles stands between the two lovers, joining the hands of Harry and Jess (as if in blessing), re-enacting the familiar transaction in women-as-property requiring a patriarchal authorizer. Perhaps the production composed this moment to encapsulate a healthy multicultural Britain, one in which the monarch gladly invites British citizens of all hues into the family. This tableau with King Charles at the center telegraphs the fantasized welcoming embrace of a benevolent and resolutely post-imperial nation. However, the odd discomfort triggered by this effort at inclusivity is deepened when Jess finally speaks at scene's end as she utters a solitary word, a feeble, "okay," in response to Harry's query, "Okay?" The compressions of this scene obviously diminish Jess and cut short the historical agency she might wield, while "surprising" the audience with a progressive monarch eager to "get beyond" the nation's racist past. Ironically then, this particularly cringeworthy scene underscores a carelessness regarding race enacted by the playwright, director, and production team, who still manage to shift agential authority from the silenced black female to the magnanimous white male.

In the final scenes of the adapted film, the race of Jess intrudes again on the diegesis to thwart the effort to depict a thriving multicultural present and future history. As characteristic of all the scenes including Jess, the televisual film offers a condensed version of her dismissal from Harry, the royal family, and the nation. When Jess finds that a seat has not been reserved for her at William's coronation, Harry confronts her in a tight cathedral alcove to end their relationship. Seen tearfully walking away from the Abbey, Jess's narrative arc has run from agential truth-teller at the start to excluded, rejected outsider no longer embraced as a member of the family: "Jess' racialized fate suggests that perhaps the notion of family, whether national or in terms of blood, has always implied this potential for exile, as she walks away alone through the gathering crowds" (MacDonald 173). Both the creators of *The Hollow Crown: The Wars of the Roses* and of *King Charles III* enjoy a level of plausible deniability when it comes to the exclusion of these two black women at film's end; they can claim that they simply work with the material authored by another. Queen Margaret is not present at the end of Shakespeare's play when Henry VII initiates the Tudor dynasty, nor does Bartlett imagine in 2017 a scripted scenario where Harry abandons the royal family for love (though true future history has made that speculative possibility a fact for Prince Harry and his biracial wife, Meghan Markle in 2020).[12] Excuses and plausible deniability simply ring hollow in the face of the overwhelming evidence from a third-millennium performed history canon that too rarely depicts inclusive stories of the nation's past. And, for those of us invested in the circulation of Shakespeare's art, Bartlett's contemporary reinvention of the dramatist's history canon should concern us as a warning about how little that genre and its adaptations have been impacted by post-colonial historiography and critical race theory.

A Future for History?

King Charles III confronts the fragility of democracy by means of the play's reflections on networked and digital surveillance culture and the erosion of the Fourth Estate's liberties. The play's obvious anxiety over democracy in crisis should be in deep sympathy with a concomitant interest in how racisms threaten liberty. Bartlett's play confronts important questions about democracy's vulnerabilities—for example, about what happens to democracy as privacy erodes and the press's ability to expose the powerful diminishes—and should thus be concerned with how a racially unequal society harms collective freedom, security, and prosperity.[13] Gilroy explains that "making critical, historical, and philosophical encounters with racism productive….requires seeing 'race' as moral as well as political and analyzing it as part of a cosmopolitan understanding of the damage that racisms are still doing to democracy" (*Postcolonial* 33). Unfortunately, Bartlett short-changes the drama's insights by scripting a history play that does not take advantage of its postmodern context to represent in greater precision the historical subjectivity of non-whites and to examine the ways in which institutional racism contributes to an imperiled democracy. Indeed, for evidence of Gilroy's prescience regarding racism's continued assault on democracy, one need look no further than the Brexit vote to leave the European Union—the contentious referendum that united together racist, isolationist, nationalist, nostalgic middle-class Tories, and left-behind Labour voters to heed the call, "Take Back Control." That famous slogan embeds a nostalgic longing for a monochromatic, unified British past, preferably one in which the colonial-imperial might of Britain unapologetically issued orders across much of the globe. Such a pseudo-historiography must be replaced with an account that represents the cosmopolitan nature of British history and identities—never monolithic and always-already multiethnic, "a network of interdependent histories" (Said 19). We must strive to articulate and enact Said's concept of "intertwined and overlapping histories" as "an alternative both to a politics of blame and to the even more destructive politics of confrontation and hostility" (18), making good on what many years ago Alan Sinfield identified as the "potential for reproduction and intervention—for cultural struggle and change" inherent in popular culture and its iterations of Shakespeare (277). As Diana E. Henderson urges, scholars and practitioners should become contemporary "collaborators" with Shakespeare to achieve "diverse representations…deserving of thoughtful consideration" whereby "modern performance then functions neither as a mere reiteration of a nostalgic past (be it textual, sexist, or national) nor as a narcissistic love affair with a falsely conceived present" (258).

And that imperative returns us to the question of Shakespearean history and why it appears so hard to adapt and perform even a "future-history" play that recognizes and values multicultural British identities. Staging history often demands a period-specific verisimilitude that can trouble efforts to reimagine the nation's story in more inclusive ways; however, Bartlett's contemporary setting should afford a context where such need not be the case, and, indeed, the BBC adaptation does include more non-white actors than the stage performance. Nonetheless, as demonstrated in the nostalgia of the kebab scene and in the treatment of Lawrance's Jess, unless artists, creatives, and scholars participate in Gilroy's "oppositional reflection" concerning historiography and white supremacism, we will not overcome the race trouble in Shakespearean history. I will draw to a close by suggesting a number of reasons that performed and adapted Shakespearean history still too often reverts to affirming a white supremacist conception of the nation.

What *is* the Trouble with History?

1 As so many scholars have noted (discussed in Chapter One), the history plays participate in the nation-building project of early modern England and, as Carol Mejia LaPerle, reminds us, "race animates some of the most fundamental issues of inclusion and exclusion" (90) informing the nation's "imagined community." Crucial to a foundational conceptualization of Britain, the history plays too often have been operationalized to justify the empire and its white supremacist predication, baggage that vexes efforts to tell a new story by repurposing these key texts.

2 Indeed, a long-standing tendency to use Shakespearean history and performance as gatekeeper of white culture and authority infects the performance history of these plays, locating "actors of color outside of dramatic imaginings and reconceptualizations of English history and genealogy" (Chakravarty 204).

3 Textual traces in the history plays of casual racism and a recurring, early modern white/black moral and aesthetic binary examined famously by Kim F. Hall have long been mobilized for white supremacism. Scholars have demonstrated that these plays are rife with racist and white supremacist assumptions that have been encoded in the institutions of the former British empire.

4 Assertions of facticity and the imperiousness of truth claims—for example, "Henry VI was not African"—have made alternative casting and scripting difficult. What Ian Smith characterizes as "fetishizing historical accuracy" in scholarship transpires in the performance of history as well, and, as he points out, doing so, "is to claim the high moral ground of sound scholarship, a position from which to disguise resistance to race work, from

which to promote a singular perspective and methodology as acceptable while placing firm restrictions on others" ("We are Othello" 120).

5 A paucity of knowledge about the always-already racial and ethnic diversity of Britain and its history may explain the whiteness of many history play productions.[14] Numerous historians such as Peter Fryer correct that ignorance: "There has been a continuous black presence in this country for something like 500 years....And white historians, almost without exception, have done their best to deprive black people of their history, too. They have consistently belittled or wiped out the black past" (Fryer, *Aspects* 5).

6 Worse yet, a willful suppression of the stories of black and brown persons who lived, worked, and died in Britain since the Roman occupation may also be to blame: "This is not simply a case of historical amnesia. The parts of British history in which black people were active participants, as well as those in which they were the exploited victims, have been erased and the story of the black presence in Britain remains obscure and even disputed despite more than fifty years of archival discovery and historical scholarship" (Olusoga 10).

7 The tyranny of a realistic aesthetic—especially in televisual adaptation—dissuades creative teams from exploring color-conscious casting more systematically, perhaps fearful that audience members and viewers will complain about a lack of historical accuracy. Since productions often earn the "quality television" label by means of historical verisimilitude in costuming, location, lighting, and design, color-conscious casting decisions might disrupt the period drama's illusion of authenticity and thus its claim to a quality that rivals or, as Ramona Wray asserts, "exceeds the cinematic" ("Shakespeare" 14).

8 Lastly, the examples (regardless of mimetic mode) discussed in this book demonstrate that a lack of both will and imagination to re-present the history plays informed by a twenty-first century, postcolonial vantage point bedevils productions at major institutional venues. On this note, I will point to a worthy exception, the Globe's 2019 staging in the Sam Wanamaker Playhouse of *Richard II*, directed by Lynette Linton and Adjoa Andoh and performed entirely by women of color (the subject of this book's epilogue).

Though undeniably imbricated in oppressive structures of white supremacism, Shakespeare's history plays also spotlight and critique the exclusionary mechanisms by which nations cohere at the peril of those deemed "outsiders." Even a play such as *Henry V,* which has done long service in aid of unquestioning patriotism, chronicles how England's near neighbors—Wales, Scotland, and Ireland—perceive her efforts to assert hegemonic Britain much to their individual detriment. From this dramatic polyvocality, producers and adaptors should take courage and embark on transformational approaches that would not replicate the casual and overt racisms of the play texts but confront audiences with those traces and nation-building strategies. As Ayanna Thompson suggests concerning three of the most troubling plays in the Shakespearean canon—*The Taming of the Shrew, Othello*, and *The Merchant of Venice*—"we will be in a position where we can maybe rewrite the endings, change the plays, have other plays enter into the major canon and some of them fall out" ("All that Glisters"). Jenna Steigerwalt adds: "Only through criticism, honest conversations, and active work with race in performance can the pervasive and casual racism of Shakespeare's plays and today's world be overcome" (434). To that end, I would like to close with a modest list of practices designed to support a more thorough-going renovation of the representational modes associated with performed Shakespearean history.

What Can We Do About the Trouble with History?

1 Nontraditional and color-conscious casting must continue with recovered history in mind and attention directed expressly towards, as Margo Hendricks urges, "race as a performative act" (524). It is imperative that white and non-white persons *see* non-whites embodying the nation's history in roles across the power spectrum.[15] The ideological disruptions of such casting must carry on ethical work defining and negotiating the multicultural nation. However, such casting should not be insistently colorblind; we cannot allow audiences to pretend that race does not matter or is inconsequential. Worse yet, such productions should not permit audience members and viewers to think that "not seeing" race marks them as liberal-minded progressives who have achieved a post-racial superiority when, in fact, they simply instantiate the "color-blind racism" that Eduardo Bonilla-Silva rightly critiques.[16] As Michel de Certeau asserts, "Thus the past is the fiction of the present" (10); representations of the past inevitably depict the present, and I would add that a Shakespearean historiography worth preserving should perform and anticipate the future a nation hopes to create. Nontraditional casting of non-whites and women in the roles of historical authority figures from the past necessarily invites an audience to envision anew who wields power and whose voices should be heard. It is vital that this reimagining of power happens under the auspices of Shakespeare's iconic status as national poet and historiographer. However, these productions should be more than a fantasy space in which we project backwards a multicultural world onto the medieval and early modern past. While history confirms that Henry VIII was white, the archives also reveal that his court and London were home to a multicultural population (as discussed in Chapter Five). In light of this, nontraditional casting of the history plays achieves multiple functions and requires intersecting interpretive frames—insisting that the right to enact and retell the nation's story belongs to all bodies (an essential right for the purposes of interrogating and claiming power) *and* unearthing a silenced history of the real, lived experience of multicultural British citizens from

the discarded shards of historiography. Such casting demands that audiences and viewers oscillate between two poles of interpretive reference—one in which we push the boundaries of received history's verities *and* one in which we learn that some of those verities need correction, refinement, and inclusive expansion to address the silences and omissions of previous tellings. Francesca T. Royster characterizes such an approach to race and history in the conceptual casting of Edward Hall's *Rose Rage* (Chicago Shakespeare Theater, 2003): "Conceptual casting practices use ethnic and female actors cast in roles to give the play greater resonance. This technique heightens the space of the stage to create new worlds. There is a split between the theatrical and actual, though that split is not entirely clean" (228). Such approaches would also dislodge the faulty assumption of whiteness as *a priori* and race-neutral; this would necessarily expose whiteness as a work in progress throughout the nation-building of the history plays themselves, complicating the "assumption of early modern English history as a story of stable white identity" (Royster 230). Thus, we move between a non-realistic construct (knowing that Henry V was not African but admiring Adrian Lester's performance of Shakespeare's fictionalized history) and a realist frame properly informed by the neglected archival evidence that non-white persons have long been part of (though too often ignored) the British national narrative.

2 Creative teams at institutional outlets of performed and filmed Shakespeare must diversify: this means diversity of gender, race, and ethnicity from the artistic directors, to casting directors, cinematographers, editors, lighting designers, musicians, and the various craftspeople building sets and sewing costumes both for stage companies and major televisual corporations. Thompson explains the necessary structures for such mindful coordination in the context of a theater company:

> For a holistic approach to nontraditional casting within the multicultural classical company, the artistic director or a director of diversity initiatives (or a similar position) needs to function as the coordinator. The point is that this person needs to be in a position in which he/she is at the table for all of the major decisions because the casting models employed will affect every aspect of the company's season.
>
> (*Passing* 92)

3 The policy call by *The Future of Multi-Ethnic Britain* (2000) for improved diverse representation at the highest levels of arts organizations remains largely unanswered. Until creative teams of both stage, film, and televisual institutions do not replicate the self-affirming echo-chambers of white privilege, mindful casting and discussion of cast signification will always be inadequate.

4 Race "breaks" into performance must be planned and scripted. The diegesis of drama is already a fictional convention; we need not pretend that

even plays ostensibly detailing the lives of historical people attain a substantially different level of facticity than a play like *Othello*. Such "race breaks" like that noted in Nicholas Hytner's *Henry V* (2003) and discussed in Chapter Two signal to audience members that they *should* be seeing, processing, and reflecting on the semiotic meanings of race—both non-white and white races alike.

5 The abundant casual racism and sexism of the Shakespeare canon must be mindfully handled. Ambereen Dadabhoy notes that "Shakespeare's plays exhibit this conventionality and mainstreaming of racial difference by deploying racialized language in scenes where we find no overtly racialized characters" (1), pointing out that "racial Othering is not unusual in the Shakespearean corpus"(2). Indeed, Patricia Akhimie baldly puts it, "Shakespeare employs racist humor....a lot" (51). Some passages may best be deleted, but an honest acknowledgment of this tainted heritage of white supremacism and sexism demands that not all such references be sanitized. Recognizing our compromised literary canon means preserving some of that casual racism and sexism, but doing so with a difference.[17] Both white and non-white actors on stage and on film should "react" to the lines, guiding audiences and viewers not to laugh at the "jokes" of racism and misogyny but rather to condemn how such language infects discourse and high art. Additional text, the eloquently raised eyebrow, a starting back, the spoken undertone of dismay all can guide audiences to an honest appraisal of the canon and the ways that racism and sexism lurk in the discourses of the West's great art. These lines should not hover in a "business-as-usual" manner over a performance.

6 Playbills and other paratextual materials such as websites and social media platforms must acknowledge casting approaches. As Geoffrey Way has demonstrated, such digital sites, "offer a means of crafting a guided user experience," access which should go beyond marketing and reifying Shakespearean cultural value to provoke audience engagement with representational choices. If Richard III is played by an Indian actor in a British production, then the playbill needs to confront and analyze the socio-cultural impact of that decision. This does not define the actor's contribution solely by his/her race but rather serves to dispel the dangerous myth that audiences can truly not see race. Indeed, just as neoliberalism and nationalism joined in an unholy alliance after 9/11 in ways detrimental to multiculturalism, so the tacit agreement to ignore visible race actually undermines progressive efforts to achieve social equality and equity.

7 As many others have pointed out, audience education must be part of the process. With the stage, this can take a variety of forms: actor post-production interviews, workshops, talk-backs, etc. I think here of the approach to audience education which Vanessa I. Corredera attributes to Keith Hamilton Cobb during stagings of his play, *American Moor*; Cobb's performances feature post-show talk-backs and interviews taking on "the intellectual and emotional labour" (54) to help "well-meaning white

people who want to become anti-racist allies" ("Lessons" 55). Television and film afford similar opportunities through "bonus" materials and "extras" featured on DVDs or streamed on tie-in website platforms and YouTube channels.

8 Film and televisual production teams and adaptors of the history plays should more consistently jettison heritage-style filming and period settings in order to "transplant" the plotting into other more contemporary contexts. Though not without its flaws, Hytner's *Henry V* stands as a ready example of the fruitful interrogations and discoveries possible when Shakespeare's medieval history acquires a twenty-first-century *mise-en-scène*. This increases the plausibility of non-whites and women in traditionally white male leading roles, and it offers more opportunity to interrogate who controls the narration of history and how that historiography determines national identity.

9 More creative re-writing of the Shakespeare history canon of plays should occur. Following examples such as *Rosencrantz and Guildenstern are Dead* (Stoppard, 1966), *A Thousand Acres* (Smiley, 1991), or *Ophelia* (Klein, 2006), Shakespeare's history plays could be retold from the point of view of a lower-class person, a key female character, or a person of color who represents the actual, historical presence of non-aristocrats, women, and non-whites in late-medieval and early modern England. In that way, such retellings would "imaginatively transform Shakespeare in ways that may extend his relevance and authenticity for those often excluded from thoughtful representation on his page and stage" (Corredera, "'How Dey'" 35). For example, how might *Henry VIII* alter if one of Catherine of Aragon's black ladies-in-waiting were positioned centrally (as in Starz's Philippa Gregory adaptation, *The Spanish Princess*, 2019) to guide viewers in an understanding of Henrician Court politics?

I humbly suggest that these practices might just better represent the richness of the multicultural, ever-changing, continually "*re*invented" (Appiah, *The Lies* 102) nation and mobilize Shakespeare's iconicity without an accompanying nostalgia for imagined homogeneity or lost greatness. These tactics could assist audiences and viewers in recognizing that multiplicity and diversity do not deplete the nation or signal a thinning out or threat but instead generate surplus, abundance, and a concept of belonging not predicated upon the exclusion and oppression of "outsiders."

Notes

1 For example, Michael Billington notes that as the play progresses, it "has acquired a borrowed grandeur through its Shakespearean form"; and Dominic Cavendish asserts: "He [Bartlett] makes knowing, deft references to many of Shakespeare's political works—including the Henries, Richard II, Macbeth and King Lear." Ben Brantley's review of the New York production observes, "And for Bardophiles,

'King Charles III' provides the bonus of confirming the immortal topicality of Shakespeare."

2 Richard Wilson notes the timeliness of *King Charles III*'s plotting: "Bartlett's Shakespearean verse drama coincided with speculation that the Prince of Wales would persist with his hobbyhorses, such as alternative medicine and kitsch architecture, on succeeding the Queen. So, the plot is not so far-fetched when Charles appears at the bar of the House of Commons, like his seventeenth-century namesake, to dissolve parliament" (90).

3 Joyce Green MacDonald observes concerning the multiethnic crowd shots early in the film: "Much more than its original London staging, the television film emphasizes to us that the future history of Britain is multiracial" (169).

4 In the Sam Mendes and Kevin Spacey Old Vic staging of *Richard III* (2011), a similar faux multiculturalism can be detected: "This faux globalism garnishes performance with the gloss of a non-Western culture or history but resolutely follows English stage traditions and, more worryingly, reinvigorates distinctly European stereotypes of the non-Western cultures from which it borrows" (Pittman, "Too Soon").

5 Indeed, Nadine El-Enany cites British involvement in Commonwealth nations as further evidence that, "Britain remains a state embedded in colonial relations that are widely considered to be historical, or not known to have existed at all" (212).

6 That John of Gaunt's imagery ghosts much of the play can be confirmed by a direct echo when Bartlett's King Charles muses, "Whatever many like to think, there is / A wise and ancient bond between the Crown / And population of this pleasant isle" (57–58).

7 Quotations from *Charles III* are taken from the printed text when identified by page number; however, when the teleplay differs from the printed text, quotations are author transcription from the DVD recording of the televised version.

8 In a monograph overview of Rupert Goold's career, Sarah Grochala points to post-2008 austerity cuts as one explanation of the Almeida Theatre's lack of diversity: "The biggest challenge Goold has faced as artistic director of the Almeida is financial. In 2011, the Arts Council cut the theatre's National Portfolio Organisation (NPO) funding by 39 per cent" (81). Citing the impact of inflation on cost of living, Grochala contends that, "One of the impacts of this is a decrease in the diversity of artists, as those from economically deprived backgrounds find it 'harder and harder to get by'. Financial pressures put pressure on ticket prices and consequently also on the accessibility of theatre to a more diverse audience, who become increasingly excluded as ticket prices increase" (81). In her afterword to the book, Grochala describes a more recent stock-taking by Goold that goes beyond blaming austerity to, instead, recognizing his own privileges that blinded him to the overwhelming whiteness of productions under his tenure as Artistic Director at the Almeida. She writes that, "acknowledging his own privilege," Goold understands: "'Right now I'm sort of anti the narrative because I'm a white middle-aged man from public school, who went to Cambridge' (Goold 2018b). He is aware that 'somebody like me isn't the voice people want to hear on the political argument because we've heard enough of those voices'" (147).

9 An anonymous editorial for *The Guardian* summarizes the range of Shakespearean analogues: "Mr. Bartlett's blank-verse drama is a riff on the Shakespearean history play: he has given us a Prince Charles tinged with Lear and Richard III; a Duchess of Cambridge perfumed with Lady Macbeth; and a Prince Harry very obviously drawing on his namesake, Prince Hal of Henry IV, who hangs around taverns with his raffish pals only to abandon them brutally when duty calls" ("The Guardian View").

10 Patricia Hill Collins explains that the hyper-sexuality of the Jezebel functions as a "controlling image" or recurring stereotype of black women: "A final controlling

image—the jezebel, whore, or 'hoochie'—is central in this nexus of controlling images of Black womanhood. Because efforts to control Black women's sexuality lie at the heart of Black women's oppression, historical jezebels and contemporary 'hoochies' represent a deviant Black female sexuality" (89).

11 In the Royal Shakespeare Company broadcast of director Simon Godwin's *Hamlet* (2016), Aebischer detects serious problems in the lighting scheme for the production's black cast, noting "in its technology a bias" that renders the performances of BAME actors "inherently less visible, legible and (re)markable than those of their lighter-skinned peers" (*Shakespeare* 190). She observes that, "cameras had difficulties adjusting for darker skin tones, especially in scenes where darker- and lighter-skinned performers shared the frame: the equipment was geared towards defining the lighter faces sharply, whereas darker faces could, at times, become 'illegible'" (182).

12 In a piece for *RadioTimes*, Huw Fullerton notes the uncanny manner in which Bartlett *did* in some ways accurately predict a "future history," in his Prince Harry subplot, though given that the love interest was originally played by a white actor, Bartlett's drama did not anticipate the racist reactions to Markle. Fullerton explains that Kensington Palace's statement condemning press treatment of Markle (8 Nov. 2016) was released "the day before the first readthrough of the TV version of the play," heightening for the cast the "relevance and importance of the project."

13 For example, in the context of American anti-black violence, Ruben Espinosa urgently states: "in the process of such continuous acts of violence and killing, what we are witnessing is the slow dying of our democracy" (*Shakespeare* 141).

14 Fryer asserts: "There were Africans in Britain before the English came here. Some were soldiers in the Roman imperial army that occupied the southern part of our island for three and a half centuries. Others were slaves"; "Besides African soldiers and slaves, there may well have been officers (*praefecti*) from the flourishing towns of north Africa serving in Roman Britain in the second and third centuries" (*Staying* 1, 2).

15 As Fryer insists, "Here too white people need to know something about black history, since for us it furnishes a version of British history that strongly challenges *our* national sense of smugness and self-righteousness, *our* avowal of fair play" (*Aspects* 6).

16 Bonilla-Silva explains that colorblind racism features the following characteristics: "(1) the extension of the principles of liberalism to racial matters in an abstract manner, (2) cultural rather than biological explanation of minorities' inferior standing and performance in labor and educational markets, (3) naturalization of racial phenomena such as residential and school segregation, and (4) the claim that discrimination has all but disappeared" (42).

17 Akhimie argues that, on the one hand, the racism fueling humor in Shakespeare, "is the hard edge of…race thinking because our laughter solidifies the power and reach of our prejudices." However, on the other hand, such "Comedy may also present the opportunity to laugh those prejudices out of fashion or to undermine their logic or their appeal" (52). In contrast to the long-standing critical tendency to ignore these lines or the performance traditions that either quietly delete or glide quickly over them, Akhimie urges, "Rather than working to foreclose the pain of racist humor in Shakespeare's comedies, we can explore the wound" (56). I would contend that just as an honest engagement with racist humor in the comedies can expose, "the production and maintenance of groups, processes of inclusion and exclusion, and of hierarchization" (56), so too must this occur within the performed history plays, and urgently so, precisely because they deal with how people groups coalesce via inclusion, exclusion, and hierarchization into the nation.

7 Epilogue

The Case of Two Richards

"For God's sake, let us sit upon the ground
And tell sad stories of the death of kings."
(*Richard II*)

This book began in 2012 when, as part of writing about Series One of *The Hollow Crown* (2012), I read the Runnymede Trust's report, *The Future of Multi-Ethnic Britain* (2000). In that first article about *The Hollow Crown*, I struggled to reconcile the cautious optimism of the *FMEB* and its gentle policy recommendations for a recalibration of the nation's story with the all-too-limited representational imagination found in the Neal Street Productions' adaptations of Shakespeare's second tetralogy. Of course, as has already been acknowledged, the world changed drastically between the release of the report in 2000 and *The Hollow Crown* airing—terrorist attacks in the United States, United Kingdom, and Europe, the invasions of Afghanistan and Iraq, and a global financial crisis along with the crippling austerity measures that followed. By the time I received sabbatical release in 2018 to research this book, the world had also witnessed a refugee crisis sparked by the wars in the Middle East and a march towards far-right nationalism—confirmed by the Brexit vote and the election of Donald J. Trump in 2016. These events thus helped frame the date parameters of my own interest in gender and race in performances of Shakespeare's history. I want to conclude this book's observations with a brief consideration of another policy document, this one produced in the shadow of Brexit in late 2016, *The Casey Review: A review into opportunity and integration* (December 2016), and two iterations of *Richard II*: one from the Netflix Windsor family costume drama, *The Crown* ("Tywysog Cymru," Dir. Christian Schwochow, 2019), and the second a performance of *Richard II* in the Sam Wanamaker Playhouse at Shakespeare's Globe directed by Adjoa Andoh and Lynette Linton (2019). These three artifacts underscore and instantiate the central concerns of this book as well as point a way forward that might just address the trouble with history.

2000–2016: Dis-Integration

Commissioned by Prime Minister David Cameron and Home Secretary Theresa May in 2015 "to undertake a review into integration and opportunity

DOI: 10.4324/9781003043065-7

in isolated and deprived communities," *The Casey Review* represents a substantial policy retreat and reorientation from the liberal-leaning proposals of Bhikhu Parekh's *FMEB* report (Casey 5). This should not be surprising given Cameron's well-known advocacy of a "muscular liberalism" rejecting multiculturalism as a failed societal enterprise.[1] Dame Louise Casey elaborates in her foreword to the published review:

> I approached this task hoping that by improving integration and the life chances of some of the most disadvantaged and isolated communities, we could also inject some resilience against those who try to divide us with their extremism and hate.
>
> (5)

Repeatedly, Casey positions the "findings" as designed to "save" the nation from the extremes of both Islamic fundamentalists and European far-right fascism. Perhaps the most troubling aspect of the review is its glaring tendency to single out Muslim communities in example after example when "reporting" on the successful or unsuccessful integration of immigrant communities. Writing for *The Guardian*, Matthew Taylor counts 249 references to Muslims in the 200-page report; in contrast, he notes that Polish communities, for example, are mentioned only fourteen times. This disproportionate referencing of Islamic communities confirms the review's biased assumption that such immigrants are singularly unsuited to assimilation into so-called British values. Dame Casey summarizes the discoveries she and her unnamed team members made over the course of 800 interviews:

> I also found...worrying things including high levels of social and economic isolation in some places and cultural and religious practices in communities that are not only holding some of our citizens back but run contrary to British values and sometimes our laws.
>
> (5)

She admits, almost as a badge of honor, that the so-called hard truths of her report exert pressure on "Muslims of Pakistani and Bangladeshi heritage" (6). *The Casey Review* received enthusiastic accolades in some quarters for the "bravery" of its assertion that Muslim cultural values often contravene Britishness: "Ukip's immigration spokesman, John Bickley, welcomed what he described as a 'damning' report. 'It pulls no punches and is an excoriating critique of the Labour, Conservatives and Liberal Democrat parties' support of mass immigration, multiculturalism and political correctness'" (M. Taylor). Though produced under Conservative auspices, the review actually recycles arguments endemic to the "social exclusion" policies of Tony Blair's New Labour government. Sivamohan Valluvan characterizes Casey's review as "preoccupied with charting the many liberal deficits that primarily Muslim communities were putatively suffering from," arguing that, "for all its affected grandstanding about speaking hard truths, the report was in fact simply another iteration of much of the policy intervention and political hyperventilation that suffused the post-2001…era in British politics" (*The Clamour* 71–72). Though presented as a review intended to foster tolerance as a British value, a national virtue threatened by Islamic and far-right extremists alike, the review's habitual spotlighting of Muslim communities and their isolation plays conveniently into the hands of far-right new nationalists of the UKIP variety.

The Casey Review also instantiates the all-too-familiar amnesia about colonial-imperial sins of the past (a forgetfulness fueled by the desire for racial innocence) and a frankly reprehensible inhospitality in the present, opting instead to concentrate on how immigrant communities and their individual members are the source of their own isolation. In contrast to the Parekh report's insistence that the monoethnic hue of British history and identity must be revisited and retold to account for a widely multiethnic citizenry, unsurprisingly, Casey's evaluations and recommendations never concede the white supremacist underpinnings of the nation's story. One segment briefly acknowledges the biased representation of Muslims in the media but quickly transitions to examining levels of access to the Internet and the pathways on the Internet employed by bad actors to radicalize young Muslims (76). Valluvan and Virinder S. Kalra identify the review as part of,

> a resurgent integration conceit…that trades on an unequivocally nationalist premise: presuming that the coherence and integrity of the nation, in its distinctly majoritarian sense, is being imperiled by the excess presence of "alien" cultures (not least, Muslims) incompatible with the national polity—alien cultures that are in need of remedial redress and/or active proscription.
>
> (2397)

To counter this perceived dissonance between immigrant cultural values (read Muslim here) and the British nation, the review offers a proposed "integration oath" administered to "immigrants intending to settle in Britain" (17). Such an oath implies that the onus falls upon immigrants to adjust and adapt but denies the nation's obligations of hospitality. Very little in Dame Casey's review, unlike Parekh's *FMEB* report, acknowledges that "integration" is inhibited not solely by immigrant community values or reluctance but too often by the "host" nation and its racisms.[2]

So what does this have to do with Shakespearean historiography and performance? In its denial of systemic racism and its failure to acknowledge the impact of colonialism in the past and the persistence of neocolonialism in the present, *The Casey Review* has everything to do with history and nation—the subject matter repeatedly under examination in Shakespeare's dramas. *The Casey Review* documents, so precisely, the callous spirit of 2016 when Vote Leave campaigners promised to make Britain great again by denying economic interdependency with Europe and closing the nation's doors to any and all who might dare to seek refuge in that "fortress built by Nature for herself / Against infection and the hand of war" (*Richard II* 2.1.43–44). More importantly, the review demonstrates a strongly homogenous understanding of the United Kingdom that inadequately accounts for its long-standing cosmopolitan and multicultural communities, as well as the diversity of the four home nations themselves—England, Northern Ireland, Scotland, and Wales. Preoccupied with the "failure" of black and brown Muslims to share common "British" values, *The Casey Review* appears to assume that the predominantly white citizens of the home nations replicate Britishness in non-threatening ways that do not require assessment by the audit.

A Welsh Correction?

Episode Six of *The Crown*'s Season Three directly confronts such assumptions by centering on a Welsh desire for home rule and rejection of hegemonic Britishness. Written by James Graham and Peter Morgan, "Tywysog Cymru" weaves the identity struggles of Charles (Josh O'Connor) on the brink of his 1969 investiture into the ceremonial title, Prince of Wales, with those of the Welsh people whose lost sovereignty helped create Great Britain. As imagined by the episode, Prince Charles also desires autonomy and self-governance but strains against his repressive family and royal destiny; "Tywysog Cymru" manifests this struggle by pitting his theatrical aspirations at Cambridge against his responsibility as Prince of Wales to "represent" the nation. Bookended by a stage performance of *Richard II*, the episode arc begins backstage in Cambridge, takes a reluctant Charles to Wales for language instruction, depicts his investiture as Prince of Wales and the speech he delivers in Welsh, and then concludes first at Buckingham Palace and then finally in Cambridge for a performance of *Richard II*. Though the episode cleverly pairs the concerns of Shakespearean historiography and nation-building with the coming of age of Charles, it ultimately does little to unsettle the whiteness of Britain's history and citizenry and thus, by extension, of Shakespeare's text. Indeed, this episode and the seasons of *The Crown* in general constitute a repeatedly missed opportunity to move beyond the soapy voyeurism of royal-watching to explore the postcolonial remnants of Britain in the twentieth century. Relied upon as a lens through which to view Charles's coming of age and familial agon, *Richard II* does not prompt a wholesale reconsideration of the cost of nationhood to the individual home nations nor to women and people of color. Rather, the episode re-centers focus on the burdens of a hyper-white patriarchal royal heir, making even its sympathetic portrayal of the Welsh struggle for autonomy yet another mechanism to mirror Charles's plight and psychology.

Camera movement, position, and framing combine to establish the weakness of Charles's subject position and his desire for escape and authentic self-expression. All the markers of heritage film appear in the lush visual qualities and *mise-en-scène* of *The Crown*'s production values as this episode begins backstage with Charles and his colleagues preparing to perform *Richard II*.[3] Opening on costumed white male actors touching up their make-up at dressing room mirrors while warming up their voices, the camera glides in its unobtrusive grace around the room to settle over Charles's right shoulder to view his reflection in the mirror as he rehearses *sotto voce* the "hollow crown" monologue. The mirror device operates throughout the episode—in the actors' green room, the palace audience chamber, and the Queen's dressing room—underscoring the performative display of monarchy and slyly echoing Richard II's request, "command a mirror hither straight, / That it may show me what a face I have / Since it is bankrout of his majesty" (4.1.265–267). In addition, shots repeatedly frame Charles within rigidly symmetrical spaces and capture him against a variety of backgrounds that minimize and even trivialize him. When Charles learns he must leave Cambridge for a term to study Welsh in a publicity and appeasement endeavor prior to his investiture, the episode positions him centrally and alone on a sofa dwarfed by a largescale royal family portrait behind him. Arrayed opposite Charles in carefully balanced and height-dependent order, his assembled family confronts him with this news stressing the young prince's disempowerment and enmeshment within a dynastic structure that denies him personal freedom. A longshot of the entire palace chamber taken from a slightly higher angle places Charles in the center of the frame subject to the gaze of his family and the viewing audience. Thus, the episode establishes the vulnerability and neutered agency of this most privileged of young men through the mechanics of its elegant, heritage-style filming.

Even as the episode grants space to the republican advocacy of Charles's Welsh language tutor, Edward Millward (Mark Lewis Jones), it takes up devolution as a mirror for Charles's own desire to escape the all-encompassing and homogenizing power of the British monarchy and its imperatives. Indeed, Millward complains that the Crown, "Imposes a kind of uniformity that by default, yes, suppresses Welsh identity with a ubiquitous Britishness." Charles's affinity with the Welsh contest for autonomy humanizes him for the viewer, and the camera's tendency to linger on a lonely, stooped Charles in shot after shot reinforces that sympathy. For example, during a family dinner at the home of his tutor, Charles responds to the warmth of the domestic scene yet still is viewed in the scene's parting image through the narrow rectangular "pass through" window connecting the kitchen to the dining room. Moved both by his tutor and the history of Wales he begins to learn, Charles crafts an addition to his investiture speech celebrating the unique and independent identity of the Welsh people, a speech that implies unspoken affinity between the stunted prince and his mother's subject peoples. This plot element reinforces that though the episode takes up the matter of Shakespearean history—the burdens of monarchy and a stifling British hegemony—these concerns remain subordinate to the coming-of-age narrative centered on the diffident young white man. Furthermore, this plotting parallel establishes a false equivalency between the hamstrung agency of Charles and the struggles of Wales that papers over serious questions of privilege.

Charles's revised investiture speech articulates the right of Welsh people to a distinct identity, but in its call for self-determination, Queen Elizabeth (Olivia

Colman) perceives coded critique of the constraints her son likewise experiences. Film technique continues to build sympathy for Charles who has successfully mastered Welsh to burnish the monarchy's public image and yet suffers as the butt of his mother's coldness. When he returns to receive his mother's praise for his effective speech, he is dwarfed by the symmetrical staircases of the palace before proceeding to his mother's rooms, a reminder of how little he rates within the royal institution. As the Queen chastises her son for voicing an individualized perspective that she insists will be regarded by none, the camera captures the verbally reduced and alienated Prince Charles through the open woodwork of a boudoir chair and the bend of the Queen's arm and then in the reflection from her dressing table mirror. Despite his maturing residence in Wales, the young prince remains as visually confined as at the episode's outset—his only escape of a sort will manifest on stage as Richard II. O'Connor begins a voiceover of "From within the hollow crown" as continuity editing carries the viewer from the palace back to Cambridge and the bookended green room scene. In ermine and thick white stage make-up, Charles prepares at his mirror until a cut reveals him midway through the speech on stage at "farewell, king! / Cover your heads." (3.3.170–171). The episode closes on Charles's recitation of, "subjected thus, / How can you say to me, I am a king?" By ending with this Shakespearean question, the episode reinforces the central irony it has spotlighted—that this man who will be king possesses very little autonomy. Though knowing in its recirculation of Shakespeare's history, the episode (while reinstating the question of Welsh sovereignty, language, and culture) does not push the history genre beyond comfortable masculine-centered confines—it remains content to use both Shakespeare and the Welsh as yet another means by which to tell the coming-of-age story of privileged white men. Though admittedly at times the object of ridicule, the Welsh remain unintegrated and unassimilated throughout the history plays, a stubborn resistance to the hegemonic enforcement of incipient Britishness that casts doubt on the emergent nation.[4] Alas, too predictably, *The Crown*'s substitution of Charles's plight for the larger questions of home rule sidesteps the potential for self-examination latent in Shakespeare's historiography.

Histories Remembered

In contrast, Shakespeare's Globe Theatre presented in its 2019 *Richard II* a substantial and creative transformation of Shakespearean history, modeling an inclusive and robustly interrogative form of history-making. Without doubt, the Andoh and Linton co-directed production heeded the call made by Parekh and his colleagues in 2000 for historiography that would face "the issue of racism, confronting Britain's selective amnesia about its former empire" and better represent "the diverse composition of its present population" (*The Future* 163). Differing from the many examples of half-hearted, inattentive, and even racist colorblind casting discussed in this book, the Globe production in the Sam Wanamaker Playhouse insisted that viewers "see" black and brown bodies as they performed Shakespeare's early modern version of medieval history. As Geraldine Heng has argued, we cannot combat racism until its structures are rendered visible, making colorblind strategies undeniably inadequate tools for anti-racist agendas: "…race, like the structure of power exercised by even would-be benign forms of colonial privilege, can only be made visible when the conditions of privilege inhabited by those who wield power are not invisible, natural, and the norm" (Heng 2). Andoh and Linton's production powerfully confronted the complexities of intersectional identity by casting all roles with women of color and working with an entirely female crew of color.

The all-female cast corrected the performance practices discussed throughout this book that frequently comply with patriarchal strictures on women's agency. Too often the butt of patriarchal jokes in the history plays—either as untrustworthy vessels for procreation or upstart and monstrous threats to masculine authority—women in this *Richard II* gathered a gravitas and sororal community often denied them in these nation-defining texts. For example, Act One, Scene Two's pleading widow, the Duchess of Gloucester (Sarah Lam), did not call for vengeance in utter isolation—the lone female voice sandwiched between two scenes in which performative masculinity is made aggressively manifest. In this frequently trimmed scene (cut in *The Hollow Crown*, for example), the Globe's Duchess did not prevail successfully on John of Gaunt (Doña Croll) to enact vengeance on her dead husband's behalf, but she was not left utterly to the justice of God as in the text. Quite literally, she was not the only woman in a man's world. John of Gaunt, her kinsman, was, of course, also female, and more provocatively, Croll transformed from Gaunt into the vociferous agent, the Duchess of York, whose advocacy on her son's behalf succeeds later in the play. In addition to the way gender resonated through doubling and created fruitful ventures for female agency rather than historical dead-ends, Romola Nuttall notes enriched possibilities in the text's imagery: "The all-female cast brought new resonances to the playtext, particularly in references to children, wombs and bleeding" (4), reclaiming language appropriated by the play's men. Much as the trick of crossdressing in Shakespeare demonstrates the constructed nature of gender identity and its dependence on a vocabulary of signifying mannerisms and costumes, so these cross-dressed and gender-bending women underscored the inherent arbitrariness that has dictated all power, authority, and sway be assigned to one biological sex. Moreover, the production validated the claims of women, and women of color especially, to positions of authority by staging female ascendency and rule so utterly.

These power-wielding women of color achieved much more than simply forcing audiences to "see" black and brown females on stage ruling medieval history; through the performers as well as the set design, costuming, and promotion, the staging also recovered the oft-ignored history of British colonial-imperialism. This deliberate approach de-naturalized the gender *and* racial status quo and rendered absolutely visible the whiteness of Shakespearean theater and the national story often conveyed. Quite literally, Andoh, Linton, and their team had to contest with a space designed without question for white acting bodies. In multiple interviews, Andoh raises the problematic decision taken by Dominic Dromgoole (Shakespeare's Globe artistic director, 2006–2016) to paint the interior of the Sam Wanamaker Playhouse black, a color that undermines the visibility of black actors. Andoh declares:

> That does not work for people of colour in space lit purely by candlelight. Black sucks the light out of the space and unless you light extremely fiercely, when *we of colour* are onstage it's a radio play. Subliminally it says people of colour are not meant to be on this stage and by extension nor in this audience.
>
> (68)

Responding to this structurally unwelcoming space, Andoh explains:

> I had everything clad in bamboo; first, because bamboo is a material you would find in East Asia, South East Asia, Africa, the Middle East and the West Indies—mirroring the geographical histories of the bodies onstage; secondly because Bamboo is light in colour, and light bounces off bamboo, which would help us enormously.
>
> (68–69)

In interview after interview, Andoh catalogues details of performance from the playing space, set design, costuming, props, and music that transmit racialized and gendered meaning. As a practitioner, Andoh models an attention to the semiotics of race and gender triggered by every aspect of performance, an attention to the material of productions that must also inform the analytical methodologies of adaptation and appropriation scholars—methods that this book endeavors to practice. Just as Andoh exemplifies, scholarship of performance must ask, "What story about the nation is advanced by every detail of a production?"

By casting largely diasporic actors from the former British Empire, Andoh and Linton excavated and centralized complex and interdependent narratives constituting an all-too-often forgotten part of the nation's historical continuum. In doing so, Andoh and Linton practiced a method of history-telling envisaged by Edward Said, who argues that redressing the wounds of colonial-imperialism necessitates an exploration of "intertwined and overlapping histories" (18). Described as "the residuum of a dense, interesting history," Said argues that

> these traces of the past in the present point the way to a study of the histories—the plural is used advisedly—created by empire, not just the stories of the white man and woman, but also those of the non-whites whose lands and very being were at issue, even as their claims were denied or ignored.
>
> (21)

In a podcast reflection for Shakespeare's Globe, Andoh explains the objective of the production:

> I wanted for us as an audience and a cast to get involved in a thought experiment that says what happens if you tell the story of England out of the mouths of women and people of color, women of color who are generally the bottom of the heap in social hierarchies, particularly women who are in this country because at some point this country went to their countries through empire and either took them, or their goods, or their natural resources and through them prospered as a nation.
>
> ("This sceptred")[5]

A sampling from the cast's backgrounds confirms the varied postcolonial histories embodied in this profoundly intentional iteration of *Richard II*: for example, British-Ghanaian Andoh (Richard II), Jamaican-British Doña Croll (John of Gaunt / Duchess of York), Indian-British Ayesha Dharker (Aumerle), Iranian-British Leila Farzad (Queen), British-Chinese Sarah Lam (Duchess of Gloucester/Bushy/Willoughby/Gardener), and British-Trinidadian Indra Ové (Mowbray/Northumberland). The production brought those personal histories to the stage by creating ancestor portraits to line the playhouse perimeters—visible invocations of the performers' actual "female antecedents" whose stories informed the journey of each participant to that moment and that staging of Shakespeare's history ("This sceptred"). Through this collective embodied history, the production recovered the voices of women of color who have been, as Joyce Green MacDonald contends, "effaced, muted, repressed in Shakespeare" (7).[6] This diverse gathering of artists formed a postcolonial "cultural survival of the people" (243–244): "For it is by living on the borderline of history and language, on the limits of race and gender, that we are in a position to translate the differences between them into a kind of solidarity" (Bhabha 244). Such a solidarity produces the "Counter-narratives of the nation that continually evoke and erase its totalizing boundaries—both actual and conceptual" to disrupt "those ideological manoeuvres through which 'imagined communities' are given essentialist identities" (213). By adapting *Richard II* through the histories of diasporic citizens, Andoh and Linton created an ameliorative counter-narrative and modeled highly self-aware dramaturgical approaches that began to correct the appalling representational failures traced throughout this book.

Just as the diverse group of actors bore their personal histories onto the stage, so the costuming, props, and musical instruments (all originating from the many lands occupied and exploited by Great Britain) made the colonial-imperial history appear as a palimpsest legible underneath, through, and over the medieval Wars of the Roses. The costuming and props, described by Nuttall in her review as "generally Oriental and Asiatic," gestured to the diverse cultures represented by the actors and their heritages: "No costume was the same yet all shared an appropriation of male dress in the use of trousers and tunics" (3). But rather than flatten out difference, the references to colonial history and formerly colonized cultures imported those worlds into the telling of Shakespearean history, insisting on the play text's imbrication within that long line of national narratives and global interdependence. Andoh describes the production's goal to "synthesize lots of different cultures," identifying her crown as Ashanti, her costume as an Indian prince's, and the musical instruments as originating from China, Southeast Asia, and West Africa ("This sceptred"). This *Richard II* enacted medieval English history so that an audience might also simultaneously see and account for Britain's former colonial-imperial lands and their peoples. Universalizing so as not to diminish the particular, the production invited the audience to abstract out of its historiography the trans-historical strategies of power and nation-building dramatized by *Richard II* and, importantly, to reckon with the specific iteration of those strategies again and again throughout Britain's long colonial-imperial history. Though the production team members very precisely accounted for the pastiche of referents accrued by means of costuming, props, and music, critics might rightly worry that this well-intentioned *Richard II* ran the risk of careless exoticizing in the long, de-particularized Orientalist tradition of European art. Andoh and Linton's production endeavored to facilitate a post-imperial education to counter persistent belief in the empire's positive global impact; in 2016, 43 percent of the British public still "considered the British Empire to have been a good thing" (El-Enany 213). What might have enhanced the pedagogical function of the performance would have been a more detailed website that catalogued the nations and traditions referenced by the production choices. Something akin to the "Locations of Wolf Hall" website discussed in Chapter Five would have helped to counter a tendency to flatten the very specific nations the cast and crew of *Richard II* referenced. Such institutional infrastructure would support the aims of the artists and assist audience member learning and understanding.[7]

Keenly aware their production run would coincide with 29 March 2019, the date on which the United Kingdom was originally set to leave the European Union, the directors, cast, and crew confronted the very isolationist, racist, and sexist nationalism which led to the 2016 referendum vote. In promotional images and in a final *coup-de-théâtre*, the production deployed England's St. George's cross flag to reference this troubling nationalism. Promotional photos for the production superimposed a headshot of Andoh over the flag, an image the actor-director proudly describes as "…my big brown face in front of the flag of St. George" (68). An avid football fan and England supporter, Andoh claims the St. George's cross flag as her own and intended the production's imagery as a rebuttal to those who would use that emblem as exclusionary rather than inclusive: "I wanted to say, 'This is our flag as well. We built this nation, so let us have a conversation with the audience in which we reflect on the state of the nation'" ("This sceptred"). Reclaiming the image from its association with racist football hooligans in order to invite others to see themselves as part of a more expansively understood national history and identity, Andoh did not avoid or naïvely ignore the undercurrents of hate mobilized by the flag. Indeed, the final scene directly confronted the violence of the symbol and edited the play text's language to indict white supremacy for its multitude of sins remembered. As actors applied a white powder to their faces, King Henry IV (Sarah Niles) intoned the last lines of the play, replacing the text's "sullen black incontinent" with "bloodless white incontinent":

> Come mourn with me for what I do lament,
> And put on [bloodless white] incontinent.
> I'll make a voyage to the Holy Land,
> To wash this blood off from my guilty hand.
> March sadly after, grace my mournings here,
> In weeping after this untimely bier.
>
> (5.6.47–52)

The edited speech highlights how the black/white moral and color binary scripted into early modern imagery can and should be reworked—in this case black's association with death transformed into white (a fact suited to the cultural practices represented by these diasporic women but also sadly all-too-apt when accounting for white supremacy's deadly costs). In addition, performed by this group of black and brown women, the prospect of Henry IV's expiation through a crusade to the Holy Land resonated critically, a fact emphasized by the application of whiteface and the keening wail of the final moments. This cast of performers made it impossible not to flashforward from Richard's death to the colonial occupation of the Middle East, the enmeshment in innumerable conflicts over the resources of that region, the unending War on Terror, and the refugees seeking asylum from the disruption sown by the US-led wars in Afghanistan and Iraq. As a seemingly contrite Henry IV concluded, the blood-red cross of St. George unfurled across the bamboo backdrop to link the past and the present in a painful continuum of nation-building, exploitation, and grief. This highly self-aware reckoning contrasts markedly with the conclusion of Michael Boyd's *III Henry VI* (2000). As I discuss in Chapter Two, that production closed on the bloody stain left behind by the body of David Oyelowo's titular monarch, a tableau that could have been mindfully expanded to signal the nation's legacy of slavery and colonialism. But while those possibilities remained largely submerged in the Boyd production and dependent upon the audience members' knowledge of Oyelowo's Nigerian heritage, the cost of nationalism to women and non-whites could not be avoided in the final moments of Andoh and Linton's *Richard II*.

Telling Sad Stories of the Death of Kings

Emmanuel Levinas asserts with characteristic direct and yet strangely elusive elegance, "All encounter begins with a benediction, contained in the word 'hello,'" urging humans to take as primary and foundational before all ontological categorization, "the well-intentioned relation toward the other" (*Alterity*

98). Turning that greeting-as-blessing into concrete practice, Kwame Anthony Appiah offers conversation as a vital tool to move from initial encounter to facilitate mutual understanding, though not always agreement, across differing people groups, alliances, and values. For Appiah, "conversation" is both literal and metaphorical, a term to describe practices and world-dispositions that signal honest "engagement with the experience and the ideas of others," simply helping "people get used to one another" (*Cosmopolitanism* 85). Appiah habitually cites works of the creative imagination as matter that fuels the moral and ethical labor of conversational interaction, advancing storytelling and analytical discussion as crucial to human intra- and intercultural rapprochement. He writes:

> Conversations across boundaries of identity—whether national, religious, or something else—begin with the sort of imaginative engagement you get when you read a novel or watch a movie or attend to a work of art that speaks from some place other than your own.
>
> (85)

He argues that the art of storytelling and an accompanying analytical dialogue about those stories provides a means by which humans align themselves to the life-worlds of others, constituting "one of the ways we maintain the social fabric, the texture of our relationships" (*Cosmopolitanism* 29). Appiah's advocacy for storytelling to build understanding and even, on occasion, consensus reinforces the ethical power that performed works of the literary imagination can wield, fostering dialogue and carving relational pathways in the hardened substrate of nationalism's exclusionary practices. Shakespeare's history plays and their performed iterations, when responsibly and creatively conceived, can make good on that promise to nurture individual and communal flourishing through art and dialogue. These plays should remind us that "no local loyalty can ever justify forgetting that each human being has responsibilities to every other" (Appiah, *Cosmopolitanism* xvi), responsibilities that begin by revisiting the omissions of past sins (Michel de Certeau's historiographic remains), tracing their corrosive impact in the present, and shaping new stories of a people that imagine and enact a healthier shared life together.

For me as a scholar, professor, and enthusiast of these vast, sprawling, and vexed plays, I believe it is vital that the radical and disruptive potential of Shakespeare's history plays—their clear-sightedness regarding the perils of nationalism and the victims of the nation's coalescence—must be staged provocatively to disrupt their imbrication in white supremacist and sexist understandings of Shakespeare and the nation. Furthermore, even as the plays predict the harm of incipient nationalism, they simultaneously inscribe poisonous complicities with racial and gender oppression—both ideological and material—that must be acknowledged and reconsidered rather than whitewashed or ignored. It is also essential to recognize that the failures of representation in performances of Shakespearean history cut across aesthetic styles—from heritage period settings to modernized retellings to rhizomatic reimaginations. Clearly, the problems do not derive from stylistic approach or a heritage gate-keeping of faux authenticity and accuracy. Sadly, they originate from a white supremacist and misogynistic political and artistic culture that cannot admit a history shared with and defined by a cosmopolitan and multiethnic population. Though clever and polished, *The Crown*'s reinvention of *Richard II* ultimately remains entranced by the so-called plight of white male coming of age. Rather than remain impervious to calls for a history that revisits the agential role of women and people of color, more engagements with Shakespeare's historiography must follow the example of Andoh and Linton in creating a hospitable and welcoming nation—not one, like *The Casey Review* that simply spotlights the failure of non-white "outsiders" to conform. Productions like the Globe's *Richard II* instantiate the "complex cultural dialogue" Seyla Benhabib calls for, which "focus[es] on the interpenetration of traditions and discourses and disclose[es] the interdependence of images of the self and the other" (*The Claims* 41). Jean E. Howard and Phyllis Rackin observe that

> Shakespeare's representations of England's medieval past...have done more to shape popular conceptions of English history than the work of any professional historian. In short, Shakespeare not only represents the greatness of his nation's heritage; he also serves in the popular imagination as the leading historian of England's past.
>
> (10)

Given this fact, performances must self-reflectively and self-consciously transform that high-impact site, directing the social and cultural capital of Shakespeare to represent more accurately the multiethnic national past to ensure its healthy future and to cast a wary eye on the enduring exclusionary strategies of nationhood. These texts must be adapted, appropriated, and performed in radically different ways, or we simply have not learned the lessons offered by Shakespeare's contested nations.

Notes

1 In a well-known speech to the Munich Security Conference, Prime Minister David Cameron suggested that the rise of "homegrown" Islamic extremism resulted from the failure of multicultural policy—blaming the enclave separatism he associated with such policy as a bar to full integration of Muslims into a set of so-called British values. The Prime Minister argued that young male Muslims, "find it hard to identify with Britain...because we have allowed the weakening of our collective identity." Contrasting his stance with that of the "soft left," Cameron elaborated: "Under the doctrine of state multiculturalism, we have encouraged different cultures to live separate lives, apart from each other and apart from the mainstream. We've failed to provide a vision of society to which they feel they want to belong. We've even tolerated these segregated communities behaving in ways that run completely counter to our values." The Prime Minister claimed that a "hands-off tolerance" ultimately "leaves some young Muslims feeling rootless." Thus, in an extraordinary turn of reasoning, Cameron insisted that a critical cause of Islamic terrorism in Britain was,

in fact, the policy of multiculturalism, a policy he willfully misinterpreted as separatism despite the highly detailed policies of intersubjective exchange advanced in 2000 by Parekh and the members of the Runnymede Trust. Driving to his conclusion, Cameron insisted: "we need a lot less of the passive tolerance of recent years and a much more active, muscular liberalism"; the "genuinely liberal country," he contended, "believes in certain values and actively promotes them. Freedom of speech, freedom of worship, democracy, the rule of law, equal rights regardless of race, sex or sexuality." David Theo Goldberg neatly summarizes how Cameron turned the threat of terrorism into a war on former multicultural policy initiatives: "The dance with multiculturalism lasted all of a quarter-century, trailing off at the twentieth century's end and the start-up culture of the new millennium. British Prime Minister David Cameron, backed up by German Chancellor Angela Merkel, declared 'war on (state) multiculturalism,' blaming it for fomenting 'extremist ideologies' and 'home-grown Islamic terrorism'" (23–24).

2 Indeed, as Parekh and his collaborators argue in the *FMEB* report concerning the Blair administration's social exclusion policies: "But if a focus on the margins and boundaries means that there is no pressure for change at the centre, or in society's principal power relationships and hierarchies, the benefits of inclusion may be slight" (79).

3 Throughout *The Crown*, Shakespeare operates as an elite in-group shorthand for white British men (as mentioned briefly in Chapter Four).

4 For example, in the case of *Henry V*'s Welshman, Fluellen, Ruben Espinosa observes: "Wales and the Welsh are undeniably alien, and thus, Fluellen exists as the site of cultural otherness, a foreigner embedded in the play's English culture—one who refuses to assimilate, who upholds his cultural traditions, and who, in the process, appears to believe that he has something to offer and teach his 'host' society" ("Fluellen's" 74).

5 Audio podcast content has been transcribed by the author.

6 "Writing black women's stories into reworked Shakespeares is a way of writing them into a history that has worked to efface or misvalue them, their works, and their lives" (MacDonald 4). Andoh and Linton achieve what Shanelle E. Kim similarly calls for—a concerted transposition of anti-black "Shakespearean objects" to be "reappropriated into new networks that assert black subjectivity" (172).

7 This interplay between the particular iterations of postcolonial identities walks a representational fine line that provokes the ubiquitous question of Shakespeare's universality. Andoh and Linton achieve a cultural pastiche highly attuned to the individual identities and histories their staging references, mindful not to paint specificity into universality. This approach avoids the dangers of a progressive universalizing optimism such as that voiced by Kiernan Ryan. While admirable, Ryan's claim that the plays "invite us to view the way things were in Shakespeare's time from *an egalitarian standpoint* that is still in advance of our time" and "which dissolves the assumptions that underpin the hierarchical society his drama depicts," underestimates the racist and sexist ideological discourses circulating in the texts (15). In response, Vanessa I. Corredera argues that, "Assertions of universality thus gloss over Shakespeare as an alienating entity – a shibboleth for approved 'high' culture often imagined as white" ("'How Dey'" 28). Indeed, Peter Erickson and Kim F. Hall caution that Ryan's assertions constitute a "disappearing act" whereby the "universalism practiced by Ryan characterizes Shakespeare's resolutions of the stress points and tensions of racial difference as readily carrying over and automatically applicable to the removal of race problems in our contemporary culture," thus rendering an interrogation of race in the early modern period seemingly unnecessary (5). Andoh and Linton heed Erickson and Hall's call, instead, for "more emphasis on race, not less" (5), though additional institutional infrastructure at Shakespeare's Globe would render more transparent the labor of this remarkable production.

Works Cited

Abdelkader, Engy. "A Comparative Analysis of European Islamophobia: France, UK, Germany, Netherlands, and Sweden." *Journal of Islamic and Near Eastern Law* 16:1 (2017): 29–63.

Abrams, Josh and Jennifer Parker-Starbuck. "A 'United' Kingdom: The London 2012 Cultural Olympiad." *PAJ* 35:*1* (2013): 19–31.

Acocella, Joan. "Tudor Tales: Hilary Mantel reconsiders the life of Thomas Cromwell." *The New Yorker*, 19 Oct. 2009.

Aebischer, Pascale. *Screening Early Modern Drama: Beyond Shakespeare*. Cambridge University Press, 2013.

Aebischer, Pascale. *Shakespeare, Spectatorship and the Technologies of Performance*. Cambridge UP, 2020.

Akbar, Arifa. "Lucian Msamati on Amadeus: 'Colour-blind casting? I want you to see my colour.'" *The Guardian*, 24 Jul. 2020.

Akbar, Arifa. "Winsome Pinnock meets Jasmine Lee-Jones: 'Some UK theatres have never staged a black British play.'" *The Guardian*, 25 Jun. 2020.

Akhimie, Patricia. "Racist Humor and Shakespearean Comedy." *The Cambridge Companion to Shakespeare and Race*. Ed. Ayanna Thompson. Cambridge University Press, 2021. 47–61.

"All that Glisters is not Gold." *Code Switch*. Hosted by Gene Demby and Shereen Marisol Meraji with Ayanna Thompson as guest, NPR, 21 Aug. 2019. Transcript.

Amis, Martin. *The Second Plane September 11: Terror and Boredom*. Alfred A. Knopf, 2008.

Anderson, Benedict. *Imagined Communities: Reflections on the Origin and Spread of Nationalism*. Rev. Edition. Verso, 2006.

Andoh, Adjoa. "Practitioner Perspective: Adjoa Andoh." *Shakespeare and Gender: Sex and Sexuality in Shakespeare's Drama*. Eds. Kate Aughterson and Ailsa Grant Ferguson. Bloomsbury, 2020. 65–72.

Andoh, Adjoa and Lynette Linton. *Richard II*. Perf. Adjoa Andoh, Doña Croll, Ayesha Dharker. Shakespeare's Globe, Sam Wanamaker Playhouse, 2019. Swinging the Lens. YouTube.

Anthias, Floya and Nira Yuval-Davis. "Introduction." *Woman-Nation-State*. Eds. Nira Yuval-Davis and Floya Anthias, Cons. Ed. Jo Campling. St. Martin's Press, 1989. 1–15.

Appiah, Kwame Anthony. *Cosmopolitanism: Ethics in a World of Strangers*. W. W. Norton, 2006.

Appiah, Kwame Anthony. *The Lies that Bind: Rethinking Identity Creed, Country, Color, Class, Culture*. Liveright Publishing, 2018.

Arendt, Hannah. *The Human Condition*. 2nd Ed. The University of Chicago Press, 1998.

Assmann, Jan. "Collective Memory and Cultural Identity." *New German Critique* 65 (Spring-Summer 1995): 125–133.

Auslander, Philip. *Liveness: Performance in a Mediatized Culture*. London: Routledge, 2008.

Bak, Greg. "Different Differences: Locating Moorishness in Early Modern English Culture." *The Dalhousie Review* 76:2 (1997): 197–216.

Baker, David J. *Between Nations: Shakespeare, Spenser, Marvell, and the Question of Britain*. Stanford UP, 1997.

Baldo, Jonathan. *Memory in Shakespeare's Histories: Stages of Forgetting in Early Modern England*. Routledge, 2012.

Balibar, Étienne. "Racism and Nationalism." *Race, Nation, Class: Ambiguous Identities* by Étienne Balibar and Immanuel Wallerstein. Verso, 1991. 37–67.

Bandura, Albert. "Exercise of Human Agency Through Collective Efficacy." *Current Directions in Psychological Science* (2000): 75–78.

Bandura, Albert. "Toward a Psychology of Human Agency." *Perspectives on Psychological Science* 1:2 (2006): 164–180.

Barthelemy, Anthony Gerard. *Black Face Maligned Race: The Representation of Blacks in English Drama from Shakespeare to Southerne*. Louisiana State UP, 1987.

Bartlett, Mike. "How I wrote King Charles III." *The Guardian*, 20 Sept. 2014.

Bartlett, Mike. *King Charles III: A Future History Play*. Theatre Communications Group, 2015.

BBC. "Black actor cast as English king." BBC News. 19 Sept. 2000.

BBC. *The BBC's Diversity Strategy 2011–2015*. May 2011. Web: bbc.co.uk/diversity/pdf/Diversity_strategy.

Bell, Fiona. "Joan of Arc in Part 1 of *Henry VI*, and Margaret of Anjou in Parts 1, 2, and 3 of *Henry VI* and in *Richard III*." *Players of Shakespeare 6: Essays in the Performance of Shakespeare's History Plays*. Ed. Robert Smallwood. Cambridge University Press, 2004. 163–183.

Benhabib, Seyla. *The Claims of Culture: Equality and Diversity in the Global Era*. Princeton Univeristy Press, 2002.

Benhabib, Seyla. "In Defense of Universalism. Yet Again! A Response to Critics of *Situating the Self*." *New German Critique* 62 (1994): 173–189.

Benhabib, Seyla. *Situating the Self: Gender, Community and Postmodernism in Contemporary Ethics*. Routledge, 1992.

Bennett, Susan. *Theatre Audiences: A Theory of Production and Reception*. 2nd Ed. Routledge, 1997.

Berry, Ralph. *Shakespeare in Performance: Castings and Metamorphoses*. New York: St. Martin's Press, 1993.

Betteridge, Tom. "Henry VIII and Popular Culture." *Henry VIII and His Afterlives: Literature, Politics, and Art*. Eds. Mark Rankin, Christopher Highley, and John N. King. Cambridge University Press, 2009. 208–222.

Bhabha, Homi K. *The Location of Culture*. Routledge, 2010.

Bhattacharyya, Gargi et al. *Empire's Endgame: Racism and the British State*. Pluto Press, 2021.

Billington, Michael. "King Charles III—a flawed premise but royally entertaining." *The Guardian*, 10 April 2014.

Blackwell, Anna. *Shakespearean Celebrity in the Digital Age: Fan Cultures and Remediation*. Palgrave Macmillan, 2018.

Boehmer, Elleke. *Stories of Women: Gender and Narrative in the Postcolonial Nation*. Manchester University Press, 2005.
Boffey, Daniel and Toby Helm. "Vote Leave embroiled in race row over Turkey security threat claims." *The Guardian*, 21 May 2016.
Bonilla-Silva, Eduardo. "The Linguistics of Color Blind Racism: How to Talk Nasty about Blacks without Sounding 'Racist.'" *Critical Sociology* 28:1–2 (2002): 41–64.
Boyd, Michael (dir). *I Henry VI*. DVD Recording. Stratford-upon-Avon: Royal Shakespeare Company. 6 Jan. 2001. Shakespeare Birthplace Trust.
Boyd, Michael (dir). *1 Henry VI*. Promptbook. Stratford-upon-Avon: Royal Shakespeare Company2001. Shakespeare Birthplace Trust.
Boyd, Michael (dir). *2 Henry VI*. DVD Recording. Stratford-upon-Avon: Royal Shakespeare Company 6 Jan. 2001. Shakespeare Birthplace Trust.
Boyd, Michael (dir). *2 Henry VI*. Promptbook. Stratford-upon-Avon: Royal Shakespeare Company2001. Shakespeare Birthplace Trust.
Boyd, Michael (dir). *3 Henry VI*. DVD Recording. Stratford-upon-Avon: Royal Shakespeare Company. 6 Jan. 2001. Shakespeare Birthplace Trust.
Boyd, Michael (dir). *3 Henry VI*. Promptbook. Stratford-upon-Avon: Royal Shakespeare Company. 2001. Shakespeare Birthplace Trust.
Boyd, Michael. "Director's Note." *Henry* VI. Program book. Royal Shakespeare Company. Stratford-upon-Avon, UK. 2006.
Branagh, Kenneth (dir). *Henry V*. MGM Home Entertainment, 2000. DVD.
Brantley, Ben. "Review: In 'King Charles III,' Glimpsing the Near Future of Monarchy." *The New York Times*, 1 Nov. 2016.
Brown, Emma. "The Theater Director." *Interview*, 9 Jan. 2015.
Brown, Maggie. "Sam Mendes: BBC Worldwide rejected 'Hollow Crown' Shakespeare Films." *The Guardian*, 2 July 2012.
Brown, Mark. "Students take Hilary Mantel's Tudor novels as fact, says historian." *The Guardian*, 31 May 2017.
CNN. "Bush makes historic speech aboard warship." CNN.com. 1 May 2003.
Calbi, Maurizio. *Spectral Shakespeares: Media Adaptations in the Twenty-First Century*. Palgrave Macmillan, 2013.
Cameron, David. "PM's speech at Munich Security Conference." GOV.UK. 5 Feb. 2011.
Cardwell, Sarah. *Adaptation Revisited: Television and the Classic Novel*. Manchester University Press, 2002.
Carson, Christie. "Creating a critical model for the twenty-first century." *Shakespeare and the Digital World: Redefining Scholarship and Practice*. Eds. Christie Carson and Peter Kirwan. Cambridge University Press, 2014. 226–237.
Cartmell, Deborah. *Interpreting Shakespeare on Screen*. Macmillan Press, 2000.
Casey, Dame Louise. *The Casey Review: A review into opportunity and integration*. OGL, 2016.
Cavendish, Dominic. Review of King Charles III. "Attendance is Compulsory." *The Telegraph*, 3 Oct. 2014.
Césaire, Aimé. *Discourse on Colonialism*. Trans. Joan Pinkham. Monthly Review Press, 2000.
Chakravarty, Urvashi. "What is the History of Actors of Color Performing in Shakespeare in the UK?" *The Cambridge Companion to Shakespeare and Race*. Ed. Ayanna Thompson. Cambridge UP, 2021. 190–207.

Clements, Kevin P. "Authoritarian Populism and Atavistic Nationalism: 21st-Century Challenges to Peacebuilding and Development." *Journal of Peacebuilding & Development* 13:3 (2018): 1–6.

Collins, Patricia Hill. *Black Feminist Thought: Knowledge, consciousness, and the politics of empowerment.* Routledge, 2009.

Connor, Phillip and Jens Manuel Krogstad. "Key Facts about the World's Refugees." *Pew Research Center*, 5 Oct. 2016.

Cook, Amy. *Casting the Bodies of Tomorrow on Shakespeare's Stages Today*. Cambridge University Press, 2020.

Cooke, Dominic (dir). *The Hollow Crown: The Wars of the Roses. Henry VI: Part I.* NBC Universal, 2016. DVD.

Cooke, Dominic (dir). *The Hollow Crown: The Wars of the Roses. Henry VI: Part II.* NBC Universal, 2016. DVD.

Cooke, Dominic (dir). *The Hollow Crown: The Wars of the Roses. Richard III.* NBC Universal, 2016. DVD.

Cooke, Dominic (dir). "The Making of *The Hollow Crown*." *The Hollow Crown: The Wars of the Roses.* NBC Universal, 2016. DVD.

Cooper, Charlie. "Vote Leave Campaign video 'doctored' to include fake screams of woman." *The Independent*, 20 June 2016.

Corredera, Vanessa Ivette. "Faces and Figures of Fortune: Astrological Physiognomy in Tamburlaine Part 1." *Early Modern Literary Studies* 18:1–2 (2015).

Corredera, Vanessa I. "'How Dey Goin' to Kill Othello?!': *Key & Peele* and Shakespearean Universality." *Journal of American Studies* 54 (2020): 27–35.

Corredera, Vanessa I. "Lessons for Whiteness: Keith Hamilton Cobb's *American Moor*." *Shakespeare* 17:1 (2021): 54–57.

Corredera, Vanessa. "'Not a Moor exactly': Shakespeare, *Serial*, and Modern Constructions of Race." *Shakespeare Quarterly* 67 (2016): 30–50.

Crenshaw, Kimberlé. "Mapping the Margins: Intersectionality, Identity Politics, and Violence against Women of Color." *Stanford Law Review* 43:6 (July 1991): 1241–1299.

Crowl, Samuel. *The Films of Kenneth Branagh*. Westport, CT: Praeger, 2006.

Dadabhoy, Ambereen. "Skin in the Game: Teaching Race in Early Modern Literature." *Studies in Medieval and Renaissance Teaching* 27:2 (2020): 1–15.

Davies, Serena. "The BBC's The Hollow Crown, Set Visit." *The Telegraph*, 29 Jun. 2012.

De Certeau, Michel. *The Writing of History*. Trans. Tom Conley. Columbia University Press, 1988.

Desmet, Christy. "Recognizing Shakespeare, Rethinking Fidelity: A Rhetoric and Ethics of Appropriation." *Shakespeare and the Ethics of Appropriation*. Eds. Alexa Alice Joubin and Elizabeth Rivlin. Palgrave Macmillan, 2014. 41–57.

Desmet, Christy and Sujata Iyengar. "Adaptation, appropriation, or what you will." *Shakespeare*, (2015): 1–10.

Dobson, Michael. "Shakespeare Performances in England, 2003." *Shakespeare Survey* 57 (2004): 258–289.

Doran, Gregory (dir). *Richard II.* Perf. David Tennant, Nigel Lindsay, Oliver Ford Davies, Marty Cruickshank. Stratford-upon-Avon: Royal Shakespeare Theatre, 13 Nov. 2013. Opus Arte, 2014. DVD.

Doran, Gregory, Catherine Mallyon, Erica Whyman, and Jo Davies. "Daily Mail review". Royal Shakespeare Company. <https://www.rsc.org.uk>.

Duffy, Eamon. *The Stripping of the Altars: Traditional Religion in England 1400–1580*. 2nd Ed. Yale University Press, 2005.

Dyer, Richard. *White: Twentieth Anniversary Edition*. Routledge, 2017.

Edgar, David. *Plays: Two*. Methuen Drama, 1990.

El-Enany, Nadine. *(B)ordering Britain: Law, race and empire*. Manchester University Press, 2020.

Eliot, George. *Daniel Deronda*. The Modern Library, 2002.

Ellis-Petersen, Hannah. "Even Holbein would recognize it: Hilary Mantel hails BBC's Wolf Hall." *The Guardian*, 11 Dec. 2014.

Elliott, Tomas. "Shakespearean Seriality: The 'Hollow Crown', the 'Wooden O', and the 'Circle in the Water' of History." *Adaptation* 12:2 (2018): 69–88.

Erickson, Peter. "Afterword: The Blind Side in Colorblind Casting." *Colorblind Shakespeare: New Perspectives on Race and Performance*. Ed. Ayanna Thompson. Routledge, 2006. 241–249.

Erickson, Peter and Kim F. Hall. "'A New Scholarly Song': Rereading Early Modern Race." *Shakespeare Quarterly* 67 (2016): 1–13.

Escobedo, Andrew. *Nationalism and Historical Loss in Renaissance England: Foxe, Dee, Spenser, Milton*. Cornell University Press, 2004.

Espinosa, Ruben. "Fluellen's Foreign Influence and the Ill Neighborhood of *King Henry V*." *Shakespeare and Immigration*. Eds. Ruben Espinosa and David Ruiter. Ashgate, 2014. 73–89.

Espinosa, Ruben. *Shakespeare on the Shades of Racism*. Routledge, 2021.

Eyre, Richard (dir). *The Hollow Crown: Henry IV, Part I*. Perf. Jeremy Irons, Tom Hiddleston, Simon Russell Beale. NBC Universal, 2012. DVD.

Eyre, Richard (dir). *The Hollow Crown: Henry IV, Part II*. Perf. Jeremy Irons, Tom Hiddleston, Simon Russell Beale. NBC Universal, 2012. DVD.

Fazel, Valerie and Louise Geddes. "Introduction: The Shakespeare User." *The Shakespeare User: Critical and Creative Appropriations in a Networked Culture*. Palgrave Macmillan, 2017. 1–22.

Final Report of the IOC Coordination Commission: Games of the XXX Olympiad, London 2012. International Olympic Committee. August 2013.

Finn, Patrick. "The Politics of Culture: The Play's the Thing." *Almost Shakespeare: Reinventing His Works for Cinema and Television*. Eds. James R. Keller and Leslie Stratyner. McFarland, 2004. 7–21.

Fleming, Crystal M. *How to be Less Stupid About Race: On Racism, White Supremacy, and the Racial Divide*. Beacon Press, 2018.

Flinders, Matthew. "The Politics of Public-Private Partnerships." *BJPIR* 7 (2005): 215–239.

Flood, Alison. "David Starkey dropped by publisher and university after racist remarks." *The Guardian*, 3 July 2020.

Földváry, Kinga. "'Sad Stories of the Death of Kings': *The Hollow Crown* and the Shakespearean History Play on Screen." *The Cambridge Companion to Shakespeare on Screen*. Ed. Russell Jackson. Cambridge University Press, 2020. 105–118.

Freeman, Thomas S. "Introduction: It's only a Movie." *Tudors and Stuarts on Film: Historical Perspectives*. Eds. Susan Doran and Thomas S. Freeman. Palgrave Macmillan, 2009. 1–28.

Fryer, Peter. *Aspects of British Black History*. Index Books, 1993.

Fryer, Peter. *Staying power: The history of black people in Britain*. Pluto, 1984.

Fullerton, Huw. "Did King Charles III predict the Prince Harry/Meghan Markle romance?" *Radio Times*, 6 July 2017.

Furness, Hannah. "Wolf Hall is 'deliberate perversion' of history, says David Starkey." *The Telegraph*, 26 Jan. 2015.

Gaby, Rosemary. "'The days that we have seen': History and Regret in *Henry IV, Parts One* and *Two, The Hollow Crown* (2012)." *Shakespeare and Emotions: Inheritances, Enactments, Legacies*. Eds. R. S. White, Mark Houlahan, and Katrina O'Loughlin. Palgrave Macmillan, 2015. 231–239.

Gerzic, Marina. "Re-fashioning Richard III: Intertextuality, Fandom, and the (Mobile) Body in *The Hollow Crown: The Wars of the Roses*." *From Medievalism to Early-Modernism: Adapting the English Past*. Eds. Marina Gerzic and Aidan Norrie. Routledge, 2019. 188–206.

Gilroy, Paul. *Postcolonial Melancholia*. Columbia University Press, 2005.

Gilroy, Paul. *There Ain't No Black in the Union Jack: The Cultural Politics of Race and Nation*. Routledge, 1992.

Goddard, Lynette. "Will we ever have a black Desdemona?: Casting Josette Simon at the Royal Shakespeare Company." *Shakespeare, Race and Performance: The Diverse Bard*. Ed. Delia Jarrett-Macauley. Routledge, 2017. 80–95.

Goldberg, David Theo. *Are We All Postracial Yet?* Polity, 2015.

Goodhart, David. "Too diverse?" *Prospect* 20 (Feb. 2004).

Goold, Rupert (dir). *The Hollow Crown: Richard II*. Perf. Ben Whishaw, Rory Kinnear, Patrick Stewart. NBC Universal, 2012. DVD.

Goold, Rupert (dir). *King Charles III*. Drama Republic/BBC/Masterpiece, 2017. DVD.

Grandage, Sarah. "Imagining England: Contemporary Encodings of 'this sceptred isle.'" *This England, That Shakespeare: New Angles on Englishness and the Bard*. Eds. Willy Maley and Margaret Tudeau-Clayton. Ashgate, 2010. 127–146.

Greenblatt, Stephen. *Hamlet in Purgatory*. Princeton University Press, 2001.

Greenblatt, Stephen. "Review of *Wolf Hall*. 'How It Must Have Been.'" *The New York Review of Books*, 5 Nov. 2009.

Greenblatt, Stephen. *Tyrant: Shakespeare on Politics*. W. W. Norton, 2018.

Griffiths, Melanie and Colin Yeo. "The UK's hostile environment: Deputising immigration control." *Critical Social Policy* (Jan. 2021): 1–24.

Grochala, Sarah. *The Theatre of Rupert Goold: Radical Approaches to Adaptation and New Writing*. Methuen, 2021.

"The Guardian View on King Charles III: A Foreboding Play." Editorial. *The Guardian*, 12 May 2017.

Habib, Imtiaz. *Black Lives in the English Archives, 1500–1677: Imprints of the Invisible*. Ashgate, 2008.

Hadfield, Andrew. "Race in Shakespeare's Histories." *The Cambridge Companion to Shakespeare and Race*. Ed. Ayanna Thompson. Cambridge University Press, 2021. 62–76.

Hall, Kim F. *Things of Darkness: Economies of Race and Gender in Early Modern England*. Cornell University Press, 1995.

Hall, Stuart. "The West and the Rest: Discourse and Power." *Formations of Modernity*. Eds. Stuart Hall and Bram Gieben. Open University, 1992. 275–318.

Hampton-Reeves, Stuart and Carol Chillington Rutter. *The Henry VI Plays*. Manchester University Press, 2006.

Harris-Perry, Melissa V. *Sister Citizen: Shame, Stereotypes, and Black Women in America*. Yale University Press, 2011.

Hartley, Andrew James. *Shakespeare and Political Theatre in Practice*. Palgrave Macmillan, 2013.

Hatchuel, Sarah. "Leading the Gaze: From Showing to Telling in Kenneth Branagh's *Henry V* and *Hamlet*." *Early Modern Literary Studies* 6:1 (2000).

Hatherley, Owen. *The Ministry of Nostalgia*. Verso, 2016.

Hattenstone, Simon. "David Oyelowo: 'Nowhere on Earth has been better at covering up racism than Great Britain.'" *The Guardian*, 16 Dec. 2020.

Haynes, Toby (dir). *Brexit*. HBO Max. 2019.

Hawkes, Terence. *Meaning by Shakespeare*. Routledge, 1992.

Helgerson, Richard. *Forms of Nationhood: The Elizabethan Writing of England*. University of Chicago Press, 1992.

Henderson, Diana E. *Collaborations with the Past: Reshaping Shakespeare across Time and Media*. Cornell University Press, 2006.

Hendricks, Margo. "Visions of Color: Spectacle, Spectators, and the Performance of Race." *A Companion to Shakespeare and Performance*. Eds. Barbara Hodgdon and W. B. Worthen. Blackwell, 2008. 511–526.

Heng, Geraldine. *The Invention of Race in the European Middle Ages*. Cambridge University Press, 2018.

Herrin, Jeremy (dir). *Bring up the Bodies*. DVD Recording. Stratford-upon-Avon: Royal Shakespeare Company. 2014. Shakespeare Birthplace Trust.

Herrin, Jeremy (dir). *Bring up the Bodies*. Promptbook. Stratford-upon-Avon: Royal Shakespeare Company. 2014. Shakespeare Birthplace Trust.

Herrin, Jeremy (dir). *Wolf Hall*. DVD Recording. Stratford-upon-Avon: Royal Shakespeare Company. 9 Jan. 2014. Shakespeare Birthplace Trust.

Herrin, Jeremy (dir). *Wolf Hall*. Promptbook. Stratford-upon-Avon: Royal Shakespeare Company. 2014. Shakespeare Birthplace Trust.

Higgins, Charlotte. "What Danny Boyle's Olympics opening ceremony said about Britain's cultural landscape." *The Guardian*, 28 July 2012.

Higson, Andrew. *English Heritage, English Cinema: Costume Drama since 1980*. Oxford University Press, 2003.

Higson, Andrew. "Re-presenting the National Past: Nostalgia and Pastiche in the Heritage Film." *Fires were started: British Cinema and Thatcherism*. Ed. Lester Friedman. University of Minnesota Press, 1993. 109–129.

Hirsch, Afua. *Brit(ish): On Race, Identity and Belonging*. Jonathan Cape, 2018.

Hodgdon, Barbara. *The End Crowns All: Closure and Contradiction in Shakespeare's History*. Princeton University Press, 1991.

Hodgdon, Barbara. *The Shakespeare Trade: Performances and Appropriations*. University of Pennsylvania Press, 1998.

Holderness, Graham. *Cultural Shakespeare: Essays in the Shakespeare Myth*. University of Hertfordshire Press, 2001.

Holderness, Graham. "Radical Potentiality and Institutional Closure: Shakespeare in Film and Television." *Political Shakespeare: Essays in Cultural Materialism*. 2nd Edition. Eds. Jonathan Dollimore and Alan Sinfield. Cornell University Press, 1994. 206–225.

Holderness, Graham. *Shakespeare: The Histories*. St. Martin's Press, 2000.

Howard, Jean E. and Phyllis Rackin. *Engendering a Nation: A Feminist Account of Shakespeare's English Histories*. Routledge, 1997.

Hughey, Matthew W. "Cinethetic Racism: White Redemption and Black Stereotypes in 'Magical Negro' Films." *Social Problems* 56 (2009): 543–577.

Hytner, Nicholas (dir). *1 Henry IV*. Costume Bible. London: National Theatre. 2005. National Theatre Archive.

Hytner, Nicholas (dir). *1 Henry IV*. DVD Recording. London: National Theatre. 27 Aug. 2005. National Theatre Archive.

Hytner, Nicholas (dir). *1 Henry IV*. Promptbook. London: National Theatre. 2005. National Theatre Archive.

Hytner, Nicholas (dir). *2 Henry IV*. DVD Recording. London: National Theatre. 27 Aug. 2005. National Theatre Archive.

Hytner, Nicholas (dir). *2 Henry IV*. Promptbook. London: National Theatre. 2005. National Theatre Archive.

Hytner, Nicholas (dir). *Henry V*. Costume Bible. London: National Theatre. 2003. National Theatre Archive.

Hytner, Nicholas (dir). *Henry V*. DVD Recording. London: National Theatre. 2003. National Theatre Archive.

Hytner, Nicholas (dir). *Henry V*. Promptbook. London: National Theatre. 2003. National Theatre Archive.

Hytner, Nicholas (dir). *Henry V*. Rehearsal Notes. London: National Theatre. 2003. National Theatre Archive.

Hytner, Nicholas. *Balancing Acts: Behind the Scenes at the National Theatre*. Vintage, 2017.

Jackson, Russell. "'This England': Shakespeare at Stratford-upon-Avon, Winter 2000–2001." *Shakespeare Quarterly* 52 (2001): 383–392.

Jaggard, Isaac and Ed Blount (print.). *Mr. William Shakespeares Comedies, Histories, and Tragedies*. Published according to the true original copies. London: *Early English Books Online*. 1623.

James, Heather. *Shakespeare's Troy: Drama, Politics, and the Translation of Empire*. Cambridge University Press, 1997.

Jewell, K. Sue. *From Mammy to Miss America and Beyond: Cultural Images and the Shaping of US Social Policy*. Routledge, 1993.

Johnson, Allan G. *Privilege, Power, and Difference*. 2nd Ed. Boston: McGraw Hill, 2005.

Johnson, David. *Shakespeare and South Africa*. Clarendon Press, 1996.

Joubin, Alexa Alice and Elizabeth Rivlin. "Shakespeare and the Ethics of Appropriation." *Shakespeare and the Ethics of Appropriation*. Eds. Alexa Alice Joubin and Elizabeth Rivlin. Palgrave Macmillan, 2014. 1–20.

Joseph, Paterson. *Julius Caesar and Me: Exploring Shakespeare's African Play*. Methuen, 2018.

Jowett, John (Ed). *Sir Thomas More*. Bloomsbury, 2011.

Kamaralli, Anna. "Daunted at a Woman's Sight?: The Use and Abuse of Female Presence in Performances of the Histories as Cycles." *Shakespeare Survey* 63 (2010): 172–183.

Kamps, Ivo. "Possible Pasts: Historiography and Legitimation in *Henry VIII*." *College English* 58:2 (1996): 192–215.

Karremann, Isabel. *The Drama of Memory in Shakespeare's History Plays*. Cambridge University Press, 2015.

Kennedy, Dennis. "Shakespeare and Cultural Tourism." *Theatre Journal* 50 (1989): 175–188.

Khair, Tabish. *The New Xenophobia*. Oxford University Press, 2016.

Kidnie, Margaret Jane. *Shakespeare and the Problem of Adaptation*. Routledge, 2009.

Kim, Shanelle E. "'Intermission!': Reading Race in the Objects of *Key & Peele*'s 'Othello Tis My Shite.'" *Variable Objects: Shakespeare and Speculative Appropriation*. Eds. Valerie M. Fazel and Louise Geddes. Edinburgh University Press, 2021. 167–191.

Kirwan, Peter. "*The Hollow Crown: Henry V* @ BBC2." *University of Nottingham Blogs.* University of Nottingham. 23 Jul 2012.

Kolkovich, Elizabeth. "Queering Poins: Masculinity and Friendship in *Henry IV, The Hollow Crown*, and the RSC's 'King and Country'." *Shakespeare Bulletin* 36:4 (2018): 635–656.

Kosminsky, Peter (dir). *Wolf Hall.* Perf. Mark Rylance, Damian Lewis, Claire Foy. Playground Entertainment/Company Pictures. 2015. Blu-ray.

Kosminsky, Peter (dir). "*Wolf Hall*: Bringing it to the Screen." *Wolf Hall.* 2015. Playground Entertainment/Company Pictures. Blu-ray.

Kosminsky, Peter (dir). "*Wolf Hall*: History and Design." *Wolf Hall.* 2015. Playground Entertainment/Company Pictures. Blu-ray.

Kosminsky, Peter (dir). "*Wolf Hall*: The People the Politics." *Wolf Hall.* 2015. Playground Entertainment/Company Pictures. Blu-ray.

Kundnani, Arun. "Multiculturalism and its Discontents: Left, Right and Liberal." *European Journal of Cultural Studies* 15:2 (2012): 155–166.

Lanier, Douglas. *Shakespeare and Modern Popular Culture.* Oxford University Press, 2002.

Lanier, Douglas. "Shakespearean Rhizomatics: Adaptation, Ethics, Value." *Shakespeare and the Ethics of Appropriation.* Eds. Alexa Alice Joubin and Elizabeth Rivlin. Palgrave Macmillan, 2014. 21–40.

LaPerle, Carol Mejia. "Race in Shakespeare's Tragedies." *The Cambridge Companion to Shakespeare and Race.* Ed. Ayanna Thompson. Cambridge University Press, 2021. 77–92.

Laskow, Sarah. "The Racist History of Peter Pan's Indian Tribe." *Smithsonian Magazine*, 2 Dec. 2014.

Lawson, Mark. "*The Hollow Crown*: As Good as TV Shakespeare Can Get?" *The Guardian*, 29 June 2012.

Leberg, Dan. "*The Hollow Crown*: Quality Television and Colonial Performances." *Reception* 10 (2018): 27–49.

Lehmann, Courtney. "Crouching Tiger, Hidden Agenda: How Shakespeare and the Renaissance are Taking the Rage Out of Feminism." *Shakespeare Quarterly* 53 (2002): 260–279.

Lehmann, Courtney. *Shakespeare Remains: Theater to Film, Early Modern to Postmodern.* Cornell University Press, 2002.

Lemons, J. Stanley. "Black Stereotypes as Reflected in Popular Culture, 1880–1920." *American Quarterly* 29:1 (Spring 1977): 102–116.

Lester, Adrian. *Adrian Lester on Henry V. Shakespeare on Stage: Thirteen Leading Actors on Thirteen Key Roles.* Interview by Julian Curry. Nick Hern, 2013. E-book.

Letts, Quentin. "Lusty revival has two waggy stars." Review of *The Fantastic Follies of Mrs Rich. The Daily Mail*, 6 Apr. 2018.

Levinas, Emmanuel. *Alterity and Transcendence.* Trans. Michael B. Smith. Columbia University Press, 1999.

Levinas, Emmanuel. *Ethics and Infinity: Conversations with Philippe Nemo.* Trans. Richard A. Cohen. Duquesne University Press, 1985.

Levinas, Emmanuel. *Otherwise than Being or Beyond Essence.* Trans. Alphonso Lingis. Duquesne University Press, 1998.

Lister, David. "Shakespeare got the new BBC chief his job." *The Independent*, 14 July 2012.

Little Jr., Arthur L. "Re-Historicizing Race, White Melancholia, and the Shakespearean Property." *Shakespeare Quarterly* 67:1 (2016): 84–103.

Livingstone, David. "Silenced Voices: A Reactionary Streamlined *Henry V* in *The Hollow Crown*." *Multicultural Shakespeare* 12 (2015): 87–100.

"Locations of *Wolf Hall*." *Masterpiece*. PBS. 2015.

Loehlin, James N. *Henry V*. Manchester University Press, 1997.

Loehlin, James N. *Henry IV: Parts I and II*. Palgrave, 2008.

"London 2012 Festival and Cultural Olympiad on the BBC." BBC Media Centre. 18 Mar. 2014.

Loomba, Ania. *Shakespeare, Race, and Colonialism*. Oxford University Press, 2002.

López, Fernando Bravo. "Towards a definition of Islamophobia: approximations of the early twentieth century." *Ethnic and Racial Studies* 34:4 (2011): 556–573.

Lorde, Audre. *The Selected Works of Audre Lorde*. Ed. And Introd. Roxane Gay. W. W. Norton, 2020.

Lurie, Kathryn. "Playing the Man Who Shot Hamilton." *The Wall Street Journal*, 6 Aug. 2015.

MacDonald, Joyce Green. *Shakespearean Adaptation, Race and Memory in the New World*. Palgrave Macmillan, 2020.

MacLeod, Emily. "Prosthetic Properties: The Materiality of Race and Gender in *The Hollow Crown: The Wars of the Roses*." *Variable Objects: Shakespeare and Speculative Appropriation*. Eds. Valerie M. Fazel and Louise Geddes. Edinburgh University Press, 2021. 151–164.

Maley, Willy and Margaret Tudeau-Clayton. "Introduction 'To England send him': Repatriating Shakespeare." *This England, That Shakespeare: New Angles on Englishness and the Bard*. Routledge, 2016. 1–20.

Maley, Willy. *Nation, State and Empire in English Renaissance Literature: Shakespeare to Milton*. Palgrave Macmillan, 2003.

Manning, Alan and Sanchari Roy. "Culture clash or Culture Club? National Identity in Britain." *The Economic Journal* 120 (2010): F72–F100.

Mantel, Hilary. "Adaptation." *The BBC Reith Lectures, No. 5*. Stratford-upon-Avon: BBC Radio 4. 11 July 2017.Transcript.

Mantel, Hilary. *Bring up the Bodies*. Picador, 2012.

Mantel, Hilary. "Can These Bones Live?" *The BBC Reith Lectures, No. 4*. Exeter: BBC Radio 4. 4 July 2017. Transcript.

Mantel, Hilary. "The Day is for the Living." *The BBC Reith Lectures, No. 1*. Manchester: BBC Radio 4. 13 June 2017. No Transcript.

Mantel, Hilary. "The Iron Maiden." *The BBC Reith Lectures, No. 2*. London: BBC Radio 4. 20 June 2017. Transcript.

Mantel, Hilary. "Royal Bodies." *London Review of Books* 35:4 (21 Feb. 2013).

Mantel, Hilary. "Silence Grips the Town." *The BBC Reith Lectures, No. 3*. Antwerp: BBC Radio 4. 27 June 2017. Transcript.

Mantel, Hilary. *Wolf Hall*. Picador, 2009.

Marcus, Leah S. *Puzzling Shakespeare: Local Reading and its Discontents*. University of California Press, 1988.

Martin, Philip (dir). "Misadventure." *The Crown*. Season 2. Writ. Peter Morgan. Perfs. Jeremy Northam and Anton Lesser. Netflix. 8 Dec. 2017.

Mbembe, Achille. *Necro-Politics*. Trans. Steven Corcoran. Duke University Press, 2019.

McIntosh, Peggy. *White Privilege: Unpacking the Invisible Knapsack*. Wellesley Centers for Women. Wellesley College, 1989.

Mckenzie, Lisa. "The class politics of prejudice: Brexit and the land of no-hope and glory." *The British Journal of Sociology* 68:S1 (2017): S266–S280.

McClintock, Anne. *Imperial Leather: Race, Gender and Sexuality in the Colonial Contest.* Routledge, 1995.

McMillin, Scott. *Henry IV, Part One.* Manchester University Press, 1991.

McLaughlin, Eugene and Sarah Neal. "Misrepresenting the Multicultural Nation: The Policy-making Process, News Media Management and the Parekh Report." *Policy Studies* 25:3 (2004): 155–174.

Meyer, Allison Machlis. "'Accidental' Erasure: Relocating Shakespeare's Women in Philippa Gregory's *The Cousins' War* Series." *Shakespeare / Not Shakespeare: Reproducing Shakespeare.* Eds. Christy Desmet, Natalie Loper, Jim Casey. Palgrave Macmillan, 2017. 259–274.

Miles, Robert and Annie Phizacklea. *White Man's Country: Racism in British Politics.* Pluto, 1984.

Monteiro, Lyra D. "Race-Conscious Casting and the Erasure of the Black Past in Hamilton." *Historians on Hamilton: How a Blockbuster Musical is Restaging America's Past.* Eds. Renee C. Romano and Claire Bond Potter. Rutgers University Press, 2018. 58–70.

Morgan, Michael L. *The Cambridge Introduction to Emmanuel Levinas.* Cambridge University Press, 2011.

Morrison, Toni. *Playing in the Dark: Whiteness and the Literary Imagination.* Vintage Books, 1992.

Morse, Ruth. "*The Hollow Crown*: Shakespeare, the BBC, and the 2012 London Olympics." *Linguaculture* 1 (2014): 7–20.

Mullin, Romano. "'You Think You Know a Story…': Reframing the Tudors on Television in the Twenty-First Century." *Adaptation* 12:2 (2018): 89–104.

NBC. "The Complete London 2012 Opening Ceremony." *London 2012 Olympic Games.* YouTube. 27 Jul. 2012.

Neill, Michael. "Post-colonial Shakespeare? Writing Away from the Centre." *Post-Colonial Shakespeares.* Eds. Ania Loomba and Martin Orkin. Routledge, 1998. 164–185.

Nochlin, Linda. *The Politics of Vision: Essays on Nineteenth-Century Art and Society.* Harper & Row, 1989.

Nubia, Onyeka. *England's Other Countrymen: Black Tudor Society.* Zed, 2019.

Nuttall, Romola. "Review of Shakespeare's *Richard II* (Directed by Adjoa Andoh and Lynette Linton) at Shakespeare's Globe, Sam Wanamaker Playhouse, London, 2019, Broadcast by Swinging the Lens on YouTube April 2021." *Shakespeare* (June 2021): 1–5.

Olivier, Laurence (dir). *Henry V.* The Criterion Collection. Home Vision Cinema, 2006. DVD.

Olusoga, David. *Black and British: A Forgotten History.* Macmillan, 2016.

O'Neill, Stephen. "Finding Refuge in *King Lear*: From Brexit to Shakespeare's European Value." *Multicultural Shakespeare* 19:34 (2019): 119–138.

Orford, Peter. "*The Hollow Crown: Henry V.*" *A Year of Shakespeare: Re-living the World Shakespeare Festival.* Eds. Paul Edmondson, Paul Prescott, and Erin Sullivan. New York: Bloomsbury, 2013. 243–246.

Orgel, Stephen. "The Authentic Shakespeare." *Representations* 21 (1988): 1–25.

Orkin, Martin. "Possessing the Book and Peopling the Text." *Post-Colonial Shakespeares.* Eds. Ania Loomba and Martin Orkin. Routledge, 1993. 186–204.

Orkin, Martin and Alexa Alice Joubin. *Race.* Routledge, 2019.

Owen, Jonathan. "Trevor Nunn defends all-white Shakespeare histories." *The Independent,* 15 Aug. 2015.

Owen, Paul and David Smith. "Nigel Farage says Brexit and Trump win are 'beginning of global revolution.'" *The Guardian*, 24 Feb. 2017.

Oyelowo, David. *Henry VI, Part* I. Faber and Faber, 2003.

Pao, Angela C. *No Safe Spaces: Re-Casting Race, Ethnicity, and Nationality in American Theater.* University of Michigan Press, 2013.

Parekh, Bhikhu (chair). *The Future of Multi-Ethnic Britain. Report of the Commission on the Future of Multi-Ethnic Britain.* The Runnymede Trust. Profile Books, 2000.

Parekh, Bhikhu. "Reporting on a report." *Runnymede Trust Bulletin* 326 (June 2001): 1–8.

Parekh, Bhikhu. *A New Politics of Identity: Political Principles for an Interdependent World.* Palgrave Macmillan, 2008.

Pathak, Pathik. "The Trouble with David Goodhart's Britain." *The Political Quarterly* 78:2 (2007): 261–271.

Patterson, Annabel. "'All is True': Negotiating the Past in *Henry VIII.*" *Elizabethan Theater: Essays in Honor of S. Schoenbaum.* Eds. R. B. Parker and S. P. Zitner. University of Delaware Press, 1996. 147–166.

Penlington, Amanda. "'Not a man from England': Assimilating the Exotic 'Other' Through Performance, from *Henry IV* to *Henry VI.*" *This England, That Shakespeare: New Angles on Englishness and the Bard.* Eds. Willy Maley and Margaret Tudeau-Clayton. Ashgate, 2010. 165–183.

Perry, Keith. "Hilary Mantel denies warning the BBC over Wolf Hall adaptation." *The Telegraph*, 12 Dec. 2014.

Phelan, Peggy. *Unmarked: The Politics of Performance.* Routledge, 1993.

Pittman, L. Monique. *Authorizing Shakespeare on Film and Television: Gender, Class, and Ethnicity in Adaptation.* Peter Lang, 2011.

Pittman, L. Monique. "Colour-Conscious Casting and Multicultural Britain in the BBC *Henry V* (2012): Historicizing Adaptation in an Age of Digital Placelessness." *Adaptation* 10:2 (2017): 176–191.

Pittman, L. Monique. "Resisting History and Atoning for Racial Privilege: Shakespeare's Henriad in HBO's *The Wire.*" *The Routledge Handbook of Shakespeare and Global Appropriation.* Eds. Christy Desmet, Sujata Iyengar, and Miriam Jacobson. Routledge, 2020. 378–387.

Pittman, L. Monique. "Too Soon Forgot: The Ethics of Remembering in *Richard III, NOW*, and *House of Cards.*" *Borrowers and Lenders* 13:1 (2020).

Pittman, L. Monique, Vanessa I. Corredera, Kristin N. Denslow and Karl G. Bailey. "'Were I human': Beingness and the Postcolonial Object in *Westworld*'s Appropriation of *The Tempest.*" *Variable Objects: Shakespeare and Speculative Appropriation.* Eds. Valerie M. Fazel and Louise Geddes. Edinburgh University Press, 2021. 85–107.

Pocock, J. G. A. "The Limits and Divisions of British History: In Search of the Unknown Subject." *The American Historical Review* 87:2 (1982): 311–336.

Potter, Lois. "English and American Richards, Edwards, and Henries." *Shakespeare Quarterly* 55:4 (2004): 450–461.

Potter, Lois. "The Second Tetralogy: Performance as Interpretation." *A Companion to Shakespeare's Works.* Vol. 3. *The Histories.* Eds. Richard Dutton and Jean E. Howard. Blackwell, 2006. 287–307.

Poulton, Mike. *Wolf Hall and Bring Up the Bodies: The Stage Adaptation.* Picador, 2014.

Powell, Enoch. "Rivers of Blood." Speech to Conservative Association Meeting, Birmingham. 20 April 1968. Channel 4.

Purcell, Stephen. *Shakespeare and Audience in Practice.* Palgrave, 2018.

Putting Quality First. BBC Trust. December 2010. <http://www.bbc.co.uk/bbctrust/assets/files/pdf/review_report_research/strategic_review/final_conclusions>.

The Cronicle History of Henry the fift. Printed by Thomas Creede, for Tho. Millington and John Busby, 1600. London: *Early English Books Online.*

Rabkin, Norman. "Rabbits, Ducks, and *Henry V.*" *Shakespeare Quarterly* 28 (1977): 279–296.

Rackin, Phyllis. *Stages of History: Shakespeare's English Chronicles.* Cornell University Press, 1990.

Rackin, Phyllis. "Women's Roles in the Elizabethan History Plays." *The Cambridge Companion to Shakespeare's History Plays.* Ed. Michael Hattaway. Cambridge University Press, 2002. 71–85.

Ramey, Corinne. "*Wolf Hall* Viewers Flock to the Soundtrack." *Wall Street Journal*, 9 April 2015.

Rattansi, Ali. "On Being and Not Being Brown/Black-British: Racism, Class, Sexuality and Ethnicity in Post-imperial Britain." *Interventions* 2:1 (2000): 118–134.

Reflections on the Cultural Olympiad and London 2012 Festival. Arts Council England and London Organising Committee of the Olympic and Paralympic Games. April 2013.

Renan, Ernest. "What is a Nation." *Becoming National: A Reader.* Eds. Geoff Eley and Ronald Grigor Suny. Oxford University Press, 1996. 42–55.

Reynolds, Peter. "Unlocking the Box: Shakespeare on Film and Video." *Shakespeare in the Changing Curriculum.* Eds. Lesley Aers and Nigel Wheale. Routledge, 1991. 189–203.

Rogers, Amanda and Ashley Thorpe. "Interview with the RSC's Hannah Miller, Head of Casting, and Kevin Fitzmaurice, Producer." *Contemporary Theatre Review* 24:4 (2014): 486–493.

Rogers, Jami. "The Shakespearean Glass Ceiling: the State of Colorblind Casting in Contemporary British Theatre." *Shakespeare Bulletin* 31:3 (2013): 405–430.

Rokison-Woodall, Abigail. *Shakespeare in the Theatre: Nicholas Hytner.* Bloomsbury, 2017.

Rosenthal, Daniel. *The National Theatre Story.* Oberon Books, 2013.

Rothwell, Kenneth S. *A History of Shakespeare on Screen: A Century of Film and Television.* 2ed edition, Cambridge University Press, 2004.

Royster, Francesca T. "The Chicago Shakespeare Theater's *Rose Rage*: Whiteness, Terror, and the Fleshwork of Theatre in a Post-Colorblind Age." *Colorblind Shakespeare: New Perspectives on Race and Performance.* Ed. Ayanna Thompson. Routledge, 2006. 221–239.

Rubin, Gayle. "The Traffic in Women: Notes on the 'Political Economy' of Sex." *An Anthropology of Women.* Ed. Rayna Reiter. Monthly Review Press, 1975. 157–210.

Rutter, Carol Chillington. "Of Tygers' Hearts and Players' Hides." *Shakespeare's Histories and Counter-Histories.* Eds. Dermot Cavanagh, Stuart Hampton-Reeves, and Stephen Longstaffe. Manchester University Press, 2006. 182–197.

Ryan, Kiernan. *Shakespeare's Universality: Here's Fine Revolution.* Bloomsbury, 2015.

Said, Edward. *Culture and Imperialism.* Vintage Books, 1993.

Sanchez, Melissa E. "Bodies that Matter in *Richard II.*" *Richard II: New Critical Essays.* Ed. Jeremy Lopez. Routledge, 2012. 95–116.

Sandberg, Eric. "Hilary Mantel's *Wolf Hall*(s) and the Circulation of Cultural Prestige." *Adaptation, Awards Culture, and the Value of Prestige.* Eds. Colleen Kennedy-Karpat and Eric Sandberg. Palgrave Macmillan, 2017. 55–73.

Schama, Simon. "What historians think of historical novels." *The Financial Times*, 13 Feb. 2015.

Schwochow, Christian (dir). "Tywysog Cymru." *The Crown*. Season 3. Netflix. 2019.

Scuira, Leonardo. "Brexit Beyond Borders: Beginning of the EU Collapse and Return to Nationalism." *Journal of International Affairs* 70:2 (2017): 109–123.

Shakespeare, William and John Fletcher. *King Henry VIII, or All is True*. Ed. Jay L. Halio. Oxford University Press, 1999.

Shakespeare Unlocked. BBC. July 2012 <www.bbc.co.uk/arts/shakespeare>.

Shakespeare, William. *I Henry IV. The Riverside Shakespeare*. Eds. G. Blakemore Evans et al. Houghton Mifflin, 1974. 847–885.

Shakespeare, William. *II Henry IV. The Riverside Shakespeare*. Eds. G. Blakemore Evans et al. Houghton Mifflin, 1974. 886–929.

Shakespeare, William. *Henry V. The Riverside Shakespeare*. Eds. G. Blakemore Evans et al. Houghton Mifflin, 1974. 930–975.

Shakespeare, William. *I Henry VI. The Riverside Shakespeare*. Eds. G. Blakemore Evans et al. Houghton Mifflin, 1974. 596–629.

Shakespeare, William. *II Henry VI. The Riverside Shakespeare*. Eds. G. Blakemore Evans et al. Houghton Mifflin, 1974. 630–670.

Shakespeare, William. *III Henry VI. The Riverside Shakespeare*. Eds. G. Blakemore Evans et al. Houghton Mifflin, 1974. 671–707.

Shakespeare, William. *Henry VIII. The Riverside Shakespeare*. Eds. G. Blakemore Evans et al. Houghton Mifflin, 1974. 980–1018.

Shakespeare, William. *Richard II. The Riverside Shakespeare*. Eds. G. Blakemore Evans et al. Houghton Mifflin, 1974. 805–841.

Shakespeare, William. *Richard III. The Riverside Shakespeare*. Eds. G. Blakemore Evans et al. Houghton Mifflin, 1974. 712–764.

Shakespeare, William. *The Tempest. The Riverside Shakespeare*. Eds. G. Blakemore Evans et al. Houghton Mifflin, 1974. 1611–1638.

Shakespeare, William. *Troilus and Cressida. The Riverside Shakespeare*. Eds. G. Blakemore Evans et al. Houghton Mifflin, 1974. 448–498.

Sharrock, Thea (dir). *The Hollow Crown: Henry V*. Perf. Tom Hiddleston, John Hurt, Melanie Theirry. NBC Universal, 2012. DVD.

Siddique, Haroon. "David Starkey widely criticized for 'slavery was not genocide' remarks." *The Guardian*, 2 July 2020.

Sierakowski, Slawomir. "Benhabib: Nobody wants to be a refugee." Interview in *Krytyka Polityczna & European Alternatives. PoliticalCritique.org*. 21 Sept. 2015.

Silverstone, Catherine. *Shakespeare, Trauma and Contemporary Performance*. Routledge, 2011.

Sinfield, Alan. "Heritage and the market, regulation and desublimation." *Political Shakespeare: Essays in Cultural Materialism*. Eds. Jonathan Dollimore and Alan Sinfield. Cornell University Press, 1994. 255–279.

Sirkeci, Ibrahim. "Transnational Döner Kebab Taking over the UK." *Transnational Marketing Journal* 4:2 (2016): 143–158.

Smith, Ian. "We are Othello: Speaking of Race in Early Modern Studies." *Shakespeare Quarterly* 67 (2016): 104–124.

Smith, Ian. *Race and Rhetoric in the Renaissance: Barbarian Errors*. Palgrave Macmillan, 2009.

Smith, Steven Rathgeb. "Privatization, Devolution, and the Welfare State: Rethinking the Prevailing Wisdom." *Restructuring the Welfare State: Political Institutions and Policy Change*. Eds. Bo Rothstein and Sven Steinmo. Palgrave MacMillan, 2002. 78–101.

Spencer, Charles. "A tale for our time summons the blood." *Telegraph*, 15 May 2003.

Spivak, Gayatri Chakravorty. "Can the subaltern speak?" *Marxism and the Interpretation of Culture*. Eds. Cary Nelson and Lawrence Grossberg. University of Illinois Press, 1988. 271–313.

Starks-Estes, Lisa S. "From Face to Facebook: Levinas's Radical Ethics and 'Shakespeare Friends.'" *Borrowers and Lenders* 10:1 (2016).

Steigerwalt, Jenna. "Performing Race on the Original-Practices Stage: A Call to Action." *Shakespeare Bulletin* 27 (2009): 425–435.

Stewart, Heather and Rowena Mason. "Nigel Farage's anti-migrant poster reported to police." *The Guardian*, 16 June 2016.

Straw, Jack. "Speech at the Launch of the Parekh Report." *Runnymede Bulletin* 324 (Dec. 2000): 2–4.

Suzuki, Mihoko. *Metamorphoses of Helen: Authority, Difference, and the Epic*. Cornell University Press, 1989.

Tatspaugh, Patricia. "Review of *Henry V* at the Olivier Theatre, London, May 6 - August 20, 2003. Dir. By Nicholas Hytner". *Shakespeare Bulletin* 21:4 (Winter 2003 2003): 100–104.

Taylor, Charles. "The Politics of Recognition." *Multiculturalism: Examining the Politics of Recognition*. Ed. Amy Gutmann. Princeton University Press, 1994. 25–73.

Taylor, Matthew. "Casey report criticised for focus on UK Muslim communities." *The Guardian*, 5 Dec. 2016.

Terris, Olwen. "Shakespeare and British Television." *Shakespeare Survey* 61 (2008): 199–212.

"The Total Audience Report: Q1 2016." The Nielsen Company. 27 June 2016.

"This sceptred isle." *Such Stuff: The Shakespeare's Globe Podcast*. Season 2, Episode 6. 29 Mar. 2019.

Thomas, Ebony Elizabeth. *The Dark Fantastic: Race and the Imagination from Harry Potter to the Hunger Games*. New York University Press, 2019.

Thompson, Ayanna. *Passing Strange: Shakespeare, Race, and Contemporary America*. Oxford University Press, 2011.

Thompson, Ayanna. "Practicing a Theory/Theorizing a Practice: An Introduction to Shakespearean Colorblind Casting." *Colorblind Shakespeare: New Perspectives on Race and Performance*. Ed. Ayanna Thompson. Routledge, 2006: 1–24.

Thompson, Ayanna. "To Notice or Not To Notice: Shakespeare, Black Actors, and Performance Reviews." *Borrowers and Lenders* 4:1 (Fall/Winter 2008–2009).

Touré. *Who's Afraid of Post-Blackness? What it Means to be Black Now*. Free Press, 2011.

Trouillot, Michel-Rolph. *Silencing the Past: Power and the Production of History*. Beacon Press, 1995.

Uberoi, Varun and Tariq Modood. "Has Multiculturalism in Britain Retreated?" *Soundings* 53 (Spring 2013): 129–142.

Valluvan, Sivamohan. *The Clamour of Nationalism: Race and nation in twenty-first-century Britain*. Manchester University Press, 2019.

Valluvan, Sivamohan. "Defining and Challenging the New Nationalism." *Juncture* 23:4 (2017): 232–239.

Valluvan, Sivamohan. "New Nationalism and Old Ideologies." IPR blog. 7 April 2017.

Valluvan, Sivamohan and Virinder S. Kalra. "Racial Nationalisms: Brexit, borders and Little Englander Contradictions." *Ethnic and Racial Studies* 42:14 (Nov. 2019): 2393–2412.

Vaughan, Virginia Mason. *Performing Blackness on English Stages, 1500–1800.* Cambridge University Press, 2005.

Vergil. *The Aeneid.* Trans. Sarah Ruden. Yale University Press, 2008.

Vertovec, Steven. "Multiculturalism, culturalism and public incorporation." *Migration and Social Cohesion.* Ed. Steven Vertovec. An Elgar Reference Collection, 1999. 222–255.

Viswanathan, Gauri. *Masks of Conquest: Literary Study and British Rule in India.* Columbia University Press, 1989.

Volf, Miroslav. *Exclusion and Embrace: A Theological Exploration of Identity, Otherness, and Reconciliation.* Revised and Updated. Abingdon Press, 2019.

Votava, Jennie M. "Through a Glass Darkly: Sophie Okonedo's Margaret as Racial Other in *The Hollow Crown: The Wars of the Roses.*" *Shakespeare Survey* 73 (2020): 170–183.

Waldstreicher, David. and Jeffrey L. Pasley. "*Hamilton* as Founders Chic: A Neo-Federalist, Antislavery Usable Past?" *Historians on Hamilton: How a Blockbuster Musical is Restaging America's Past.* Eds. Renee C. Romano and Claire Bond Potter. Rutgers University Press, 2018. 137–166.

Walsh, Brian. *Shakespeare, the Queen's Men, and the Elizabethan Performance of History.* Cambridge University Press, 2009.

Way, Geoffrey. "Peeking Behind the Digital Curtains: Shakespearean Performance Institutions, Social Media, and Access." *Borrowers and Lenders* 10:1 (Spring/Summer 2016).

The West Wing. Season 3. NBC, 2001–2002. *Netflix.*

White, Hayden. "Historiography and Historiophoty." *American Historical Review* 93:5 (1988): 1193–1199.

Williams, Zoe. "Nationalism can be a good thing." *The Guardian*, 8 May 2018.

Willis, Susan. *The BBC Shakespeare Plays: Making the Televised Canon.* University of North Carolina Press, 1991.

Wilson, August. *The Ground on which I Stand.* Theatre Communications Group, 1996.

Wilson, Richard. "The Madness of King Charles III: Shakespeare and the Modern Monarchy." *Critical Survey* 29:2 (2017): 76–93.

Wingfield, Nick. "Amazon challenges Netflix by opening Prime to Monthly Subscribers." *The New York Times*, 17 Apr. 2016.

"*Wolf Hall*: Filming on Location." *Masterpiece.* PBS. 20 April 2015.

"Wolf Hall Q&A with Hilary Mantel and Claire Foy." British Film Institute. YouTube 12 Jan. 2015.

Wolterstorff, Nicholas. *Art in Action: Toward a Christian Aesthetic.* Eerdmans, 1980.

Womack, Peter. "Imagining Communities: Theatres and the English Nation in the Sixteenth Century." *Culture and History 1350–1600: Essays on English Communities, Identities and Writing.* Ed. David Aers. Wayne State University Press, 1992. 91–145.

Woodward, Carl. "Sheila Atim Interview." Mr Carl Woodward.com. 17 Nov. 2018.

Woolf, Daniel. *The Social Circulation of the Past: English Historical Culture 1500–1730.* Oxford University Press, 2003.

Wray, Ramona. "*Henry V* After the War on Terror." *Shakespeare Survey* 72 (2019): 1–15.

Wray, Ramona. "Henry's Desperate Housewives: *The Tudors*, the Politics of Historiography, and the Beautiful Body of Jonathan Rhys Meyers." *The English Renaissance in Popular Culture: An Age for All Time.* Ed. Greg Colón Semenza. Palgrave Macmillan, 2010. 25–42.

Wray, Ramona. "Shakespeare and the new discourses of television: quality, aesthetics, and *The Hollow Crown*." *Cahiers Élisabéthains* XX:X: 2021: 1–17.

Wright, Patrick. *On Living in an Old Country: The National Past in Contemporary Britain*. Oxford University Press, 2009.

YouTube. "Brexit: 10 Most Interesting Ads by the 'Vote Leave' Campaign." FactPoint-Video. 16 June 2016.

Index

Abdelkader, Engy 80
absolutism 8, 105
Abu Ghraib 78
accent snobbery 65
Acocella, Joan 158
adapting historical novels 163–169
Aebischer, Pascale 38, 196
Akbar, Arifa 76–77
Akhimie, Patricia 203
Akrout, Edward 129
Akuwudike, Jude 73, 75–77
Alexander Hamilton 36
alienation 76, 133, 152
aliens 133–146; at the border 133–137; as invaders 137–146
"All the Henrys and Richards, too, for that matter" 1–5
All Is True 158–159
Almeida Theatre 183–184, 187, 191
Amadeus 76
Amazonian threat 60–61, 63
ambivalence 42–45
American Minstrelsy 86
American Moor 203
Amis, Martin 18
analepsis 167–168
Anderson, Benedict 6, 134–135
Andoh, Adjoa 39, 42, 200, 207, 212–217, 219
Anthias, Floya 7
anti-EU voter fervor 20
anti-Islamic sentiment 2
anti-racism 204
anti-Semitism 132
anti-totalitarianism 17
Appiah, Kwame Anthony 6, 218
Arendt, Hannah 30, 32
Armstrong, Joe 108
Arne, Thomas 43
Arthurian legends 24
artistic representation 26
asserting authenticity 163–169
Assmann, Jan 121
Association of Police Officers 80–81
atavistic nationalism 8, 10, 16, 133
Atim, Sheila 117
audience resistance 55–56
austerity 11, 152
austerity nostalgia 120
authentic Shakespeare 119
authenticity 130; asserting 163–169; inauthenticity of white history 177–178; of locations 130, 143, 165, 167–168
authoritarianism 18

Baartman, Saartje 139
Bak, Greg 171
Baker, David 23–24
Balibar, Étienne 7
BAME actors 54–55, 58, 71, 85
Bandura, Albert 117
Barrie, J. M. 120
Barrit, Desmond 74
Bartlett, Mike 10, 41, 183–185, 187–192, 194–199
Battle of Britain 43
Bazely, Paul 130
BBC 10, 38, 57, 159–160, 163–165, 183–184; *Hollow Crown* series 1 94–127; Tudor casting 163–164; *Wars of the Roses* 128–156
Bell, Fiona 57, 59–65, 68
belonging 44–45, 148, 189
Benhabib, Seyla 29–32, 51, 143, 219
Bennett, Susan 55–56
BFI *see* British Film Institute
Bhabha, Homi K. 42–43

Bhattacharyya, Gargi 98, 152–153, 188
Bible 80
Bickley, John 208
bigotry 36, 136
black sacrifice 115
blackface 120–121, 158, 172–177
blackness 75–78, 85–86, 171
Blackwell, Anna 129
Blair, Tony 12, 50, 67, 74, 188, 208
Blake, William 96
Blanke, John 171
"blind spots" 33, 121, 169, 183; *see also* colorblind casting
Boehmer, Elleke 7
Bond, James 95
Bonilla-Silva, Eduardo 201
Bonneville, Hugh 142, 146
Booker Prize 160
boundary-drawing 38
Boyd, Michael 49–93, 140, 183, 185, 217; seeing and not seeing 53–59
Boyle, Danny 95–100, 111, 120–121
Branagh, Kenneth 88, 96–97, 104, 109, 111, 113, 121
Brand Britain 9, 38
Brayben, Kate 192
"Breaking Point" 132–133, 150
Brexit: The Uncivil War 43
Brexit 2, 6, 10–11, 20–21, 39–40, 44, 68, 121, 128, 131–137, 143, 147, 151–154, 169–170, 182, 188–190, 198, 207–220
Bring Up the Bodies 157–181
British Broadcasting Corporation *see* BBC
British Film Institute 165
British Kebab Awards 190–191
British multiculturalism 16–21
British Museum 94, 102
British nation 94–127, 157–181; history of 157–181
Britishness 9, 12–17, 19–21, 23–24, 37–38, 51–52, 58, 116, 118, 211; identification with 19–20
Brolin, James 1
Buckley, Jeff 5
bunker mentality 150, 186; *see also* Brexit; Vote Leave
Burford, Priyanga 184
Bush, George W. 80

Cade, Jack 66–67, 131, 153–154
Caliban 96–97
Call the Midwife 95
Callender, Colin 166–167
Cameron, David 40, 120, 131–133, 188, 190–191, 207–208
case of two Richards 207–220; dis-integration (2000–2016) 207–210; histories remembered 212–217; telling sad stories 217–219; Welsh correction? 210–212
Casey, Louise 208–209
Casey Review 207–210, 219
casual racism 203
catharsis 83
Catholicism 24–25
cause–effect problems 162
Cavendish, George 157–159
Certeauvian gap 25, 44
character doubling 63–65, 68, 187
chauvinism 60, 65
Chernow, Ron 36
Chillington Rutter, Carol 54, 59, 65–66
Claims of Culture 51
class 3, 53–59, 65–68; resistance in history 65–68; unrest 66
Clegg, Nick 190
clownishness 67–68
coalition invasion of Afghanistan 69–70, 78
Cobb, Keith Hamilton 203
coded racism 21
Cohen, Leonard 5
collective agency 117
Colman, Olivia 211–212
colonial aggression 8
colonial mentality 12
colonial-imperialism 7–8, 58, 96
color of war 68–69
"color-blind racism" 34, 201
color-conscious casting 49
colorblind casting 3–4, 11, 33–35, 40–41, 49–50, 54–60, 66–77, 84–88, 103, 111, 130–131, 137–140, 144–148, 183–185
comeuppance 61
Commission on the Future of Multi-Ethnic Britain 12, 14–16, 21, 39, 51–54, 67, 70, 89
Commission for Racial Equality 16–17
Complete Works Festival 58
conflation of practices 18
consciousness of doubleness 25
constitutional monarchy 105
constructedness 89
Cooke, Dominic 129–130
Corbyn, Jeremy 190
Cordery, Richard 64
Corredera, Vanessa 37, 203–204

Covillault, Jérémie 129
Crenshaw, Kimberlé 51
Croll, Doña 213, 215
Cromwell, Thomas 158, 160–161, 164–165, 167–168, 170–174, 176–178
crossdressing 213–214
Crow, Jim 86
The Crown 42, 210–212, 219
cultural amnesia 170
cultural appropriation 191–192
Cultural Diversity Network 101
Cultural Olympiad 39, 94–127
cultural representation 13, 53
Cumberbatch, Benedict 43, 129–130
Cummings, Dominic 43
curated bogeymen 153

Dadabhoy, Ambereen 203
Daily Mail 35
Daily Telegraph 14–16, 56, 78, 161
Daniel Deronda 21
Darabont, Frank 114
D'Arcy, Sarah 59
darstellen 26
Davies, Jo 35–6
de Certeau, Michel 22–23, 25, 27, 82, 89, 182, 201, 218; Certeauvian gap 25
death of kings 217–219
deliberative democracy 29
democratic equality 31
Dench, Judi 129, 133–135, 148–149
Desmet, Christy 10
Dharker, Ayesha 215
Dickens, Charles 4, 95
diegesis of drama 168, 202–203
differentiation 22
Dillane, Richard 57
diminishment 106
dis-integration 207–210
disappearing Moor: adapting Mantel 163–169; Hilary Mantel's historiography 160–163; inauthenticity of white history 177–178; "take back control" 169–177; white privilege blind spots 169–177
disempowerment 7, 131, 140
disenfranchisement 20
disequilibrium 68
diversity 19, 55, 58, 68, 71, 86–87, 101
Dobson, Michael 75, 82–83
Dobson, Gary 98
Dockery, Michelle 108
Doran, Gregory 35–36
Downie, Penny 81–83
Downton Abbey 142, 146
dreadlocks 74
Dromgoole, Dominic 214
du Jeu, Félicité 74, 83
Dunbar, Adrian 142, 146
Duncan, Lindsay 106
Dyer, Richard 77, 188, 193

Edgar, David 4–5
editorial independence 102
El-Enany, Nadine 133
Elgar, Edward 96
Eliot, George 21–22
Elliott, Tomas 107
embodied history 25, 215
empowerment 19
Englishness 9, 14, 37–38, 51–52
Entwistle, George 102
epistemic fallacy 29
epistemological ascendancy 111
equal opportunities 13
Equality Act 2010 102
equivocal interiority 7
Erickson, Peter 32–33
Escobedo, Andrew 24–25
Espinosa, Ruben 32–33, 116
ethics 10, 23, 28–32, 56
ethnic diversity 49, 111–118
ethnicity 17–18
European continental actors 129
evasions 84–88, 95–100, 189–191; and Shakespeare 95–100
exceptionality 178
exclusionary racism 21, 189
exclusivity 88
exteriorization 7–8
extremism 2–3, 6, 17, 208–209
Eyre, Richard 104–105, 108

fair play 15
false binary 19
Fantastic Follies of Mrs. Rich 35
Farage, Nigel 11, 132, 150
Farzad, Leila 215
fascism 188
faux multiculturalism 185, 219
Fazel, Valerie M. 10
female characterization 58–60
female participation 105
feminism 7, 148
feminist theory of nationalism 7
fetishizing 18, 178, 199
fictionality 107
Finney, Gavin 166

flawed racial representation 87
fledgling Great Britain 24
Fleming, Crystal M. 34
Fletcher, John 157–158, 164, 168–169
FMEB *see* Commission on the Future of Multi-Ethnic Britain
Földváry, Kinga 128
foreignness 133
Forms of Nationhood 37
"fortress Britain" 52–53, 88, 128–156, 186, 210
Fourth Estate 198
Foy, Claire 168
fragmentation 17–18
Frances-Morgan, Laura 140
Francis, Geff 58
Fryer, Peter 200
fundamentalism 208
Future of Multi-Ethnic Britain 11–16, 21, 27, 39, 51, 65, 67, 70–71, 202, 207–209; *see also* Parekh, Bhikhu
future of multiethnic Britain 51–3

Gambon, Michael 88
Geddes, Louise 10
gender 3, 18, 26, 53–65, 94–127, 182–206; diversity 105–106; equality 18; hierarchies 26; intersections with nation and race 182–206; intersections of 191–198; in Michael Boyd's *Henry VI* cycle 59–65; norms 26; politics 104–111; seeing and not seeing 53–59
gender-blind casting 183
gendered derision 167
genetic realism 154
genital mutilation 62–63
Gilroy, Paul 8, 14, 16, 41, 43, 73, 134, 177, 185–186, 198–199
glass ceiling 50
global contrary movements 6–11
global power relations 23
globalization 6
Globe Theatre 38–39, 119, 158–159, 166, 200, 212–215, 219
Goddard, Lynette 55, 57, 59
Goldberg, David Theo 44–45
good nationalism 121
Good Society 95
Goodhart, David 17–19, 188
Goold, Rupert 41, 104–108, 110, 183–184, 187, 191
GOSH *see* Great Ormond Street Hospital for Children
Goulding, Richard 195
Gove, Michael 132
Graham, James 210
Great Chain of Being 134
Great Ormond Street Hospital for Children 120
Greenblatt, Stephen 158–159
The Green Mile 114
Gregory, Philippa 204
Guardian 95, 121, 132, 208
Guy, John 161

Habib, Imtiaz 171
Haddon Hall 143
Hadfield, Andrew 37
Hall, Edward 202
Hall, Kim F. 61, 140, 199
Hall, Stuart 22–23
"Hallelujah" 5
Hamilton 36, 55
Hampton-Reeves, Stuart 54, 59, 66
Hannan, Daniel 43–44
harbinger of progress 95–100
Harewood, David 85–86, 88
Harmon, Mark 5
Harris, Pippa 94–95, 104, 128–129
Harris-Perry, Melissa V. 139–140, 145
Hart, Darren 85–86
Hartley, Andrew James 38
Hatchuel, Sarah 111
hate crimes 80–81
Hatendi, Nyasha 184, 187–191
Hatherley, Owen 120
Hatley, Tim 79
Hawes, Keeley 147, 149, 151
Haynes, Toby 43
hegemonic identifiers 96
Helgerson, Richard 23, 37
Henderson, Diana H. 198–199
Hendricks, Margo 76, 201
Heng, Geraldine 26, 173, 213
Henriad 104–111, 118
Henry IV parts I and II (Hytner, 2005) 84–88
Henry V 2–3, 24, 68–69, 84–88, 111–118, 200, 203–204; Hytner production (2003) 68–69; racial representation 111–118
Henry VI cycle (Boyd, 2000–2001) 32, 53–59, 66, 185
Henry VIII 9, 158–159
heritage films 158–159, 166–167, 176, 178
Herrin, Jeremy 174
heteronormativity 114
Hiddleston, Tom 102, 109, 114

Higgins, Charlotte 95
Higson, Andrew 159, 167, 176
Hill Collins, Patricia 138–139
Hirsch, Afua 89
histories remembered 212–217
historiography 160–163
historiophoty 177
history of evasion 95–100
Hodgdon, Barbara 118–119
Hogg, Ian 74
Holderness, Graham 118–119
Hollow Crown 10, 84, 192, 197, 213; BBC Shakespeare for inclusive Britain 100–104; cultural politics of 104–111; gender politics and 104–111; *Henry V* 111–118; selective memory 118–121; series 1 94–127; series 2 128–156; Shakespeare as harbinger of progress 95–100
homoeroticism 114–115
homogenization 191
horizons of expectations 56
Hostile Environment Policy 97, 112
"Hottentot Venus" 139
Howard, Jean E. 26, 104–105, 109, 137, 219
Hughes, Tom 106, 112
Hughey, Matthew W. 114
human culture 28–32
The Human Condition 32
Hurt, John 110
hyper-sexualization 60
Hytner, Nicholas 49–93, 183, 203–204; *Henry V* 68–69

"I ask no less than power" 191–198
iconicity 119, 182, 204
identity crisis 41
ideological dislocation 188
illegal immigrants 97
imagined community 25, 134–135
immigration 21, 97
imperial aphasia 98
imperialism 4–5, 7–8, 54
inauthenticity of white history 177–178
incendiary imagery 189
inclusive Britain 53, 100–104; Shakespeare for 100–104
inclusive casting 67–69; *see also* colorblind casting
Industrial Revolution 96, 98
inequality 52–53, 60, 67–68, 150–152
inertia 70
insecurity 18
institutional neglect 55
institutional racism 75, 711
insularity 131
integration 207–209
intercultural rapprochement 218
interdependence 19, 25, 170, 198, 208–209
interlocking oppressions 117
internal exclusion 7–8
international alliances 3, 16
internecine conflict 134, 151
intersectional identity 213
intersections 182–206
intersubjectivity 28–32
intransigence of historical fact 33
inviolability 131, 136
invisibility 4, 58, 77
Irons, Jeremy 103
"The Iron Maiden" 169–170, 178
"Isaac and Ishmael" 2
Islam 2–3, 6, 17–18, 80, 143, 208–209
Islamic State 11, 132
Islamophobia 39–40, 80
"Isles of Wonder" 95–96, 100
isolationism 134, 150, 154, 170, 216
Iwuji, Chuk 58

Jackson, Russell 64
Jaws 168
Jeremiah, Ivanno 130, 150–151
"Jerusalem" 96
Jim Crow *see* Crow, Jim
jingoism 12, 116
Johnson, Allan G. 117
Johnson, Boris 191
Johnson, David 166
Joseph, Paterson 100, 111–117, 150
Joubin, Alexa Alice 10

Kalra, Virinder S. 209
Kamaralli, Anna 60–62, 104–105
Kamps, Ivo 169
Karremann, Isabel 27
Keen, Will 168
Kennedy, Dennis 118–119
Khan, Akram 99
Kidnie, Margaret Jane 9–10, 101
King Charles III 182–185, 187, 192–194, 197–198
King John 9
King Lear 154, 193
Kinnear, Rory 106
Kirwan, Peter 107
Kissoon, Jeffery 85–86
Kolkovich, Elizabeth 114
Kosminsky, Peter 157, 164–165
Kundnani, Arun 16–18

l'affaire foulard 143
Lam, Sarah 213, 215
Lanier, Douglas 9, 119, 178
LaPerle, Carol Mejia 199
lasciviousness 139, 195
Lawley, Sue 175
Lawrance, Tamara 41, 184, 192, 195, 199
Lawrence, Doreen 98
Lawrence, Stephen 98
Leberg, Dan 110, 119
"left-behind" voter thesis 152
legitimacy 55–60
Leicester, Margot 196
Les Miserables 3
Lesser, Anton 113, 158
Lester, Adrian 39, 49–50, 68–69, 71–77, 88, 202
Letts, Quentin 35–36
Levinas, Emmanuel 28–29, 32, 217–218
Lewis, Damian 158
Lewis Jones, Mark 211
liberalism 16–20, 34, 99, 120–121, 185, 208
Life and Adventures of Nicholas Nickleby 4–5
liminal spaces 55–56
Line of Duty 146
Linton, Lynette 39, 42, 200, 207, 212–217, 219
literary inventiveness 161
little island 129, 153
Lloyd, Harry 168
Loehlin, James N. 85
London Review of Books 192
Lurie, Kathryn 36

McArdle, Aiden 58, 61
Macbeth 149, 193–194
McClintock, Anne 6–7
MacCulloch, Diarmaid 169–170
MacDonald, Joyce Green 184–185, 196–197, 215
Macfadyen, Matthew 85
McGuckin, Aíslin 59
McIntosh, Peggy 117
Mckenzie, Lisa 152
McLaughlin, Eugene 14–15
MacLeod, Emily 141
McMillin, Scott 103
McMullan, Tim 196
Macpherson Report 98
"make-believe" 21–22
Maley, Willy 186
Mallyon, Catherine 35–36
Manning, Alan 19–20
Mantel, Hilary 41, 157–169, 192–194; adapting novels of 163–169; historiography of 160–163
Margaret of Anjou 137–146
marginalization 51, 146–147
marketability 130
Markle, Meghan 197
marriage mores 18
Mason, Rowena 132
Mason Vaughan, Virginia 77–78
May, Theresa 97, 207
Mbembe, Achille 7–8
memory 6
Mendes, Sam 94–95, 102, 128–130
Merchant of Venice 201
metonymy 121
Meyers, Jonathan Rhys 163
Middleton, Catherine 192–196
Miles, Ben 140
Miles, Robert 98
Miliband, Ed 190
millennial threshold 49–93
Miller, Hannah 174
mimetic reproduction 105, 176, 200
Miranda, Lin-Manuel 36, 55
misogyny 44, 121, 138, 143–144, 203, 219
mission accomplished? 5, 70–73, 80
Mitchell, Jeff 132
Modood, Tariq 19
Monteiro, Lyra 36–37
moral culpability 8
moral righteousness 80
"morbidity of heritage" 8
More, Sir Thomas 160, 171, 177
Morgan, Michael L. 28–29
Morgan, Peter 210
Morrison, Toni 72
Msamati, Lucian 76–77, 111
Mullin, Romano 176
multicultural backlash 16–17, 19–20
multiculturalism 6, 11–21, 31, 36, 50, 56, 69–73, 77, 88–99, 116, 150–151, 176–177, 191–198; British 16–21, 50, 69–73
multiethnic casting 4, 174–177; *see also* colorblind casting
multiethnicity 11–12
muscular liberalism 208
mutual obligation 28–29

Naiambana, Patrice 58
narcissism 199

nation 11–16, 53–59, 182–206; intersections of 182–206; in Michael Boyd's *Henry VI* cycle 59–65
nation-building 8–9, 83, 104, 133, 192
National Health Service 95, 98, 120–121, 132, 150, 189–191
national inviolability 131, 136
national rebranding 170–171
national solidarity 19
National Theatre 38, 49, 59, 68–70, 76, 78–81, 109, 183; *Henry V* at (2003) 68–69
National Trust 159
nationalism 2, 6–8, 15, 17–21, 100, 120–121, 131, 143, 153, 216
nationhood 5, 8–10, 12, 15, 23, 88, 103, 120, 134, 187
naturalism 111
Nazi Germany 104
NBC Universal 102–103, 121
Neal, Sarah 14–15
Neal Street Productions 94–95, 103–104, 117, 128–131, 154, 207
Negro, Dyego 171
negro ex machina 115
neoliberalism 6, 153
neverland bricolage 49
New Labour 14, 50, 75, 89, 152, 208
New Nationalism 6, 10–11, 20–21, 44, 187–190
New Politics of Identity 19, 31
New York Review of Books 158
New Yorker 158
NHS *see* National Health Service
Niles, Sarah 217
9/11 *see* September 11, 2001
Noble, Cecilia 73
non-stereotyping 103
non-traditional casting 72, 201–202; *see also* colorblind casting
Norris, David 98
Norway 21
nostalgia 1–2, 169, 185, 189; *see also* Brexit; Vote Leave
NT *see* National Theatre
Nubia, Onyeka 170
Nunn, Trevor 183
Nuttall, Romola 213

objectification 7
Occidentalism 97, 215
O'Connor, Josh 42, 210
Odom Jr., Leslie 36
Ogbomo, Ann 59
Okonedo, Sophie 41, 130–131, 138–149, 151–152, 154, 192
Oliver, Stephen 4
Olivier, Laurence 44, 88
Olusoga, David 98, 171, 200
Olympic Games 94–103, 116, 120–121
on seeing/not seeing 53–59
O'Neill, Stephen 154
Ophelia 204
opportunism 26, 191
oppositional reflection 185, 199
Orgel, Stephen 159–160
Orientalism 69, 132, 215–216
Othello 201, 203
other-worldliness 147
otherness 3, 21–22, 31, 37, 60, 63–65, 112, 203–204
outsider's timely utility 75, 146–151, 200
Ové, Indra 215
ownership of national history 130
Owusu, Jude 130
Oyelowo, David 32–34, 39, 49–50, 54–58, 65, 67–68, 185, 217

palimpsests 63
panegyric 135
Pao, Angela C. 33–34, 183
Parekh, Bhikhu 12–13, 15–16, 19, 21, 27, 31–32, 51, 54, 57, 65, 67, 70–71, 208–209, 212–213; *see also Future of Multi-Ethnic Britain*
Parry, Hubert 96
particularism 12–13
pastiche 95, 98–99, 120–121, 216
paternalism 184
Pathak, Pathik 19
patois 73–76
"Patriotic Song" 5
patriotism 4, 15
Patten, Chris 102
Penshurst Place 165
Penlington, Amanda 58, 74
performing multiethnic nation's history 32–37
performing race 73–78
Peter Pan 120
Pew Research Center 131–132
Phillips, Trevor 16–17, 34
Phizacklea, Annie 98
pictorialism 167
Pigott-Smith, Tim 194–195
Pinnock, Winsome 76
Poésy, Clémence 107, 129
political correctness 20

"Posse Comitatus" 1–5
Postcolonial Melancholia 8, 14, 41, 43, 185–187, 189–190
postcolonialism 7, 11
Potter, Lois 26
Poulton, Mike 41, 157, 174–176, 178
Powell, Enoch 188–189
Powellism 188
Power, Ben 113–115, 117, 129
power-brokering 69, 186
powerlessness 20
privilege 118, 169
problematics of colorblind casting 111–112, 186–188
progressivism 36
prolepsis 167–168
promiscuity 60
Protestantism 24–25
Pryce, Jonathan 168
public reaction 15–17
Public Sector Equality Duty 102
puncturing colorblind claim 73–78
Putting Quality First 101
Pyke, Elaine 59
pyromancy 145–146

Quayle, Anthony 103

race 51–59, 73–78, 94–127, 131–133, 157–206; baiting 131–133; *Bring Up the Bodies* 157–181; *Hollow Crown series* 1 94–127; intersections with nation and gender 157–206; intersections of 182–206; seeing and not seeing 53–59; seeing performance of 73–78; *Wolf Hall* 157–181
race neutrality 73–74, 78
race performativity 75–76
race-baiting 131–133
race-blindness 34
racial categorization 77
racial coding 176
racial discrimination 12
racial hierarchies 26
"racial nonracialism" 44–45
racial othering 21
racial prejudices 20
racial purity 131, 136, 142
racial representation 3, 11, 58, 87, 111–118
racial semiotics 118; *see also* semiotics of race
racialization 14
racism 6–7, 15, 17, 40, 53, 55, 59, 67, 71–72, 75, 121, 132, 138–139, 150–151, 176, 188–189, 216
racist humor 203, 213
Rackin, Phyllis 24, 26, 104–105, 109, 116, 137, 142, 219
Ramey, Corinne 166
Ramm, John 174
Rattansi, Ali 136
re-casting 58
reality of discourse 22
recalibrating the past 176–177
reciprocity 18
recursion to Shakespeare's history 49
recycling bodies 67
Reformation 24–25, 163, 169–170
refuge of *Hollow Crown* 128–156
refugee invaders 131–146, 150
refugees 27, 132
reinventing nation 204
Reith Lectures 161–164, 169, 175, 178
religious affiliations 17–18
Renaissance 24, 77, 157, 163–164, 169, 177
Renan, Ernest 6, 95
renegotiating self 31–32
representation 11–16, 27, 111–118; racial 111–118
representing nation's history: "All the Henrys and Richards, too, for that matter" 1–5; ambivalence 42–45; British multiculturalism in wake of terror 16–21; intersubjectivity, ethics, human culture 28–32; methodology 38–42; multiculturalism, nation, representation 11–16; performing multiethnic nation's history 32–37; Shakespeare's contested nations 6–11; Shakespeare's telling nation's history 21–28; a word on terminology 37–38
resurgent nationalism 131, 143
"Rethinking the National Story" 51–52
reticence 57
Reynolds, Peter 73
Richard II 39, 183–184, 200, 207, 210, 212–213, 215–217
Richard Plantagenet 3, 136, 148
Riley, Charlotte 192–196
"Rivers of Blood" speech 188
Rivlin, Elizabeth 10
Robb, David 168
Robinson, Lucy 142
Rogers, Jami 50, 54–55
Rokison-Woodall, Abigail 68
Rose Rage 202
Rosencrantz and Guildenstern Are Dead 204
Rowling, J.K. 95, 99, 120
Roy, Sanchari 19–20

Royal Shakespeare Company 4, 32, 35–36, 38, 49, 53–59, 68, 94, 140, 157–158, 174, 183, 185
Royster, Francesca T. 26, 202
RSC *see* Royal Shakespeare Company
"Rule, Britannia!" 43
Runnymede Trust 10–13, 207
Rylance, Mark 158, 166–167

Said, Edward 185–186, 198, 214–215
Sam Wanamaker Playhouse 42, 200, 207, 212–214
Sanchez, Melissa E. 105
sanctification 61
Sandé, Emeli 99
sanitization 158
scapegoating 3, 7–8, 19, 137
Scarborough, Adrian 85
"sceptred isle" 187, 215–216
Schadenfreude 148
Schama, Simon 94, 160–161
Schiller, Ginny 183
second-order narratives 30
seeing performance of race 73–78, 176
selective memory 118–121
self-actualization 114–115
self-congratulatory liberalism 121
self-construction 53, 66, 134–135
self-definition 51
self-determination 211–212
self-examination 1
self-exclusion 50
self-harm 136
self-identity 28, 78
self-narration 23, 51
self-protection 135
self-reflection 23, 58, 99, 110, 112
self-righteousness 41–42
self-sabotage 44, 137
self-satisfaction 34, 72
self-understanding 16
semiotics of race 34–35, 56–57, 118, 195
September 11, 2001 1–5, 10–11, 16, 18, 39, 49, 69, 80, 203
7/7 terror attacks 10, 16, 84, 188
sexism 60–61, 67, 82, 121, 138–139, 167, 216
sexuality 27, 50, 60, 64, 66
Shaffer, Peter 76
Shakespeare Memorial Theatre Company 103
Shakespeare Plays 100, 103
Shakespeare Quarterly 178
Shakespeare Retold 100–101
Shakespeare Survey 75
"Shakespeare Unlocked" 94, 103, 110–111, 119
Shakespeare, William 1–5, 8–11, 21–32, 36, 49–59, 100–104, 157; anniversary of death 128–131; history plays 23, 25–27, 32, 36, 50, 56, 116, 183; for inclusive Britain 100–104; telling nation's history 21–28
"Shakespearean rhizomatics" 9, 178
Sharrock, Thea 104–105, 110–118, 139
Sheen, Martin 1
Sherlock 129
shrewishness 108
siege sensibility 2
Silverstone, Catherine 71, 81, 84
Simms, Stephen 113
Sinfield, Alan 198
Singhateh, Faz 71
Sirkeci, Ibrahim 190–191
skepticism 16, 19
Skyfall 95
"slant" authenticity 165; *see also* authenticity
slave trade 96, 139, 186
slave-owning 7
Smiley, Jane 204
Smith, Ian 178, 199
social exclusion 67–68, 75, 152, 208
social "glue" 17–19
social praxis 23
solidarity 188
Sorkin, Aaron 1–2, 5, 194
sovereignty 20, 131, 211–212
The Spanish Princess 204
Spencer, Charles 71
Spivak, Gayatri Chakravorty 26
staging multiethnic nation 49–93; class resistance in history 65–68; color of war 68–69; evasions 84–88; future of multiethnic Britain 51–53; gender and nation in Boyd's cycle 59–65; mission accomplished? 70–73; past as prologue 88–89; puncturing colorblind claim 73–78; on seeing and not seeing 53–59; who tells your story? 78–84
Starkey, David 161
Starks-Estes, Lisa 28
Steed, Tim 43–44
Steen, Tafline 195–196
Steigerwalt, Jenna 175, 201

stereotyping 59–60, 73, 75, 77–78, 82, 84, 86, 103, 106, 138–139, 146–147
Stewart, Heather 132
stock-taking 11
Stoppard, Tom 204
Straughan, Peter 157
Straw, Jack 12, 14–15, 53
Sturridge, Tom 142
subjectivity 28, 51, 105
Suchet, David 106
Suffragette Movement 97
"Summary of the Vision" 52
superiority 17, 44, 134, 186
Suzuki, Mihoko 137–138
system of representation 22–23

taboo 27
"Take back control" 131–133, 169–1670, 177, 198
taking stock 11
Taming of the Shrew 201
Tatspaugh, Patricia 82
Taverner, John 166
Taylor, Matthew 208
Teale, Owen 116
telling nation's history 21–28
telling sad stories 217–219
terminology for Shakespeare 37–38
Terris, Olwen 101
terrorism 144
"That England, that was wont to conquer others" 185–191
Thatcher, Margaret 152, 188
Thierry, Melanie 109, 129
thingification 171–172, 175
"This England" 54, 88, 189
"this fortress built by nature" 128–156, 210
Thomas Wolsey, Late Cardinal, His Life and Death 157
Thompson, Ayanna 34–35, 57, 111–112, 115, 201–202
Thompson, Emma 109
Thompson, Mark 85, 102
A Thousand Acres 204
threat 18
Tillyard, E. M. W. 103–104
timely utility 146–151
tokenism 116
Tolkien, J. R. R. 95
"Too Diverse?" 17
totalitarianism 18
Touré, 76
Travelex 70, 72
Troilus and Cressida 133–136, 138, 142
trouble with history 182–206; future for history? 198–199; "I ask no less than power" 191–198; what can we do about the trouble? 201–204; what *is* the trouble? 199–201
Troughton, David 141
Trouillot, Michel-Rolph 161, 182
Trump, Donald 2, 11, 18, 182, 207
The Tudors 162–163
Turkey 132–133, 136, 191; acceptance in to EU 132
Twitter 132
"Tywysog Cymru" 210

Uberoi, Varun 19
UK Independence Party 11, 208–209
UK Labour Force Survey 19–20
UKIP *see* UK Independence Party
ultra-right-wing parties 6
unreality of discourse 22
unsettling acoustic 65
upper-class elitism 35

Valluvan, Sivamohan 20–21, 132, 143, 186–187, 190, 208–209
van Kampen, Claire 158, 166, 168
ventriloquism 41, 187, 189–190
verisimilitude 107, 130, 158, 176, 183, 200
vertreten 27
vilification of outsiders 8
violations of history 65; *see also* colorblind casting
violence 52–53, 61–64, 67, 151, 216–217
visibility 4, 17, 147
Votava, Jennie M. 26, 131
Vote Leave 2, 6, 21, 43, 131–133, 136–137, 147, 150–153, 177, 191, 198, 209–210

wake of terror 16–21
Wall Street Journal 36, 166
Walsh, Brian 25, 164
war in Iraq 11, 49, 69, 78–80, 135
war on terror 1, 4–6, 39, 49, 80, 99
Wars of the Roses 1–4, 128–156, 183, 197; aliens at the border 133–137; Margaret of Anjou 137–146; outsider's timely utility 146–151; "take back control" 131–133; what is forgotten 151–154
Way, Geoffrey 203
"web of narratives" 30
Weber, Stanley 129
wedge issues 18
Welsh correction? 210–212

West Wing 1–5, 194; Season Three 1–5
"The West and the Rest" 22–23
what can we do about the trouble with history? 201–204
what is forgotten 151–154
"What is a Nation?" 6
what *is* the trouble with history? 199–201
what's past is prologue 88–89
Whishaw, Ben 107, 134
White Cliffs 133–6, 143, 154
White, Hayden 177
white history 177–178
White House 1–2
White, Lee 73
white privilege blind spots 169–177
white racial imagery 77
white racial purity 131, 136, 142
white supremacy 34, 50, 72, 75, 78, 88, 138–140, 170, 184–185, 200, 217–218
whiteness 14–15, 56, 58, 77–78, 83–84, 170–171, 176, 178, 188
whitewashing 69
who tells your story? 78–84
Whyman, Erica 35–36
Williams, John 168
Williams, Zoe 121
Wilson, August 34
Wilson, Lambert 129
Windrush generation 73–74, 77, 97, 112
Wiseman, Debbie 166, 168
witch hunts 2
Wolf Hall 10, 157–181, 183
Womack, Peter 8
women of color 200
"women on top" 3, 6–7
women's emancipation 143–144
Wood, Clive 62
Woolf, Daniel 23–24
World Shakespeare Festival 94, 128
World Trade Center 5, 16
Wray, Ramona 102, 107, 200
Wright, Patrick 8, 159
Writing of History 22

xenophobia 39, 43, 121, 132, 152, 154, 170

YouTube 121
Yuval-Davis, Nira 7

For Product Safety Concerns and Information please contact our EU representative GPSR@taylorandfrancis.com
Taylor & Francis Verlag GmbH, Kaufingerstraße 24, 80331 München, Germany

www.ingramcontent.com/pod-product-compliance
Ingram Content Group UK Ltd.
Pitfield, Milton Keynes, MK11 3LW, UK
UKHW040034090825
461685UK00024B/1583
9781032252483